Introducing Adobe® Photoshop® Elements

Lisa Lee

Contents
at a Glance

A Division of Pearson Technology Group
201 W. 103rd Street
Indianapolis, Indiana 46290

Introducing Adobe® Photoshop® Elements

International Standard Book Number: 0-7897-2629-7

Library of Congress Catalog Card Number: 2001090314

Printed in the United States of America

First Printing: September 2001

04   03   02   01   4   3   2   1

Trademarks

All terms mentioned in this book that are known to be trademarks or service marks have been appropriately capitalized. Que Publishing cannot attest to the accuracy of this information. Use of a term in this book should not be regarded as affecting the validity of any trademark or service mark.

Adobe is a registered trademark of Adobe Systems, Incorporated.

Photoshop is a registered trademark of Adobe Systems, Incorporated.

Warning and Disclaimer

Every effort has been made to make this book as complete and as accurate as possible, but no warranty or fitness is implied. The information provided is on an "as is" basis. The author and the publisher shall have neither liability nor responsibility to any person or entity with respect to any loss or damages arising from the information contained in this book.

Publisher
Robb Linsky

Acquisitions Editor
Laura Norman

Development Editor
Laura Norman

Project Editor
Tonya Simpson

Copy Editor
Kezia Endsley

Indexer
Rebecca Salerno

Proofreader
Kaylene Riemen

Technical Editor
Toby Anne Malina

Team Coordinator
Cindy Teeters

Interior Designer
Ann Jones

Cover Designer
Alan Clements

Page Layout
Ayanna Lacey

Contents

About the Author

Lisa Lee is the author of several best-selling computer books about topics ranging from Macintosh computers to Adobe Photoshop. She also has written more than 1,000 tutorials about all kinds of consumer hardware products, operating systems, and applications.

She is an amateur photographer, cartoonist, painter, musician, and Web designer. Visit her Web site at `www.flatfishfactory.com` to view her latest projects.

Dedication

This book is dedicated to Mike Neil.

Acknowledgments

Thanks to all of my fellow photographers who contributed to this book. Sairam Suresh, Bobby Joe, Neal Tucker, Kieca Mahoney, and especially Julie Ann Lee: you are all great photographers. Thanks for giving me permission to use your photos in my book!

Thank you, Mom, for trusting me with so many of your sacred photos. And, special thanks to Marta Justak, for being such a supportive, invaluable agent and friend.

A big thank you to the wonderful team at Que Publishing for being so helpful, and for helping me put together such a great book. Thanks to Beth Millet for asking me to write this book. And special thanks to Laura Norman for being such an expert editor and manager of this book's layout and design. Finally, thanks to all the teams at Que who helped put this book together and make it out into the world.

Tell Us What You Think!

As the reader of this book, you are a valued, important critic and commentator. As an author I encourage you to take the time to share your thoughts, likes, and dislikes about my book. As a publisher, Que Publishing values your opinion and wants to know what we're doing right, what we could do better, what areas you'd like to see published, and any other words of wisdom you're willing to pass our way.

You are welcome to send your comments to me at lisalee@spies.com and let me know what you did or did not like about my book.

Que Publishing would also like to hear from you. You can fax, email, or write directly to the editor.

Please note that neither of us can help you with technical problems related to Photoshop Elements. You'll want to contact Adobe's support staff regarding technical issues or product support. Due to the high volume of email we receive, neither of us might be able to reply to every message.

When you write, please include this book's title, *Introducing Adobe Photoshop Elements*, and author, Lisa Lee, as well as your name and phone or fax number. Your comments will be reviewed and shared with the folks who worked on this book.

Fax: 317-581-4666

Email: feedback@quepublishing.com

Mail: Laura Norman
         Que Publishing
         201 West 103rd Street
         Indianapolis, IN 46290 USA

introduction

Adobe introduced Photoshop Elements in Spring 2001. It's Adobe's replacement for Photoshop LE, which is most commonly bundled with scanners. Obviously, Photoshop Elements doesn't have all the features you'll find in Photoshop. However, you will find a few new things that you won't find in Photoshop, such as the Red Eye Eraser Tool, Shortcuts and Options toolbars, and Photomerge Wizard. There are also tools such as Adjust Backlighting and Fill Flash that enable you to darken or lighten midtones in an image. What's most important, Photoshop Elements enables you to apply many of the same top-notch photo-editing techniques that make Photoshop so popular.

About *Introducing Adobe Photoshop Elements*

Digital imaging has evolved from simple bitmap graphics, such as the first icons used with Macs, to full-blown, full-color image editing. Since those early days of black-and-white bit flipping, high-cost scanners and digital cameras have plummeted in price while exponentially improving in image quality, performance, and features. Today, people can use digital cameras to instantly share exciting, fresh images on the Web, or convert old, damaged photos into digital images using a flatbed or film scanner. Photoshop Elements enables you to enhance images with effects, put together an old yearbook online, or digitize your family tree without having to worry about dirt, dust, and aging affecting your digital images.

I can't believe how many years I've been learning about digital images and trying to improve my digital imaging editing skills. First, I spent years experimenting with black-and-white and color photography. Years ago, I remember how disappointed I was when I took my first 640×480 digital pictures with Apple's QuickTime camera. Today, I have a three-megapixel camera, and I take only digital pictures.

The point I want to make is that working with digital images is much easier and affordable today than it ever was. Programs like Photoshop Elements make working with digital images easy to learn and produce satisfying results. However, easy doesn't necessarily mean fast. Photoshop Elements won't keep you from spending a lot of quality time perfecting an image and experimenting with images, new and old.

Photoshop Elements is both an easy-to-use and sophisticated application. It enables you to try a quick fix on an image, as well as perform some heavy-duty image editing, beginning with hours of experimentation, which extends into days of fine-tuning. Keeping this range of tasks in mind, I've designed this book for those who have opened their first scanner or digital camera and have little experience working with digital images. Or, if you already have a scanner or digital camera, and upgraded to Photoshop Elements from another application, you'll learn how to use combinations of tools to improve or create new digital images.

Who Is This Book For?

My hope is that you, the reader, can sit down and start doing something with Photoshop Elements by first understanding some of the basic concepts of digital imaging, and then following a set of steps, or a variation on a set of steps, in this book. I'd also like to think the examples in this book will inspire you to extend your creativity. I try to write books that teach some useful skills, produce tangible results, and show you that computers can do great things if you take the time to explore what's possible.

But, like Photoshop Elements, this book isn't for the total beginner—someone just sitting down with his or her very first computer. If you're familiar with a Windows or Macintosh computer and can learn quickly, this book is for you. Of course, if you're already a Photoshop expert, you might have already figured out the major differences between these two programs. If that's the case, this book can show you how to apply many of those swanky Photoshop techniques using Photoshop Elements.

Photoshop Elements might have fallen into your hands for one of the following reasons:

- It came preinstalled or bundled with a computer/scanner or computer/digital camera purchase.
- Looking for a low-cost, full-featured digital imaging application, you purchased Photoshop Elements.
- You mastered Photo Deluxe but aren't quite ready for Photoshop.
- Graphics and imaging applications are fun and you want to do something cool with digital images. Photoshop Elements looks like it's fun to use!

Regardless of how you acquired Photoshop Elements, this book can show you how to do both simple and sophisticated tasks. You'll learn how to correct images, combine or create new images to compose a new kind of photo album, or share great-looking photos with your friends and family.

How to Use This Book

I had two goals in mind when I put this book together. Because this book is about Photoshop Elements, my first goal was to introduce you to the digital imaging features in the program. The examples and steps in this book are just one of the many ways you can work with digital images. My second goal was to introduce you to working with digital images. This involves using a small combination of tools, observation skills, and a little creativity. With a little luck, my examples will help you design and create your own pictures that you can share with others.

This book is divided into five parts. The first three parts show you how to get images into and out of Photoshop Elements. These are basic skills that you might already be familiar with if you've used other graphics applications. The last two parts make up the larger portion of the book. They show you how to do some more complicated, advanced tasks. You can read this book from cover to cover, as a reference, or go to any particular chapter you like. You can find a gallery of images from this book on my Web site at www.flatfishfactory.com/ipse/index.htm.

tip

Tips highlight something new, something cool, something helpful, and something true.

note

Notes point out a related tidbit of information about a chapter topic.

caution

Cautions warn you about potential pitfalls or tell you ways to troubleshoot a potential problem.

Except for the system requirements and installation sections, all the screen shots created for this book were created with Windows 2000. The Macintosh and Windows versions of Photoshop Elements are similar, so Mac users should be able to follow along. Tool shortcuts and menu command shortcuts are included for both Windows and Mac. Macintosh keyboard shortcuts appear as (Command-C), and Windows keyboard shortcuts appear as [Ctrl+C].

You'll find tips, notes, cautions, and sidebars throughout this book. Each contains different kinds of helpful hints. Some chapters also contain variations on a set of steps, which take a particular skill, such as color correcting, and show you how to adjust the exposure and hot spots in an image in addition to learning how to fine-tune brightness and contrast settings for an image.

Your Mileage Can Vary

In a perfect world, this book would be all things to all Photoshop Elements owners. I realize, however, that I'll fall short explaining a technical doodad, or skimp on coverage about filter effects. Hey, if you want to see what all the filters look like in Photoshop Elements, open the Filters palette and choose All from the drop-down menu. You won't find out how to use every single one in this book! Because I'm cutting to the chase, I might as well tell you, there's no coverage of how to create Jackson Pollack–style brushes, or how to create the perfect collage or montage.

Also, sidebars point out some interesting factoids that are related to the local chapter topic.

The Contents of This Book

Introducing Adobe Photoshop Elements takes you from ground zero to cloud nine. The book begins by taking you through some of the more elementary features, such as understanding the work area, and some simple tasks such as resizing or auto-correcting the tonal range of an image. It then gradually introduces you to using combinations of tools to correct, repair, and combine digital images into animation or panoramic photos.

Most of the book focuses on building on fundamental techniques for improving, correcting, combining, or creating great-looking digital pictures. Each part of this book introduces you to a different digital-imaging element of the program, from scanning and printing images to color correction and animation.

Part I—Photoshop Elements Setup

It doesn't take a rocket scientist to set up Photoshop Elements. In fact, you can skip to Part II if you aren't interested in how the work area is laid out, or how different tools and windows are related to each other in the work area. If you do want to customize a preference or turn off a setting, you can always come back and revisit these chapters.

Chapter 1—Get that puppy installed on your computer. If you're not sure whether your computer meets or beats the system requirements for Photoshop Elements, I'll show you how to check your Mac or Windows computer. If you've already installed the program, move along to Chapter 2.

Chapter 2—Familiarize yourself with all the tools, menus, and windows in the work area.

Chapter 3—Find out how to change the color, tool, and program settings in this chapter.

Chapter 4—Explore the built-in Photoshop Elements help systems installed on your computer.

Part II—Scanning and Acquiring Images

Working with digital images is a two-part task. First, you must get the image into your computer. Then, you can edit, save, or print it. Depending on the state the image is in, this first part can be a difficult task. However, in most cases, acquiring an image is fairly straightforward and relatively easy, just as opening, saving, and printing an image is relatively easy when you know what you're doing, and possibly why you're doing it.

Chapter 5—Install the software for your scanner, and then discover how to connect and control your scanner. More importantly, import photos or film negatives into the work area.

Chapter 6—Learn a bit about digital cameras, and then find out how to connect, view, and download images from a digital camera.

Part III—Opening, Saving, and Printing Images

For those of you who take photos that look great as-is, you can learn how to view, save, and print them in Photoshop Elements. I've also thrown in some simple tweaking tasks, so you can quickly straighten or automatically correct an image.

Chapter 7—Open sesame, or Open As sesame. Find out how to open and convert image files. Image modes and resolution for printers, monitors, scanners, and cameras are also explained in this chapter.

Chapter 8—Explore the exciting world of file formats and learn how to optimize and save the right file for printing or for the Web. Also, find out how to upload images to a Web server.

Chapter 9—Get the scoop on how to print images with grayscale or color printers. Print a folder of files to a contact sheet using the built-in Automate command. Also, learn how to create picture packages showing one picture multiple times in different sizes, all on the same page.

Part IV—Correcting and Combining Images

Start taking a walk on the wild side of digital imaging. Take a scanned or camera-captured image and learn how to work with color. You also learn how to fix numerous kinds of color-related problems using the arsenal of tools in the toolbox and menus.

Chapter 10—Take a short course and learn how to interpret all the colors in front of your eyes. Work with the palettes that enable you to control color for any open image.

Chapter 11—Jump into a slew of color-correction techniques, and consider a few variations that can help bring an old photo alive.

Chapter 12—Experiment with filters and effects to enhance digital pictures. Learn how to hide things you don't want to see, and bring out objects or areas in a picture.

Chapter 13—Combine, remove, and perform advanced correction techniques by taking full advantage of layers, copy and paste commands, and the Clipboard.

Chapter 14—Add a title, or enhance text by putting an image inside each character. Use the shape and drawing tools to make your mark on an image.

Chapter 15—Repair old photos scanned in from negatives or damaged photo paper.

Chapter 16—Create complex pictures and recipes that can help you experiment with any previous set of tasks to pump up an image.

Part V—Designing Complex Images

After you've primed and polished your images, you can go the distance and learn more advanced tasks, such as animating your images or creating a Web photo gallery.

Chapter 17—Put together two or more images and create animation, or more precisely, an animated GIF.

Chapter 18—Stitch together two or more pictures and create a panorama. Photoshop Elements has a built-in tool, the Photo Merge Wizard, that magically combines similar photos to create a panorama.

Chapter 19—Use drawing and text tools with Layer Styles to create Web-ready graphics combined with your digital pictures.

Chapter 20—Create a Web photo gallery out of any folder full of images. Photoshop Elements can generate HTML and JavaScript code, as well as resize your image files.

Glossary—You'll find definitions for most of the acronyms and Photoshop Elements terms used in this book in the glossary.

part

I

PHOTOSHOP ELEMENTS SETUP

Installing Photoshop Elements

Before you can start using Photoshop Elements, you need to install it. Actually, before you consider installing Photoshop Elements, be sure to check the system requirements for Photoshop Elements and check to see if your computer meets or beats them. One thing to keep in mind when you're working with digital pictures is that more memory, a larger hard drive, and a faster processor all make it easier for you to edit larger images.

System Requirements

System requirements for software are the amusement-park equivalent of being a certain height to go on a roller-coaster ride. If you're taller than the height limit, you'll enjoy the ride problem-free. If you're shorter than the height limit, you probably won't enjoy the ride, and if you go on the ride, you might endanger yourself.

note
To find out more about color, and color requirements for your computer, go to Chapter 10, "Digital Images and Color."

tip
Adobe has announced that a Carbonized or Cocoa version of Photoshop Elements should be available for Mac OS X in the spring of 2002.

Of course, software isn't nearly as dangerous as an amusement-park ride. If your computer system doesn't meet Adobe's requirements, Photoshop Elements might perform slowly, or not be able to perform at all. On the other hand, if your computer system meets the requirements, enjoy the ride! Although Photoshop Elements might not blast wind onto your cheeks, you will find lots of thrills as you learn to work with digital pictures.

Macintosh System Requirements

The following list contains Adobe's minimum requirements for running Photoshop Elements on a Macintosh computer.

- Power PC Processor
- Mac OS 8.6, 9.0, 9.0.4, or 9.1
- 150MB of available hard drive space
- A color monitor with at least 256 colors; a monitor resolution of 800×600 pixels
- A CD-ROM drive
- At least 64MB (with virtual memory on) of available memory

How do you know if your computer meets these requirements? You can use the system software on your Mac to view your computer's hardware configuration. The following sections show you how to view your processor, memory, disk space, and monitor configuration (see Figure 1.1). The following Macintosh instructions apply, in general, to Mac OS 8.6 through Mac OS 9.1. However, depending on the type of Macintosh you have, the name of the Monitors control panel might vary slightly.

Figure 1.1
You can view the
Macintosh hardware
information in the Apple
System Profile
Application.

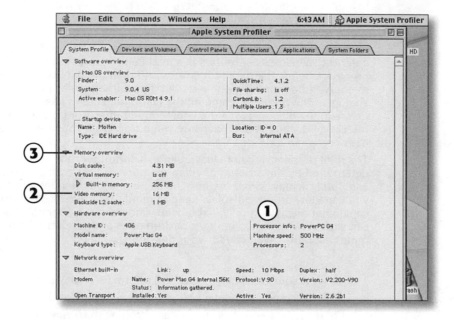

① Processor info

② Video memory

③ Memory info

What Is Video Memory?

Video memory consists of a set of chips connected to your computer's logic board. It enables your computer to process video for your computer display, and works with the operating system's monitor settings to determine how many colors can be viewed on your screen.

The more technical term for video memory is VRAM, or video random access memory. This type of chip is similar to memory, or DRAM (dynamic random access memory), which is used by a computer to run the operating system and applications on a computer.

When a computer wants to send video to the computer screen, the image data first is sent to the processor. Macs use Power PC processors, and Windows computers use Intel Pentium processors. The processor sends the data to memory, and then the data is sent to video memory. Video memory converts the digital image information into analog data. When the image on the computer screen needs to be updated, the display reads the latest frame buffer from the video memory. Computers can have anywhere from 1MB to 2MB of video memory, up to 8MB or 16MB.

The total number of colors viewable on a computer monitor will be determined by the amount of video memory and the capabilities of the computer display. Video memory helps determine the number of colors you can view on your display. Keep in mind that most displays are capable of displaying only 24-bit color. Choosing a higher color depth can slow down your computer's performance and can limit the maximum resolution available for your desktop.

note

If you're running Mac OS X, choose About This Mac from the Apple menu to view the memory and processor information for your Macintosh computer.

To view your computer's hardware information in Mac OS 9, click the Apple menu and choose Apple System Profiler (refer to Figure 1.1). Then click the System Profile tab to view the processor, memory, disk, and video information. Click the Devices and Volumes tab to view the amount of available disk space on each hard drive connected to your Mac.

Another way to view the amount of memory available on your Mac is to click the Apple menu and choose About This Computer (see Figure 1.2). The amount of physical memory installed on your computer appears beside the Built-in Memory field. The Largest Unused Block is the amount of free memory on your Mac. Photoshop Elements requires at least 64MB of memory if virtual memory is on. Go to the Memory control panel to turn virtual memory on.

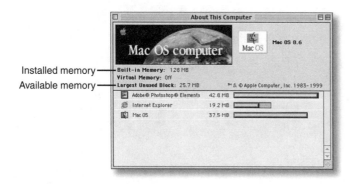

Installed memory

Available memory

Figure 1.2
You can view the amount of installed and available memory in the About This Computer window. Although the Mac OS 8.6 window is shown here, this window is similar in any version of Mac OS 9, including Mac OS 9.1.

Virtual Memory

Virtual memory enables a computer to store data on your hard drive instead of in physical memory, or DRAM. Physical memory refers to the actual memory chip, or DIMM, installed on the computer's logic board. On the other hand, virtual memory uses your hard drive to swap the contents of system and application memory into physical memory.

As you open and edit image files, Photoshop Elements uses its own form of virtual memory, which Adobe refers to as a *scratch disk*. Photoshop Elements can work with up to four different scratch disks to store image data on your drive. Because access to the hard drive is considerably slower than access to physical memory, the higher you set virtual memory, the more disk space will be used, and the slower your computer will become.

Apple recommends turning on virtual memory, setting it to approximately 1MB higher than the amount of physical memory installed on your Macintosh computer. For best results, you should have at least 128MB of physical memory installed on your Mac.

Monitor and video settings can be viewed and modified from the Monitors control panel. To open the Monitors control panel (or the Monitors & Sound control panel if you're running Mac OS 8.6), click the Apple menu, choose Control Panels, and then select Monitors. The Monitors control panel opens (see Figure 1.3).

Figure 1.3
Choose the number of colors and the size of your desktop from the Monitors control panel.

The Monitors control panel window consists of two main areas, Color Depth and Resolution. The Color Depth settings enable you to set how many colors Mac OS can display on-screen. The Resolution settings enable you to set the size of the desktop. Adjust the number of colors or the size of the desktop by choosing one of the settings from the following list:

- Choose Thousands or Millions of colors in the Color Depth section of the window.

- Choose 1024×768 as your desktop size. Although you can use a smaller desktop size, 1024×768 is recommended. Adobe only requires an 800×600 desktop.

Know Your Monitor

Although you might be able to select Thousands or Millions of colors in the Monitors control panel, the monitor connected to your Mac must also be able to display 16- or 24-bit color if you actually want to see all the full range of colors.

Windows System Requirements

Adobe's system requirements for Windows are similar to the Mac system requirements. However, the hardware requirements for Windows are totally different than those for the Mac. Also, virtual memory, one of the memory-related features in Windows, is always on. Windows requires 64MB to run Photoshop Elements in addition to the standard amount of memory required to run Windows 98, NT, 2000, or Me.

The following list contains Adobe's minimum system requirements needed to run Photoshop Elements on a Windows computer:

- Pentium Processor
- Windows 98, Windows 98 Second Edition, Windows Millenium Edition, Windows NT 4.0 (with service pack 4, 5, or 6a, and Internet Explorer 4, 5, or 5.5), or Windows 2000
- 150MB of available hard drive space
- Color monitor with at least 256 colors and a resolution of 800×600 pixels
- A CD-ROM drive
- At least 64MB of available memory

Depending on the flavor of Windows you're using, you can view your PC's hardware configuration by choosing a software application, control panel, or Properties menu command. Right-click the My Computer icon on your desktop, and then choose Properties from the shortcut menu to view the memory and operating system information.

The System Properties window opens, as shown in Figure 1.4. By default, the General tab is displayed. View the version of the Windows operating system in the System section of this window. The amount of physical memory installed in your computer appears at the bottom of the window.

Physical memory is installed on the computer's logic board. Virtual memory stores memory information on your hard drive, and physical memory stores memory information on Dynamic Random Access Memory (DRAM) chips. Windows uses physical and virtual memory to process data on your computer.

To find out how much drive space is available on your computer, open the My Computer window, and then right-click a hard drive icon in the My Computer window. Select Properties from the hard drive icon's shortcut menu. The Hard Drive Properties window opens. View the amount of used and available disk space in this window.

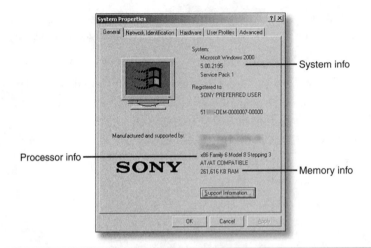

Figure 1.4
You can view Windows hardware information in the System Properties window.

Right-click the desktop and choose Properties from the shortcut menu to view the video and color information in Windows. The Display Properties window opens. Click the Settings tab in the Display Properties window (see Figure 1.5). Here, you can set the number of colors viewable in Windows. You can also change the size of the desktop if you like.

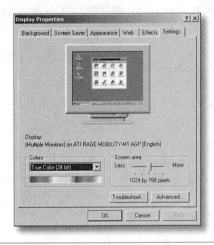

Figure 1.5
You can view and modify the video and color information for your computer from the Settings tab of the Display Properties window.

Installing Photoshop Elements

Photoshop Elements is one of the few software packages that includes an installer application for Macs or Windows computers on one CD. If you have a Mac and a PC, you can install Photoshop Elements on both computers and not worry about buying two copies of the same application. Is that a great deal, or what?

DVD-ROM Drives Are CD-ROM-Friendly

You can use a DVD-ROM drive or a CD-ROM drive to install Photoshop Elements onto your computer. DVD-ROM drives can read CD-ROMs in addition to DVD movies, or DVD media disks.

If your computer doesn't have a built-in CD or DVD drive, you can use an external CD or DVD-drive to install Photoshop Elements.

If you've downloaded the 30-day trial version of Photoshop Elements, simply double-click the installer icon to start the installer application. The following sections show you how to install Photoshop Elements from the CD-ROM.

Installing on a Macintosh Computer

The installer application for Photoshop Elements is similar to many other software application installers. You double-click the installer icon to start the installer application (see Figure 1.6). Then follow the on-screen instructions to install Photoshop Elements onto your Mac's hard drive.

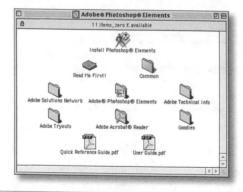

Figure 1.6
Double-click the Install Photoshop Elements icon to start the installer application.

Déjà Vu?

If you're not sure whether Photoshop Elements is already installed on your hard drive, you can search for it. You can start Sherlock to search your Mac. Alternatively, you can choose Find from the File menu in the Finder.

Type Photoshop Elements into the text field in the Sherlock window. Press the Find button (Mac OS 8.6) or magnifying glass button (Mac OS 9) to start the search. If Photoshop Elements appears in the search results, you can select its icon in the Items Found (Mac OS 8.6) or Sherlock (Mac OS 9) window and view its location on the hard drive.

When the installer application has started, it introduces you to different installation options for Photoshop Elements. The following steps walk you through the installation process:

1. Choose the language you want Photoshop Elements to use from the Select Language window. Then click Continue.

2. The License Agreement window appears (see Figure 1.7). Click the arrows located on the right side of the window to scroll through the license agreement as you read it. If you agree with the terms of the license agreement, click Accept. If you disagree, click Decline to exit the installer application.

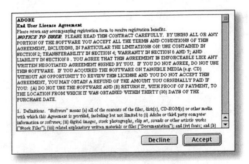

Figure 1.7
Read the license agreement to find out about Adobe's terms of use for Photoshop Elements.

3. If you clicked the Accept button in the previous step, the Read Me window appears (see Figure 1.8). When you have finished reading the Photoshop Elements information, click Continue.

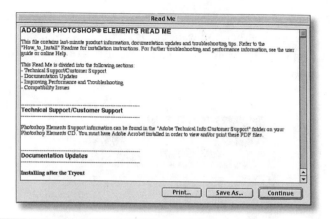

Figure 1.8
The Read Me file contains helpful documentation and support information.

4. The Install Photoshop Elements window appears. Easy Install, located in the pop-up menu in the upper-left corner of the window, is the default installation (see Figure 1.9).

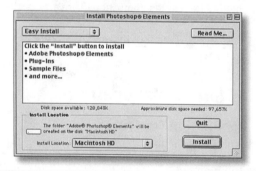

Figure 1.9
An Easy Install places Photoshop Elements on your Mac.

5. Click the Install button to install Photoshop Elements onto your hard drive.

6. A dialog box appears asking you to type in the serial number for Photoshop Elements. The serial number is located on the back of the Photoshop Elements CD-ROM jewel case. Type the serial number into the dialog box and then click OK to exit the dialog box.

7. After Photoshop Elements is installed, the installer application will ask whether you want to install the SVG plug-in (see Figure 1.10). Follow the on-screen instructions and wait for this software to install.

note

The SVG plug-in file enables your browser to view images created with the W3 (World Wide Web Consortium) XML language known as SVG. Find out more about SVG by visiting Adobe's Web site at www.adobe.com/svg.

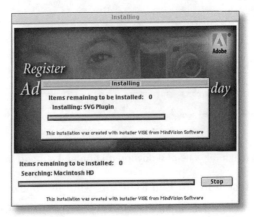

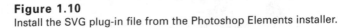

Figure 1.10
Install the SVG plug-in file from the Photoshop Elements installer.

8. When the installation completes, click Quit to exit the installer application.

Choosing a Hard Disk Location

Macintosh Installation Options

For most folks, the Easy Install option puts everything they'll need to run Photoshop Elements on their Mac. However, if you want to reinstall part of Photoshop Elements, you can do so with the Custom Install option in the installer application.

You can also select a particular folder to install Photoshop Elements on your hard drive. This feature is available for both Easy and Custom installs. If you've already installed Photoshop Elements on your Mac, don't worry. You can simply move the Photoshop Elements folder to another folder on your hard drive instead of re-running the installer application.

The following sections show you how to select a folder from the installer application.

If you want to install Photoshop Elements to a specific folder on your Macintosh computer's hard drive, click the Install Location pop-up menu located at the bottom of the install window.

1. Click the Install Location pop-up menu and choose Select Folder, as shown in Figure 1.11. A dialog box opens.

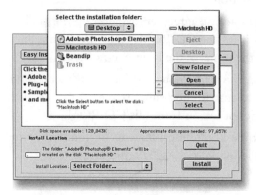

Figure 1.11
Choose a specific location on your hard drive for an Easy or Custom install.

2. Double-click the hard drive icon to navigate your hard drive. You can click the New Folder button to create a new folder on your hard drive.

3. Select the folder to which you want to install from the left window list. Then, click the Select button. The dialog box closes, and the newly selected folder appears in the Install Location area of the Install window.

Removing Photoshop Elements

The Photoshop Elements installer application does not have a Remove option. Therefore, you have to select the Adobe Photoshop Elements folder icon on your hard drive and drag it to the Trash to remove it from your Macintosh computer.

Installing on a Windows Computer

When you first insert the CD-ROM, the Adobe Photoshop Elements CD splash screen will most likely appear. If not, you'll need to double-click the My Computer icon on your desktop and

caution
Although you can move the Photoshop Elements folder around on your Macintosh hard drive, I don't recommend moving the Photoshop Elements folder around on your Windows hard drive. Windows relies on several different settings, which expect Photoshop Elements to be in a particular folder.

then double-click the CD-ROM drive icon to start the installer. Follow these steps to install Photoshop Elements on your PC:

1. Click the Next button, and you'll be taken to a window that asks you to select a country where you purchased the software. Select the appropriate language for the country, and then click the Next button.

2. Next, a license agreement window appears. This license agreement is for the CD-ROM. Click the Accept button if you agree with the terms of the license agreement.

3. Next, an Adobe Photoshop Elements menu window appears. You can install Photoshop Elements, Acrobat Reader, or a PostScript Driver from this CD-ROM.

4. Click the Photoshop Elements button in the window to start the Installation Wizard (see Figure 1.12).

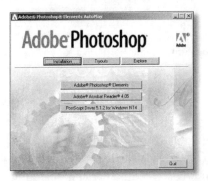

Figure 1.12
Click the Photoshop Elements button to start the Installer Application Wizard.

5. Wait for the Installer Application Wizard to start. Choose the language you want to install from the Select Language window. Then click Continue.

6. The License Agreement window appears. Click the arrows located on the right side of the window to scroll through the license agreement as you read it (see Figure 1.13). If you agree with the terms of the license agreement, click Accept. If you disagree, click Decline to exit the installer application.

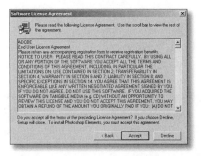

Figure 1.13
Read the license agreement to find out about Adobe's terms of use for
Photoshop Elements.

7. The Adobe Photoshop Elements Setup window appears. Typical
   is selected by default (see Figure 1.14).

Figure 1.14
The Typical installation places Photoshop Elements on your Windows PC.

8. Click the Browse button if you want to select a different folder
   to which to install.

9. Next, you can choose the image file formats that Photoshop
   Elements will open by default (see Figure 1.15). If you have
   other graphics applications installed on your hard drive, you
   might not want to allow Photoshop Elements to open every
   graphics file format on your computer. By default, Photoshop
   Elements will open only its native PSD file format, as well as
   EPS files. If you aren't sure, leave the default selections. Click
   the Next button to continue.

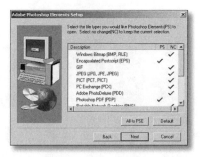

Figure 1.15
Select the image file formats you want Photoshop Elements to open.

10. A dialog box appears asking you to type your user information for Photoshop Elements. Type your first and last name and the serial number into the corresponding text fields. The serial number is located on the back of the Photoshop Elements CD-ROM jewel case. Then click OK to exit the User Information window.

11. Next, click Install to install Photoshop Elements onto your hard drive.

12. When the installation completes, click the Finish button to exit the installer application.

Removing Photoshop Elements

You can remove Photoshop Elements from your Windows computer as you can any other installed application. Click the Start menu, and then choose Settings, Control Panels, Add/Remove Programs. Select Adobe Photoshop Elements in the Add/Remove Programs window. Then, click the Remove button. Follow the on-screen instructions and wait for Windows to delete the software from the hard drive.

Starting Photoshop Elements

Now that you've installed Photoshop Elements onto your Macintosh or Windows computer, you're ready to start it. Mac OS and Windows provide several ways for you to start an application. One way is to double-click the Photoshop Elements application icon. The following sections show you how to start Photoshop Elements on a Macintosh and Windows 2000 computer.

Starting the Macintosh Version

You're two clicks away from starting Photoshop, once you open the Photoshop Elements folder, that is. Double-click the Adobe Photoshop Elements application icon to start this application. If your Macintosh computer has enough memory and disk space available, you will see the Photoshop Elements work area.

Of course, there are other ways you can start this application, too. For example, you can create an alias to the Photoshop Elements application icon and place it on your desktop. Then, you simply double-click the alias to start Photoshop Elements instead of having to navigate your hard drive. Alternatively, you can open the Adobe Photoshop Elements folder and place it at the bottom of your desktop, turning it into a pop-up window.

Photoshop Elements and Mac OS X

If you're using Mac OS X, you can install and start Photoshop Elements using the same steps you use if you have Mac OS 8.6 or Mac OS 9. Simply double-click the Photoshop Elements application icon. The Mac OS 9.1 classic environment will start under Mac OS X, and you'll see the Photoshop Elements work area, shown in Figure 1.16.

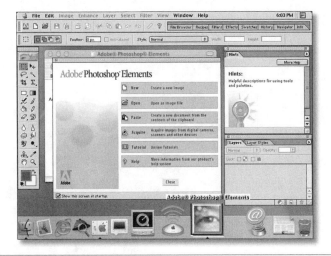

Figure 1.16
Starting Photoshop Elements in Mac OS X is similar to the Mac OS 9 experience.

Starting the Windows Version

There are many ways to start Photoshop Elements in Windows. The most accessible way is to navigate to the application through the Start menu. However, you can also use Explorer, or the Find application to locate the Photoshop Elements executable on your Windows computer.

The Photoshop Elements install wizard creates an entry in the Start menu in Windows. To open Photoshop Elements, click the Start menu, choose Programs, and then choose Adobe. If you have more than one Adobe application installed in Windows, you'll see a folder for each application in the hierarchical view of the Start menu. Select the Photoshop Elements folder and then choose Adobe Photoshop Elements.

Navigating the Work Area

The work area encompasses the Photoshop Elements desktop space. The menu bar, toolbox, palettes, document window, shortcuts bar, and options bar each bring a unique set of features to this application. As you work with different types of image files, you will find there are several kinds of work-flow processes that you can follow in the Photoshop Elements work area.

One of the tasks you'll find yourself doing often is opening an image, whether it's to determine its dimensions, to combine it with other images to create a presentation, or to simply print it. Of course, you also can modify any image using the toolbox or palette tools. Finally, you might want to save the image in one or more image file formats so that you can publish the image on a Web site or for print, or save all the internal Photoshop data to edit later.

Before taking a look at how you want to use Photoshop Elements to explore these workflow processes, you'll take a tour of the work area. Workflow processes are covered in more detail in Parts II through IV of this book.

Introducing the Work Area

One of the first things you'll notice about the menu bar area is that it looks like a sandwich. Two additional bars are located right below the menu bar: the toolbar and options bar. The menu bar itself contains a healthy total of 10 menus. Located directly below the menu bar is the shortcuts bar, which holds (you guessed it) shortcuts to tasks such as printing, cutting, pasting, and going to Adobe Online. Just below the shortcuts bar you'll find the options bar. The options bar's contents change depending on which tool you choose in the toolbox.

Over to the left of the work area, you'll find the indispensable toolbox. If you've seen Photoshop or other graphics applications, the toolbox items will look familiar to you. The toolbox contains selection, drawing, editing, and color-selection tools. You can apply these tools to any open document window. A document window is created whenever you open an existing image or create a new one.

Another common item from Photoshop that also exists in Photoshop Elements is the palette. A palette is a floating window. It's the type of window that you can drag around, but it won't get lost in a crowd of windows. A palette is always in front of all the other image windows in the work area. The palette well (on the right end of the shortcuts bar) houses all the palettes when they aren't in use. To use a palette, simply drag it from the palette well onto the work area (see Figure 2.1).

note
You can close a palette window by clicking in its Close box. The X icon, located in the top-right corner of the palette, marks the Close box if you're running Windows. Mac users can click on the left square in the title bar of the palette to close it.

Figure 2.1
The palette well resides
in the shortcuts bar
alongside the shortcut
icons.

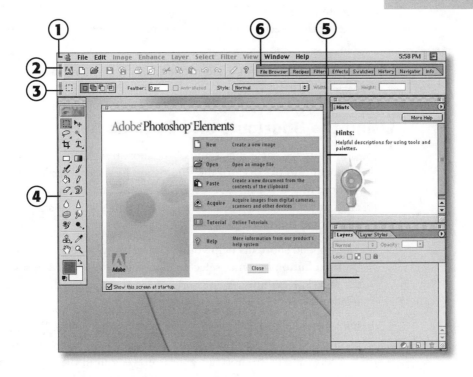

① Menu bar   ④ Toolbox

② Shortcuts bar   ⑤ Palettes

③ Options bar   ⑥ Palette well

At the bottom of the work area is a status bar. The status bar displays information about the document window, such as the size of the front-most image, as well as its dimensions. You can customize the status bar to show one of the following data items: document dimensions, document sizes, document profile, scratch size, efficiency, timing, and current tool. If you're running Windows, you can view help text for the selected toolbox tool in the right portion of the status bar.

The following section explores the tools in the shortcuts and options bars.

Using the Shortcuts and Options Bars

The shortcuts bar brings some of the most frequently selected menu commands to the front of the Photoshop Elements user interface. You can quickly open, save, or print a document in a single mouse click instead of having to click and select a menu command or learn a keyboard shortcut.

Not only do shortcuts help you save time, they're also smart! Each shortcut button becomes selectable only when certain conditions are met. For example, most shortcuts require an open document window.

Each shortcut button has two states, active and inactive. For example, if you haven't selected part of an image in the image window, the cut, copy, and paste shortcuts appear grayed out in the menu bar and will not be selectable. Similarly, if you haven't modified an image file, the Save shortcut will be inactive.

Show and Hide Commands

You can hide or show the shortcuts and options bars by choosing the Hide or Show Shortcuts or Hide or Show Options command from the Window menu.

Choose Show or Hide Tools if you want to show or hide the toolbox.

If you press the Tab button once, you can hide all palettes, in addition to the toolbox, shortcuts bar, and options bar. Press the Tab button once more, and presto—they're back!

The following list (starting from the left of the shortcuts bar) gives you a brief description of each button and its function:

- **Adobe Online**—Click on this button to visit Adobe's Web site. You will need to click on the links to locate and view the latest information available about Photoshop Elements, including information about software updates and third-party plug-in information.

- **New Document**—Open the New Document window by selecting this shortcut button.

- **Open Document**—Navigate your hard drive and select an existing image file to open in the work area.

- **Save Document**—If you've made any changes to an image file, select this shortcut button to save your changes.

- **Save for Web**—The Save for Web window enables you to customize a file you want to save for the Web. Select a Web file format for an image, and preview settings in the Save for Web window by clicking this button.

- **Print Document**—When you're ready to print your image, click this shortcut button to send the image file to a color or black-and-white printer.

- **Print Preview Document**—Preview a document before sending it to the printer by choosing the Print Preview shortcut button.

- **Cut, Copy, and Paste**—These shortcut buttons become active whenever you apply a selection tool to a document window.

- **Step Backward/Step Forward**—Pressing one of these buttons moves you backward or forward through tasks performed on the document, logged in the History palette.

- **Show/Hide Rulers**—Pressing this button will make vertical and horizontal rulers appear on the left and top edges of the document window.

- **Help Contents**—Clicking the Help button opens a browser window and brings up the HTML-based help contents for Photoshop Elements.

Separated At Birth?

The options bar works right alongside each tool located in the toolbox. That is, the buttons in the options bar change depending on which tool you click in the toolbox. After a tool is selected, you can adjust any available settings from the options bar. Click in a text box, click and drag a slider control, or select an item from a drop-down menu list to customize the selected tool.

Introducing the Toolbox Tools

The toolbox contains two vertical rows of tools. Although this window opens by default on the left side of the work area, you can drag and drop the toolbox window anywhere on your desktop. If you have two monitors connected to your computer, you can place the toolbox in one monitor and the document window on the other screen. You can choose Hide Tools from the Window menu if you don't want the toolbox open in the work area.

Before you start clicking away on those tools, remember that only one tool at a time can be applied to the image window. And finally, the foreground and background colors, shown at the bottom of the toolbox, also affect the way the tool can be applied to an image. Most tools, except for the eraser tool, apply the foreground color to the document window.

A total of 38 tools are available in the toolbox, but you can see only 24 of them. Why? Well, some tools are hidden in the toolbox. Simply click and hold down the mouse over the desired tool to view its hidden alternatives. A small arrow appears in the lower-right corner of the tool if any hidden tools share that space.

For example, the Rectangle Marquee Tool, located in the upper-left corner of the toolbox, shares its space in the toolbox with the Elliptical Marquee Tool. When you're using the Rectangle Marquee Tool, the Elliptical Marquee Tool remains hidden in the toolbox.

The good news is that each tool in the toolbox has a shortcut key. You can press a shortcut to select a tool in the toolbox. This enables you to switch tools with the press of a button. You don't have to hunt for an icon and then click on the toolbox icon every time you want to pick a new tool. If more than one tool shares a shortcut, you can hold down the Shift key and then press the shortcut key to cycle through each tool that shares the same keyboard shortcut. For example, if you want to select the Rectangular Marquee Tool, press the letter M on the keyboard. If you want to choose the Elliptical Marquee Tool, hold down the Shift key and press M again. The icon in the toolbox will change as you cycle through each tool that shares a particular keyboard shortcut.

Toolbox tools, shown in Figure 2.2, can be grouped into five general groups of tools: selection, drawing, effects, miscellaneous, and Color-Picker tools. The following list summarizes the four general groups of tools stored in the toolbox:

- **Selection Tools**—Select an area by shape, define a shape with a lasso tool, or select pixels by color using these handy tools.

- **Drawing and Painting Tools**—Choose the Paintbrush, Pencil, or Airbrush Tool and customize the brush settings and other options before you draw or paint over an image. Shape tools enable you to create simple geometric shapes that also can be added to any photo.

- **Effects Tools**—Remove red-eye, or apply a blur or sharpen tool to an image with a custom-sized brush or darken or lighten (burn or dodge) pixels in the image window. There are several effects tools you can choose from.

- **Additional Tools**—Magnify or zoom out from the contents in the image window. Select a foreground or background color, or clone a pattern of pixels to another part of the image window. This group of additional tools consists of the tools located at the bottom portion of the toolbox.

tip
Beside each tool name is the command-key shortcut you can use to quickly select that tool from the toolbox. To view a tool's name and shortcut, place the cursor over a tool in the toolbox. Let it hover over a tool for a few seconds. The tooltip will appear, and the shortcut letter will appear to the right of the tool's name. Press the shortcut key to select a tool from the toolbox.

Figure 2.2
Thirty-eight tools are
stored in the toolbox.
Click on an icon to select
a tool.

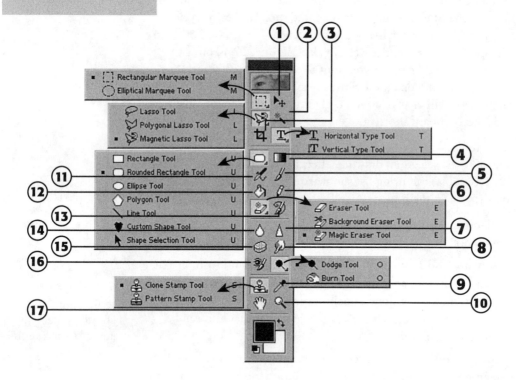

①	Move Tool (V)	⑩	Zoom Tool (Z)
②	Magic Wand Tool (W)	⑪	Airbrush Tool (J)
③	Crop Tool (C)	⑫	Paint Bucket Tool (K)
④	Gradient Tool (G)	⑬	Impressionist Brush (A)
⑤	Paintbrush Tool (B)	⑭	Blur Tool (R)
⑥	Pencil Tool (N)	⑮	Sponge Tool (Q)
⑦	Sharpen Tool (P)	⑯	Red Eye Brush Tool (Y)
⑧	Smudge Tool (F)	⑰	Hand Tool (H)
⑨	Eyedropper Tool(I)		

Choosing Pixels with Selection Tools

Selection tools enable you to choose all the pixels in an image, or one or two pixels. Five kinds of selection tools are available in the toolbox. Each one can help you quickly select all or part of an image's pixels. After pixels are selected, you can edit them by using a menu command or by applying color correction or filter tools to the selected pixels.

No Tool Is an Island

After you select a tool in the toolbox, take a peek at the options bar, located just below the shortcuts bar below the menu bar. Some tools have more options than others. But these options, which also can be viewed from the Preset Manager window, enable you to customize the way a tool works.

But wait, there's more! You can find out more about a tool from the Hints palette. Choose Show Hints from the Window menu, or select the Hints tab from the palette well located in the shortcuts bar.

The following list explains what each selection tool in the toolbox can do (see Figure 2.2):

- **Marquee Tool (M)**—Select an area in a rectangle or circular shape with this tool. The Elliptical Marquee Tool shares this space in the toolbox.

- **Move Tool (V)**—Click and drag one or more image objects in the document window with this frequently used tool.

- **Lasso Tool (L)**—The Polygonal and Magnetic Lasso tools enable you to click around the shape or color of an object you want to select in the image window.

- **Magic Wand Tool (W)**—Click on a color with this tool to select all touching pixels of that color in a document window.

- **Crop Tool (C)**—Select part of an image by applying the Crop Tool to an image file. The Crop Tool enables you to select a rectangular area of an image and removes any image area outside the cropped area.

tip
To find out more about how to add text and graphics to an image, see Chapter 14, "Adding Text and Shapes to Images."

Working with an Image in the Document Window

Before you can use the selection tools, first you'll need to create a new document window or open an existing image file. When a document window is open, you can pick a tool from the toolbox and experiment with selecting, drawing, or editing images. The drawing and painting tools enable you to work with vector and bitmap graphics and combine then with an image.

What are vector and bitmap images? Vector images are mathematically calculated graphics such as shapes, or line art–type images created by programs such as Adobe Illustrator. Vector images can be resized without losing the clarity of the images. On the other hand, bitmap images, including digital photos, consist of groups, or matrices, of pixels. Bitmap images are not easily resized. For example, if you try to enlarge a bitmap image, you'll start to see square-ish chunks of colors appear. This is called *pixelation*. In contrast, vector graphics are more adept at rising to this occasion.

Of all the tools in the toolbox, drawing tools offer you the most ways to be creative (see Figure 2.3). You also can add text, apply a gradient (a range of two or more colors that blend together), or blend layers of images together with Photoshop Elements' tools.

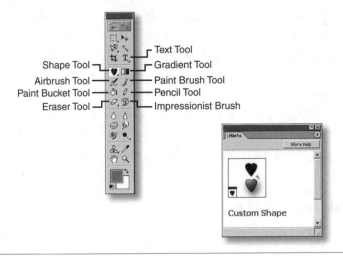

Figure 2.3
The tooltip for each tool appears in the Hints window, or if you hover over the tool's icon in the toolbox.

The following list provides a brief description of the toolbox's drawing tools:

- **T** **IT** **Horizontal and Vertical Type Tool (T)**—Text objects are a special kind of vector graphic. You can continue to modify text after you add it to a document by selecting the Text Tool, and then selecting the text you want to edit. However, if you convert the text into a bitmap, the Type Tool will not affect the bitmap text.

- **Shape Tool (U)**—Add a vector graphic to an image using one of six shape tools: rectangle, rounded rectangle, ellipse, polygon, line, or custom shape tools. Or, modify a shape with the Shape Selection Tool.

- **Gradient Tool (G)**—A gradient consists of two colors where one fades gently into the other from one end of the selected area to the opposite end. You can use the Gradient Tool to create a virtual sunset, focused lighting, or other effects by placing a gradient over the Fill area of a shape or graphic in the image window.

- **Airbrush Tool (J)**—Scatter pixels as you draw with this tool. The color of the pixels is determined by the foreground color of the color well. The longer you hold down the mouse, the more pixels will be added to the image window.

- **Paintbrush Tool (B)**—Experiment with different brush sizes, tips, and colors. You can choose a custom brush tip for this tool from the options bar.

- **Paint Bucket Tool (K)**—Fill an area with a solid color using the foreground color from the color well combined with the Paint Bucket Tool.

- **Pencil Tool (P)**—If you don't need a straight line, or want to replace one colored pixel with a new color, try using this tool.

- **Eraser Tool (E)**—Shares its space with the Background Eraser and the Magic Eraser. The eraser tool can be applied to a single layer or across all layers in the image window. The background eraser can remove the contents in the background layer of the image. The Magic Eraser replaces the color you click on with the foreground color in the image window.

tip

To find out more about layers, go to Chapter 13, "Working with Layers and Layer Styles." To find out more about how to work with graphics, go to Chapter 14, "Adding Text and Shapes to Images."

- 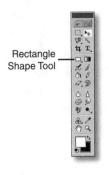 **Impressionist Brush (A)**—Use this tool to paint with stylized brush strokes. You can customize the brush, blending mode, opacity, style, fidelity, area, and spacing of the tool in the options bar.

Most tools in the toolbox are bitmap tools, except for the Shape and Type Tools. Figure 2.4 shows a Shape Tool placed over the bitmap image in the image window. As you draw or add graphics to an image, a new layer is created for each graphic object in the Layers palette. You can combine vector and bitmap graphics into the same image file.

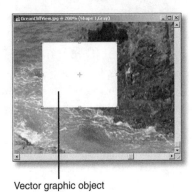

Rectangle
Shape Tool

Vector graphic object

Figure 2.4
Add a vector graphic object to an image file by applying a Shape Tool to the document window.

Vector and Bitmap Graphics

Vector and bitmap graphics are equally easy to work with. However, vector graphics are mathematically calculated whereas bitmaps are made up of static pixels. You can apply sophisticated tonal range and color tools, as well as filters and effects to bitmap graphics in Photoshop Elements. Vector graphics are better when you plan to grow or shrink a graphic. Text and shape objects are vector objects in Photoshop Elements. Although there are no limits to the size of a bitmap or vector graphic, vector graphics tend to create smaller-sized image files.

Several effect-related tools are also located in the toolbox. Some of these tools, such as the Blur and Sharpen Tools, can also be found in the Filter menu. The Red Eye Removal Tool is one of the new, cool features in Photoshop Elements. The effect-related tools are as follows:

- **Blur Tool (B)**—Add a localized blur effect to a particular set of pixels by applying this tool to an area of pixels.

- **Sharpen Tool (P)**—Like its big brother the Sharpen filter, this tool compares like-minded pixels and changes their color to try to create the illusion of a sharper, crisper image.

- **Sponge Tool (Q)**—With the right color and blending setting, this tool can act like a wet sponge. Click on a color, and then drag this tool over a different color to sponge the first color onto the next one.

- **Smudge Tool (F)**—Click on a color and drag this tool to smudge a color over another. Some of the pixels below the original position of the tool will remain, while others move along with the brush to create a smear, or smudge effect.

- **Red Eye Brush Tool (Y)**—Click and drag this tool over a photo of someone with red eye, and wipe the red away!

- **Dodge/Burn Tool (O)**—Tweak the shadows, midtones, or highlights of an image using these handy tools.

Going Back in Time with the History Palette

As you work on an image, it's possible to lose sight of your original goal for the image. If you want to undo or go back to a previous state of the image (as long as you don't close the image file), you can open the History palette and select a previous state of the document and jump back in time. Scroll and zoom changes are not saved in the History palette.

tip

To find out more about how to correct colors with the Dodge and Burn Tools, go to Chapter 17, "Creating Complex Images."

In addition to the invaluable effect tools, don't forget to try the Clone Stamp or Pattern Stamp Tools. These tools enable you to quickly duplicate a pattern or matrix of pixels in an image, and then apply that pattern elsewhere in the same image. Other tools that can help you select and control key elements are briefly explained in the following list:

- **Clone Stamp/Pattern Stamp Tool (S)**—Hold down the (Option) [Alt] key and drag the cursor over an area of an open image file you want to clone. This becomes the sample point for the tool. You can apply the tool to another location in the open image, and the sampled pixels will be applied wherever you click and drag the tool in the selected layer of the image window (see Figure 2.5). The Pattern Stamp Tool enables you to apply a pattern as a brush in the image window.

- **Eyedropper Tool (I)**—Use this tool to pick a foreground or background color in the document window.

- **Hand Tool (H)**—If you're working on a large or magnified document, select this tool to move the image around within the viewable area of the document window.

- **Zoom Tool (Z)**—Magnify a specific area of an image by selecting this tool, and then clicking in the document window. Hold down the (Option) [Alt] key to demagnify the image. Double-click this tool to restore the view to 100%.

- **Foreground Color**—The left color square displays the color of a shape, pen, or pencil. It can be added to the selected layer in the image window using the Brush or Paint Bucket Tools.

- **Background Color**—The color square located immediately to the right of the foreground color. This color appears when you select and delete an area in the document window.

Figure 2.5
The Clone Stamp Tool enables you to perform some amazing bitmap cloning. In this example, I've created a clone of the sheep on the right.

Different Ways to Apply the Clone Stamp Tool

Some of the toolbox tools can sample pixels across layers. Although most of the examples in this book apply the Clone Stamp Tool across layers, you can do the same with the Magic Wand, Smudge, Blur, and Sharpen Tools. The following list describes the Clone Stamp Tool settings available in the options bar:

- **Brush Settings**—Click on the brush stroke to open a drop-down menu. Choose a new brush size or stroke, or customize and save your own brushes.

- **Blending Mode**—Choose the blending mode to be applied when the Clone Stamp Tool applies the sampled pixels. See Chapter 13 to find out more about blending modes.

- **Opacity**—Set the transparency level of the applied pixels for the Clone Stamp Tool. Lower values add more transparency.

- **Alignment**—Apply the entire sampled area once to the target area. When the mouse is released, any other areas you choose to apply the tool are relative to the first area you applied the tool. Uncheck this option if you want to apply a particular sampled area multiple times to different images.

- **Use All Layers**—Check this option if you want to sample pixels from any other layer in the image. But only apply the Clone Stamp Tool to a correction layer.

- **Brush Options menu**—Click on the brush button located in the right side of the options bar to view or choose new Brush Dynamics settings for the Clone Stamp.

The Pattern Stamp Tool

The Pattern Stamp Tool is located with the Clone Stamp Tool in the toolbox. You can apply a pattern, selectable from the options bar, to the image window with the Pattern Stamp Tool. Like the Clone Stamp Tool, you can choose a custom brush size, and adjust the blending mode and opacity settings for the Pattern Stamp Tool.

Working with Palettes

Tucked away in the palette well on the shortcuts bar are 11 palette windows. Each palette is represented by a tab, and each tab can be pulled away from the shortcuts bar and opened into a standalone palette window in the work area. To activate a palette, click on its tab. When a palette window is closed, its tab will reappear in the palette well. If a palette window is open in the work area, you can view or use it as you like.

Palette windows are designed to make it easier for you to access features in Photoshop Elements. For example, the File Browser window enables you to view a thumbnail image of a previously viewed file. Simply double-click on an image to open it in the work area (see Figure 2.6).

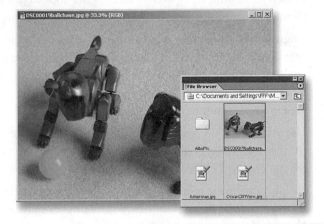

Figure 2.6
The File Browser palette enables you to double-click on an icon to open a file.

Grouping and Ungrouping Palettes

If you like a particular combination of palettes, you can click and drag each one onto a single palette window to group them together. Each palette window can host additional palettes if you drag and drop one palette window over another. Similarly, you can separate grouped palettes by dragging a palette tab away from its shared window.

The following sections explore the palette windows you'll find in the work area. You'll find out more about how to use a palette as you read through the rest of this book and work through the sample exercises.

Introducing Palettes

Each of the 11 palette windows is stored in the palette well. You can hide or show a palette by choosing its name from the Window menu, or by clicking on its tab in the palette well. You also can click and drag each palette into the work area. If you click on a palette's close box, its tab will reappear in the palette well.

Each palette well performs a specific function. For example, the File Browser palette enables you to preview and open an image file. The Hints and Recipes palettes contain helpful information about the tools in the toolbox and how to use them to correct color and apply effects to an open image.

Palettes also have some similarities. For example, the drop-down menu for a palette is located in the upper-right corner of the window. A right-arrow icon appears in the tab of a palette located in the palette well, or as a round button icon in the floating palette window. Click the drop-down menu button to view unique menu commands for each palette. Some palette windows, such as the Layers, Filters, and Swatches palettes, also have a small set of icon buttons located at their bottom. You can click the icon to change the view of the contents in the palette or to perform a command.

The following list introduces you to each of the palette windows in Photoshop Elements:

note
If you see a right-arrow icon in a palette, this means that the palette contains a palette menu. Click on the arrow icon to view the menu list. Items in the menu list can vary based on the contents of the active palette.

- **File Browser**—View and open an image file stored on any local or networked drive on your computer. You can use this palette to navigate the image files stored on a hard drive or CD-ROM.

- **Recipes**—Learn how to apply one or more tools in Photoshop Elements by following the steps in this palette window. Choose a set of recipes from the drop-down menu, and then click on a link to view the set of steps for a particular task.

- **Filters**—Preview or apply filters to the selected area of an image by clicking on a button in this palette window.

- **Effects**—Preview or apply an effect from this palette.

- **Layer Styles**—Customize the way a selected object looks by choosing a layer style.

- **Swatches**—Store groups of colors in custom palettes in this handy palette window (see Figure 2.7). You can pick a color from an existing color palette or add your own custom colors to a color palette.

Figure 2.7
Create and experiment with custom colors using the Swatches palette.

- **History**—As you apply tools, menu commands, or changes from a palette to an image, each task is logged as an entry in the History palette. Click on an entry to revert the document to a previous state.

- **Navigator**—You canadjust the view of the image as it appears in the image window. Click and drag the red rectangle in this palette window to pan to different areas of an image.

- **Info**—View X and Y coordinates for your cursor as it hovers over any area in the image, or view the color information below the cursor.

- **Layers**—The Layers palette enables you to view each image object, hidden or showing in the image window. Layers enable you to modify images in separate layers, preserving the original image until you're ready to flatten and optimize the final image. You can add, view, or remove layers using the buttons at the bottom of the palette.

- **Hints**—Read all about any tool you select from the toolbox or any palette in the palette well. This palette is a floating dictionary!

Using the Info, History, and Navigator Palettes

Although each palette window can be used as a standalone tool, two or three can work together to help you streamline your work flow (see Figure 2.8). For example, if you want to view color information and navigate around an image file, you can open the Navigator and Info palettes in their own separate windows. Simply glance at the open palette window to find out a particular color in an image, or zoom into or out of a picture. You also can keep track of the changes you make to an image by opening the History palette.

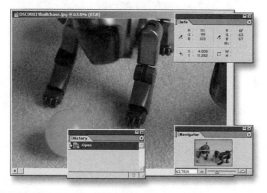

Figure 2.8
View document information in the Info, Navigator, and History palettes.

tip
You can combine two or more palettes into a single palette window. Click on the tab of a palette and drag and drop it over the tab area of a second palette window if you want both palettes to share the same window.

Drag and drop the second palette toward the bottom of a palette window if you want to stack two palette windows one above the other in the work area.

The Info palette enables you to view location and color information in the image window. If you want to pinpoint the location of a particular pixel or create an exact match for a color, you can use the Eyedropper Tool, combined with the Info palette, to get the job done! Click on the tab for the Info palette, and then select the Eyedropper Tool from the toolbox. Move the Eyedropper Tool over the active image window. The cursor location and RGB and hexadecimal color information update as you move the cursor around the image window.

Most tasks you perform in Photoshop Elements are stored as states in the History palette. The History palette only records the tasks you perform while it's open in the work area. If you save or close the file and then reopen it, the previous history will be cleared. You can click on an item in the History palette's window list to revert the image window to a previous state. You also can drag and drop a history state over the image window to revert the image to a previous state.

The Navigator palette enables you to change the view of the open image. A thumbnail image of the open document appears in the Navigation palette. You can drag the slider control to zoom into or away from the contents of the image window, or you can type a number into the View text box to change the view in the image window. A red rectangle marks the current view in the palette. You can click and drag the rectangle to pan to a new location of the image in the document window.

Customizing Images with the Recipes, Filters, and Effects Palettes

Filters and effects enable you to customize an image. You can preview each filter or effect from the palette window (see Figure 2.9). A filter or effect can be applied once, or multiple times to the same image. You also can apply more than one filter or effect to any image. The image window must be in RGB mode before you apply a filter or effect.

A filter is less complex than an effect. Fifteen groups of filters are installed with Photoshop Elements. Each filter has a unique way of changing an image. Effects, on the other hand, are made up of several filters and a few other items. Four groups of effects are available in the Effects palette. Drag and drop a filter or effect onto the image window to watch it go.

note

The History, Info, and Navigator palettes enable you to find out precisely what you're looking at (in terms of color, document history, and magnification level) in the document window.

note

To find out more about how to work with filters and effects, go to Chapter 12, "Applying Filters and Effects."

Figure 2.9
Preview Effects and Filters before applying them to an image. Recipes show you
how to apply a tool or perform a task.

Viewing Objects in the Layers Palette

Any image opened in Photoshop Elements is opened in a single
layer, called the Background layer. If you copy or create a new layer
or paste another image into the document window, a new layer is
created for each image object. Each new layer is placed above the
background layer.

You can view all layers in a document in the Layers palette (see
Figure 2.10). The Layers palette enables you to select a specific
layer, as well as adjust transparency settings and blending modes for
one or all layers. You also can drag and drop layers within the Layers
palette to change the order of layers in the document.

note
To learn more
about how to work
with layers and the
Layers palette, go
to Chapter 13,
"Working with
Layers and Layer
Styles."

Figure 2.10
Each object or adjustment layer in a document appears in the Layers palette.

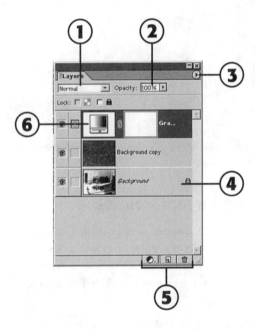

① Blending mode
② Transparency setting
③ Layer pop-up menu
④ Background layer
⑤ Layer command shortcuts
⑥ Image object layer

A Closer Look at the Document Window

You might have noticed that the document window is the center of attention in the work area. But it's pretty obvious that you can't do much with Photoshop Elements if you don't have an image file open. In addition to presenting the image file, the document window also displays some general information about the image file (see Figure 2.11). It has the standard scroll and size controls found in most Windows or Mac OS windows.

Figure 2.11
You can view some general information about each image file open in the work area. The filename and color mode of the image window appear in the title bar. The document size of the active window appears in the left side of the status bar.

Viewing Color Mode and Image Size Information

The document window displays the size of the open image, as well as its image mode. Photoshop Elements supports four image modes: RGB, grayscale, indexed color, and bitmap. Each image mode has its own way of managing the color information in the image file. In most cases, a scanned image, or an image from a digital camera, will be created as an RGB image and opened in RGB image mode in Photoshop Elements.

note
To find out more about color modes, see Chapter 10, "Digital Images and Color."

When you open an image file, Photoshop Elements changes the document view (also known as the magnification level) so that you can view the entire image in the work area. The actual width and height of the image, in pixels, can be viewed by holding down the mouse button while the cursor is over the middle section of the status bar (see Figure 2.12).

Figure 2.12
Customize the information that appears in the status bar of a document window.

Working with the Document Window

Each document window, which I also call an image window, can be moved, resized, hidden, opened, or closed. When a new document is created or an existing image file is opened, Photoshop Elements opens the contents of the file into memory. As you change an image, your changes are stored on a scratch disk on your hard drive.

The name of the file appears in the title bar of the window. You can move a window by clicking in the window's title bar and dragging it to a new location in the work area. The status bar located at the bottom of the window can be configured to show information about the open file. The Macintosh version of Photoshop Elements shows the document status at the bottom of each document window. The Windows version shows the status of the active window in the status bar located at the bottom of the work area.

You can have more than one document window open at once in the work area. The text in the title bar of the active window will be black, and not gray. The active image window usually is the front window in the work area. You can apply tools and commands only to the active image window. Any windows open behind or beside the active window are—you guessed it—inactive. If you don't plan to work with an inactive window, you might want to close it to free up memory.

If you modify the image, Photoshop Elements will ask you if you want to save the changes to the file on your hard drive when you close the document window, or exit Photoshop Elements. If you want to preserve any layer information or custom Photoshop settings and pick up where you left off when you next work with this image file, you can save the file as a Photoshop file. You also can save the image file in one of many commonly used graphics file formats for Web or print.

note
To find out more about how to save files, go to Chapter 8, "Saving and Sharing Files."

Navigating Menu Commands

The menu bar consists of 10 menus in the work area. Each menu in the menu bar represents a group of commands that can enable you to apply a specific graphics tool to all or part of an image. For example, the Filters menu contains groups of filters and effects that, when applied to an image, can create cool-looking effects. The following sections give you an overview of each menu command in Photoshop Elements.

Introducing File Menu Commands

Some of the menu commands, such as New, Open and (Quit) [Exit] will seem familiar to you if you've used other Windows or Mac OS applications. Photoshop Elements has an extended set of commands in its File menu, more so than most applications. For example, you can optimize an image for the Web by choosing the Save for Web command, or preview an image by choosing the Print Preview command. The following list introduces you to each command that resides in the File menu:

- **New**—Opens the New document window, enabling you to define the exact dimensions, image mode, and resolution.

- **Open/Open As**—Opens an image file. The Open As command enables you to convert an image file into a supported Photoshop Elements file format. For a complete list of supported file formats, see Chapter 7, "Creating, Opening, and Converting Images."

Open Sesame

There are a few more ways you can open an image file in the work area. You can use the Copy command in Photoshop Elements or another application to move a file to the Clipboard. Then, paste it into a new image window.

You also can choose the Open Recent command from the File menu. A list of previously opened files will appear in the menu list. Choose a file to open it.

If you want to create a panorama, choose the Photomerge command from the File menu. To find out how to create a panorama, go to Chapter 19, "Stitching Together a Panorama."

- **Close**—Closes the active window.

- **Save/Save As**—Use this command, and use it often, to save a native Photoshop file or any other supported file format. For a complete list of supported file formats, see Chapter 8, "Saving and Sharing Files." The Save As command enables you to choose a new name and file format for the file you want to save.

- **Save for Web**—Optimize an image for the Web by opening the Save for Web window. You can save a GIF, JPEG, PNG-8, PNG-24, or animated GIF from this window.

- **Revert**—Removes any changes made to the document, returning it to its original contents when it was first opened. This tool can only revert the document to its last-saved state.

- **Place**—Enables you to place an imported PDF, Illustrator, or EPS file, or an image stored in the Clipboard, into a specific place in the document window.

- **Import**—Select this command to control a scanner or camera device that works with installed TWAIN software. A list of installed TWAIN plug-ins can be found in the Import menu.

- **Export**—Save an image file using the Export menu command. You can install plug-in files that enable you to export an image file to a custom file format.

- **Automate**—Choose from creating an automated contact sheet, picture package, or Web photo gallery, or run a simple automated task, such as resizing photos on a batch of image files.

- **File Info**—Add caption, copyright, URL, and EXIF information to a document. EXIF information displays camera, scanner, or other device-specific information related to the image file.

- **Print Preview, Print**—Print commands enable you to preview the page layout, configure the way the document will print, and then send the image to the printer as a print job.

- **Page Setup**—Enables you to choose portrait or landscape orientation for the open image file, select the paper size, and scale of the active image window.

- **(Quit)/[Exit]**—Terminates the Photoshop Elements application.

Exploring Edit Menu Commands

Commands in the Edit menu might seem even more familiar to you if you're a big cut, copy, and paste user. If these commands don't ring a bell, don't worry, you'll learn how to use them soon enough! The following list summarizes what each of these handy commands can do:

- **Undo**—Select this command once to reverse the previous task or command performed on the document window. You can perform multiple undo commands. Set the number of undo tasks from the General Preferences window.

- **Step Forward/Backward**—Redo the previously undone task by choosing Step Forward. Undo the previous task by choosing Step Backward.

- **Cut**—Removes the selected area from the document window and puts it into the Clipboard. The Clipboard is a part of the Windows and Mac operating system used to store temporary data.

- **Copy/Copy Merged**—Creates a copy of the selected area in the document window and places it in the Clipboard. Copy Merged enables you to copy all the layers in the selected area.

- **Paste/Paste Into**—Places the image stored in the Clipboard into a new layer in the document window. The Paste Into command places the image from the Clipboard into a selected area in the document window.

- **Clear**—Deletes the selected image and its layer from the document window. However, you can revert the document by opening the History palette or by choosing the Undo command from the Edit menu.

- **Duplicate Image**—Creates an exact copy of the selected image object.

- **Fill/Stroke**—The Fill command enables you to adjust content and blending settings for the fill or color after you've applied a tool to an image. The Stroke command enables you to customize a stroke after it has been applied to an image.

- **Define Brush/Pattern**—These commands enable you to select a customized brush stroke or pattern and save it as a custom brush or pattern.

- **Purge**—Clear the Undo, Clipboard, Histories, or all three types of settings from the Purge command's submenu.

- **Color Settings/Preset Manager/Preferences**—Customize the color management, tools, and your work preferences by choosing these menu commands. To find out more about how to use these valuable features, go to Chapter 3, "Customizing Adobe Photoshop Elements."

Image Menu Commands

Perform the equivalent of a facelift or liposuction with one or more of the commands you'll find in the Image menu. Go to Chapter 11, "Tonal Range and Color Correction," to find out how to use the Image menu commands with your images. Each selection in the Image menu list contains a short list of mission-critical tools that can make your images look marvelous!

The following list provides a brief explanation of what each menu item can do:

- **Rotate**—Flip or turn an image on its side by choosing one of the commands from this menu.

- **Crop**—Use this tool to define new boundaries for the open image and reduce its dimensions.

- **Resize**—Adjust the image or canvas size of an image by choosing the Image Size or Canvas Size commands from this menu. Choose Scale to adjust the size of the selected area in the image window. Or choose Reveal All to show any hidden images stored in the Layers palette.

- **Mode**—Change the number of colors available to an image. Choose from RGB, Grayscale, Bitmap, or Indexed Color modes.

- **Adjustments**—Choose one of the commands in this menu to reduce the number of pixels in an image by defining a reduced set of colors to apply to the open image.

- **Transform**—Skew or distort an image, or change a selected image's perspective.

- **Histogram**—Enables you to view the tonal range distribution for each or all color channels in the open image.

Adjusting Images with the Enhance Menu Commands

Image is everything in Photoshop Elements. But even if your image looks great, you can use the tools in the Enhance menu to make it look even better. It's sort of the equivalent of adding makeup to a facelift. After all, the devil is in the details, right?

The following list contains a brief description of each menu item in the Enhance menu:

- **Auto Levels**—Photoshop Elements will automatically correct the tonal range of colors in an image when this option is selected. Sometimes, this feature can save you time by quickly correcting colors rather than you having to do it manually.

- **Auto Contrast**—Automatically correct the contrast levels in an image with this command.
- **Adjust Backlighting**—Manually adjust washed out colors in the background of an image using this feature.
- **Fill Flash**—Brighten shadowed areas of an image with this command.
- **Color**—Adjust the hue, saturation, and lightness of colors in an image, or replace or remove colors using the Color menu commands.
- **Brightness/Contrast**—Manually adjust the brightness and contrast levels of an image with this command. The submenu options in this selection open either the Brightness/Contrast dialog box or Levels dialog box for making the adjustments.
- **Variations**—The Variations window enables you to experiment with color adjustment. You can make changes to Shadows, Midtones, Highlights, and Saturation, and view the results as you manually adjust colors.

Layer Menu Commands

Layers enable you to organize, combine, and edit images in a document. Although you can use the Layers palette to adjust many of the layers settings, many additional commands are also stored in the Layers menu. The following list summarizes Layer menu commands:

- **New**—Create one of four possible kinds of new layers.
- **Duplicate Layer**—Create a copy of a layer by selecting a layer, and then choosing this menu command.
- **Delete Layer**—Remove a layer from a document.
- **Rename Layer**—Give each layer a unique name. You also can double-click on a layer to open the Layer Properties window. Then type in a new name for the selected layer.
- **Layer Style**—Apply or modify a layer style by choosing one of the commands in this submenu.
- **New Fill Layer**—Add a solid-color, gradient, or pattern layer to a document.

- **New Adjustment Layer**—Experiment with Levels, Brightness/Contrast, Hue/Saturation, Gradient Map, Invert, Threshold, and Posterize settings to adjust the tonal ranges of an image.

- **Layer Content Commands**—The Change Layer Content and Layer Content commands enable you to modify adjustment or fill layers that exist in the Layers palette.

- **Type**—Format a text layer in a document by choosing one of the commands in this menu. The Warp Text command enables you to create some cool-looking text effects.

- **Simplify Layer**—Some layers can contain more than one element. Choose this command to merge complex layers into a simple, single-object layer.

- **Group with Previous/Ungroup**—Keep layers together or apart by choosing one of these two commands.

- **Arrange**—Change the order of the selected layer in the Layers palette. The Background layer cannot be moved, although any other layer can be moved freely.

- **Merge Layers**—Merge all layers below the selected layer in the Layers palette.

- **Merge Visible**—Combine all layers marked with the eye icon into a single layer. Invisible layers will remain unchanged.

- **Flatten Image**—Merge all layers in a document into a single layer.

note
To find out more about how to use layers, go to Chapter 13.

Using the Select Menu Commands

Before you can view or edit part of an image, you'll need to select it. The following list provides a brief summary of the selection menu commands:

- **All**—Select everything in the active document window.

- **Deselect**—Deselect everything in the active document window.

- **Reselect**—Well, you get the picture by now. This command reselects the previously selected image.

- **Inverse**—Select all parts of the image except for the currently selected area.

- **Feather**—Blend the edges of the selected image object into the pixels surrounding the selected area.
- **Modify**—Adjust the border, or expand, smooth, or contract a selected area of an image.
- **Grow**—Extend the edges of the selected area.
- **Similar**—Change the pixels of the edges of the selected area to be more like the color of the surrounding pixels.

Adding Effects from the Filter Menu

Wow! Have you ever seen so many menu options in a menu list? The Filter menu stores all the plug-in files installed with Photoshop Elements. Plug-in files can be used to extend the capabilities of Photoshop Elements. Select an image layer in the Layers palette, and then choose one of the many commands in the Filter menu to stylize an image. The following list provides a brief overview of each group of filters and effects installed with Photoshop Elements:

- **Repeat Last Effect**—The previously selected filter or effect will appear at the top of the Filter menu. Press (Command)/[Ctrl]+F to reapply the filter or effect to the selected area of the document.
- **Liquify**—Apply several kinds of distortion effects to specific areas of an image.
- **Artistic**—Apply neon glow, colored pencil, smudge stick, rough pastels, and other artistic stroke effects to an image.
- **Blur**—These filters smooth out pixels by averaging the color of pixels located beside hard edges, lines, or shaded areas.
- **Brush Strokes**—Apply another variation of brush strokes to an image, similar to the artistic effects.
- **Distort**—Each distort effect takes a shape, such as a sphere, and applies a specific effect, such as pinch, ripple, or shear, combined with the shape to distort an image.
- **Noise**—Add pixels to an image to reduce the clarity of an image. This filter can be used to minimize sharp color or tonal contrasts in an image.

- **Pixelate**—Group pixels to a specific shape or size to create a unique effect.

- **Render**—Add a lens flare, lighting effect, or a 3D effect to an image by applying a render effect.

- **Sharpen**—Sharpen filters work in contrast to Blur filters, increasing the contrast of nearby pixels to bring out an image.

- **Sketch**—Apply a texture or stroke to an image to enhance it. Works similarly to the Artistic and Brush Stroke filters.

- **Stylize**—Apply a painted effect to an image with options such as Emboss, Diffuse, Solarize, Glowing Edges, Trace Contour, or Wind filter.

- **Texture**—Intensify the depth or substance of an image by applying selections such as Grain, Patchwork, Stained Glass, or Texturizer filters to an image.

- **Video**—De-interlace or change an image to NTSC colors with video filters.

- **Other**—Create your own filter effects by choosing the Custom filter, or choose DitherBox, High Pass, Maximum, Minimum, or Offset filter to apply a color adjustment filter to an image.

- **Digimarc**—Image files can be saved with a unique indentification, or watermark. This filter enables you to search for a digimarc watermark in an image.

Customizing Output with the View Menu Commands

View commands enable you to change the way an image appears in the document window. As you work with an image, you might need to magnify part of it or measure a certain area. Some of the commands in this menu enable you to do just that. The following list describes each menu option and its use:

- **New View**—Opens a second, duplicate window of the image in the active window.

- **Zoom In**—Magnifies the image in the document window.

- **Zoom Out**—Reduces the size of the image in the document window.

- **Fit on Screen**—Adjusts the size so that the full image fits in the document window.

- **Actual Pixels**—Changes the view to 100%, or the unaltered view of the image in the document window.

- **Print Size**—Defines the printed dimensions of the image file. Changes the image in the document window to the way it will appear if printed.

- **Selection Edges**—Enables you to view or not view a dash-line marquee when a selection tool is applied to the image window.

- **Show/Hide Rulers**—Shows or hides a horizontal and vertical ruler on the document window.

- **Show/Hide Grid**—Adds or removes a grid in the document window.

- **Snap**—Helps align an object being placed in the image to the nearest grid cell.

- **Show/Hide Annotations**—If an image contains annotation data, you can view or hide this information by selecting this command.

Opening and Closing Palettes with the Window Commands

Photoshop Elements enables you to work with more than one image file at a time. Windows folks can use the commands in the Window menu to help organize all the open documents in the work area. Each palette window also can be selected from the Window menu. The following list contains a brief description of the commands in the Window menu. The palette commands are not included in this list as they were covered in the previous section.

- **Cascade**—Overlaps each window from the left corner of the work area toward the right. This menu item is available only in the Windows version of Photoshop Elements.

- **Tile**—Resizes each open window so that you can view each open image in the work area. This menu item is available only in the Windows version of Photoshop Elements.

- **Arrange Icons**—Aligns minimized images (Windows only) in the work area. This menu item is available only in the Windows version of Photoshop Elements.

- **Close All**—Closes all document windows. This menu item is available only in the Windows version of Photoshop Elements.

- **Show/Hide Tools**—Shows or hides the toolbox.

- **Show/Hide Options**—Shows or hides the options bar.

- **Show/Hide Shortcuts**—Shows or hides the shortcuts bar.

- **Show/Hide Quick Start**—Opens or closes the Quick Start window.

- **Show/Hide Status Bar**—Shows or hides the status bar in the work area. This menu item is available only in the Windows version of Photoshop Elements.

- **Reset Palette Locations**—Returns the palette windows to their original locations in the work area.

note
The Help menu is also located in the menu bar. To find out more about the Help menu commands, go to Chapter 4, "Using the Quick Start Window and the Help System."

Customizing Adobe Photoshop Elements

It's okay to go ahead and use Photoshop Elements as-is. However, as you become more familiar with it, you might want to customize some of its settings. Now, you might be wondering exactly what kinds of settings can be customized. For starters, you can customize the way an image file is opened or choose whether the cursor matches the brush size or remains constant regardless of how many pixels a tool applies to an image.

Photoshop Elements has three general groups of customizable settings. The first group of settings has to do with color management. The second group corresponds to brush, gradient, and pattern-related settings. Finally, you can work with eight windows of user preference settings.

Adjusting Color-Management Settings

Somehow, a term involving color combined with management just doesn't sit well with me. When I think of color, I think of red, blue, and yellow. When I think of management, I think of a business, desks, payroll, a water cooler, phones, and a photocopier.

But if you think about how a computer manages color, and compare that to the way a monitor, printer, camera, or scanner manages color, it might seem as though each device is running its own color-management business. For example, if you pick a certain green color on your computer monitor, it might look light blue when you print it to your color printer. Similarly, if you take a picture of a red apple with a camera, it might appear greener when you print that picture to a color printer, depending on how you set up your computer's monitor and printer software.

The following sections explain how color-management settings work in Photoshop Elements. If you're not sure which setting to choose, choose the default setting: No Color Management.

Back Up Original Images

Before you get all excited about working with color images and start modifying an image with Photoshop Elements, make a copy of that file onto your hard drive. If you plan to make several modifications to an image file, it's helpful to keep a backup of the original nearby on your local hard drive.

However, the best method for backing up a file is to copy it to an external drive, such as a Zip disk or CD-R media, or to a tape backup drive connected to your computer over a network. If the hard drive stops working, you can always install Photoshop Elements on a new computer, restore your backup files, and continue working on your image files. After you've created a copy of the original image file, you can make all the changes you like without worrying about making an irreversible mistake. If you make a mistake, you can always start over with the original.

Operating System Color Settings

Some operating systems, such as Mac OS 9 or Mac OS X, support color management for input and output devices, such as a scanner or printer. This is important in that it helps to ensure that the colors you are seeing onscreen when you create your images are the same colors that appear when the image is seen in print or on the Web. To customize the color settings for Mac OS, open the Color Sync control panel.

Windows and Linux do not have an equivalent technology to Color Sync. However, Photoshop Elements enables you to save an image file with an ICC color profile, which, in essence, does the same thing.

Before you can add a color profile to an image you want to save, first you must select the Color Settings command, located in the Edit menu, shown in Figure 3.1. Choose the Limited Color Management radio button if you plan to save files for the Web. The Limited Color Management setting will give you the option, on the Save or Save As dialog box, to save an sRGB IEC61966-2.1 color profile for a Web image. Click the Full Color Management radio button to save an Adobe RGB (1998) Color profile to an image you want to print.

Figure 3.1
Although No Color Management is the default for the color settings, your color images might still print colors fairly close to the way they appear onscreen.

In addition to choosing a color management setting for Photoshop Elements, you can customize the operating system settings on your computer monitor so that you can view as many colors you like. The maximum number of colors you can view on your monitor is limited by the amount of video memory installed on the monitor or on your computer. To adjust the number of colors viewable on your computer, open the Display Settings control panel if you're using Windows, or open the Monitors (or Monitors & Sound) control panel if you're using a Mac. Choose a minimum of thousands (16-bit) or millions (24-bit) of colors.

The size of your desktop affects how much of an image file you can view. Choose a minimum desktop size of 800×600 pixels. Depending on the average size of the image you'll be working on (the average two-megapixel camera creates a 1024×768 pixel image file), choose a desktop size that displays the most colors. This provides the best processor performance in addition to a healthy dose of desktop real estate.

What's the Size of Your Desktop?

The desktop size desktop represents the number of pixels that you can view on your computer monitor. However, the larger the desktop size, the smaller each pixel will become. The result? Eye strain.

In a nutshell, it's tough to work with large image files on small computer monitors desktop (for example, 13- or 15-inch monitors). Although you might be able to view the full color spectrum on any size monitor, smaller monitors limit how much of the image you can view and access.

If working with small pixels or squinting your eyes doesn't appeal to you, choose a larger desktop size for your computer screen. I use a 1600×1200 pixel desktop on a 17-inch monitor with one of my Windows computers.

note
Photoshop Elements enables you to choose one of four different image modesfor an image file. Each image mode determines how many colors will be used to create the image in the active image window. To use most of the commands and tools, the image will need to be in RGB, or red, green, and blue mode. Grayscale, Indexed Color, and Bitmap are the other three image modes available.

Limited Color Management

Photoshop Elements can assign a color profile to an image file. The type of color profile assigned to an image depends on which setting you choose in the Color Settings window. The image mode selected for the image file also determines which color profile is saved with the file.

If you're planning to create images for the Web, select the Limited Color Management option. When you're ready to save an image file, choose Save As from the File menu. Then check the ICC Profile if you're using Windows, or the Embed Color Profile if you're using a Mac in the Save As window. Photoshop Elements will generate a color profile for Web graphics and save it along with the image file. Select any additional options you want to apply to the file. When the file is saved, it will contain color profile information.

Web Graphics and Image Optimization

If you want to optimize an image before saving it as a Web graphic, choose the Save for Web command from the File menu. The Save for Web dialog boxis chock-full of tools that enable you to create a great-looking image in a relatively small file size. An (Embed Color Profile) [ICC Profile] check box also appears if you choose in this dialog box to save the image as a JPEG file.

Full Color Management

If you plan to print an image, choose Full Color Managementfrom the Color Settings dialog box. The Full Color Management option assigns a print-related color profile to the image file if you check the Color Profile check box in the Save As window before saving the image. To find out more about color management, see Chapter 10, "Digital Images and Color."

Choosing Settings in the Preset Manager

Customize settings for brushes, swatches, gradients, and patterns from the Preset Manager window. Choose Preset Managerfrom the Edit menu to open the Preset Manager window. The Preset Type drop-down menu contains Brushes, Swatches, Gradients, and Patterns. Each of these menu options changes the available settings that appear in the Preset Manager window.

Preset Shortcuts

Press (Command) [Ctrl]+1, 2 , 3, or 4 to go directly to the Brushes, Swatches, Gradients, or Patterns Preset window in the Preset Manager window.

In the upper-right corner of the Preset Manager window is a right-arrow icon. Click on this icon to view a drop-down menu for each Preset. You can change the window list view, load another group of settings into the window list, or choose a custom command specific to each preset. The Load and Save Set buttons enable you to save and open custom settings so you can re-use your presets with other documents or share them with other Photoshop Elements users.

Each set of brushes, gradients, swatches, or patterns is stored in a folder located in the Presets folder of the Adobe Photoshop Elements folder on your hard drive. For example, each set of brushes is stored in a separate file in the Brushes folder of the Presets directory. To create a new set of brushes, patterns, gradients, or swatches, select one of the items in the window list, and then click the Save Set button. Type a name for the file, and save the file to your hard drive. Brushes are saved as .abr files, patterns as .pat files, gradients as .grd files, and swatches as .aco files. If the file is placed in the

note

If Limited Color Management is selected in the Color Settings window, Photoshop Elements will attach an sRGB IEC61966-2.1 color profile to the image being saved. sRGB IEC61966-2.1 will appear beside the ICC Profile check box name in the Save As dialog box. If you open this image file in another graphics application, it will be capable of producing a more accurate set of colors than if the color profile had not been saved with the file.

corresponding Brushes, Gradients, Color Swatches, or Patterns folder in the Presets folder, its name will appear in the drop-down menu list in the Preset Manager window.

Presets in the Options Bar

You also can access brush, swatch, gradient, and pattern settings from the options bar if a tool that uses these presets is selected in the tool-box.

Brushes

You can choose the default brush settings for the Brush tool (B) from the Brushes Preset Manager window. Upon first glance, you'll notice that each type of brush setting has a number below it. The number represents the number of pixels that brush will apply to the canvas. Click on a brush in the window to pick the style or stroke settings you want to use.

Double-click a setting to open its Brush Name window. View the name of the brush, or type a new name into the Name text box.

Where to Find Brushes

Each group of brushes that appears in the drop-down list in the Preset Manager window is stored on your hard drive in the Presets, Brushes folder in the Photoshop Elements folder. Photoshop Elements stores brush files as ABR files.

The menu for the Brushes Preset Manager enables you to reset or replace brushes, choose a custom view for the window list, or load several brushes (Assorted Brushes, Calligraphic Brushes, Drop Shadow Brushes, Faux Finish Brushes, Natural Brushes 2, Natural Brushes, or Square Brushes) into the window list. You can view only one group of presets at a time in the Preset Manager window (see Figure 3.2).

Learn How to Use Drawing Tools

To find out more about how to use the drawing tools, go to Chapter 14, "Adding Text and Shapes to Images."

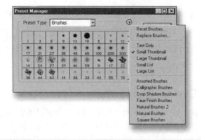

Figure 3.2
Choose from a huge list of brush sizes and strokes in the Preset Manager
window.

Choosing Swatches in the Preset Manager

The Swatches Preset Manager window determines which set of
swatches appears in the Swatches palette (see Figure 3.3). Photoshop
Elements includes seven sets of swatches you can load into the
Swatches palette: Mac OS, VisiBone, VisiBone2, Web Hues, Web
Safe Colors, Web Spectrum, and Windows.

Click the arrow button to view each swatch set, and select an item
from the menu list to change the swatch set in the Preset Manager
window. Each swatch set represents a group of colors stored in a file
in the Color Swatches folder, located in the Presets folder. Click the
Save Set button to create your own swatch set and save it as a file on
your hard drive. Click the Load button to select a swatch set file
stored on your hard drive.

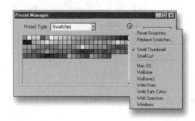

Figure 3.3
Choose a group of colors to work with from the Swatches Preset Manager
window.

note
Remember the
swatch set you've
selected in the
Swatches Preset
Manager window.
The name of the
current swatch set
will not appear in
the Swatches
Preset Manager
window or the
Swatches palette
window.

To view the hexadecimal value of a color, click on a color square in the Swatches window. The tooltip for the color contains the hexadecimal value of the color. You also can double-click a color to view its hexadecimal value.

Where to Find Color Swatches

Each group of color swatches is stored in the Presets folder, located in the Photoshop Elements folder. All the color swatches that appear in the drop-down list in the Preset Manager window are stored in the Color Swatches folder located in the Presets folder on your hard drive. Photoshop Elements stores swatch files as ACO files.

The drop-down menu for the Swatches contains two view options, Small Thumbnail and Small List. You also can reset or replace swatches from the drop-down menu.

Gradients

A *gradient* consists of two or more colors that gradually blend into each other. When Gradients is selected as the Preset Type, each square in the window contains a gradient map (see Figure 3.4). When you select the Gradient tool (G) from the toolbox, you can assign a gradient map to the selected area in the image window. You can choose the default gradient maps that appear in the options bar settings from the Gradients Preset Manager window.

Figure 3.4
Select a set of gradients to work with from the Gradient Preset Manager window.

Where to Find Gradients

Each group of brushes that appears in the drop-down list in the Preset Manager window is stored on your hard drive in the Presets, Gradients folder in the Photoshop Elements folder. Photoshop Elements stores groups of gradients in GRD files. Choose the Save Set button in the Preset Manager window to create a custom group of gradients.

View gradient maps in one of five views: Text Only, Small Thumbnail, Large Thumbnail, Small List, or Large List. You can access these views from the arrow drop-down menu. You also can reset or replace gradients by choosing the Reset Gradients or Replace Gradients commands from the drop-down menu list. Click the Load button and select a gradient file, or choose one of the gradient sets from the drop-down menu to load one of eight built-in gradient map sets: Color Harmonies 1, Color Harmonies 2, Metals, Noise Samples, Pastels, Simple, Special Effects, or Spectrums.

note
You cannot apply gradient tools to images in Bitmap, Indexed-Color, or 16-bits per channel mode.

Patterns

You can apply the Patterns in the Preset Manager window (see Figure 3.5) to an image by adding a pattern Fill Layer to it. You can choose from two pre-installed groups of patterns: Patterns and Patterns 2. You can reset or replace patterns from the arrow drop-down menu or change the format of the view for the Patterns window list.

Figure 3.5
You can choose from two groups of patterns in the Patterns Preset Manager window.

tip
To find out more about how to apply a pattern to an image file, go to Chapter 14, "Adding Text and Shapes to Images."

Where to Find Patterns

Each group of patterns that appears in the drop-down list in the Preset Manager window is stored on your hard drive in the Presets, Patterns folder in the Photoshop Elements folder. Photoshop Elements stores patterns in the PAT file format. PostScript patterns are stored as AI, or Adobe Illustrator, files.

Personalizing Your Preferences

Photoshop Elements enables you to customize the way a document opens, how the cursor behaves with tools, how transparent areas are visualized in the document window, how rulers and grids behave, how the program uses memory, and which hard drives are used as scratch disks. All these settings are grouped into eight preference windows. Each setting can be accessed one at a time from the Preferences window.

The following sections introduce you to the preference settings. Each Preferences window contains a set of five buttons located to the right of the Preferences window. Click the Prev or Next button to view the next set of preferences. If you want to view the HTML help files in a browser window, click the Help button. Click the OK button to save your changes, or click Cancel to exit the Preferences window without saving any of your changes.

General Preferences

To open the Preferences window, choose Preferences from the Edit menu or press (Command-K) [Ctrl+K].. The General preferences window contains settings for the Color Picker and Undo feature, 11 check boxes you can choose from to customize various ways the work area behaves, and two buttons that enable you to reset warning messages and tools (see Figure 3.6).

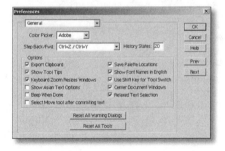

Figure 3.6
Choose from a long list of check boxes to customize the way the work area behaves. You also can choose the Color Picker or set the number of undo steps and history states.

Preferences for Saving Files

Change the way image files are saved in the Saving Files Preferences window. For example, when you save a file, Photoshop Elements creates a thumbnail image along with the image file. On a Mac, the image file's icon becomes a tiny image of the actual picture. On a Windows computer, you can preview each image in the Open dialog box. In the Saving Files Preferences window, you can tell Photoshop Elements to ask when saving, or never save a thumbnail image with a file. You also can change the formatting of the file extension, choose file compatibility with older versions of Photoshop files, and set how many recently opened files appear in the File, Open Recent submenu (see Figure 3.7).

note
If you're using the Macintosh version of Photoshop Elements, you'll find a few more check boxes in the Saving Files Preferences window. You can save a Macintosh or Windows Thumbnail preview image for the file's icon. Check the corresponding Icon, Macintosh Thumbnail, or Windows Thumbnail check box to choose the settings you want.

You also have the option of always, never, or being asked if you want to add the file extension to the name of the image file being saved.

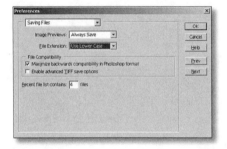

Figure 3.7
Adjust your image previews, file extension-naming scheme, and Photoshop file compatibility in the Saving Files Preferences window.

Preference Window Shortcuts

Navigate through the eight preferences windows by clicking in the drop-down menu window, and then pressing the up or down arrow keys on your. You also can use the (Command) [Ctrl]+1–8 keys to go directly to a preference window.

Display & Cursors

The cursor changes depending on which tool is selected. For example, the selection, drawing, and text tools use unique tool pointers to enable you to apply the tool to the image. Selection tools use crosshairs for tool pointers, the Text Tool uses an I-beam, and drawing tools use the Brush Size icon.

Tool Pointer Shortcut

Press the Caps Lock key to switch between standard and precise cursors if you're using a selection, drawing, or text tool from the toolbox.

You also can adjust the appearance of tool pointers in the Display & Cursors Preferences window. Choose Standard if you want the cursor to remain a constant size as you use a tool, or choose Precise if you want the cursor to reflect the actual pixel size of the brush (see Figure 3.8). Choose the Brush Size radio button if you want the Painting Cursors to change to match the number of pixels of the selected brush size that will be applied to the canvas.

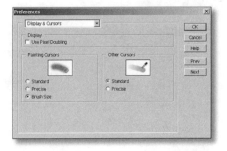

Figure 3.8
View the current Display & Cursor settings to change the way tool pointers appear.

Transparency

Transparency represents the absence of color in an image—typically the background layer. You can adjust the transparency of an image layer by increasing or decreasing its opacity value from the Layers palette. A value of zero renders a transparent (or invisible) image. Photoshop Elements uses a gray-and-white checkered pattern to represent transparency. You can customize the grid size and colors in the Transparency Preferences window (see Figure 3.9). Choose from a small, medium, or large grid, or change the grid colors as you like. Preview the transparency pattern in the square on the right.

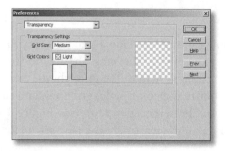

Figure 3.9
Edit the default gray and white transparency pattern to suit your needs.

Units & Rulers

You can adjust the units of the ruler in the Units & Rulers Preferences window (see Figure 3.10). Choose the measurement and type formats, or choose between PostScript or Traditional Point/Pica size. If you've added columns to a document, you can adjust the width and gutter sizes of the columns in this preferences window, too.

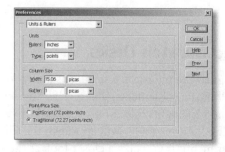

Figure 3.10
You can customize the rulers, column size, and point/pica size in the Units & Rulers Preferences window.

Picas, Points, and PostScript

Type size can be measured in *picas* or *points*. A point is approximately 1/72 of an image in a 72 pixel-per-inch (ppi) image. 72-point text in a 72dpi image appears as a 1-inch tall image. A pica is approximately 12 points in a 72ppi image.

The Point/Pica size option in the Units & Rulers Preferences window enables you to choose the point size definition for printing. If you're printing to a PostScript printer, choose PostScript (72 points per inch) in the Units & Rulers Preferences window. If you're not printing to a PostScript printer, choose traditional (72.27 points per inch).

tip
To find out more about transparency and opacity settings, go to Chapter 13, "Working with Layers and Layer Styles."

Grid

Each window can show or hide a grid to help you align your objects. You can view the grid by choosing Show Grid from the View menu. To have your images snap to the grid, choose Snap from the View menu. Customize the color, style, gridlines, and subdivisions of the gridin the Grid Preferences window (see Figure 3.11). Click on each drop-down menu to view or choose new settings.

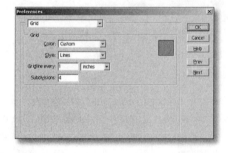

Figure 3.11
Create a custom grid if you need to align images to create a custom document, such as a contact sheet.

Plug-Ins and Scratch Disks

Adobe designed the plug-in file format as a way to extend the capabilities of Photoshop Elements. There is a Plug-ins folder located in the Photoshop Elements folder on your hard drive. Any plug-in files located in the Plug-ins folder will appear in the Filter menu or in the File, Import menu. If you take a closer look at the Plug-Ins folder, you'll notice that plug-in files are grouped into folders. The TWAIN plug-ins, which are explained in more detail in Chapters 5 and 6, are stored in the Import-Export folder of the Plug-Ins folder. If you click the File, Import menu, you'll see each TWAIN plug-in file in the Import menu list.

If you want to use an additional plug-in folder, you can check the Additional Plug-Ins Directory check box in the Plug-Ins & Scratch Disks Preferences window (see Figure 3.12). Click the Choose button and navigate through your hard drive to select the secondary plug-ins folder. A secondary plug-in folder enables you to access another group of plug-in files from the Filter or Import menus.

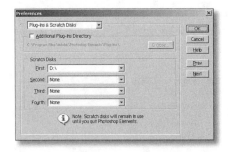

Figure 3.12
Add a second directory to extend filter effect or TWAIN plug-ins available to the work area, or assign additional scratch disks to Photoshop Elements from this Preferences window.

To Use New Plug-Ins and Scratch Disks...

You must (Quit) [Exit] Photoshop Elements, and then restart the application to use the secondary plug-ins or additional scratch disks selected in the Preferences window.

As you work with an image, Photoshop Elements uses available hard disk space as a scratch diskThe scratch disk works similarly to virtual memory, storing information about the original image, as well as any edits you make to it. Naturally, the scratch disk size will grow as you continue to modify or combine images. Also, each image you open increases the size of the scratch disk.

By default, Photoshop Elements chooses the startup drive as the primary scratch disk. You might want to choose an external, or second drive, to use as the secondary scratch disk. You can select up to four scratch disks, enabling you to work on a single image longer, or a larger image faster, without running out of disk space, on a single drive. Choose each scratch disk from the Plug-ins & Scratch Disks Preferences window.

Memory & Image Cache Preferences

If the previous section about scratch disks didn't give you a hint about how large image files can be, the Memory & Image Cache Preferences window will give you some hard numbers to work with. If you're using a Mac, you'll be able to adjust the Cache settings only from this window. Windows users also can adjust the amount of

caution

If you see an error message appear in Photoshop Elements indicating your hard drive is full, Photoshop Elements is telling you it has run out of scratch disk space. You might not be able to save the file on which you're working. You can free up some disk space by closing any other open image files or by deleting other files on your hard drive.

If you want to avoid running out of scratch disk space, you can attach an external drive and assign it as a secondary or third scratch disk before you start working with Photoshop Elements.

79

memory allocated to Photoshop. Figure 3.13 shows that 117MB, or 50% of the memory on my PC, is allocated to run Photoshop Elements.

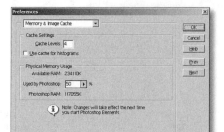

Figure 3.13
Adjust the cache settings and the amount of memory available to Photoshop Elements from the Memory & Image Cache Preferences window.

tip
You can reduce the size of a file without sacrificing image quality by optimizing the image. Choose Save for Web from the File menu to open the Save for Web dialog box, which contains several optimization tools. For example, you can save the file as a JPEG image and choose a file compression setting that reduces the file size. You can shave thousands of bytes off an image by optimizing it. To find out more about optimizing an image file, go to Chapter 8, "Saving and Sharing Files."

How Much Memory Is Enough?

Assume that the average picture scanned in or captured by a digital camera is stored in a 1MB file. When Photoshop Elements opens this file, it creates red, green, and blue channels for the image. Each channel comprises about one third of the image. Most 1MB files grow into 9MB files in the work area. As you edit it or add new layers with other images, the file size can grow larger and larger.

If you plan to work on large image files, you can improve Photoshop Element's performance by increasing the amount of memory allocated to the program when it starts. On a Windows PC, you can set how much memory on the computer can be dedicated to Photoshop Elements in the Memory & Image Cache Preferences window. On a Mac, select the Photoshop Elements icon, and then choose Get Info from the File menu. Select Memory from the Show pop-up menu, and then double or triple the amount of memory in the Preferred Size text box.

If you're still wondering how much memory is enough, remember that you can never have enough memory installed on your computer. However, a ballpark estimate is to double the amount of memory you'll think you'll need and buy as much memory as you can afford.

Photoshop Elements creates a cache to store frequently used data, such as a histogram. See Chapter 10 for an explanation about histograms. Each time you need to view an item stored in the cache, Photoshop Elements displays the cached information instead of recalculating the data each time you open a histogram window or access a frequently used image layer. By using the cache, Photoshop Elements can perform tasks faster, which is a good thing.

4

Using the Quick Start Window and the Help System

The Quick Start window automatically opens whenever you start Photoshop Elements. Simply click on a button to create a new window, open, paste, or acquire an image, or quickly access the tutorial and Web Help pages. If you need to look up a topic or want to access other help resources, a complete listing of help options is located in the Help menu. Choose one of the menu items in the Help menu if you want to access Adobe's online Web help pages, visit a support group, or just take a peek at all the help resources available for Photoshop Elements. This chapter shows you what each button can do in the Quick Start window, and then gives you a brief explanation of all the helpful commands located in the Help menu.

Introducing the Quick Start Window

When you first start Photoshop Elements, the Quick Start window will appear in the middle of the work area. There are six buttons you can choose from; each enables you to jump right into a document or view HTML help or tutorial files. The following list explains each button in the Quick Start window, which appears in Figure 4.1:

- **New**—Create and open a new document window and choose the dimensions, resolution, and color mode of the document.

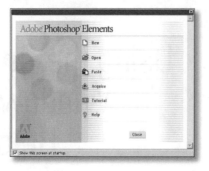

Figure 4.1
Bring an image into the work area with a single click, or access tutorials or help from the Quick Start window.

note
The Quick Start window automatically closes after any button is selected. Choose Show Quick Start from the Window menu to open the Quick Start window.

- **Open**—Open an existing image file stored on your hard drive.
- **Paste**—If an image is stored in the Clipboard, choosing this button pastes it into its own, new window.
- **Acquire**—Control a scanner or camera and download an image into a new image window.
- **Tutorial**—Learn how to use some of the advanced features in Photoshop Elements.
- **Help**—Open the HTML help files in a browser application by choosing this Quick Start button.

Creating a New Document and Opening a File

Click the New button in the Quick Start window if you want to create an empty document window. Before you type in the width and height of the document, select the unit of measurement you want to use to determine the size of the document. Choose from pixels, inches, centimeters, points, or picas. The example in Figure 4.2 shows the dimensions in pixels, which is the typical unit of measurement for an image. Fill in the rest of the settings you want for your new window, and then click OK. A blank image window will appear in the work area.

tip
If you do not want the Quick Start window to appear when you start Photoshop Elements, uncheck the Show This Screen At Startup check box.

Figure 4.2
Type the width and height of your new document in the New window.

note
The Width text box in the New window enables you to use the columns measurement in addition to pixels, inches, centimeters, points, and picas.

There are four ways you can open an image window in the work area using the Quick Start window. You can click the New or Paste buttons to create a new image window, or click the Open button to open an image file stored on your hard drive. The fourth way to open an image window is to choose the Acquire button. View and select a TWAIN plug-in from the Import Source window list, and then use the digital camera's software to download an image from the external device into a new window in the work area. The Acquire button enables you to import images from cameras and scanners.

To open an image file on your hard drive, click the Open button and the Open dialog box will appear. On a Windows computer, you can preview a thumbnail image in the Open dialog box, and then open any image files stored on your computer's hard drive. If you have a Mac, the Open window enables you to open a file in its original file format, or open it as a different kind of file. For example, if you want to open a JPEG file as a PSD file, you can select the image file and then choose the file format you want it to open as from the Format pop-up menu in the Mac's Open dialog box.

Pasting a File from the Clipboard

note
For Windows users, to open a file in a different file format, you have to use the Open As command from the File menu.

The Copy and Paste commands, located in the Edit menu, enable you to share images or text from other applications with Photoshop Elements. You also can use these commands to duplicate the same image over and over in an image window, or paste it to a new image window.

Before you can paste an image, first you must select an image or portion of an image, and then choose the Copy command from the Edit menu. The Copy command places the selected image into the Clipboard, which is part of the Windows and Macintosh operating system software.

note
To find out more about how to work with the Copy and Paste commands, go to Chapter 16, "Experimenting with Composite Images."

Click the Paste button in the Quick Start window to place the selected image into a new image window in the Photoshop Elements work area. The new window will contain the pasted image. The image will open in a new window in the work area. That's right, you can simply click on one button instead of having to select the Open command from the File menu, and then pressing (Command)/[Ctrl]+V, or choosing Paste from the Edit menu.

Acquiring Images

Before you can use the Acquire command to control a camera or scanner, you must install the TWAIN plug-in for that device. You also will need to connect a USB or serial cable to the digital device and computer.

Some vendors provide a separate installer program for the TWAIN plug-in and others install it as part of a software application that comes bundled with the camera or scanner. Most camera and scanner vendors advertise whether a TWAIN plug-in is bundled with a camera or scanner product. If you're shopping for a camera or scanner and don't plan to use a card reader to copy your files to your computer, purchase a camera or scanner that comes with a TWAIN plug-in. This will enable you to control the device using Photoshop Elements.

Click the Acquire button in the Quick Start window to access any connected devices, as shown in Figure 4.3. The Import Source window will open. A list of TWAIN plug-in files installed on your hard drive will appear in the window list. Choose a device from the Select Import Source window, and bring an image directly into the work area.

note
See Chapter 5, "Scanning Images into Photoshop Elements," for more information on working with scanned images. See Chapter 6, "Acquiring Images from a Camera," for details on working with a digital camera.

Figure 4.3
A list of TWAIN plug-ins appears in the Select Import Source window if you click the Acquire button in the Quick Start window.

The software that appears when you acquire an image will be the software created specifically for the digital camera or scanner. Select the images you want to view or save in the work area. Then download them to your hard drive.

The rate at which an image is acquired depends on what kind of cable is used to connect the camera or scanner to the computer. Most of the newer cameras and scanners have a USB connector, which supports a faster data transfer rate than its predecessor, the serial port. Some of the higher-end scanners, in the $1,000 price range, also have a FireWire (1394) port available for connecting to a computer. FireWire ports can support the faster data transfer rates between a digital device and a computer. If the computer does not have a USB port, you will need to download images over the serial port. Most digital cameras will include a USB-to-serial adapter cable. However, newer cameras tend to support only USB connections.

note
It's okay if the camera batteries run out of juice while you're copying images to your computer. The image files will remain on the camera's storage card whether batteries are in or out of the camera. If you don't want to repeatedly download files, or have your download session interrupted due to a shortage of batteries, put a fresh set of batteries into the camera or use an A/C adapter specifically made for your camera.

Viewing Tutorials

Click the Tutorials button if you want to learn how to use some of the more advanced features (see Figure 4.4). You can, for example, walk through some basic step-by-step examples in a browser application that show you how to use layers, create a multi-picture panorama, or produce an animation. You also can jump to Adobe's Web site and view more online tutorials there. Of course, this book contains all that and more, so read on!

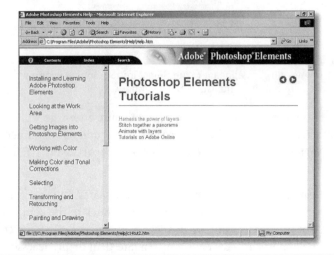

Figure 4.4
A few advanced tutorials are installed with Photoshop Elements. Click the Tutorial button to view the tutorials in a browser application.

Accessing the Help System

Help files are installed onto your computer along with the Photoshop Elements program. To properly view and use these Web pages, you must select a Help command in Photoshop Elements. Click the Help button in the Quick Start window to open a browser window and view the help information, as shown in Figure 4.5. The help content contains definitions for terms, in addition to steps that show you how to use the features in Photoshop Elements. Much of this information is also located in the Photoshop Elements manual.

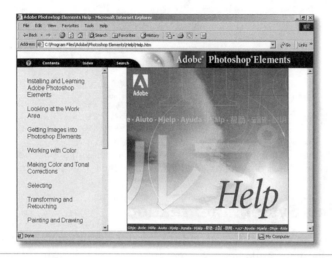

Figure 4.5
Access the built-in Help system by clicking the Help button in the Quick Start window. The Help system is covered in more detail later in this chapter.

Viewing the Version, System, and Support Information

note
To view the Help Web pages, you must have Netscape Navigator, version 4.0, or Internet Explorer 4.0 or higher installed on your computer. If you need to upgrade the browser on your computer, you can download the latest version from www.netscape.com or (www.microsoft.com/mac/ie) [www.microsoft.com/ie].

Click the Help menu to view all the help resources available for Photoshop Elements. All the help systems and help options are stored in the Help menu, including a command to open the Tutorials. In addition to the elaborate Help system installed with Photoshop Elements on your hard drive, Adobe provides an online support area and message boards for Photoshop Elements owners.

The Help menu enables you to access the Web-based Help content or view the serial number for Photoshop Elements. The System Info command, for example, enables you to open the System Info window. You can view your system's vital statistics, such as which version of the operating system is running (see Figure 4.6). You can use this information to help troubleshoot software issues that might arise with Photoshop Elements or your computer.

Figure 4.6
The Help menu contains menu commands that can tell you about Photoshop Elements and your computer, as well as open the built-in help system.

note
The Help Contents and Photoshop Elements Tutorials commands located in the Help menu open the same browser Web pages as the Tutorial and Help buttons located in the Quick Start window.

Viewing System Information

Photoshop Elements can tell you all about your computer. Click the Help menu, and choose System Info to open the System Info window (see Figure 4.7). Here you can see all kinds of detailed information about Photoshop Elements and your computer's processor, memory, and operating system. This information can be especially helpful when you (or a help technician) are troubleshooting hardware or software problems you encounter when running Photoshop Elements. Click the Copy button if you want to copy the text data to the Clipboard. Then, open a Notepad or text file and choose the Paste command from the Edit menu to paste the system information into the open window. Save the file to your hard drive, or print the information and keep it with your software product records.

Figure 4.7
View your computer's processor, operating system, and memory configuration in addition to your Photoshop Elements settings in the System Info window.

Locating Support Information

Some day you might need to replace your Photoshop Elements CD-ROM or contact Adobe for other support-related questions. Select the Support menu command from the Help menu, and you'll be taken to Adobe's support Web site, as shown in Figure 4.8. You can search Adobe's knowledge base, read technical guides and tutorials online, or post a question in Adobe's Support Exchange.

Figure 4.8
Visit Adobe's support Web site to find the latest information about Photoshop Elements.

Choose Updates to view any upgrades available for Photoshop Elements. You can download updates from Adobe's Web site through this menu option. Your computer must be connected to the Internet to use the Updates dialog box. Adobe Online is another Web-based help system available to you: You can access additional tutorials and technical guides and find out about user forums. Finally, you can choose Register from the Help menu if you want to register your copy of Photoshop Elements with Adobe or to print the registration form. Registering this program enables you to access Photoshop Elements' technical support services.

Using the Help System

A folder full of Help pages is installed with Photoshop Elements. These files are stored in the Help folder in the Adobe Photoshop Elements folder on your hard drive. If you want to read more about a particular feature, or search the information available about a certain topic, you can choose Help Content from the Help menu. Your system will start your default browser program and load the HTML-based help system in a browser window. You can navigate the help content as you would a Web page. Most of the information in the bundled manual can be found in the Help Web pages. You also can check the index of this book.

Searching for a Help Topic

The search engine in the help content works similarly to other Internet search engines. First, open the Help Content pages by clicking the Help button on the Quick Start menu or by selecting Help, Help Contents (see Figure 4.9). Wait for the browser to start and load the help content. Click the Search link in the browser window. If you've visited Yahoo! or Google.com, typing a word or words and clicking the Search button are very familiar. You can use search for any topic in the Photoshop Elements help content using this search feature.

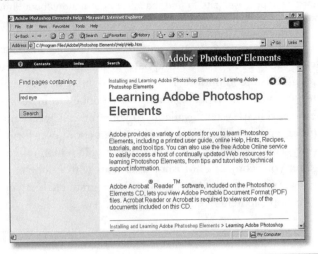

Figure 4.9
Search for a help topic by typing a word or words into the Search text.

A list of help items matching your search will appear in the left column of the browser window. Click on a topic to view more information, which will appear on the right side of the window. Each help page has a pair of arrow buttons in the upper-right corner of the content window. These buttons enable you to move to the previous or next pages in a help topic. Figure 4.10 shows the Search page for the Help system.

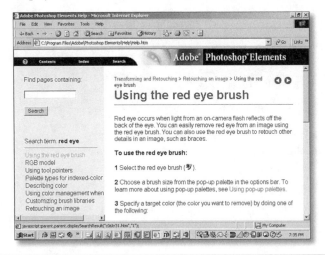

Figure 4.10
A list of search results will appear in the left column of the Search help page. Click one of the help links to read all about it.

Finding a Help Topic in the Index

Another way to find information in the Help Content pages is to use the index. Click on the Index link in any help page to view the index list in the left column of the browser window. Click on a letter, located to the right of an index topic, to view all items that start with that letter.

Click on any of the topics in the left column to read more about it. Figure 4.11 shows the index for the letter G, and the selected help information on the right.

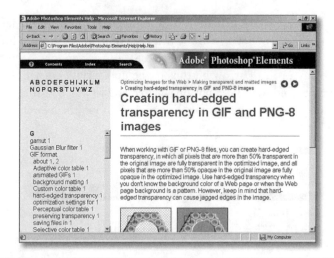

Figure 4.11
Click on a letter in the Index help page and view help topics alphabetically.

part

II

SCANNING AND ACQUIRING IMAGES

Scanning Images into Photoshop Elements

Scanners are computer peripheral devices that connect to your computer. Unlike digital cameras, you must connect a scanner to a computer to capture an image. Most current scanner models use a USB (Universal Serial Bus) connection. Older models used the parallel port on a PC or a SCSI (Small Computer System Interface) port on a Mac. Today's scanners are affordable and offer high-resolution image capture capabilities.

If you're taking traditional 35mm photographs, or if you want to convert a photo album of pictures into digital images, a scanner is your best bet for converting those analog images into digital ones. Most scanners are bundled with TWAIN plug-in software, enabling you to control the scanner in Photoshop Elements. This chapter introduces you to scanners and explains how to bring scanned images into the work area.

Overview of Scanner Products

Scanners were initially designed to bring printed images and text into computers. The first scanners were based on dot-matrix printers and were introduced in the early 1980s. These scanners were very slow and produced a unique-looking image that were nothing close to what today's scanners can produce.

Like television and cameras, the first scanners were only capable of capturing grayscale images. In the early 1990s, grayscale scanners were expensive, ranging in price from around $2,000, dropping to around $300 by the end of the millennium. These first scanners were also heavy, and the bundled software initially was not very easy to use. These scanners were created before the Web supported images. The main reason for scanning an image was to be able to print it to a black-and-white or grayscale printer.

Scanners use a moving bar of light to read an image, line by line, into your computer. The bar, which holds a horizontal array of sensor chips, moves from the top to the bottom of the scanable area, usually a piece of glass, line by line. The light bounces off the scanned image into a charge-coupled device (CCD) or complementary metal oxide semiconductor (CMOS) sensor chip. These sensor chips measure the amount of light and pass their data along to other processor chips, which turn the light information into digital data that can be interpreted by software installed on your computer.

Over the years, scanners have evolved into low-cost, easy-to-use, high-resolution add-ons to Windows and Macintosh computers. Not only can you scan line art and text, but you can also scan full-color images. You can post the scanned, digital files to a Web server or print the original or modified file to a grayscale or full-color printer. The following sections briefly describe the most commonly used, and available, scanners.

Scanners and Digital Cameras

Both scanners and digital still and motion cameras use charge-coupled device sensor chips to convert light into digital data. Scanners capture this data line by line, whereas digital cameras capture the data all at once. Both kinds of devices also can use three CCDs in a device to capture red, green, and blue data through separate CCD chips to capture ultra high-quality images. CMOS (complementary metal oxide semiconductor) is another type of light-sensing chip that is used in some digital cameras.

Flatbed Scanners

Some flatbed scanners have a scan area of around 8.5×14 inches. There isn't a standard for how big or small the scan area can be, so don't be surprised to find a variety of scanner shapes for business cards, photos, 8.5×11, or legal documents. Most scanners take the form of a rectangular-shaped box with a lid that exposes a plate of glass covering the top of the box. Inside the box is a mechanism that moves across the length of the box. Flatbed scanners are probably the most inexpensive and commonly used type of scanner. Figure 5.1 shows the front and top of the Epson 640U and Canon 1220U scanners. A typical $100 model flatbed scanner can capture a 600×2400 dots-per-inch image.

Scanning Film Versus Paper

The light that scans an image in a flatbed scanner is projected at an angle so that a CCD can capture the reflected image. If you're scanning a film negative with a flatbed scanner, it's possible to capture the glare of the glass in addition to the image on film. Photo scanners use a black background without any glass surface, reducing exposure to glare as the image is scanned.

Figure 5.1
Flatbed scanners are affordable and offer a wide range of imaging capabilities.

Drum scanners are the more expensive cousins of flatbed scanners. They can scan documents at higher resolutions and create color-separated images. The image you want to scan is wrapped around a drum, which is rotated at high speeds. An intense, focused light duplicates the image.

The quality of a scanned image depends on several factors, as follows:

- The quality of the glass platen, or copyboard, combined with the quality of the lens components pointed at the CCD in the scanner. Although the quality of the lens components plays a bigger role in determining the quality of the scanned image, the glass platen sits right smack in between the lens and the image being scanned. If the glass is pock-marked, wavy, or scratched, these etchings will appear in the digital output from the scanner.

- The number of sensor chips, located in the horizontal bar, that scan the image. The quality of the sensor chips helps determine the scanable resolution of the image. However, the number of sensor chips used to scan the image also contributes to what the scanner can do. The more sensor chips in the scanner bar, the higher the resolution the scanner can capture.

  Most scanner vendors don't advertise how many sensor chips are in the scan bar. Look for the highest, non-interpolated resolution the scanner is capable of capturing to get a general idea of the limitations of the sensor chips in any particular scanner model.

- The distance the horizontal bar moves before scanning another line of the image.

- The quality of the CCD, which determines how color is interpreted by the scanner. Most scanners can capture a minimum resolution of 600 dots per inch (dpi). Scanners that capture lower resolutions, such as 300 dpi, probably use lower-quality CCDs, whereas scanners that can capture 1200 or 2400 dpi with 48 bits of color are using higher-quality CCDs.

- The software bundled with the scanner. Many scanners bundle more than one application. In addition to the TWAIN plug-in software, you can install applications such as Photoshop Elements to edit scanned images. Other applications that might be bundled enable you to scan text documents, catalog your images, or create a digital photo album on your hard drive.

- The capabilities of the software installed on the computer. Photoshop Elements helps tremendously with correcting the orientation of an image, as well as with color or image correction.

Interpolated Versus Actual Scanning Resolution

Some scanners are bundled with software that enables the scanner to capture higher resolutions than the CCDs are capable of capturing. How does this work? Scanners capture analog data, and then convert it into digital data. After the image becomes digitized, a software algorithm can be applied to each pixel in the image, comparing its color to the pixels immediately around it. This process is called *interpolation*.

Scanner software can interpolate an image scanned at 600 dpi and generate a 900 dpi image based on the 600 dpi scanned data. For most scanned images, you probably won't be able to tell whether the image was scanned purely with CCDs or interpolated to a higher resolution using scanner software. However, if you want to capture as much image detail as possible with a scanner, look at the actual scanning resolution for a scanner, and not the software-capable scanning resolution.

Film and Handheld Scanners

If you have slides or film negatives you want to convert into digital images, you can spend a little more money on a photo scanner. Figure 5.2 shows an HP photo scanner that's relatively affordable at less than $500. Higher priced models are available and can cost several thousand dollars. The photo scanner also uses light, combined with a CCD, to scan a printed image on paper or an image on film. It can scan photos at 300 dpi or film at up to 2400 dpi.

You can use a flatbed scanner to scan film, too. However, first you'll need to attach a transparency unit to compensate for the short depth of field of the flatbed scanner. Both flatbed and photo scanners can easily generate precise 36-bit color images. However, photo scanners enable you to capture multiple frames of film with a little more ease than a flatbed scanner. Photo scanners also do not rely on glass to capture an image, so this is the optimal device for converting film into digital media.

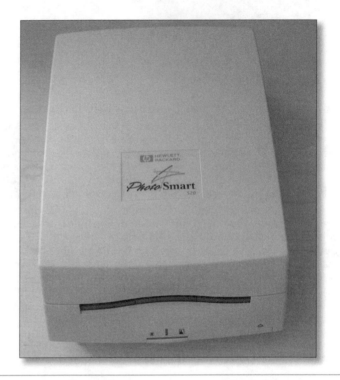

Figure 5.2
The HP Photo Smart scanner can scan film, slides, and print media.

Other kinds of scanners are business card and handheld scanners. You can even buy a pen that scans text into your computer. Handheld scanners place the optics and the CCD in the palm of your hand. However, this means it's up to you to move the device horizontally or vertically to capture an image or text. Even if you can feed an image into a handheld scanner, the size of the scanable image is limited to the optically exposed area of the handheld device. Unless you intend to scan small images, you're better off with a bigger scanner.

Differences Between Cameras and Scanners

The most obvious difference between a camera and a scanner is that you have a lot more freedom to pick and choose an image with a digital camera. Cameras also can capture an image much faster than a scanner. They do have one thing in common: both convert analog light into a digital image, which you can view or edit on a computer. The scanner is more of an extension of the computer, whereas a camera is easier to use as a mobile image-taking machine.

If you're planning to take new photos, you'll probably prefer to use a digital camera instead of a scanner to bring images into your computer. If you prefer to use a 35mm camera to take pictures, or if you have a wealth of documents, negatives, or existing photos, a flatbed or film scanner is probably the best way to bring your photos into a computer.

One of the more noticeable differences between the resulting image created by a camera is that you don't have to worry about dealing with dust specs or paper texture with the final image. Although scanners can capture high-quality images, the largest limitation is the medium itself. Images can inherit some of the more subtle appearances of the paper on which the image is printed, especially when the photo has been torn or folded. Fortunately, you can correct these visual glitches using Photoshop Elements.

The following list highlights some of the main issues to consider when choosing between a digital camera and scanner:

- **Image resolution**—The number of pixels that compose the height and width of the digital image.

- **Image size**—The actual file size of the image, usually measured in megabytes (MB).

- **Image clarity**—When viewed, the sharpness of the colors and content in the image. The type of monitor can affect how an image appears on a computer.

- **Color depth**—The number of colors that capture and display the image.

- **Printability**—The resolution of the image in regards to the resolution supported by the printer. For example, printing text or line art often requires a higher resolution printer, up to 600 or 1200 dpi, compared to a color graphic or photo, which can be printed at up to 360 dpi.

Although both cameras and scanners use software that enable you to capture images at a certain resolution, scanners use samples per inch (spi) to measure resolution. Digital cameras usually refer to the captured image in megapixels, or number of total pixels determined by multiplying the width and height of pixels in an image.

It gets even more confusing if you want to print an image. Printers use the measurement of dots per inch (dpi). However, it isn't an easy task to convert spi or megapixels into dpi. Formatting an image for the Web is probably the easiest of all these tasks. You can save an image at 72 to 75 dpi to make it Web-ready. The best way to tell whether you've selected the correct settings for an image is, of course, to view the final output.

Installing Plug-In Files

As mentioned in the previous section, there are two main types of plug-in files you can install with Photoshop Elements. The most common kind of plug-in is a filter or effect. To find out more about filters and effects, go to Chapter 12, "Applying Effects and Filters."

The second kind of plug-in is what you'll need to acquire images from your scanner or digital camera directly into Photoshop Elements. All plug-in files are located in the Plug-ins folder, which is in the Photoshop Elements folder. The Import/Export folder is where TWAIN plug-ins are stored. TWAIN plug-ins enable you to acquire images from the Import menu into the work area.

The following sections show you how to install a TWAIN plug-in for an HP scanner device. However, these steps are similar for installing any TWAIN plug-in into Photoshop Elements.

Installing Plug-In Software

If you're using Windows 98 Special Edition or Windows 2000, plug your scanner or camera into your computer's parallel, serial, or USB port. Windows will notice a new device is connected to the computer and open the Found New Hardware Wizard (see Figure 5.3). Insert the CD for the device into the CD-ROM drive, and then click the Next button. Mac users can install the TWAIN plug-in software by

tip
If you're new to digital photography, you might want to pick up a copy of *The Absolute Beginner's Guide to Digital Photography* by Richard Lynch (Que Publishing) to help you get more familiar with your digital camera's hardware and software features.

tip
Looking for more information about scanners and scanning techniques? *The Scanning Workshop* by Richard Romano (Que Publishing) is a book that can help you learn how to get the best digital images out of your scanner.

placing the TWAIN plug-in file in the Plug-Ins, Import/Export folder, in the Adobe Photoshop Elements folder.

Figure 5.3
When you first connect a scanner or camera to your computer, Windows will try to install software for the new hardware.

For Windows users, here are the steps you'll go through using the New Hardware Wizard:

1. The next two screens ask you how you want Windows to locate the driver software for the new device.

2. Choose the radio button that searches for a suitable driver for the device (recommended) in the Install Device Drivers window.

3. Click the Next button, and then check the CD-ROM Drive check box in the Locate Driver Files window. Be sure you have the CD-ROM from your hardware (scanner or camera) in the drive.

4. Click the Next button, and Windows will search the CD-ROM for the software driver. If a TWAIN plug-in file is on the CD, Windows will install both the driver and the TWAIN plug-in file (see Figure 5.4).

5. If Windows installs the files successfully, you'll see the Completing the Found New Hardware Wizard window. Click the Finish button to exit the wizard.

Figure 5.4
If Windows can locate a driver for the device, it will install it.

note
If you want to learn how to hook up a camera, go to Chapter 6, "Acquiring Images from a Camera."

Accessing Your New Plug-In in Photoshop Elements

You must exit or quit Photoshop Elements before you can use a newly installed TWAIN plug-in file. Photoshop Elements scans the Plug-Ins folder only when the application starts. Therefore, if you install any plug-in file while Photoshop Elements is running, you can't use the plug-in unless you quit and restart the program.

First, power on the device you want to connect to the computer, and then connect the device to the computer. Next, start Photoshop Elements. To access any of the TWAIN plug-in files, click File, Import. A submenu containing a list of devices will appear, as shown in Figure 5.5. Select one of the TWAIN plug-in files from the Import menu list. The TWAIN plug-in will open a device-specific window in the Photoshop Elements work area. Import an image into the work area.

Troubleshooting
Not all cameras and scanners come bundled with TWAIN plug-in files. If your device does not have a TWAIN plug-in file, you'll need to use the software that comes with the device to create an image on your computer. Save the images in a file format so that you can open them in Photoshop Elements.

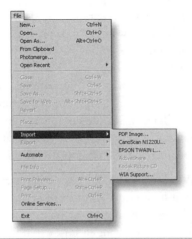

Figure 5.5
Choose Import from the File menu to view a list of installed TWAIN plug-in files.

Connecting Computers and Scanners

Now that you've learned how a scanner works, you might want to connect one to your computer and use it with Photoshop Elements. Most scanners, including photo scanners, use a USB connector. Older model scanners (before USB came on the scene) have a SCSI connector. Newer model high-end (or is that higher-cost) scanners might have a FireWire (IEEE 1394) port in addition to a USB or SCSI port. Before you can connect a scanner to a computer, first be sure the computer you want to use has a port available for the scanner you want to connect to it.

When to Upgrade Your Operating System

If you haven't upgraded to Windows 98 Special Edition, ME, NT 4.0, service pack 4, 5, or 6, or 2000, you might want to consider it, especially if the scanner—or rather, the software for the scanner—you want to purchase doesn't support your current operating system. Most scanners that work with USB ports will work with these operating systems, but there are exceptions. Check the Web site for the scanner you have or are considering for purchase and see whether it is compatible with your PC or Windows operating system.

Don't forget that Photoshop Elements requires Windows 98, NT, 2000, or ME, or Mac OS 8.6, 9.x, or Mac OS X. If you're running an earlier version of these operating systems, you'll need to upgrade to one of the supported operating systems before you can install Photoshop Elements onto your computer.

If you've never seen a USB, parallel, SCSI, or FireWire cable, it might be difficult to tell whether a particular scanner can actually connect to your computer. SCSI and parallel port connectors, on the computer, have a 25-pin connector. The SCSI connector on the scanner usually is a 50-pin port. The parallel port connector on the scanner will be similar to a 25-pin connector on a printer. Connect the SCSI or parallel cable to the computer and the scanner. Then, check the operating system and BIOS settings to be sure those ports are active before starting Photoshop Elements.

Most of the Windows and Macintosh computers made over the past few years have at least one USB port. You can identify the USB port on a PC or Macintosh computer by looking for the USB symbol, which looks like a three-pronged fork extending from a circle. There are two types of USB connectors. Your computer uses a Type A connector, which is the flat, rectangular-shaped connector. The scanner has a Type B USB connector, which is shaped like a square with the top two corners rounded in a bit more than the bottom two corners (see Figure 5.6). It looks something like a telephone jack, but don't plug anything but a USB connector into it.

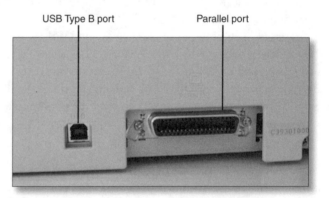

USB Type B port   Parallel port

Figure 5.6
Most scanners have only one type of computer connection. However, some models have a USB or parallel port, or a SCSI port. Be sure to configure your computer's software to work with the correct port.

Power On, and Then Connect

Connect the power cable to the scanner (if the scanner requires external power) before connecting the USB cable to the scanner or the computer. Power off the computer before connecting the USB cable to the USB port (see Figure 5.7). Some scanners, like the Canon CanoScan 1220U or Epson 640U, can be plugged into Windows 2000 or Mac OS 9 after the computer has been powered on. Newer operating systems, such as Windows 2000, ME, and Mac OS 9, support plug-and-play USB devices.

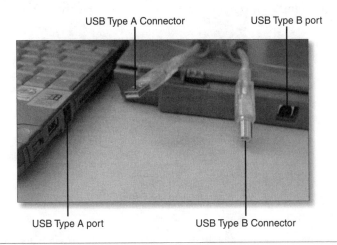

USB Type A Connector   USB Type B port

USB Type A port   USB Type B Connector

Figure 5.7
Connect the USB cable to the computer and the scanner.

SCSI Versus USB Versus FireWire

If you have a scanner that has a SCSI and a USB port, or a USB and a FireWire port, choose the faster port to connect to your computer. Assuming your scanner and computer are working reliably, the FireWire or IEEE 1394 port would provide the fastest connection, up to 400 megabits per second (Mbps), between a scanner and computer. USB supports up to 7Mpbs of throughput, which makes it faster than a SCSI or parallel port connection at up to 5Mbps.

FireWire actually is Apple Computer's name for the IEEE 1394 port. The FireWire port is slightly smaller than the USB port and, depending on the device, can be a relatively tiny port compared to SCSI and USB. FireWire ports are also used to capture full-motion digital video, and can also support high-speed, 7200 and 10,000 rpm external hard drives on computers. If you're looking for a scanner that can transfer data quickly to a computer, consider purchasing a scanner with a FireWire port.

Working with Scanner Software Settings

Start Photoshop Elements, if it isn't already running on your computer. Choose File, Import, and select the TWAIN plug-in for your scanner from the menu list. The scanner's software window will open. Different scanners have different software settings. Most scanners provide an interface enabling you to preview and scan the image placed on the scanner bed. Some scanners, such as the S20 Photo Scanner, enable you to calibrate the screen and scanner in addition to scanning an image into the computer (see Figure 5.8).

Figure 5.8
Although you can click the Calibrate Scanner or Calibrate Screen button for the S20 Photo Scanner, most scanners don't require calibration. If a software option is available, calibrate the scanner before acquiring the first image.

Scanner software features vary from scanner to scanner. For example, the HP Photo Smart scanner enables you to calibrate your scanner and monitor. Most scanners do not need to be calibrated before you scan an image.

Adjusting Scanner Settings

Place a photo or a piece of paper with text or graphics face down on the glass surface of the scanner if you're using a flatbed scanner. If you're using another type of scanner, insert a scanable document into the scanner device. Some scanners, such as the Epson 640U, will automatically scan and choose the settings for you. The HP Photo Smart scanner starts scanning when you insert a photo, filmstrip, or slide (see Figure 5.9). Other scanners require you to click a button in the work area to start the scan.

tip
To find out how to calibrate a monitor, go to Chapter 10, "Digital Images and Color."

Figure 5.9
Create a preview scan to view the output for the scanner software settings.

What Is the Best Resolution for Scanning?

Your scanner might be capable of scanning only up to a specific resolution. Assuming you have a more recent scanner capable of scanning up to 2400 dpi, try scanning an image at 600 dpi. Then compare that scan to the same image scanned at 1200 or 2400 dpi. Usually the higher dpi setting will produce the sharpest scanned image. Save the highest-quality image to your hard drive.

If you cannot see a difference between the resulting images, save each one to your hard drive. Then compare the file size of each scan. Use the Zoom tool to determine how much more image information is added to the higher-resolution images. If the 600 dpi scan looks great and creates the smallest file size of the scanned image, you might want to consider working with this setting when you scan other images.

Choosing a Resolution

If you have several images that are similar, you can choose the resolution and scanner settings for one image and scan the rest without making any major changes. However, if you have a diverse set of colors, or old and new photos, you might want to set aside a big chunk of time if you want to get the best results for each scanned image.

Consider the following issues when trying to set the optimal resolution for scanned images:

- What kind of image are you trying to scan? Consider the size of the image, and decide which resolution would be able to capture the most detail without creating an unusually large file.

- How many colors does the image have? If you're scanning a color image, you might need to configure the scanner software to capture thousands of colors instead of 256. On the other hand, you can see what happens if you scan in a color image as a grayscale or black-and-white image.

- What is the highest, noninterpolated resolution supported by the scanner? Some scanners work with bundled software to capture higher resolutions than the scanner hardware is capable of creating. You might want to compare the software-enhanced, high-resolution scans with the same image scanned at a lower resolution without the aide of the software interpolator.

- Does the computer have any display limitations that might limit your ability to view beyond a certain resolution? You might need to change your computer monitor's settings to display more colors if you want to see as much of the scanner output as possible. The computer's performance can slow down if you set it to display 24-bit color, compared to 256, or 16-bit color. The more colors the monitor has to display, the more processing power is required from the computer.

Choose a resolution in the scanner software window. Look for a resolution setting that enables you to set the spi or dpi of the image. Some software breaks down the resolution settings into horizontal and vertical resolution settings. The horizontal resolution affects the optics in the scan bar, and the vertical resolution affects how far the bar will move as it scans each line of the image.

Adjusting the Color Depth and Scan Area

The number of colors, or *color depth*, of the scanned image affects the quality of the resulting, captured image. Most scanners will automatically scan an image in color, even if the image has no color. You can adjust the software settings to scan a black-and-white image if you like. The scanner does not have any sensors built into its optical array that can distinguish a color image from a black-and-white one; it simply captures the image placed on the glass.

Although most scanners have some support of how many colors can be scanned, each uses its own software and terminology to describe color depth. For example, the CanoScan N1220U uses the term Color Mode to describe its color depth settings: Black and White, Grayscale, Color (Photos), Color (Documents), or Text Enhanced. The Epson 640U uses the term Image Type to describe its color depth options: Color Photo, Color Document, Black & White Photo, or Black & White Document.

The important thing to remember here is that you want to pick a color depth that matches the photo placed on the scanner. For example, if you're scanning a black-and-white image, choose a grayscale or black-and-white color depth. If you're not sure which color depth to choose, choose a setting as close to 16- or 24-bit color as possible. The higher the color depth value, the more color data will be captured when the image is scanned. For example, scanning an image at 24 bits will capture more color information than a 16-bit scan.

Experiment with different color depth settings with different kinds of images. You can scan photos, line art, sketches, text, two-color, or full-color images at different color depth settings to see how your scanner reacts to different capture modes. I capture almost all my images in color, and remove or add colors with Photoshop Elements.

The resolution setting also affects how the image will be scanned. The higher the resolution, the more color information the scanner will try to capture. If you're not sure at what resolution to start scanning an image, choose 600 dpi. Scan and save the image, and then change the resolution to 1200 or 2400 dpi and save this second image. Open each image and place them side by side on your desktop. If you cannot see any improvement in the 1200 or 2400 dpi image, you might want to continue to scan additional images at 600 dpi. However, if you plan to edit images, the higher resolution settings will enable you to do more precise image editing than an image scanned at a lower resolution.

tip

Be sure to adjust the color settings for your computer's operating system and monitor before you scan an image. Both Windows and Mac OS enable you to customize the resolution or desktop size. You also can set the color depth, or number of colors that can be displayed onscreen. To find out how to check your system settings, see Chapter 1, "Installing Photoshop Elements." If you want to learn more about how to work with color, see Chapter 10, "Digital Images and Color."

Comparing SPI to PPI

Scanners capture images using the measurement of samples per inch (spi). However, your computer monitor displays an image in pixels, or 72 pixels per inch. You might wonder whether a sample and a pixel are the same size.

Sadly, the answer is no, they are not the same size. In fact, there isn't an easy way to compare the quality of a scanned image to an image viewed on your computer monitor. The final results depend on the output of your printer, the settings and capabilities of your computer monitor, and your ability to choose the software settings that create the best possible images.

Previewing and Setting Up for the Scan

To create a preview of an image, before you actually scan it into your computer, click the Preview Scan or Preview button in the Scanner software window. Don't be surprised if your scanner does not have a preview option available. If the scanner software doesn't support a preview mode, click the Scan button and wait for the image to be scanned into the work area.

Some scanner applications, such as the Epson 640U, enable you to let the scanner do all the thinking for you with a full-service auto-scan feature. You might need to turn or flip the image on the scanner bed if you want to straighten the scanned image. If you want to avoid creating unnecessary scans, check to see whether the scanner you are planning to buy includes a preview option in its software package.

After you have created the preview scan, you can apply the selection tools to choose the specific area you want to scan into the work area (see Figure 5.10). Reducing the area being scanned reduces the amount of time you must wait for the scanner to complete its job.

After the scanned image is captured and viewable in the work area (see Figure 5.11), you can save it to your hard drive. Choose Save from the File menu, and then type a name for the image file and save it to your hard drive. Now you can experiment with the image by applying one of the tools in the toolbox, or add a new layer to the image file if you don't want to make any permanent changes to the original image.

Figure 5.10
If the scanner software
provides tools, you can
select the area you want
to scan.

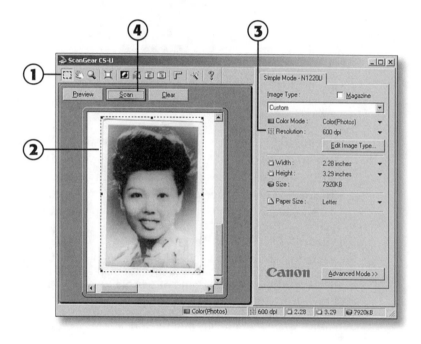

① Selection tool   ③ Resolution settings

② Marquee   ④ Scan button

Figure 5.11
The resulting file contains the image you selected in the scanner software window.

Photoshop Elements opens scanned images in RGB mode, enabling you to work with red, green, and blue color information: 24 bits of image data on the canvas. You can apply any menu command or tool to any part of an image in RGB mode. To find out more about the image modes in Photoshop Elements, go to Chapter 10.

Shouldn't This Look Prettier?
Scanners might be able to create luscious 36-bit and 48-bit color images, but most monitors are capable of displaying only 24-bit color, or millions of colors. You might not be able to see the additional colors captured by the scanner, but Photoshop Elements enables you to work with all the color information captured by the scanner. You will see the difference when you edit or print the image.

Scanning Different Kinds of Images

Film, slides, color photos, or old monochrome photos all can be scanned into Photoshop Elements. After you scan a few images, you might start to notice something they all have in common: dust. You might need to gently dust the surface of the print or negative, as well as the glass surface on the scanner, before placing and scanning the image. Try to avoid using your hands, cloth, or tissue to remove dust from the surface of the scanner. For best results, hold a can of compressed air about six to ten inches from the glass and use the canned air to clear the surface of the scanner.

Choose the scanner settings you want to apply to the scanned image. Then preview the image in Photoshop Elements. If the image is slightly crooked, you can try to straighten it in the scanner. However, you also can use Photoshop Elements to vertically or horizontally correct an image's alignment.

If you're working with a damaged, bent, or warped photo or image, you might try to flatten the image by placing it in a plastic jacket or folder. A flat image is optimal for scanning. It encourages the scanner to produce consistent, accurate colors throughout the captured image. Don't hesitate to run several preview scans, and try to scan the best possible image as you can.

If you don't want to worry about adding glare to the scan by adding the plastic layer to the image, try scanning a test image to see how the scanner captures the damaged areas of the photo (see Figure 5.12). Then add the plastic cover to see if you can identify any differences between the two preview images.

Figure 5.12
A test scan can help you optimize settings if you're scanning worn or damaged photos.

Experiment scanning at different resolutions and with different color or grayscale settings. If you want to simulate creating a color image, try scanning an image in grayscale. Then hand-tint the image in Photoshop Elements by adding red, blue, and green adjustment layers to create a custom color image.

caution
As you scan images, try not to touch the glass on a flatbed scanner with your hand or fingers. The oil from your hand or fingertips can leave marks on the glass that will be scanned in along with your images.

tip
Layers enable you to edit an image without affecting a pixel of the original image. To find out more about layers, go to Chapter 13, "Working with Layers and Layer Styles."

Scanning the Final Image

Adjust the photo and the scanner settings until you're satisfied with the scanner output. Then, click the Scan button to bring the image into Photoshop Elements. The scanner software will bring the image into the work area in a new document window. If you're scanning a negative, the image might be difficult to recognize at first (see Figure 5.13). When the image is in the work area, you can save it as a file or apply a filter or invert the image to view the quality of the image. For best results, use a photo scanner to convert a color negative into a full-color, non-negative–looking image.

Figure 5.13
Scan a negative into Photoshop Elements and convert it into a black-and-white or color photo.

Checking Image Quality

The size of the scanned image might vary depending on the size of the original image, as well as the scanner settings selected in the software window. Use the Zoom tool to magnify the digital image to compare it to the original.

If you're disappointed by dust specs, dirt, or torn areas of the photo, you can learn how to correct these glitches in Part II of this book (see Figure 5.14).

Figure 5.14
You can scan damaged photos into a computer and remove dust, dirt, or damaged areas of the image using Photoshop Elements.

To change a black-and-white negative into a regular black-and-white (actually grayscale) image, first make the image window the active window. Then choose the Invert command from the Image, Adjustments menu. View the image in the work area, and save it if you like.

Acquiring Images from a Camera

Most digital cameras are bundled with software enabling you to download pictures from a camera to your Windows or Macintosh computer. You can use the bundled software, or you can use a media card reader to access your digital pictures. This chapter provides a brief introduction to digital cameras and shows you how to get your pictures from your camera into your computer.

Overview of Digital Cameras

Depending on how you want to interpret the data, you could say digital cameras are nothing like traditional 35mm cameras, or are a whole lot like them. The basic design of a camera involves converting light into some sort of captured image. On a 35mm camera, the captured image is stored on film. You can choose different kinds of film to capture different kinds of images, varying in range from no light, to lots of color, to fast-moving images. A 35mm camera uses lenses and a mirror to redirect a certain amount of light onto the film. It's possible to expose the film to too much light. However, given the best circumstances, the film is processed with several different chemicals, and the image is burned onto photographic paper, where you can view it.

Digital cameras skip the whole development process. This is probably the most attractive thing about digital cameras—no lines, no negatives, and no envelopes to fill out. You pay once for the storage card, and you can take as many pictures as you like.

What makes digital cameras different is that the camera relies on a chip, called a *CCD* (Charge Coupled Device), to capture the image. An alternative chip used by some cameras is the Complimentary Metal Oxide Semiconductor (CMOS) chip. Although each chip is designed differently, both kinds of chips are built to use very little power.

After the CCD captures the image, the camera writes the image to a file on a storage card. Most digital cameras use one of three types of storage cards: Compact Flash, Smart Media, or Memory Sticks (Memory Sticks are specifically used with Sony digital cameras). The CCD replaces the film, and the storage card replaces the development process of a traditional 35mm camera.

So, why isn't everyone using a digital camera? First of all, you'll need a computer to store those image files, so you can print them or post them to a Web site. Then, there are the issues of battery consumption and cost of the camera, storage media, or accessories, as well as the biggest issue of them all, image quality. The good news is that more and more people are using digital cameras.

Low-Cost Digital Cameras

For those of you looking for the digital camera equivalent of the $20 throwaway 35mm camera, you won't find one. However, there are many digital cameras in the sub-$100 to $200 price range that offer fairly decent image quality. If cost is a big issue for you, and image quality isn't, you might want to consider buying one of the bargain-priced digital cameras to see how you like working with digital pictures.

note

The full name of a Charge Coupled Device (CCD) is Interline Transfer Charge Coupled Device, or IT CCD. A CCD chip is packed with sensors. When light is focused on the sensors, or photo diodes, a charge is produced. The photo diodes accumulate and transfer the charges into the camera's image processing system. The data is processed and organized into red, green, and blue image information and stored as a file on the storage card.

The following list includes some common limitations of low-cost digital cameras:

- **Fixed Resolution**—Capture a fixed file size, or up to two different file sizes, up to one megapixel in size. Some cameras allow you to capture and save only one resolution, such as 640×480. Look for one that states a resolution of at least 1280×960 with options for higher resolution shots. The tradeoff is that fewer shots can be saved to a memory card, but if you need high quality at a low price, this is the way you can get it.

- **Fixed focus**—Digital cameras are steadily dropping in price, but some at the low end of the lower-cost cameras might have only a fixed lens or a limited range for adjusting the focus. Look for one that lists an autofocus among its features to avoid dealing with the fixed focus lens.

- **Automatic or fixed exposure settings**—If your camera has no manual settings, you might need to avoid taking pictures in low light. Don't be surprised if you don't find digital cameras with manual setting capabilities in this price range.

- **Minimal software bundle**—Most cameras include software that you install to your computer to enable you to download images from the camera to your computer. The drawback is that at this price range the software bundle might lack image-editing and cataloging features.

Buying a digital camera is similar to buying any kind of technology, such as a computer. If you're not in a hurry to buy something today, chances are you'll be able to buy the same technology for less in three to six months. Like computers, digital cameras might be able to share one or two similar components, such as batteries, and Compact Flash, Smart Media, or Memory Stick storage cards.

Mid-Range Digital Cameras

If you're willing to spend more than a few hundred dollars on a camera, you'll probably find the largest selection and widest range of features in the $500–$999 price range (see Figure 6.1). Some of the more common features in mid-range cameras include automatic and manual modes for focus, flash, shutter speed, and aperture. Most models also support two or more file formats—usually JPEG and TIFF. You'll also notice more software features built into these cameras, as well as more or better computer software bundled with them.

Figure 6.1
Three-megapixel cameras generally range in price from $500 to $999 and can create great-looking images.

The following list contains some common features found in sub-$1,000 digital cameras:

- **Low- or high-quality images, up to three or four megapixels**—Choose from a wider range of image resolutions and file sizes. Some mid-range cameras enable you to capture low-resolution video in addition to still photos.

- **Small and large file sizes**—Although you can capture only one file at a time, some cameras enable you to shoot multiple images in succession. Being able to capture smaller files gives you a little freedom to experiment with different camera-shooting options.

- **Automatic and manual focus and flash**—You will be able to control whether the flash and focus are controlled by you or the camera. This can help you work around limitations of the camera when you're trying to take a shot with multiple subjects, for example, and you can't get the camera to properly focus on either subject. Most digital cameras require you to hold the shutter button halfway down to allow the camera to focus on a subject.

- **Automatic and manual shutter speed and aperture settings**—More choices are available to you, although you might be much happier with the smarter automatic features in most mid-range cameras.

- **Filter and lens expansion capabilities**—You can purchase adapters and lenses for some mid-range digital cameras. Lenses and filters enable you to capture images with special effects, such as wide angle or fish-eye effects.

- **Software bundle**—You can view or customize the camera's settings by accessing the software controls from the built-in LCD screen. If the camera has an automatic, manual, and playback mode, the menu system will be different for each camera mode. Click the menu button to view the menu options for each camera mode. A CD-ROM containing software for downloading, editing, and printing images also will be included with the camera.

When shopping for a digital camera, try to prioritize which features are most important to you: ease of use, picture quality, picture-taking speed, the design of the camera's body, the type of media used by the camera, and cost. So many camera models in the sub-$1,000 price range are constantly changing, that it might be easier to wait, or buy the camera that produces the best picture quality for the price.

There are several other issues you should consider before buying a camera, such as

- How many pictures you plan to take per picture-taking session. Choose the file format and multiply that by the number of photos you are likely to create, and you can determine what size and how many storage cards to purchase with your digital camera.

- How long the batteries will support picture taking. No matter what comes with the camera, most have the option of using rechargeable batteries. Look for batteries specifically designed for digital cameras.

- Whether you will be taking pictures in natural light or in low- or no-light conditions. Most digital cameras tend to take better pictures in daylight. Low light conditions might or might not create clear, crisp images.

- The kind of reviews the camera has received from current owners. Visit a Web site such as www.cnet.com to see how other owners have reviewed or rated digital cameras.

- The length of time you plan to own the camera before upgrading to a new one. Is this digital camera a long- or short-term investment? If you plan to keep this camera over the long haul, are the features that are most important to you present in the camera you want to purchase?

- Whether you plan to print the pictures or post them to the Web. Review the width and height of the higher-quality images the camera is capable of taking. Is the camera capable of capturing an image that you might want to print? For example, if you want to print 8×10-inch photos with your digital pictures, is the camera capable of capturing a 1024×768 or 800×600 pixel image? If you only plan to share images on the Web, you can probably get away with capturing 640×480 pictures, enabling you to store more pictures in a picture-taking session than if you had to capture images at a larger picture size.

The physical layout of the camera can determine how often you'll use it, as well as how many pictures you'll be taking with it. For example, look at the physical size of the camera and consider how easy it is to hold, or how much it might weigh if you have to carry it on your shoulder or in a camera bag. If the camera is too heavy, too small, or if the buttons and controls are awkward to navigate, you might want to compare it with a different camera model to see whether it is a better fit for your digital photography needs.

Most digital cameras have an LCD screen in addition to a viewfinder. Note the size of the LCD screen and the physical location of the viewfinder on the camera. The larger the LCD screen, the more battery power the camera will need to drive that screen. Most cameras have an automatic timeout setting in the camera's built-in software, plus a display button enabling you to power off the LCD if you're not using it. However, it can be difficult to take a picture if you have to wait one or two seconds if you want to frame your subject before taking the picture.

Digital Camera Performance Issues and Features

There can be many things you like or dislike about a particular digital camera. Depending on what you're looking for in a camera, it can be difficult to make a purchasing decision without having a hands-on experience with the camera. As you read reviews, camera features, and specifications, you might want to consider some of the issues presented in the following list:

1. How long does it take the camera to power on or wake up the LCD display? Some cameras power on within seconds after you press the power button, while others take longer. Depending on the camera you choose, you might need to get used to giving your camera a few seconds to get juiced before taking any pictures.

2. How long does the camera take to capture an image? Some cameras can write a three-megapixel image to the storage card in one or two seconds, whereas others take three or four seconds. If you plan to take pictures of a sports or action event, you might want to wait for the right shot instead of assuming your camera will be able to capture images at your whim.

3. Is the camera excessively noisy when you use the zoom or focus settings? Some cameras take longer to focus on a subject than others. Most cameras allow you to hold the shutter button down halfway so you can watch the camera adjust focus as the subject moves around. The noise created by the lens zooming to or away from the subject might not be an issue depending on how sensitive you are to working with noisy electronic devices. Most people prefer to work with electronics that can be seen and not heard.

4. Is the sound on the camera too loud? Can you turn off or adjust the sound levels for the camera? Some cameras play a shutter click sound when you take a picture to let you know that you have captured an image to the storage media card. Most cameras enable you to turn off sound from the built-in software menu. However, not all cameras give you this option. If sound is an issue, you might want to be sure sound-controlling features are available in the camera you want to use.

If you're not sure whether to buy a certain camera model, search the Web or digital camera magazines and read reviews for similarly priced cameras. Some Web sites, such as www.cnet.com and www. amazon.com, encourage Web visitors to rate their products and say what they like or dislike. Depending on the camera, you might be able to find a Web site showing photos for a particular camera model. If possible, compare photos from different cameras to help you decide which camera is best for you.

Lens Size and Picture Quality

The CCD plays a big part in determining the quality of the image captured by a digital camera. Most digital cameras have one CCD that processes red, green, and blue color information. However, the size of the lens also contributes to the quality of the image. The more light exposed to the CCD, the more image data the CCD can process. This doesn't mean that all digital cameras that have a large lens are capable of taking great pictures. The quality of the lens, combined with the quality of the CCD, determines how accurately the camera can capture an image. In general, digital cameras with larger lenses are likely to take sharper, more accurate, colorful pictures than digital cameras that have smaller lenses.

High-End Digital Cameras

Most professional or serious 35mm photographers are likely to poo-poo low-cost and medium-range cameras and look closely at the more expensive digital cameras. These cameras have dropped in price considerably over the past year. Now you can spend $1,000–$2,000 and get a digital camera that also can use your 35mm lenses and filters. The newer models are capable of capturing 3- to 6-megapixel images.

Three Media Card Formats for Cameras

The three most popular storage card formats used with digital cameras are Compact Flash, Smart Media, and Sony's Memory Stick. All three cards can store anywhere from 4MB to 128MB of data.

Another storage card alternative is IBM's micro drive. It currently tops out at 1GB. But don't be surprised if larger micro drives arrive on the scene. This storage card format is used by high-end cameras, as well as most Canon mid-range digital cameras.

Most 2- and 3-megapixel cameras can take a sharp, colorful picture. Most of the mid-range cameras are limited to their particular picture quality because of the size of the lens. High-end digital cameras support a larger lens and may have three CCDs, one each for the red, green, and blue capture. These higher-cost cameras are capable of capturing more image data simply because more light can be captured through the larger lens, and more CCDs are available to process the image data. However, one of the trade-offs can mean these higher-cost cameras take more time to create each digital picture.

The following are some features of the high-quality digital camera:

- **High-quality images three to six megapixels or higher—** Capture larger digital images ranging in size from 1MB or 2MB to 34MB or more.

- **Large file sizes; room for significant hard disk expansion—** Some of these higher-cost cameras support more than one type of storage card. For example, you can use a 1GB IBM micro drive in addition to a 128MB Compact Flash card with this type of camera.

- **Automatic or manual focus—**Some models have more than 200 levels of autofocus, in addition to enabling you to set where in the frame the camera should focus. Most cameras focus on the subject based on the location of a light source. If you're not happy with the autofocus behavior, you can control the camera's focus manually.

- **Automatic and manual settings—**In addition to being able to adjust the aperture and shutter speed, you also can let the camera take a sequence of pictures at different settings, and pick the best shot.

- **Full-size 35mm filter and lens expansion capabilities—** Capture a wider range of images by adding any number of lens and filter combinations to the camera.

- **Generous software bundle—**At least one CD-ROM containing a robust software bundle for editing and cataloging your images will be bundled with the camera.

If you're a casual photographer and you want to create images for both the Web and print, most sub-$1,000 3-megapixel cameras will do the job. The high-quality, high-priced digital cameras really are of great value and use only to professional photographers looking to make money from the photos they take.

Bigger Isn't Always Better

Even with JPEG compression, 6-megapixel cameras can create image files that are 34MB. That's right, 34MB per picture means you'll probably want to invest in a larger Compact Flash card or Smart Media card. Some cameras can work with the IBM 1GB microdrive, which you might want to invest in if you want to take more than three pictures at a time. Don't forget to get a CD or DVD RW drive, and possibly a larger hard drive. It's also not a bad idea to increase the amount of memory allocated to Photoshop Elements.

note

Most digital cameras have a special area where you'll find a small group of connection ports (see Figure 6.2). Most cameras support video out, for example, to connect to a television, in addition to a digital out port, which is used to connect to a computer.

Connecting Computers and Cameras

Most of the newer cameras connect to a computer's USB port. Older camera models rely on the PC or Mac serial port, which is much slower compared to USB (see Figure 6.2). Because digital cameras are considerably smaller than scanners and most computer peripherals, you won't find a Type A or Type B USB connector on a digital camera. Each camera has its own custom digital, mini-USB port. Unfortunately, USB ports on cameras aren't standardized, so you may be able to share a USB cable only if you have more than one camera made by the same company. You must use the USB cable that comes bundled with the camera to connect the camera to a computer's Type A USB port.

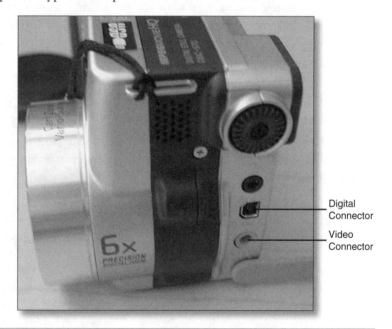

Figure 6.2
Most cameras require a custom USB connector to connect the cable to the camera. A USB or serial cable would connect to the digital connector on the camera and the USB or serial port on your computer.

Power off your camera, and connect the USB or serial cable to its digital connection port. Some cameras have a specific setting for connecting to a computer. Turn the mode dial on the camera to the appropriate mode setting (see Figure 6.3). Look for a mode setting on the camera that is to be used when downloading images—it could say play, review, or even computer.

Digital Connector

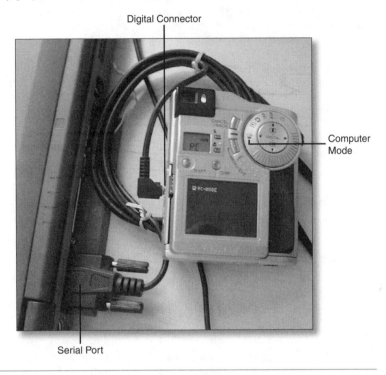

Computer Mode

Serial Port

Figure 6.3
Some cameras have a computer mode switch; others will automatically go into connect mode when powered on while connected to a computer.

Connect the other end of the cable to your computer's USB or serial port. After the cable is connected to both devices, turn the camera on. The status display or LCD screen on the camera should indicate that it is connected to a computer. However, some cameras might not have a special indicator to let you know whether it is connected to a computer.

Downloading Images and Battery Power

One of the more energy-draining tasks you can perform with a digital camera is downloading its images to a computer. You might want to put a fresh set of batteries into the camera before connecting it and downloading its images to a computer.

Another alternative is to invest in a storage card reader. Most readers cost less than $100 and enable a desktop or laptop to mount a Compact Flash card, Smart Media card, or Memory Stick card onto the Windows or Macintosh desktop. Most card readers are USB devices and require you to install software on your computer so that the computer can recognize the reader device.

Most PC and Macintosh laptops with a PC Card slot will be able to mount a Compact Flash and Smart Media card inserted into a PC card adapter. In most cases, you won't need to install any software to have your computer mount the camera's storage card as a PC Card.

Accessing Images on the Camera

Connecting a camera to a computer creates a physical hardware connection between the two devices. Next, you'll need to install software that enables your computer to communicate with the software on your camera. You can install the software from the CD-ROM that comes bundled with the camera or download some of the software from the camera manufacturer's Web site.

Setting Up the Software

Some cameras are bundled with TWAIN plug-in software, which will enable you to control the camera within the Photoshop Elements work area. Other cameras have their own custom software that you must use to download images from the camera onto your computer. If your camera falls into the latter category, follow the instructions that came with your camera, and download the image files onto your computer's hard drive. Then skip ahead to the next chapter.

Downloading Images to Your Computer

Controlling a camera in the Photoshop Elements work area is similar to the way you work with a scanner. Before you can select a device from the File, Import menu, you need to install the TWAIN plug-in software for your camera. Not all cameras have a TWAIN plug-in, so you might need to view or download files using the camera's applications before you can open them in Photoshop Elements. Choose Import from the File menu, and then select the camera from the menu list. Then, wait for the camera's software window to open in the Photoshop Elements work area.

The user interface varies depending on the camera you're using. Usually, the software user interface is very simple. When Photoshop Elements first connects to the camera, a thumbnail image of each picture on the camera is downloaded to the computer. If you want to copy the file from the camera to the computer, click the Acquire button (see Figure 6.4).

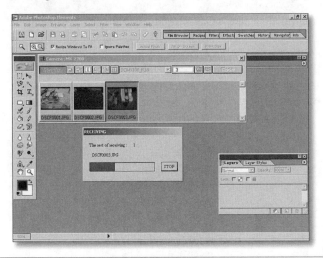

Figure 6.4
Download images from your camera to your computer in Photoshop Elements.

You might find that downloading images over a cable takes a little more time than you'd like. It will also drain your camera's batteries. If you want to copy all the files from the storage card in your camera directly onto your computer's hard drive, without viewing any of the files, you can insert the storage card into a media reader or PC Card adapter. If you're using a media card reader, you'll need to install additional software on your desktop computer so it can recognize the USB device.

If you're using a PC Card adapter, you probably won't need to install any additional software to view or copy files from the storage card to your computer. However, some PC Card adapters require you to install software to work with a particular version of Windows or Mac OS. Windows 98, 2000, and newer operating systems, as well as Mac OS 8.6 and newer operating systems, all have built-in support for reading files from storage cards (see Figure 6.5).

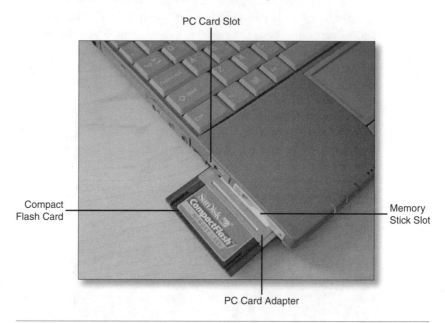

Figure 6.5
Insert the media card from the camera into a PC Card adapter to quickly access your image files.

Saving Images

After you've downloaded an image from a camera to your computer, you can choose the Save command from the File menu. Before you start modifying an image, it's a good idea to save a copy of the original image to your hard drive. After a file is saved, you can experiment with color correction or filter effects without having to worry about losing or damaging the original.

To save a file, make the file the active window in the work area. Choose Save from the File menu. Then type a name into the Save dialog box. Click on the Format drop-down menu and choose JPEG. Navigate to a folder location on your hard drive in the Save dialog box. Finally, click the Save button to save the image. Photoshop Elements will create a new image file on your hard drive.

More About File Formats

Not sure which file format to use when saving your file? Choose the JPEG file format, with the highest level of image preservation (in Photoshop Elements, choose Maximum, or 10).

To find out more about saving files, as well as Photoshop Elements-supported file formats, see Chapter 8, "Saving and Sharing Files."

Viewing the File Format

If you want to view an image on a camera without downloading it to your hard drive, you can use Photoshop Elements or the custom software that is bundled with the camera. Figure 6.6 shows the photo viewer application, Visual Flow, that opens when you insert a Memory Stick into a Sony computer. Each image scrolls up the photo view window as you move your cursor in the main window. Click on a picture to view it in more detail.

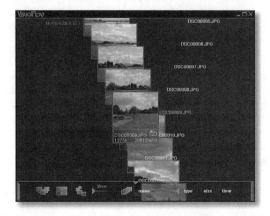

Figure 6.6
When you insert a Memory Stick into a Sony VAIO laptop, you can navigate through thumbnail images of the files stored on the card. PC Card and USB Memory Stick readers are also available for Macs and Windows computers.

If you don't want to use an application to access your image files, you can use the Explorer (Windows) or the Finder (Mac OS). Figure 6.7 shows each image on the Memory Stick card. The camera gives each image a unique filename, along with the .jpg file extension. If you're using Windows, you might not see the .jpg extension if Windows is set to hide file extension names in the Explorer windows. You simply can copy the files from the Memory Stick onto your computer. Then, open the images with Photoshop Elements to view or modify them as you like.

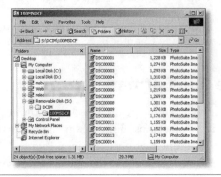

Figure 6.7
Files stored on a media card can be copied to your hard drive as you copy any other document.

Which File Format Is Best?

Most cameras capture images and then save them as JPEG files. Although some cameras also support TIFF, and multimedia files formats such as MPEG or AVI, the best file format to use for still image files is JPEG. You'll get the smallest, best-looking file sizes by using the JPEG file format on your camera, your computer, and, in most cases on your Web site, too.

After you've saved or copied a file to your computer, open it to see whether the file was saved successfully. Choose Open from the File menu to view the Open dialog box. Select the file you just saved, and then click Open. The image will open in the Photoshop Elements work area.

If the image is larger than your desktop, Photoshop Elements will resize the full image to fit on your screen. The magnification level of the image will appear in the title bar of each image window. You can use the Navigator palette to adjust the view of each image window, or select the Zoom Tool from the toolbox. Click in the image window to increase the magnification level of the image window. Or hold down the [Alt] (Option) key to zoom away from the image. If the image opens and looks as good as the original, you can close it.

Selecting Devices

If your digital camera or scanner has a TWAIN plug-in installed on your computer, you can work with each device one at a time or alternate between one or the other. There are two ways you can select a device in the work area. You can choose the device from the File, Import menu list, or you can click the Acquire button in the Quick Start window. The Select Import Source window will only open if you click the Acquire button. You can access the TWAIN plug-in–related software of each scanner or camera from the Select Import Source window (see Figure 6.8), or from the File, Import menu list. After you select a device, you can't perform any other tasks in Photoshop Elements. You must exit the camera's software window before you can access any other features in the work area.

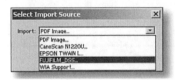

Figure 6.8
Select a device from the drop-down menu in the Select Import Source window. You can access this window if you click the Acquire button in the Quick Start window.

Be sure the device is connected to your computer before selecting it in the Select Import Source window. If the software cannot locate the device, it will ask you to connect the device. You'll need to re-select the camera from the Import submenu to re-establish a connection with the camera.

If the software is able to locate your camera or scanner, you can preview the images in the work area. The preview image is usually much larger than the image shown in the software window. If you want to scan or download several images, it might take a while.

You can view additional information about an image, or about the camera or scanner device if the device software provides these options. Figure 6.9 shows an information window from Fuji's MX 2700 digital camera software.

Figure 6.9
Different cameras offer different software features. The Fuji camera software enables you to view camera information in Photoshop Elements.

part

III

OPENING, SAVING, AND PRINTING IMAGES

Creating, Opening, and Converting Images

If there's anything an image absolutely has to have in Photoshop Elements, it's a window. Photoshop Elements places an image in a new image window whenever you open an image file, or whenever you create a new document from scratch. Each image window in the work area represents an unsaved document: a potential file that can be stored on your hard drive. You can open more than one image window if you like, enabling you to work on different images at the same time or compare variations of the same image in the work area.

Opening an image window is one of the first things to learn if you want to be an image wizard. Adobe created the Quick Start window to bring the Open, New, and Acquire commands right in front of you when you first start Photoshop Elements. You can click any of the six buttons to open a new window or existing image, or to acquire an image from a scanner or camera or view tutorials and help files.

note

To learn more about the Quick Start window, go to Chapter 4, "Using the Quick Start Window and the Help System."

If you want to create a new image window from scratch, click the New button in the Quick Start window, or choose New from the File menu. The New dialog box opens. If you already have an image file on your hard drive, click the Open button in the Quick Start menu or select the Open command from the File menu. The Open dialog box will appear. Need to download an image from a camera or scanner? No problem! Click the Acquire button and you can have a new image window open in a matter of minutes. This chapter shows you how to create a new document and open an image file.

Creating a New Document

The image window is the heart of image editing in Photoshop Elements. Photoshop Elements enables you to set the specific width and height of each window. The width and height settings in the New dialog box define the size of the canvas. You can grow or shrink the window regardless of the size of the canvas. However, more memory and scratch disk space will be required as the canvas area, resolution, and number of image layers grows.

You can create a document from scratch by choosing File, New (Command-N) [Ctrl+N]. The New dialog box will open. You can manually type the width and height of the new window and set the form of measurement you want to use for that window. If you want to create a new window that matches the dimensions of a specific image or other graphic, you can use the Copy command to transfer the image to the Clipboard. When you choose the New command from the File menu, Photoshop Elements will automatically set the width and height values in the New dialog box to match the contents of the Clipboard (see Figure 7.1). Click OK, and then choose the Paste command to place the copied image into its new window.

If you scanned or downloaded an image from a digital camera, Photoshop Elements will place the image in a new window when you open the file in the work area. By default, Photoshop Elements creates a document in RGB color mode. Almost all the examples in this book require an image to be in RGB mode, which supports millions of colors. Also, most of the tools and commands in Photoshop Elements won't work unless the image is in RGB mode. The other color modes—Grayscale, Indexed Color, and Bitmap—support 256 or fewer shades of color. To find out more about color modes (also called image modes), see Chapter 10, "Digital Images and Color."

Figure 7.1
Type a number in each text box to set the dimensions, image mode, resolution, and contents for your new document.

Located at the bottom of the New dialog box are three radio buttons enabling you to choose the content for the new window. You can set the color of the window to the background layer of the document, or choose a white or transparent background for the window. If you choose White, Photoshop Elements creates a background layer filled with pure white. Choose Transparent if you want to create a completely empty image window. You'll see a gray-and-white checkerboard pattern in the new window. This pattern represents transparent areas in the image window.

If you choose the Background Color radio button, the background layer of the new window will become the color displayed in the background swatch in the toolbox. If you're working with graphics intended for Web pages, you can set the background color to match the background color of a Web page. This can help you coordinate the colors of other images you create in the image window with the colors used on a Web page.

Choosing a Color Mode

When in doubt, assuming you have enough memory and disk space available, create a new document in RGB color mode. Most scanned images, including images created by digital cameras, work great in RGB mode.

Deconstructing the New Dialog Box

To create a new document, you will need to fill in each text field in the New dialog box. There are several settings you can customize in the New dialog box (see Figure 7.1). The following list contains a brief description of each text box and radio button available in the New dialog box:

- **Filename**—Enter the name of the new document in the Name text box.
- **Image size**—Set the width and height of the canvas area, not the image, in the New dialog box. Documents can be created in pixels, inches, centimeters, points, picas, and columns.
- **Resolution**—Enter the pixels per inch for the image window. You can also set this to pixels per centimeter.
- **Mode**—Choose the color mode for the new document. Select RGB Color, Bitmap, or Grayscale.
- **Contents**—Choose a transparent or colored background for the new window.

Demystifying Resolution and Image Size

Many of the settings in the New dialog box are also available in the Image Size dialog box. Determining the width and height of the canvas is fairly straightforward, especially when you copy and paste the image into a new document window. The more complex settings to consider when creating a new document are the resolution and image size settings.

Several meanings exist for both of these terms. *Resolution* often describes the size of a computer desktop, the scale of measurement for an image, or the dimensions of an image. *Image size* also can mean more than one thing, referring to both the size of the file on the hard disk and the size of the document in memory. The following sections contain brief descriptions of each of these definitions of resolution and image size.

What Is Resolution?

The following list summarizes the three most commonly confused uses of the term *resolution*:

- **Dimensions of the image**—The actual number of pixels wide and tall for an image. The dimensions of the image can be larger or smaller than the canvas area of the image window.

- **Number of pixels per inch**—Some monitors display images at 96 dots per inch (dpi). Older Macintosh monitors have a resolution of 72 dpi. Photoshop Elements uses the measurement of pixels per inch to represent the number of pixels displayed for each inch of a computer monitor.

- **Resolution of the display**—Set the size of your computer's desktop area from the [Display] (Monitors) Control Panel window. The resolution of your desktop, combined with the actual size of your display screen, determines how much of the image you can view on your computer monitor.

What Is Image Size?

The following list contains three definitions of image size:

- **Document size**—The canvas area of the image window.

- **Pixel size**—The actual number of pixels wide and tall of an image.

- **File size**—The size of the image file on the hard drive.

Customizing the Canvas Size

Each document created or opened in the work area has a canvas. When you open an existing image file, the canvas area matches the width and height of the image being opened. The canvas can be transparent, represented by a gray-and-white checkered pattern that indicates the absence of color. It also can be white or any color you choose.

You can view the size of the canvas by choosing the Canvas Size command from the Image, Resize menu. The Canvas Size window will open. The current file size appears at the top of the window, followed by its width and height. You can type a new width and height into the text boxes, or choose a new anchor point by clicking on one of the Anchor buttons.

note
Increasing the size of the canvas will not affect the size of any images in the image window. However, if you decrease the size of the canvas, Photoshop Elements will remove any areas of the image that are not located on the smaller-sized canvas.

When you resize or create a new document window, the width and height settings define the canvas area in addition to the dimensions of the window and image. The canvas represents the printable or publishable area of the image window. The following describes each setting in the Canvas Size dialog box:

- **New Size**—The new file size is calculated based on the new width and height values you enter into the text boxes.
- **Width and Height**—Enter a new value into the text box. Choose from percent, pixels, inches, centimeters, points, picas, or columns for the canvas measurement.
- **Anchor**—Determines the location and direction of the new canvas area. Click on a square to choose where the current document will reside when the canvas area is extended.

Document Settings for Print

Although the width and height settings determine the dimensions of an image file, the resolution setting in the New dialog box ultimately has the biggest impact on how the image will appear when you print it. Printers use the measurement of *dots per inch* (dpi). Dots refer to the way the printer places ink or toner powder onto a page to re-create the image being sent from your computer. To print a document, first you must view it on a computer screen. However, computer monitors use the pixel as their most basic form of measurement. Dots and pixels have no common ancestor, although Photoshop Elements makes it relatively easy to convert an image intended for print into an image targeted for the Web.

Computer monitors use the measurement of *pixels per inch* (ppi). The size of a pixel is different from the size of the dots referenced by printers. Digital cameras use *megapixels*, a combination of the total number of horizontal and vertical pixels captured, to determine resolution. However, when you open an image created by a digital camera, it will be set to 72 pixels per inch—the same settings as a computer screen. In the next section, I'll say more about why digital cameras and publishing to the Web are much more straightforward than printing digital images.

Scanners, on the other hand, use samples per inch to measure the data captured by the 600 to 1200 sensors located on the scanner's scan bar (below the glass on a flatbed scanner). The data captured by the sensors is combined with the vertical distance between each line of captured data. For example, you can create an image that's scanned into your computer with a resolution of 1200 dpi.

After you've scanned an image into the work area, you can click on the status bar in the work area to view the image's information (see Figure 7.2). Click the middle-left area of the status bar, located at the bottom of the work area. A window will appear displaying the dimensions of the image, as well as its image mode and resolution. Clicking on the status bar is a nice, quick way to determine the size and resolution of the image you're modifying.

note

To find out more about scanning images and working with scanner settings, go to Chapter 5, "Scanning Images into Photoshop Elements."

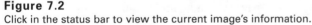

Figure 7.2
Click in the status bar to view the current image's information.

Image and Print Sizes

If you plan to share a scanned image on the Web, you can modify the scanned image at a high resolution, such as 600 dpi, and then resize it to 72 or 96 dpi (see Figure 7.3). The print dimensions of the document will not change, although the size of the image window might shrink quite a bit. Double-click on the Zoom Tool (Z) in the toolbox to resize the image to a 100% view.

Figure 7.3
Resize an image by changing the resolution in the Image Size dialog box. The image on the right is 72 dpi, whereas the image on the left was scanned in at 2400 dpi.

Document Settings for Web Images

If you're creating a new document for use on the Web, consider the width and height of the Web page for which you will be designing the image or graphics. Most images for Web pages are created at 72 or 96 dpi, because the Web visitors can view Web pages at these resolutions on their monitors—regardless of whether the image is actually a higher dpi in its electronic format.

The dimensions of the image file will affect the overall size of the Web page. Users are also limited by the connection speed of the Web visitor; the larger the image, the longer the download time for the Web page. Web pages should contain smaller, rather than larger image files, enabling your Web visitors to experience your Web graphics without waiting too long for them to download. Find out more about how to optimize Web graphics in Chapter 8, "Saving and Sharing Files."

Consider the following issues when creating a new document for use on the Web:

*   Create an image file that fits within the desktop area of the Web page. I usually save my images as 640×480 files (see Figure 7.4), expecting visitors to my Web site to have at

minimum a 800×600 pixel desktop. If a visitor arrives at your Web site and only has a 640×480 desktop, they will only be able to see part of your Web page onscreen at once. They will have to scroll around the browser window to view the full 640×480 image. If you want each visitor to view the full size of each photograph, consider creating a smaller thumbnail image for each larger image.

- A resolution setting of 72 dpi will work fine for Web graphics. In most cases, you don't have to adjust the resolution of your images captured with your digital camera to put them on a Web page.

- Set the background color of the document window to be colored or transparent. For most images, you're better off choosing a transparent background for a new image window. Alternatively, you could choose a background color for the canvas if you want to create graphics that blend in with the Web page.

Figure 7.4
The width and height of a Web document should fall within the size of the desktop and work well with the resolution setting of 72 ppi.

Photoshop Elements enables you to create images and graphics for use on the Web. To make an image file appear on a Web page, first create the image file, and then create an HTML text file and type HTML code to add the image or images to the Web page. To view the image on a Web page, you will need to copy the HTML and image file to a Web server.

You can use the Web Photo Gallery command in the File, Automate menu to create a photo album that you can share on the Web. You can view your digital images on your computer, or upload them to a Web site and share them with friends and family over the Internet. To find out more about Web pages, image files, and how to create a Web photo album, go to Chapter 20, "Creating a Web Photo Gallery."

Opening Image Files

You can open an image file in the work area in three ways. Choose File, Open [Command-O] (Ctrl+O) to open an image file in its current file format. If you want to convert a file to a different image file format, use the File, Open As command [Command-O] (Alt+Ctrl+O). You also can open an image file by dragging and dropping its icon onto the Photoshop Elements application icon on your desktop.

caution
Digital camera owners heed my words. If your camera was running low on batteries when you took that picture, you might end up with a blurry image, no matter how sharp the image appeared in the display on the camera. Remember to put in fresh batteries before going on an extensive photo shoot.

Attention Macintosh Users

The Macintosh version of Photoshop Elements does not have an Open As command in the File menu. Instead, you can perform this task in the Open window. Choose File, Open, and the Open dialog box will appear. Click on the image file you want to open. Then, choose a file format from the Format pop-up menu. The selected file will open in the format you choose in the Format menu list. For example, if you want to open a JPEG file as a PSD file, highlight a JPEG file in the window list. Choose Photoshop PDF from the Format pop-up menu. Click on the Open button, and the JPEG file will open as a native Photoshop document.

When you first open an image file, you should decide whether the quality of the image is good enough. For example, if you're scanning an image, it's better to rescan an iffy-looking image before spending hours trying to correct what could have been prevented by creating a better quality scanned image.

Why Change a Good Thing?

One of the reasons to use the Open As command is to save time. For example, if you know you want to combine two JPEG files, you can open the first image as a PSD file, and then copy the second JPEG image into the PSD file. Each image will reside in its own editable layer.

continued

A PSD file is the native file format used by Photoshop Elements. Why edit images as PSD files? Because this file format will preserve all layer information you generate as you click away on an image. If you try to save this same image as a JPEG file, the two images will be merged into one layer, preventing you from editing it in the future.

Working with Scanned Images

You can open an image file created by a scanner the same way you open any image file. However, depending on the resolution, dimensions, and file size of an image, it might not quite fit into the work area. If you're planning to repair or correct a scanned image, you'll want to keep the image at a higher resolution (see Figure 7.5). If you plan to print the scanned image, you probably don't need to change the resolution of the image file. If you plan to use the image for a Web page, you can change its resolution to 72 dpi after correcting or modifying it.

Figure 7.5
One of the benefits of working with a scanned image is that you can scan the image into Photoshop Elements at a high resolution, thus making it easier to work with.

When Bigger Is Better

Scanning an image into Photoshop Elements enables you to make detailed edits before scaling it down to a smaller size for printing or publishing to the Web. Be forewarned that the larger the document, the larger the size of the image file. This means the image takes up more space on your hard drive and will download very slowly on the Web.

continued

For example, I scanned in a color negative at 2400 dpi and ended up saving a 3GB file. The same image scanned in at 1200 dpi is less than 1GB.

I also scanned in a 4×6 photo at 1200 dpi, which resulted in a 4GB file. This file opens as a 60MB image in Photoshop Elements!

Opening Images Created by a Digital Camera

Most files created by digital cameras are JPEG files, although some cameras also can create TIFF, MPEG, or AVI files. The latter two file formats are multimedia file formats. The multimedia files usually are smaller 320×240-pixel images compared to the larger 2000×1600-pixel still images. You cannot open multimedia files in Photoshop Elements, only single-frame image files.

Choose Open from the Quick Start window or from the File menu to view the Open dialog box. The Open dialog box looks slightly different on Windows than on a Macintosh computer. However, both perform the same core task of opening image files. You can open any of the file formats that appear in the Files of Type drop-down menu. To find out more about Photoshop Elements' supported file formats, go to Chapter 8.

The Windows Open dialog box enables you to preview some JPEG files if a thumbnail is stored along with the full-size image (see Figure 7.6). The file size appears below the thumbnail image. Sorry, Mac users, you can preview images as a thumbnail icon on your desktop, but not in the Open dialog box.

tip
Hold down the Shift key to select more than one image in the Open dialog box if you want to open more than one image at a time.

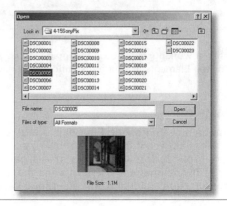

Figure 7.6
The Open dialog box enables you to view one or all image file formats supported by Photoshop Elements.

If your camera can capture 1-, 2-, or 3-megapixel images, you can open them with Photoshop Elements. When you open a megapixel image, it might seem like your desktop is a little too small to display the full-size image. This is a good thing, because it's better to have a larger image than a smaller one, especially when you want to edit the image. Photoshop Elements will adjust the magnification level of the image so that you can view the entire image in the work area. You can view the file size, resolution, width, or height of an image by clicking on the status bar of the open image in the Photoshop Elements work area.

If you want to reduce the dimensions of the digital image, choose Image Size from the Image, Resize menu. Enter a smaller number into the width and height text boxes. By default, the link icon that appears to the right of these text boxes will maintain the original proportions of the image file. You can type in a new number for the width of the document, and Photoshop Elements will automatically calculate the new height of the image.

Importing Versus Opening

Importing enables you to select specific settings for an image file being opened in the work area. For example, TWAIN plug-ins enable you to run device-specific (such as scanners or digital cameras) software in the Photoshop Elements work area, allowing you to customize an image with the device before opening it in the work area. Similarly, you can use the PDF Image command to import each image from a PDF (Portable Document Format) file. If you opened the PDF file with the Open command, the entire document will open in the image window. To find out more about PDF files, see Chapter 8.

Resizing an Image

Photoshop Elements opens an image in its original dimensions. You can either change the view of the image displayed in the image window, or permanently resize the image (see Figure 7.7). The term *resize* is used here to describe the actual width and height dimensions of the image, not its file size.

Figure 7.7
You must resize a 3-megapixel image to view it in a typical browser window.

Choose the Zoom Tool (magnifying glass icon) to zoom into and out of a document. This tool enables you to change the view of the image without affecting the image itself. Click the image to enlarge it, or hold down the (Option) [Alt] key and click to reduce or zoom away from the image.

You also can use the Navigator palette to set the magnification level of the viewable image in the document window. Click and drag the red rectangle to pan around the image window. The magnification level of the image appears in the lower-left corner of the Navigator palette and the work area. It also appears in the title bar of the image window.

If you want to change the width or height of the image, choose Image Size from the Image, Resize menu. The Image Size window opens. This window is divided into four general areas. On the right, the OK, Cancel, Help, and Auto buttons enable you to open or exit the window. You can adjust the Pixel Dimensions, Document Size, or choose a different method for Photoshop Elements to use to resample the resized image. The following list contains a brief description of each area of settings in the Image Size window:

- **Pixel Dimensions**—View the current dimensions of the image here. Enter a new width or height into the text boxes. The default behavior is to constrain the settings so that the proportions of the original image are preserved.

- **Document Size**—The actual printed size of the file. The default setting is in inches, and the width and height are constrained to preserve the original dimensions of the image.

- **Resolution**—The number of pixels per inch in the image. You can enter a new value into this text box to change the resolution of an image without changing the document size.

- **Constrain Proportions**—If this box is checked, the original proportion of the width to the height is preserved when you enter any new value in the Image Size dialog box.

- **Resample Image**—Choose the interpolation method you want Photoshop Elements to use on a resized image (see Figure 7.8). The interpolation method applies an algorithm to retain as much of the original image as possible.

tip
Click the Auto button if you'd like Photoshop Elements to automatically resize the image based on the resolution of the screen and the quality of the image.

Figure 7.8
A resized image will be resampled using the interpolation method selected from the Resample Image drop-down menu.

Converting Image Information

You might need to modify your images for several reasons. You might want to change the file type so that it matches another image with which you are going to combine it. After you open an image, you might find that you need to change the resolution, color mode, or size in order for it to fit your intended purpose. Whatever the reason, Photoshop Elements makes it fairly painless to accomplish just about any type of change you need to make.

note
When you resize an image for the Web, Photoshop Elements uses the interpolation algorithm selected in the Resample Image option in the Image Size dialog box to determine which pixels to change. Bicubic interpolation, which is the default setting, usually offers the best and fastest method of resampling an image. However, you also can choose a bilinear or nearest neighbor algorithm when shrinking or growing an image.

Opening an Image in a Different File Format

When you open an image file using the (Open) [Open As] dialog box, you can convert it to a different file format (see Figure 7.9). When it's open, you can change its image mode or dimensions to more closely match the settings of another image file. For example, if you want to take a scanned image and combine it with an image created with a digital camera, you might need to work with the resolution and image sizes to scale both images until they match. Using the Image Size dialog box to adjust the settings, you can experiment with copying and pasting an image using different resolutions in multiple image windows. Then, pick the images you want to combine and paste them into a single image window.

Figure 7.9
The (Open) [Open As] command enables you to convert a file to a specific file format when you open it. If you're running Windows, choose a file format from the Open As drop-down menu. On a Mac, choose a file format from the Format pop-up menu of the Open dialog box.

Changing an Image to a Different Color Mode

The color mode of an image determines the number of colors that can be used to display the image. Photoshop Elements enables you to work with an image in four image modes: RGB Color, Grayscale, Bitmap, and Indexed color. Most images will open in RGB Color mode. The following list matches up image modes with image files:

- Color photo—RGB Color
- Optimized color photo—Indexed Color

- Black-and-white or monochrome image—Grayscale
- Line art—Bitmap

When Not to Change Files

First, save a copy of the original image before experimenting with different image sizes or resolutions.

After an image is reduced in size, pixels are permanently removed from the image file. If you want to apply different color correction tools, filters, or effects, it will be much more difficult to do this after the image has lost a lot of its color information. If you're working with color images, work with them in RGB mode and at the largest possible image size as you can.

Converting a File for Print Output

Printing a digital image can be either a pleasant or frustrating experience. More precisely, it is a pleasant experience when you print an image that matches what you created on your computer screen. And it's frustrating when the printed image does not meet your expectations.

If the image originates from a digital camera, it was most likely created at a resolution of 72 dpi. You can adjust the width and height of the printed size of the image without changing its resolution to make the image match the dimensions of the paper on which it will be printed. Photoshop Elements will use an interpolation algorithm to resize the original so that it will retain as much color and image detail when it is printed at 300 or 600 dpi.

If you've scanned an image, you might have captured a 300 or 600 dpi or higher resolution image. Save the file as a TIFF or JPEG file format to retain the image size and quality. If you print this image to a 600 dpi printer, it will print with a much higher quality than a resized digital picture because the original image consists of more dots packed into each inch of printed paper (see Figure 7.10).

note
To find out more about printers and printing digital images, go to Chapter 9, "Printing Images."

note
When working with scanned images or images taken with a digital camera, it is necessary to preserve the original JPEG or TIFF image. Saving the original file enables you to archive the original state of the captured data so that you can easily go back to the original state if you find the edits you are making don't achieve the result you want. As you work on an image, you might find that an image you captured can be more easily edited if you change some of the scanner or camera settings and bring the image back into Photoshop Elements again.

Figure 7.10
Both of these images are 72 ppi. The image on the left was scanned, and the one on the right taken with a digital camera.

Choosing a Web File Format

One of the great things about the Web is that you can easily download images from a Web page onto your hard drive. If you have access to a Web server, you can store a backup copy of your images on the Web, and easily download an original if you lose or remove it from your hard drive. Most images on the Web are stored as JPEG or GIF files. However, some browsers can display the PNG file format, too.

The following list contains a brief description of each of these Web file formats:

- **GIF**—Pronounced with a soft g, as in "choosy mothers choose Jif," this file format is great at compressing images that have a large chunk of a single color. Images also can contain transparency, which helps an image blend in with a background color or with another image on a Web page.

- **JPEG**—This is the best file format to choose for digital images. However, JPEG images don't enable you to use transparency, like GIF and PNG files do. You can choose from varying levels of image compression and image quality using this file format.

- **PNG**—Although a less popular file format because it is not widely supported by Web browsers, it shares many of the great features of the GIF and JPEG file formats.

Saving and Sharing Files

The best thing about working with digital images is that you can preserve all the detail of an image as a file, and copy or back that file up as many times as you like. The quality of the digital image won't degenerate as the file is opened, copied, closed, or is just biding its time on your computer's hard drive.

Saving a file also means you can share it with others. You can send an image file in an e-mail or publish it on a Web page. This chapter shows you all the ins and outs of saving files, whether you want to print them or share them on the Web.

What's All the Fuss?

What can be so difficult about choosing the Save command from the File menu to save a file? Well, certain file formats retain image data better than others. For example, a JPEG file stored at a high compression rate will save a portion of the original image. A high compression rate usually results in a lower quality image, compared to the original image. However, if you choose the minimum compression rate, the quality of the image will be preserved; all the original image data will be stored in the compressed file.

When you save an image, you want to preserve all the image data so that you can edit the image with as much image and color data as possible. After you've created the final image, you can save a separate copy of the same image containing fewer colors, or only a portion of the original image. What I've just described here is the general workflow for preparing digital camera images for printing or for posting on a Web page.

Using the Save Command

If you're working with a new document, the first time you choose the Save command and assign it a name, the Save As window will appear. If you've already chosen a file format for your image file, or are saving the same file as you gradually make changes, use the Save command. The Save command, located in the File menu, replaces the existing file with all the new information of the current image file, using the same file format. If you want to choose a different file format for an image, use the Save As command—it's chock-full of file-saving options (see Figure 8.1).

Choosing the Color of the Canvas

If the Background Color radio button is selected in the New dialog box, the color that appears in the background color square located in the toolbox will be used as the background color for a new window. If the Web page you're working with uses a solid color background, you can work with images or graphics with the same color background. This can help you adjust transparency settings for each graphic object, and also choose colors that blend well with the background color of the page.

tip

Heed these words of wisdom: Save, and save often. You can edit the images, undo a change, or copy and paste other images into multiple documents without ever saving them. But there's nothing more memorable than watching your computer crash after you've spent hours of work developing an image.

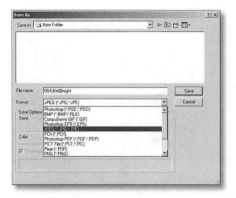

Figure 8.1
The Save As window contains a treasure trove of file formats from which you
can choose.

The color profile contains color information that can help maintain
the original captured colors as you work on the image with different
applications, or on different computers (see Figure 8.2).

You can access color management in one or more of the following
ways:

- **File format**—Choose a file format that can preserve as many
  colors as possible (see Figure 8.3).

- **Color profile**—Choose a color profile to save along with the
  file.

- **Operating system**—Mac OS uses a color-management system
  called ColorSync. Check to see whether your computer has
  color-management software available for any connected devices.

The options you choose when saving a file can affect how much data
is saved. Some file formats, such as the JPEG format, shown in
Figure 8.3, support compression, which reduces the file size of an
image. You can adjust the compression options when you first save
an image. A format options window will appear for a JPEG, GIF, or
TIFF image after you select the Save button in the Save window.
Although it's not the case for all file formats, more compression
usually means more image data is removed when the file is saved.
Basically, the smaller the image, the less image data it contains.

Figure 8.2
Save the color profile of an image so that you can preserve its color information if you copy the file to different computers, or work on it in more than one application.

Figure 8.3
Some file formats, such as JPEG and TIFF, have several file settings that enable you to control how much of the image data is saved to the file.

If you're not sure which settings to use for a particular file format, your best bet is to use as little compression as possible. For example, if you're saving a JPEG file, choose an image quality setting of 10. TIFF images can also be saved with or without compression. However, some compression formats, such as LZW compression, might not work with different graphics editors or image viewer applications.

Saving a File for Any Occasion

Photoshop Elements supports a long list of file formats. Although you can use any of these file formats to save your image, Photoshop Elements' native PSD is the only file format that enables you to continue editing multilayered images time and time again. A PSD file can store any layers or other Photoshop Elements-specific settings. Other file formats will only be able to save a single, flat layer as an image file. Flattening an image makes it much more difficult to edit later. It's better to preserve the layers of an image whenever possible, until you are positive you will no longer need to edit the file.

Supported File Formats

The following list contains all the possible file formats you can use to save your image:

- **BMP**—The bitmap image file format used most frequently with Windows computers. This is the default format used when you create a screen capture in Windows.

- **PCX**—Another graphics file format used by many Windows graphics applications.

- **PICT**—The standard file format used by Mac OS 9.1 to store captured screen shots. (Mac OS X captures screen shots as TIFF files.) PICT also is referred to as a .PCT file or PICT Resource. A PICT Resource is a type of image stored in a Mac file.

- **Photo CD**—A file format created for image files stored on Kodak's Photo CD-ROMs. If you take a roll of 35mm film, many stores can create a Photo CD of that roll of film so that you can open the images on your computer. The Photo CD contains several sets of the 35mm images. Each set contains the images stored at different resolutions, such as 640×480 pixels or 1024×768 pixels. Photoshop Elements enables you to import Photo CD images into the work area. Photoshop Elements cannot save files in PCD format.

- **GIF**—Graphics Interchange Format. GIF images use LSW compression combined with a transparency layer and a color table to store an image. Choose CompuServe GIF to save an image as a GIF file.

note

Color management enables different output devices to translate color information to preserve color accuracy. To find out more about color management, go to Chapter 10, "Digital Images and Color."

- **JPEG**—Joint Photographic Experts Group. This format supports the widest range of colors of all the image file formats. It also offers file compression, but no transparency support. Also, the more compression you apply to a JPEG file, the more image data is lost.

- **PNG**—Portable Network Graphics. An alternative to GIF or JPEG image formats. The latest versions of Internet Explorer and Netscape Navigator can display PNG files. This file format was designed to replace the GIF file format; however, it does not support animation.

- **TIFF**—Tag Image File Format. A common format used with Mac and Windows computers. You can save a TIFF file as a grayscale or color image, using no compression, or JPEG, LZW, or ZIP compression.

- **(Photoshop EPS) [EPS]**—An acronym for Encapsulated PostScript. Sound like some sort of medicine? It's not. This file format was originally created by Adobe to preserve font and line art, or vector graphic data in a file. Opening an EPS file converts the vector graphics into pixels.

- **PDD**—The native file format created by Adobe Photo Deluxe. This format is not available on the Macintosh version of Photoshop Elements.

- **(Photoshop PDF) [PDF]**—An acronym for the Portable Document Format. It is the standard file format used by Adobe Acrobat and Acrobat Reader.

- **(Photoshop) [PSD]** —The native file format for Photoshop and Photoshop Elements. This format enables you to preserve unique Photoshop Element document information, such as layers, group layer information, and other settings.

- **Raw**—This is not as much of a file format as it is a file that contains a stream of image information. This is a generic file format that can be used to transfer files between computers or applications. Compressed files, such as PICT or GIF files, cannot be opened using this format.

- **Pixar**—Pixar is the 3D computer graphics company that makes feature films with computers. Pixar also is the name of the file format used to store the custom, high-end graphics required by their sophisticated computer systems. That's right, you can use Photoshop Elements to view image files created by Pixar graphics systems.

- **Scitex**—Scitex is a type of computer used to process high-end images. The Scitex file format enables you to save your image in Photoshop Elements so that it can be viewed on a Scitex computer.

- **Targa**—The TGA file format is designed for computers that have a Truevision video board. This file format is also supported by many MS-DOS color applications. You can choose a pixel depth of 16, 24, or 32 bits per pixel.

Choosing a File Format

There are so many different formats from which to choose, it can be difficult to decide which one to use. Your best bet will be to use a format that can be viewed on a Windows or Macintosh computer, regardless of whether that computer has Photoshop Elements installed. JPEG probably will be the best file format to save your digital images. It works well for both print and the Web.

Although there might be a few exceptions, most old and new computers will have a browser application already installed. Internet Explorer and Netscape Navigator are the most popular Web browsers currently in use. Plus, they're both free. You can visit Microsoft's Web site (www.microsoft.com) or Netscape's Web site (www.netscape.com) to download the software and install it on your computer.

The following file formats can be viewed in a browser, and are the most commonly chosen file formats for saving graphics and digital images for the Web or for printing:

- **GIF**—Graphics Interchange Format. Choose this format if your image has large areas of similar or solid color, or if you're creating a Web graphic, such as a button or menu graphic. This format supports transparency. Your image can be edited into an animation if the file is saved as an animated GIF in the Save for Web window.

- **JPEG**—Joint Photographic Experts Group. This format saves images of any size. However, this format won't save any transparency settings along with the image. Use this format to save scanned or digital images for the Web or print.

- **TIFF**—Tag Image File Format. The optimal file format for publishing. Choose this format if you want to submit an image to a book publisher, or for other professional quality print jobs. You might need to install the QuickTime plug-in for your browser to view a TIFF file.

File Information

You can add copyright and caption information when you save an image. Choose File, File Info, and then choose either caption, copyright & URL, or EXIF from the Section drop-down menu. Type any caption information into the Caption window (see Figure 8.4). You can add the copyright notice or URL for the image into the Copyright & URL section of the Caption window.

Click the Section drop-down menu, and select EXIF to view any custom information saved along with the image by the digital camera. Some digital cameras store date, time, resolution in ppi, and exposure settings along with each image file. To find out more about EXIF annotations, read the documentation for your digital camera.

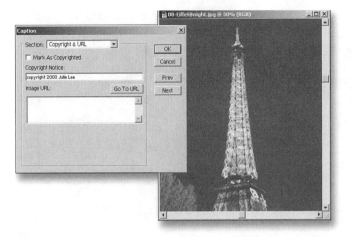

Figure 8.4
Choose File Info from the File menu to view or add copyright information to an image file. Check the Mark as Copyrighted check box and add a copyright notice to your image files.

Optimizing Images

Depending on how you want to share your images, you might need to optimize an image before you print it or save it for the Web. For example, if you're working with a group of people, you want to share your photos as-is without making any changes so that the team can decide how to proceed with each image. On the other hand, if you want to create custom images, correct portrait photos, or repair an old photo, you'll probably want to polish—or optimize—an image before you print it or share it on the Web.

Optimizing for the Web

Optimizing an image can involve several processes. The goal of optimizing an image is to minimize the file size of the image without sacrificing the quality of the image (see Figure 8.5). You can optimize an image based on a fixed file size, or enhance the quality of an image by choosing the best combination of settings for a particular file format. Photoshop Elements provides both kinds of tools that enable you to preview Web settings before you save the file.

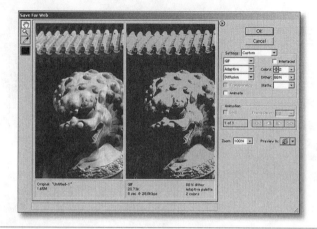

Figure 8.5
A black-and-white image is significantly smaller than the original full-color image.

File Size and Download Time

With a growing base of broadband (fast Ethernet connections) Internet access, you might not need to worry about how long someone will have to wait to download your image to their browser. Broadband connections support anywhere from 144Kbps up to 1.5Mbps connection rates—not too bad when you compare that to a 56Kbps modem, or a 10Mbps Ethernet data transfer rate.

Before you decide how to optimize an image, consider your audience, and then decide whether file size or image quality is more important for the image being optimized. If most of your visitors will have slow modem connections using traditional telephone lines, you should choose the smallest file size (around 50KB–300KB) for your image. If the quality or colors in an image are more important to your visitors, you can ignore the size of each image and focus on creating a great-looking image. In some cases, you will be able to create a great-looking image with a relatively small file size.

Another alternative might be to reduce the width and height of the image, preserving its quality but reducing the overall dimensions of the file.

Choose the Save for Web command from the File menu to preview optimization settings. You will only be able to optimize the image settings for GIF, JPEG, and PNG file formats in the Save for Web window.

If you're working with a photo image, first view different compression settings for the JPEG version. Then, compare the quality and file size of the JPEG version to a GIF version. For most pictures, you'll find that JPEG creates the smaller, better-looking image. For example, the black-and-white GIF image shown in Figure 8.5 is just barely smaller than the low-resolution, highly compressed JPEG of the same image, shown in Figure 8.6.

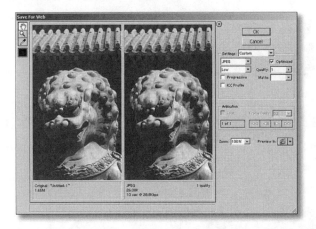

Figure 8.6
A low-resolution JPEG file isn't much larger than the black-and-white image, yet has much more image detail and color.

If you want to create an image that blends in with the background color of a Web page, select the GIF format. The file size will be a little larger than the JPEG file, but if you don't think your Web page visitors will mind waiting a few more seconds for the GIF, save the image as a GIF. Figure 8.7 shows the same image as a GIF file. The GIF version has 128 colors, versus 2 colors, as seen in Figure 8.5.

Why Save a Photo As a GIF?

In most instances, you will save a photo as a JPEG file. However, if you want to add transparency to an image you need to use the GIF file format.

The GIF file format also supports animation. To convert the layers of a file into frames of animation, choose Save For Web from the File menu. The Save for Web window will open. Choose one of the GIF items from the Settings drop-down menu, and then check the Animate check box. To find out more about how to create animation with Photoshop Elements, go to Chapter 18, "Animating Images."

tip
If you want Photoshop Elements to remember your settings in the Save for Web window, open the Save for Web window, and then hold down the [Alt] (Option) key. The OK and Cancel buttons will change to Remember and Reset. Click the Remember button if you want to save the settings in the window. Click the Reset button to revert to Photoshop Elements's recommended settings. The remembered settings will become the default setting the next time you open the Save For Web window, regardless of the image file you have open.

Figure 8.7
Increasing the number of colors in the GIF file also increases the file size and download time of the image.

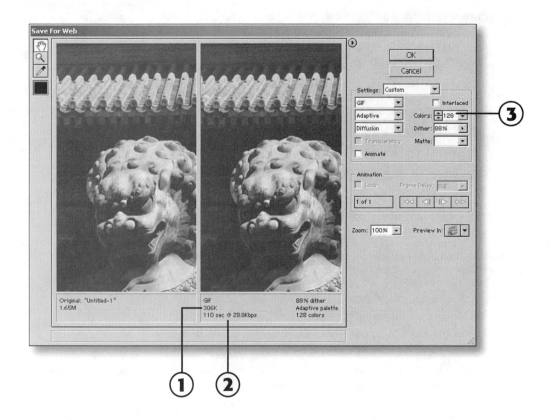

① File size

② Download time

③ Number of colors

Comparing Web File Formats

There are actually three image file formats that you should compare before picking one to save your file. PNG is an acronym for the Portable Network Graphics file format. Its biggest strength is that it can support more colors than GIF. Otherwise, it provides decent file compression compared to GIF. But JPEG tends to turn out the best image quality to image compression ratio. Figure 8.8 shows the image quality of a PNG-8 file. Compare the image quality and file size, as well as the download time with the JPEG and GIF file.

note
The PNG file format does not support animation. It was originally intended to be a patent-free replacement for the GIF format. However, if you want to create animation for the Web, only the GIF format is capable of creating a single file containing animation.

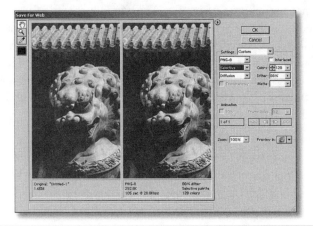

Figure 8.8
The same file saved as a PNG-8 file is slightly smaller than the GIF image with 128 colors.

Consider these issues before saving a file for the Web:

- Compare the optimized Web file format to the original. How close is the optimized file to the original?

- Compare the file size of the original image to another file format. You can open the Save for Web window and compare a GIF, JPEG, or PNG file format to the original. You also can limit the number of colors available for any of these three file formats to try to reduce the file size of the image. How much smaller is the optimized file? If you don't see much of a difference, consider saving the original file as a JPEG and posting that to the Web.

- Consider the download times for different optimized images. If the higher-quality, optimized file can download in less than 30 seconds, or a time that you consider acceptable, save the image and upload it to a Web site. If download time is not an issue for your Web visitors, you won't have to worry about file compression or loss of image quality.

Optimizing a TIFF Image File

Although you won't find the Tagged Image File Format (TIFF) as a format option in the Save for Web window, this file format is recognized by most graphics applications that run on Mac OS and Windows. A common file format ensures the image quality will look the same on any computer or application that opens it. However, TIFF files are formatted a little differently for a PC and a Mac. Fortunately, Photoshop Elements enables you to open and save a TIFF image in either format.

You can save a TIFF image with or without compression. Plus, you can choose from three different compression formats, and choose between a Mac or PC byte order for the saved image. When a TIFF file is compressed, the quality of the image is preserved. If that's not enough, you also can save transparency settings in a TIFF file.

Choose Save As from the File menu. If you want to save an open image as a TIFF file, select TIFF from the Format drop-down menu. Type a name for the file, and then click the Save button. The TIFF Options window opens. You will be able to choose compression options in this window if the Enable Advanced TIFF Save option is checked in the Saving Files Preferences window.

Click the IBM PC or Macintosh radio button to select the byte order of the TIFF file. The file will be formatted in a slightly different way depending on whether you choose IBM PC or Macintosh. The difference between Power PC and Intel processors apparently has some affect on the way TIFF files are processed. The good news is that most publishing applications, such as QuarkXpress and InDesign, can work with either TIFF format.

If the advanced TIFF option is selected in the Saving Files Preferences window, you will be able to choose between LZW, JPEG, or ZIP compression formats. Older TIFF-viewing applications will not be able to open JPEG- or ZIP-compressed TIFF files. You can use Adobe InDesign to work with these newer TIFF compression formats. LZW compression is the more common compression format applied to TIFF images.

When to Export a File

Although there aren't any Export options installed, you can still export an image from Photoshop Elements. Like importing, exporting enables you to save an image in a specific file format, such as GIF89a, which is a variation of the GIF file format, or CompuServe GIF.

You can install an export plug-in with Photoshop Elements by placing the Plug-in file in the Import/Export folder, located in the Plug-ins folder of the Photoshop Elements folder. Unfortunately, there aren't any export plug-ins installed with Photoshop Elements, so I can't demonstrate the finer points of exporting. In case you're still wondering whether to export or save, it's always best to save, and save often. However, if you need to save a file in a specific format that's only available as a plug-in, it's better to export.

Sharing Files Electronically

When you save a file, you can copy that file to a file server, send it in an e-mail, or print it. If you print your image, it's easy to show that printed picture to your friends and neighbors, or mail it to someone. Another way you can share the image is to post it on a Web site or send it attached to an e-mail message. E-mail and Web sites are both great ways to share images immediately without sacrificing too many trees. Of course, your friends, family, and neighbors must have a computer to get to your Web page, too.

Before you can share files on the Web, you'll need the following items:

* An account on a Web server. You might have received a free Web site with your Internet service provider (ISP) when you signed up for Internet access. If you are a Mac OS X user, you have space available through iTools.

- Enough disk space to store the image files you want to share. This is probably the toughest issue to work around—especially if your Internet service provider can provide only 5MB or 10MB of disk space per Web site.

- Software to connect to the Web server. Most Web servers support the File Transfer Protocol (FTP). You can upload or download image files to a Web server using an FTP application.

Sending an Image in E-Mail

tip

You can use the Save for Web window to estimate how long it might take someone to download an image attached to an e-mail message. Choose Save for Web from the File menu to open the Save for Web window. Then compare the download times for different JPEG compression formats.

If you don't have access to a Web server that can accommodate all the images you want to share, you can e-mail images. You can use a browser or a dedicated e-mail program to send or receive e-mail. Yahoo! and hotmail are probably the most popular Web sites that provide e-mail services for free. You can also download free e-mail programs from Microsoft's or Netscape's Web sites. Microsoft's e-mail application for Windows is Outlook or Outlook Express. Entourage is the latest e-mail application available for Macs, although Outlook Express is also quite popular.

E-Mail Limitations

Some mail servers limit the number of e-mail messages you keep in your e-mail account. This can affect the size of the attachments that you can send. Also, think about the people receiving your e-mail message. If they have a slow connection, it might take them much longer to download your e-mail than it took you to send it!

To send an image file with an e-mail message, add the image file as an attachment to the e-mail message. If you're using a browser to send e-mail, log in to your e-mail account, and then create or compose an e-mail message. Click the Attachments button or link in the browser window. Navigate your hard drive and select the image file you want to attach to the e-mail message. Type your message into the e-mail, and then click the Send button.

If you're using Outlook or Outlook Express, click the New button in the toolbar to create a new e-mail message. Click the Attachments button in the toolbar, or choose the Attachments command from the Insert menu. Then navigate to your hard drive and select the image file you want to attach to the e-mail. Figure 8.9 shows an image

attached to an e-mail message in Outlook Express. After the image is
attached, click on the Send button, and away it'll go!

E-Mail Attachments and File Compression

To help e-mail attachments download faster, you might want to compress a file before you send it. For example, most computers can open
files compressed in either a Zip or StuffIt archive. WinZip is one of the
more popular compression utilities available on Windows, and Aladdin
provides free copies of UnStuffit for Macs and Windows computers on
the Web. Some image files may compress into a smaller file size than
others. For example, a JPEG file already incorporates its own file compression. It will not shrink much in size if you add it to a Zip or StuffIt
archive.

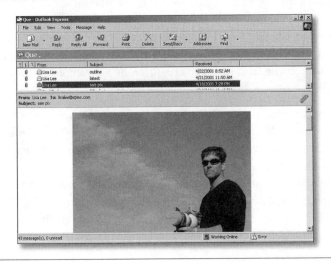

Figure 8.9
Saving a small file means a faster sending and receiving time if you send it
along with an e-mail. Outlook Express is one of several e-mail programs available for both Windows and Macintosh computers.

Using FTP Programs

Another way to share image files is to copy them to a file server or a
Web server. If you have access to a Web site, you can use an FTP
application to view and copy files to it. However, not all Web sites
will require you to use an FTP application to post files to them.
Some Web sites, for example, enable you to post or remove files
directly from your browser window.

Sharing Files on the Web

There are Web sites that provide free photo services and allow you to share your photos on their Web sites. If you're curious about sharing files on the Web, you might want to visit Kodak (www.kodak.com), www.shutterfly.com, Yahoo! (www.yahoo.com), or Microsoft Web sites (www.msn.com) to find out more about what image-sharing services are available. Most of these Web sites offer services to convert 35mm images into digital files, enabling you to download the electronic image directly from your account on their Web site.

The File Transfer Protocol (FTP) was first created as a networking tool for Unix, one of the first popular computer operating systems. Many FTP applications are available for Macintosh and Windows computers. One of the more popular FTP applications for the Mac is called Fetch. Many FTP applications are available for Windows. You might want to visit www.zdnet.com or another shareware collection Web site to review and try different FTP applications for Windows.

To share your files on a Web site, you'll need the account login and password information. You'll also need to know where the image files are located on your hard drive, so that you can upload them to the Web site. If you have problems connecting or setting up your FTP application, you can try connecting to your Web site with a browser application. Like most Web pages, if you log in to an FTP site with a browser rather than a FTP software, you'll only be able to view and download files from the FTP server.

Logging In and Uploading Files

Uploading files is the network term for copying files from a computer to a server. Start your FTP application, and then log in to your Web site. The interface will vary from one FTP program to the next. In general, you will be able to navigate the FTP server by clicking or double-clicking a folder in the FTP application's main window. Most FTP programs use the Put command to enable you to copy an image to the FTP server. Choose the Get command if you want to download a file from the FTP server to your local hard drive.

Figure 8.10 shows the application WS_FTP LE program. You can navigate to the files you want to upload in the local area of the FTP software. If you want to copy files to the FTP server, navigate to your Web server directory in the remote area of your software, and create a folder for your image files. Click on the file you want to copy from the Local System window list. Click the right arrow button to copy it from your computer to the Web server. After the images have been copied to the server, type the URL (Universal Resource Locator), also known as Web address, such as www. flatfishfactory.com, in the browser window to view or download your image files. If you can open the downloaded image on your computer, you're ready to share the URL with friends and family.

note
To find out more about how to create a photo album to share on the Web, go to Chapter 20, "Creating a Web Photo Gallery."

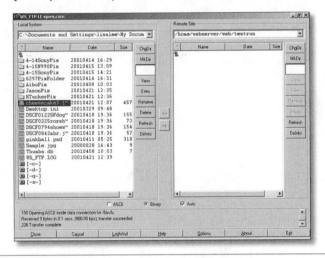

Figure 8.10
Copy a file from your computer to a Web server to share it with other Web surfers.

Printing Images

Many of today's printers enable you to print grayscale or full-color pictures on regular or photographic paper at reasonable prices. This is an exciting development for digital imaging. Even a year ago, low-cost photo printing had not dropped below the $1,000 price point. Now you can purchase a 600 dpi (dots per inch) ink-jet color printer for around $100, or get a six-color 2880 dpi printer for $499 that work equally well with Macintosh and Windows computers.

Comparing and Choosing Printers

Shopping for a printer can be an educational experience. So many printer features are available that it's tough to remember which ones are valuable and which ones aren't. A good place to start looking is at printers made by the bigger printer makers, such as Hewlett Packard, Brother, Epson, and Canon. If you're shopping for cameras and printers, read as much as you can about similar models that are fairly close in price. If

tip
There might or
might not be a
benefit to purchas-
ing a camera and
printer made by
the same manufac-
turer. Hewlett
Packard and Canon
make a full range
of printers and
digital cameras.

possible, take a look at the image quality created by the camera or
printer to see whether it meets your expectations.

Although you're more likely to purchase a printer based on its feature list, magazine reviews, or word of mouth, the best way to review
a printer is to view images printed on regular or special paper. You
also might want to compare the image printed at high and low resolutions. Ink cartridge printers usually are the more affordable printers. Because each print job relies on the ink cartridge to distribute
each dot of ink to the sheet of paper, you might get varying results
for color accuracy if you print the same image to the printer more
than once. The quality of the print head affects the quality of the
image, and the resulting image also can vary depending on how full
or empty each ink cartridge becomes as you use the printer.

Printers that use toner for either grayscale or color printing are more
capable of printing the same image consistently. Most grayscale
printers can print at 600 or 1200 dpi. One issue to consider is how
many pages per minute the printer can output. Printing an image
will tend to take longer than printing text, so if a printer is advertised
at 12 pages per minute, that rate is for printing text pages with black
ink. If you don't mind waiting for an image to print, you won't need
to invest in a faster printer.

Consider the following issues when purchasing a color printer:

- **Image quality**—Do you need to purchase special ink and paper
  to get the best printing results? Does the ink bleed when you
  print to regular paper? Also, will you be printing text documents
  along with photos, or only images?

- **Water**—Is water resistance an important feature for your prints?
  If it is, you probably want to consider a photo printer. Photo
  printers usually cost a little more than ink cartridge printers.
  Photo paper also is more expensive.

- **Fade and wear**—How long does the print retain the original
  quality of the image before color fading starts?

- **Cost**—How much do you want to spend on a printer and supplies? Is a toner-based color printer worth the additional cost in
  supplies, or is a low-cost color printer good enough to do the
  job?

- **Size and space**—Are there any space considerations you need to address with regard to the physical size of the printer you want to purchase? You might need to purchase a smaller printer if you do not have the desk space or office space for a larger printer.

  Do you plan to print on any special-sized paper, such as an envelope, postcard, legal, or 11×14-inch sheet of paper? Check to see whether you need to purchase any special add-ons to print with smaller or larger sizes of paper.

Color Versus Grayscale Printing

Printing an image in color is a little more complicated than printing to a grayscale printer. Although both kinds of printers look quite similar (see Figure 9.1) and offer high-resolution printing, color printers are by far the more complex machines. Although an image printed in color might not exactly match what you see on the screen, it might still turn out looking great. However, if you don't want to spend the time trying to fine-tune a color printer, consider having a photo shop (sorry, no pun intended), or online service convert your images to photo prints for you. For example, you can choose File, Online Services if you want to sign up with an online service and have your images sent out for printing.

caution
Don't forget to consider the price of the ink cartridges for a printer when purchasing a printer. Many sub-$200 color printers require the same ink cartridges as some higher-priced models. If you plan to print a large number of images on your printer, you might want to add in the cost of ink cartridges you'll buy, and compare the overall price of the ink cartridges with the printer before making a final purchasing decision.

Figure 9.1
The Epson Stylus Photo 1280 can print text in black and white, but also is capable of printing 11×14-inch photos on glossy paper.

tip
To find out more about color and printing, see Chapter 10, "Digital Images and Color."

Consider the following issues when printing to a color printer:

- **Sharpness of the image**—Are the brightness and contrast in the original image preserved?

- **Paper**—Is the paper on which the image is printed capable of holding the color over time? Will water ruin the quality of the print? Does the ink saturate the paper to the point of affecting the image quality?

- **Consistency**—Can you print different images with the same printer without having to constantly change or tweak printer software settings?

Viewing Printing Options

Printing an image created with a digital camera is fairly straightforward. Although digital cameras create images at 72 dpi, the images (for example, 2000×1500 pixel images) are large enough to be resized and printed on an 8.5×11-inch sheet of paper without losing much of the original image quality. If your printer is capable of printing a full range of colors, and you don't mind shelling out a few bucks for extra toner or ink cartridges and special, glossy paper, you might find yourself making your own holiday season cards someday. Figure 9.2 shows a Sony photo printer. It is only capable of printing 4×6-inch images, but at less than $500 it can print some nice-looking, photo-quality images.

Most photo printers enable you to print directly from a Compact Flash, Smart Card, or in the case of Sony's photo printer, from a Memory Stick. You can hook up a TV to view the images stored on the card, and bypass the computer altogether to print your digital pictures. This is a great way to take pictures as you travel. You can make your own postcards and send them out long before you return from your travels.

Printing a scanned image usually involves converting an image from a relatively large pixel per inch (ppi) value, such as 1200 ppi to 300 ppi. If you convert the resolution of an image to 72 ppi from a higher value and then set the image window to view an image at 100%, Photoshop Elements accurately displays the size of the image as it will fit on the paper. To find out more about color modes and resolution, go to Chapter 10, "Digital Images and Color."

Understanding Color Concepts

Every color in a digital image is derived from combining light with one or more of the three primary colors: red, yellow, and blue. Light affects the intensity of a color.

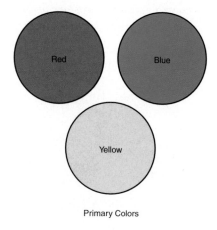

Primary Colors

Figure CS.1
Red, yellow, and blue are primary colors. They cannot be created by combining any other colors (see Chapter 10, Figure 10.1).

The color wheel represents the relationship between the primary colors and all the other possible colors in the color spectrum. Secondary colors, such as orange, purple, and green, are created by combining two primary colors. Tertiary colors, such as red-orange or blue-green, are created by combining secondary colors with primary colors.

Color Wheel

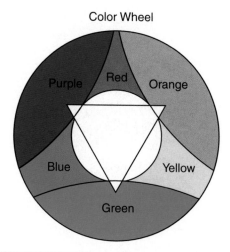

Figure CS.2
The color wheel presents the primary, secondary, and tertiary relationships for all colors in the rainbow (see Chapter 10, Figure 10.2).

Additive and Subtractive Color

Computers and other imaging devices use different methods to define colors with numbers. Computer monitors, for example, create color with an additive process based on red, green, and blue colors. The computer controls which colors are displayed by exciting phosphors on the computer screen. On the other hand, printers use a subtractive process using cyan, magenta, and black as the primary colors.

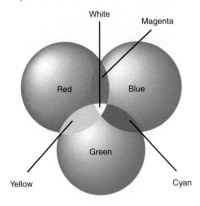

Additive Color

Figure CS.3
The three additive color primaries. Additive colors for the RGB color model are red, green, and blue. Computer monitors display color using an additive color process (see Chapter 10, Figure 10.6).

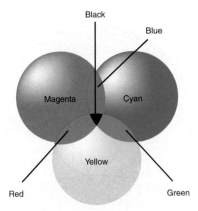

Figure CS.4
The three subtractive primary colors. The CMYK color model is based on subtractive colors. Cyan, magenta, and yellow are the primary colors, and red, blue, and green are the secondary colors. Printers create color with a subtractive color process (see Chapter 10, Figure 10.7).

Applying the Invert Command

You can flip positive and negative color values for some or all pixels in an image by applying the Invert command. For example, if you have a black-and-white image, all blacks will be changed to white and all white will be changed to black. In the examples shown here, purple is the positive color and green is its opposite, or negative, color. The Invert command changes the brightness value for each pixel to its inverse, or opposite value. For example, a value of 0 will invert to 255, or 235 to 20.

Figure CS.5
A photo of a purple orchid (see Chapter 11, Figure 11.7).

Figure CS.6
Inverting the purple orchid changes it to green, which is located on the opposite side of the color wheel (see Chapter 11, Figure 11.11).

Adjusting Hue and Saturation

The Hue and Saturation window enables you to adjust the amount of color (hue), gray level in color (saturation), and lightness values in an image. The Hue slider control represents each color in the color wheel, shown in Figure CS.2. Increasing the saturation level removes any gray levels in the color, creating a purer color tone. The lightness value can increase or decrease the brightness level of each pixel.

You can permanently change the hue and saturation levels in an image by choosing the Hue/Saturation command from the Enhance, Colors menu, or add an editable Hue and Saturation Adjustment layer by choosing this command from the Layers, New Adjustment Layers menu.

Figure CS.7
The original image before adjusting the hue and saturation settings (see Chapter 11, Figure 11.13).

Figure CS.8
The colors are a little brighter after adjusting the hue, saturation, and lightness settings (see Chapter 11, Figure 11.14).

Combining Text with Images

Photoshop Elements contains a large number of filters and effects. You also can use the type, shape, or drawing tools to add line art or text to an image. Some effects require a text object to be added to the image window, whereas others, like the Quadrant Effect, can be applied to any image.

Figure CS.9
The Quadrant Effect can add an interesting color scheme to any photo (see Chapter 12, Figure 12.20).

Figure CS.10
Combine text and graphics to give a photo new meaning (see Chapter 14).

Image Restoration

Several tools in Photoshop Elements can help you restore torn or damaged images. For example, the Clone Stamp Tool, combined with layers, filters, and color correction tools, can help you reconstruct a faded or torn photograph. Be prepared to spend time experimenting with different repair techniques and learning how to use the image editing tools as you restore one or many photos.

Figure CS.11
A folded, damaged wedding photo can be brought back to life using a few simple techniques (see Chapter 15, Figure 15.01).

Figure CS.12
After applying the Clone stamp, as well as several fill and adjustment layers, the photo looks as good as new (see Chapter 15, Figure 15.9).

Image Repair and Retouching

Photoshop Elements enables you to repair and retouch an image without making any permanent changes to the original. Through the magic of layers, you can hide or show different repair techniques or add or delete experimental layers, all while keeping the original image locked in the background layer of the Layers palette.

Figure CS.13
A torn photo where part of the subject is missing doesn't mean all is lost (see Chapter 15, Figure 15.11).

Figure CS.14
The repaired photo shows no signs of alteration, even after creating a new background (see Chapter 15, Figure 15.16).

Advanced Imaging Techniques

Select part of an image and apply the Feather Tool to the selected image. Then, copy and paste the selected image into another image window to create new compositions. Selection tools enable you to choose the pixels you want to move from one image to another. The Feather command enables you to smooth the edges of the selected image so that it can blend in with a background image. Each image pasted into an image window is placed in its own layer in the Layers palette. You can use the Move Tool to place each image on the canvas. Then merge layers together as you finalize your composition.

Figure CS.15
Composite images enable you to put two characters together who might otherwise never see eye to eye (see Chapter 16, Figure 16.9).

Figure CS.16
Create special effects by scaling an image from one picture and pasting it into another (see Chapter 16, Figure 16.11).

Figure CS.17
Use the Photo Merge command to stitch together several photos to create one beautiful panorama photo (see Chapter 19, Figure 19.1).

Figure 9.2
Sony's DPP-SV55 is a relatively low-cost photo printer that can print 4×6-inch images to special photo paper.

Choosing the Best Resolution for Printing

Scanned images work great with printers. Although there isn't a one-to-one relationship between scanner and printer resolutions, you can scan an image at 300 dpi, and then print it to a printer at 300 dpi. The scanned image should look pretty darn close to the printed image. Figure 9.3 shows a 72 ppi image that has been resized to 300 ppi. In this case, the 72 pixels per inch were converted into a smaller image consisting of 300 pixels per inch.

Figure 9.3
The original image on the left printed at 72 ppi, and the same image on the right at 300 ppi.

Paper Selection and Print Quality

Most color printers, including photo printers, require their own custom brand of glossy paper, unless you're happy with the way the color image prints to regular paper. Glossy paper usually produces the best color results and will hold the quality of the color better than regular paper. However, glossy paper is quite expensive.

Most printers that use toner cartridges enable you to print to special materials, such as an iron-on transfer or transparency. Check the printer's documentation to see whether the printer is capable of printing on manually inserted thick paper, card stock, poster board, or other special printable material. Ink-jet and thermal or dye-sublimation printers probably will not be able to print on a plastic transparency or other nonpaper-based sheets of material.

Setting Up Your System for Printing

I'd like to assume you already have a color printer connected to your computer and are ready to print an image with Photoshop Elements. However, if it has been a year or two since you bought your printer, you're likely to find low-cost, better quality printers on the market now. It might be time to upgrade.

What Makes a Printer a Printer?

Beside the printing mechanism, which is sometimes referred as the *print head* (the part that distributes ink onto paper), all printers rely on some form of ink and paper. The most common kinds of printers use toner, ink distribution cartridges, or colored plastic combined with a thermal or dye-sublimation process to create a photographic-quality image on paper. Most sub-$1,000 ink-jet printers print with regular and glossy, or specially coated paper.

There is a difference between regular color printers and photo printers. Photo printers are capable of printing on glossy paper and are optimized to print photo-quality images at more than one resolution. Regular color printers might or might not support printing on specially coated paper, and are not optimized to print photo-quality images. These printers, for example, might not recognize color management software saved with an image.

Finally, for a printer to communicate with a computer, you'll need a serial, parallel, Ethernet, or USB cable and the appropriate printer software. Printers, scanners, and cameras communicate with computers using software components referred to as *drivers*. When the drivers for

continued
a printer are installed on a computer, you can configure printer settings, such as the resolution and paper type.

Printers rely on an ink or toner distribution mechanism to put your digital image on paper. This is called the print head, or print mechanism. Some color printer models share the same print head across similarly named models. If you like the print quality of a higher cost color printer, look for a lower cost model number to see if it offers a similar print resolution with fewer printing features. Like all great computer technologies, printing technology is constantly improving. As it improves, better quality, more affordable printers become available to everyone.

More photo printers also have been introduced to the relatively large number of printers available for purchase. Although these fancy sub-$1,000 photo printers can use both regular and special glossy photograph-like paper, they usually require expensive color supplies to produce great prints. If you don't want to invest heavily in printer supplies, take a look at some of the $100 to $200 color printers. Many of these affordable models manufactured by HP and Epson are capable of producing great-looking pictures. Most of the newer color printers also support both Windows and Macintosh, so you won't have to worry about sharing or borrowing a printer if you have both kinds of computer.

Different Types of Printers

Many kinds of printer technologies are used in printers today. Most low-cost color printers use ink cartridges to distribute color on paper. These kinds of color printers apply liquid ink to regular or specially coated paper. Printing to regular paper usually causes the ink to bleed into the paper; images tend to look better when printed on glossy or coated paper. Also, some ink jet printers use all-in-one cartridges, while other use separate cartridges for each of the five colors.

More expensive color printers are modeled after grayscale LaserWriter printers. Cyan, Magenta, and Yellow (CMY) toners are combined with black toner cartridges to print full-color images on regular paper.

Many photo printers use special CMY cartridges that contain colored sheets of plastic. When you print to this type of printer, the image passes through the printer three times before you see the final image. This can take a while, but the results are beautiful colors.

Setting up your system involves connecting your printer to your computer. Most of the latest printers can connect to either the USB or parallel port on a PC, or to the USB port on a Mac. Older model printers most likely will rely on a parallel port on a PC or a serial or SCSI port on a Mac—that's if you have a direct-connection printer. Macintosh and Windows computers also can share access to a printer over a network.

After you've connected a printer to your computer, you'll need to install the software for the printer onto your computer. Most printers come bundled with a CD-ROM containing an installer application for both Mac and Windows computers. Run the installer for your printer, and follow the onscreen instructions.

Printing Digital Images

note

Photoshop Elements will print any image that appears in the image window. If you want to print the contents of a single layer, hide all other layers in the Layers palette and show the layer you want to print. This layer should be visible in the image window. Click the Print button in the toolbar to print the image layer.

Printing is printing—there's not a whole lot more to do other than click on the Print button, right? Not necessarily. For example, when printing scanned images, you might need to do a little more preparation, especially if you scanned the white borders of a photo or captured the edges of a film negative along with the picture. Even if you've already performed some of these tasks before scanning the image, you might want to make additional adjustments to fit the image on the paper.

If you scanned a slightly larger area of an image than you need to print, you can use the Crop Tool (C) to remove the outer edges of the scanned image. Choose the Crop Tool from the toolbox and click and drag the cursor around the area of the image you want to print. Then press the Return key to resize the image.

Now that you have defined the image you want to print, you can see what the image's resolution is. Click on the status bar to view the resolution of the active window. If the image is set to 72 ppi, you will see 72 pixels/inch in the status bar. Next, click the status bar again and look at the height and width of the image. The printed size of the image will appear beside the height and width values in the status pop-up window. If the printed size is smaller than the paper size on which you want to print, you might have a tough time trying to grow the dimensions of the image without harming the quality of the image.

Downsizing a large image usually brings pleasant results. Taking a large image and making it smaller usually will improve the sharpness of an image, whereas resizing a smaller image to a larger one tends to expose blurriness or cause pixelation. If you choose to print an image that appears too small, consider keeping it at its original size. Don't enlarge it unless you don't mind viewing a rougher image. Table 9.1 shows how different image sizes at 72 ppi match up with paper sizes.

Table 9.1 Comparing Image Size to Print Size at 72 ppi

Image Size	Paper Size
640×480 pixels	8.89×6.67 inches
800×600 pixels	11.11×8.33 inches
1024×768 pixels	14.22×10.667 inches
2400×1800 pixels	33×25 inches

If you've opened an image that was scanned in at a resolution higher than 72 ppi, you can scale it down in size to match the paper size on which you want to print. For example, if you scanned an image at 600 ppi, you can either use the Print Preview window or the Image Size window to resize the image. Choose Print Preview if you do not want to alter the dimensions of the file to print the image. Otherwise, type new height and width values into the Document Size text boxes in the Image Size window if you want to resize the image.

If you want Photoshop Elements to scale the image to fit onto a specific paper size, perform the following steps.

1. Choose Print Preview from the File menu. The Print Preview window opens.

2. Check the Scale to Fit Media. Type the height and width of the paper on which you want to print into the text boxes in the Print Preview window.

3. Click OK to save your changes for the image, or click the Print button to print the image.

caution
Photoshop Elements does not support CMYK color mode, only RGB, Indexed Color, Grayscale, and Bitmap color modes. You can print an RGB image to a grayscale or color printer. For best results, save the image with the Full Color Management color profile. Then customize the print settings in the Print Preview dialog box, which you'll learn more about if you continue reading this chapter. To find out more about color management, go to Chapter 10, "Digital Images and Color."

tip

To find out more about how to use the Crop Tool, go to Chapter 11, "Tonal Range and Color Correction."

tip

Pixelation is a squarish, blocky appearance that occurs when an image lacks enough color or image data to fill in those rough areas realistically. When an image is enlarged, the pixels from the original image are simply multiplied to fill in the new areas of the image. A pixelated image has the overall appearance of a low-resolution bitmap image.

If you want to permanently change the size of the image, perform the following steps.

1. Choose Image Size from the Image, Resize menu.

2. Change the resolution to match the resolution of your printer. Type a number into the Resolution text box—somewhere between 300 or 600 ppi, or at least 170 ppi.

3. Type the height and width of the paper size into the Document Size text boxes.

4. Click OK in the Image Size window.

5. Click on the status bar for the resized image. The new dimensions should appear in the status bar pop-up window.

6. Click the Print button in the toolbar to send the image to the printer.

When your images are ready to print, you can set up the printer software. On a Mac, you can select the printer from the Chooser, located in the Apple menu. Choose Page Setup from the File menu. The Page Setup window will open. Click [Properties] (Options) button in the Page Setup dialog box to open the properties window of your printer, and choose the settings you want to use. For example, select the type of paper, resolution, and whether you want to print in color or grayscale (see Figure 9.4). You also can configure your computer to handle print jobs in the foreground, one at a time, or spooled in the background.

Background Printing

Background printing enables you to send more than one print job to a printer simultaneously (see Figure 9.5). This can be helpful if you don't want to wait for each page to print. Windows and Macintosh computers have background printing built into the operating system. On a Mac, you can activate background printing from the Chooser. On a Windows computer, you can activate background printing from the printer's properties window from the Print Manager.

Figure 9.4
Print higher-quality images by choosing a different mode for the printer. In this example, you can adjust the resolution of the print job by changing the settings in the Mode area in the printer's properties window. On a Mac, you can change this setting from the Print dialog box.

Figure 9.5
Set up the printer software to spool multiple print jobs.

Printing Images from a Digital Camera

If you think about this in simple terms, your images either fit on the sheet of paper to which you want to print them, or they don't. A good example of an image that fits on an 8.5×11-inch sheet of paper is a 640×480-pixel image. You can open this image in the work area, set it to print in Landscape mode in the Page Setup window, and then print it to plain or glossy paper without having to worry about resizing or converting it.

Show and Tell

Although you can queue several print jobs to a printer, it's a good idea to print a test photo before making multiple copies of an image. You can print a test photo at a lower resolution on less expensive paper if you want to find how the image will appear on a sheet of paper. After the test image has been printed, you might want to compare it to the onscreen image to determine the quality of the printout. Or, take a close look at the printed image to determine whether it meets your needs and expectations.

Creating a Contact Sheet

A contact sheet consists of a set of thumbnail images organized in columns and rows, enabling you to preview or catalog a group of image files. If you have a folder full of image files, you can print a contact sheet. You can use contact sheets to archive all your digital photos, and compare the composition of images without having to print each one on its own sheet of paper. Choose Contact Sheet II from the File, Automate menu to open the fabulous dialog box shown in Figure 9.6.

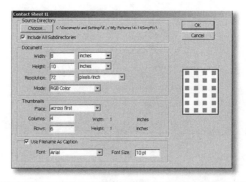

Figure 9.6
Choose the set of images you want to place on the contact sheet. Select the document, layout, and caption settings for each picture from the Contact Sheet II dialog box.

The Contact Sheet II dialog box has many bells and whistles. If you like all the default settings, select the folder containing the image files you want to put onto a contact sheet. Then customize the page layout for the contact sheet. Click OK and wait for Photoshop Elements to create a new image window with the contact sheet images.

You can customize the size of the document, as well as the resolution and image mode of the pictures you want to print on the contact sheet by selecting a new value in the corresponding field in the Document area of the dialog box. For example, choose Grayscale from the Mode drop-down menu if you want to print all the images in Grayscale mode.

Several settings enable you to lay out the images on a page, too. The image located on the right side of the Contact Sheet window will display the layout for the number of columns and rows selected in the Thumbnails text boxes. You also can view the exact size of each thumbnail image as you change the number of columns or rows for the contact sheet. Check the Use Filename As Caption check box to print the name of each file below each thumbnail image (see Figure 9.7). Unchecking this check box will enlarge each image to 1.8×1.8 inches.

tip
You can use a contact sheet to catalog image files saved to CD-ROM or removable media. Write the name of the Zip cartridge or CD-ROM on the contact sheet to enable you to quickly locate an image file.

Figure 9.7
You can catalog your images visually by printing contact sheets of them.

When you click OK, Photoshop Elements runs a batch script that resizes each image to the settings you requested. The contact sheet, shown in Figure 9.7, will appear in a new document window, which you can save and print as you like. Choose File, Print to send the contact sheet to a printer.

Printing a Fax

Although you probably won't find yourself faxing many images, Photoshop Elements won't hold you back. You can send your images to a fax instead of to a printer. On a Mac, open the Chooser and select the icon for the Fax software. On a Windows computer, choose Fax from the Name drop-down menu in the Page Setup window (File, Page Setup). When you choose the Print command, the active image will be converted to a 200×200 dpi image. Then, the fax software will process the image, which can be sent over a modem or network connection to another fax machine.

Printing to a Printer

If you have several printers set up to work with your computer, choose the printer you want to use. The Print dialog box will open whenever you choose the Print command from the File menu. The printer name appears at the top of this dialog box. You can select the quality of the image generated by the printer, choose how many copies you want to print, or print the image to a file or to the printer. Figure 9.8 shows the Print window of the Epson Stylus 740 color printer. Check each printer setting, and then click OK to print the contents of the image window.

Figure 9.8
Choosing the Print command opens the Print window of the default printer.

Printing More Than One Copy of an Image

Aspire to be a portrait photographer by printing multiple copies of an image on a single page. Choose from 20 layouts and 10 picture size combinations. To put together a picture package, choose Picture Package from the File, Automate menu. The Picture Package dialog box will open, as shown in Figure 9.9. Select the file with which you want to work, and then pick a layout, or change the resolution or mode of the image.

Figure 9.9
Print multiple copies of an image at the same or different sizes with the Picture Package command.

When you're ready to create a document with the picture package settings, click OK. Photoshop Elements creates a picture package using a script to resize the selected image and apply any settings you chose in the Picture Package dialog box. Wait for the image to be processed. When the script completes, the picture layout will appear in a new document window, as shown in Figure 9.10. Now you can save or print the picture package.

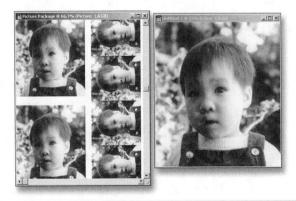

Figure 9.10
The Picture Package command creates a custom layout of an image in several different sizes and layouts.

Preparing an Image for a Photo Printer

Take a contact sheet or picture package document and print the file to a photo printer to create, you guessed it, photos. Printing to a photo printer requires the same steps as most other printers. First, you must open the document you want to print. Then, choose the correct page orientation, such as portrait or landscape. Check your printer's color and resolution settings. Unfortunately, most photo printers don't allow you to use plain paper. If you have a photo printer, such as the Epson 1280 model, print a test page with plain paper before printing to the glossy paper.

Photoshop Elements has a Print Preview command (Alt+Ctrl+P) [Opt-Command-P] that enables you to modify the position or adjust the size of the image before printing it. Figure 9.11 shows the Print Preview dialog box. Click on the appropriate setting to change it, and then click OK to exit the Print Preview dialog box. Choose Print from the File menu to send the image to the printer.

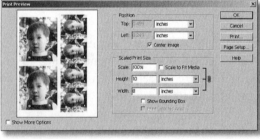

Figure 9.11
Open Print Preview window to view the position of the image on the target paper size.

tip
To find out more about how to add text to an image, go to Chapter 14, "Adding Text and Shapes to Images."

Considerations for Printing Images with Text

Adobe uses the term *type* for what you and I call *text*. The Horizontal and Vertical Type Tools (T) co-exist in the toolbox. Choose either tool from the toolbox, and then type text into the image window. You can use the Type Tool to select text in the image window, too. Text formatting options are conveniently located in the options bar.

You can use two general kinds of fonts with Photoshop Elements: scalable or PostScript fonts. Scalable fonts are similar to vector graphics. Both use a software algorithm to re-create the image, large or small. PostScript fonts are more like bitmap images. Each font is a fixed size. If you don't have a specific font size for a PostScript font, its edges will appear aliased, or jagged, both onscreen and when printed.

Figure 9.12
You can add text to an image or graphics. The text onscreen will appear.

The good news is that Photoshop Elements is smart. Text objects are created in their own layer. If you save an image, any layers will be flattened into one single layer. This means text objects are converted into bitmaps, which do not require the font to be installed on your computer in order for it to be printed. When you print an image with text, the text you see in the image window will appear exactly the same way on paper (see Figure 9.12).

Improving Printer Output

After you become familiar with the way a printer converts screen color on your computer into printed color, you probably will be able to print images faster and more accurately. Be sure to keep plenty of extra ink or toner cartridges nearby if you want to print different kinds of images or want to improve your images.

If you're looking for an easy way to improve printer output, look no further than your printer's [Properties] (Print) dialog box. If you're using Windows 2000, click the Start button, and then select the Printers menu item. The Printers window will open. Right-click the printer icon and choose Properties to open the Properties dialog box for your printer, and then try to locate the print quality settings.

Print quality settings for the Epson Stylus 1280 photo printer are shown in Figure 9.13. Higher resolution settings for the printer (without changing the resolution of the image) will result in higher-quality printouts. Click OK to save your changes. Then print a test image to see if you notice a difference. Compare a 600 dpi printed image with a 720 ppi image.

If you're using a Macintosh computer, first set up the printer for your computer. Open the Chooser application, and click the printer icon in the Chooser window. You might have to set up the printer if this is the first time you've printed to it. You might want to print a test page to make sure is properly connected to your Mac. Next, go to Photoshop Elements and open an image you want to print. Then, select the Print command from the File menu. The Print dialog box will open. Look for the printer quality settings for the selected printer. Adjust the printer settings, and print a test page at a lower and higher dpi setting. Compare the printer output and save or note the printer output settings for the printer.

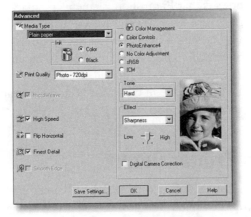

Figure 9.13
Select a higher dpi to improve the quality of the printed image.

Customizing Color Management Settings

Photoshop Elements enables you to save a color profile with an image when you save it to your hard drive. You can choose Limited color management if you want to attach a color profile for image files saved for the Web. Choose Full color management if you want to save a color profile for an image you want to print.

You also can customize the color management settings for a printer from the Print Preview window. First, open the Print Preview dialog box by choosing Print Preview from the File menu. Check the Show More Options check box. Then, choose Color Management from the first drop-down menu. The Source Space and Print Space options will appear at the bottom of the Print Preview window. Click the Profile drop-down menu to view a list of profiles for the printer. Choose Same As Source if you want the printer to use the color profile to determine the colors of the printed image. Choose Print Color Management (or PostScript Color Management if you're printing to a PostScript printer) if you want to use the print driver to manage color conversions. Otherwise, choose one of the predefined color profiles from the menu list.

If you choose one of the color profiles from the Profile menu list, the Intent drop-down menu will become active. Choose a rendering intent to determine how colors are converted to the selected profile. Choose one of the following intents: Perceptual, Saturation, Relative Colorimetric, or Absolute Colorimetric. Perceptual preserves the visual relationship between colors based on the way the human eye perceives natural color. Saturation intent favors vivid colors over color accuracy. Absolute Colorimetric preserves color accuracy over and above preserving relationships between colors. Relative Colorimetric compares the white point of the color source to the white point of the destination color space and remaps all colors based on the new value of the white point.

Adjusting Page and Printer Settings

Many of the newer photo and color printers have the option to print the image so that it covers the full sheet of paper. That's right, no borders, just a page full of ink. Choose File, Page Setup to select the printer you want to use. Then, click the [Properties] (Options) button to view the printing options. The software options will vary depending on the type of printer you're using and the software options available for that printer. In Figure 9.14, I've selected the Layout tab in the Properties window for the Epson Stylus 740 color printer. Choose the Fit to Page radio button if you want the image to fill the page selected in the Paper Size drop-down menu.

note

You might not need to use a color profile to preserve color accuracy for a printed image. Print a test image to a color printer and compare it to the onscreen image. If the printed colors meet your expectations for matching the screen colors of the image, you won't have to worry about color management issues.

Figure 9.14
Most newer printers have a Fit to Page option, which is an easy way to scale the image to fill the page.

Troubleshooting Printing Problems

Disappointed with the way your image printed? Not sure why the color isn't quite right, or why the printer output looks different from what's on your computer monitor? There are lots of things you can check. Finding a problem can take time and lots of patience. If you have Internet access, try checking the printer vendor's Web site to see if newer software is available, or visit their support site to see if there are any troubleshooting tips or known problems with your particular brand of computer.

The following list contains good starting points to check when you're unable to print:

- **Cables**—Be sure both ends of the printer cable are completely connected to each device.

- **Lights**—Check the lights on the printer. Most printers show a green light when power is on. If a print job is being processed the green light should flash. If you send a print job and the light flashes, you might need to power the printer off and on, or restart your computer.

  Other lights let you know whether the printer is out of ink or paper, if the paper jammed, or if a print job is in progress. If you don't see any lights, check the power adapter and be sure the printer is connected to a power-generating source.

- **Printer Software**—If the printing software appears to be working but the printer is not responding when you try to print to it, be sure the printer software settings are set up correctly for that printer. You might need to restart your computer and try printing without running any other applications to be sure you have plenty of memory to print.

- **Networks**—If you are unable to print to a printer that is connected to a network, try connecting the printer directly to your computer's USB, parallel, or serial port to see whether you can print to it. If you're able to print to it directly, check your network cables and try to see whether you can print using another computer on the same network. You might want to see whether a software upgrade is available for the printer or your computer's operating system.

- **Paper**—Check the paper tray and paper-pushing mechanisms in the printer. If you're unable to print in Photoshop Elements, try printing from another application or from the desktop. If you have a second computer, determine whether you can print from it.

- **Scale to Fit Media**—Check this option in the Print Preview window if you want the image to fill the printed page. Print a test page to see how the image fits the paper you want to print on. If you're trying to print a tall, thin image or a super-small image on a large sheet of paper, selecting this option will most likely distort the original image. Print a test page with this option turned on and off if you want to see the extent of any distortion that might result from scaling the image to fit on the printed page.

- **Image Quality**—Uncheck the Scale to Fit Media check box, and print the image to view the image quality of the printer output. Depending on the type of printer you're using and the type of computer monitor, you might see some degradation of image quality between the printed image and the onscreen image. The image quality of the printed image should look similar to the image you see on your computer screen. If the printed image appears much smaller or larger than what you see on your computer screen, you might need to adjust the printer settings in the

Print dialog box, or change the scale, orientation, or paper settings in the Page Setup dialog box.

- **Printer Output**—Before printing, open the Print Preview dialog box and check the settings for the Scaled Print Size of the image. Use the preview area in the Print Preview window to scale the image you want to print. Select the Show More Options check box if you want to change color management or output settings for the printed image.

- **Paper Size**— If the printed image is printed beyond the edges of the paper, or much smaller than expected, check the Paper option in the Page Setup dialog box. Choose Page Setup from the Print menu to select the paper size on which you want to print. If you're printing to an 8.5×11-inch sheet of paper, choose letter for the paper size. If the printed image seems mismatched with the paper, check to see if envelope, legal, or a different paper size is selected, and then choose the correct paper type for your print job. Also, check to see if the Scale to Fit Media option is checked in the Print Preview window.

chapter

10

Digital Images and Color

Whether you're working with grayscale or color images, you can add color or create images containing both types of color modes using Photoshop Elements. Before you start working with color, it's best to explore how color works outside and inside a computer. First, this chapter discusses color theory, and then explains how computers and other output devices such as printers use numbers and color management technology to create colors.

Color Theory

You need to spend some time understanding several color concepts before you attempt to correct color. What exactly is color? First, color is what we perceive when light is refracted off different objects. Long, medium, and short wavelengths of light trigger red, green, or blue color recognition in our eyes. Our eyes convert light into neural data, which is interpreted by our brain.

Colors also can be mixed together. Blue and yellow make green, and red and blue make purple. However, you cannot create the three primary colors by mixing two colors together: red, yellow, and blue. These three colors can be mixed together in different proportions to create the full spectrum of colors.

Representing color on a computer involves creating numeric representation for each of the primary colors, and every combination of those colors on a computer monitor. You can define color on a computer in several ways. Each method is referred to as a color space. For example, RGB is the name for the red, green, and blue color space used in Photoshop Elements.

Primary Colors

Red, yellow, and blue are the three primary colors from which all other colors are made. Red, yellow, and blue cannot be created by mixing any other two colors together. White and black are colors, too, but they represent the maximum and minimum amount of reflectivity of all three colors combined. White absorbs no color and reflects all the light to our eyes, whereas black absorbs all the colors of the rainbow, so no light reaches our eyes. You can mix white with red to lighten the initial red color. Alternatively, you can mix black with red to darken red.

In the real world, it's rare to find a pure red, yellow, or blue color. Many external factors affect the way we perceive color. The biggest factor is the medium that created the color. For example, a book probably will display different red, yellow, and blue colors than a blue ink pen, or than the blue color on a television or a computer screen. Computers, printers, scanners, and cameras each have their own way of identifying and reproducing color. (See Figure CS.1 in the color section of this book.)

note

In 1931, color scientists got together and developed a scientific model that defines color—CIE, Commission Internationale L'Eclairage, or the International Commission on Illumination (www.cie.co.at/ cie). They designed the *tristimulus* color model, which assigns hue angle, saturation, and value (or brightness) to define a color. Using this model, color can be mapped to an X, Y, or Z axis.

Despite the existence of primary colors, your chances of finding true red, yellow, or blue is slim to none. The more realistic approach is to use computers, scanners, printers, and cameras that support color models that can be converted from one device to the next, preserving as much of the original color as possible. (See Figure CS.2 in the color section of this book.)

Viewing colors on the color wheel can help you understand different relationships between colors. Secondary colors are purple, green, and orange, the colors resulting from mixing red and blue, blue and yellow, or yellow and red. Tertiary colors are mixtures of secondary and primary colors, such as yellow-orange, yellow-green, blue-purple, or red-purple. Colors located on opposing sides of the color wheel are complementary colors.

In the physical world, the color of an object is defined by the way the object reflects and absorbs light. On a computer, you can choose a color arbitrarily from the color picker window, or use the color wheel to pick a primary, complementary, or tertiary color that you want to use in an image.

Light and Color

Color perception is the result of light being reflected off other surfaces. For example, when you look at a red ball, the ball absorbs all the color of the light except red, and reflects its own color, red, which is the color you see. The more light the ball is exposed to, the more color you'll see on the ball. However, there are limits; if you shine too much light on the ball, the light will bounce off it, hiding the red color and reflecting the light instead of the color.

Natural and artificial light can affect the appearance of a color. This is most obvious when you take a digital picture during the day in natural light, and then take a picture in the evening indoors. Tungsten and fluorescent light bulbs cast a unique shade of light. Tungsten bulbs usually cast a yellow-orangish *hue*. Fluorescent bulbs, besides having an annoying low-pitched hum, cast a greenish-yellowish hue. Hues cast by artificial light can be compounded if you use a flash or have another device, such as a television, in the picture.

note
Hue and saturation define the purity of a color. Hue defines the specific attributes or intensity of a color.

Saturation defines a color in the absence of white, using differences in gray values to adjust the saturation level of a color. A highly saturated color contains very little white.

When working with digital images, think about where the light source is originating from in the picture. Are there multiple light sources? Next, try to determine the colors in the picture. Does the light wash out colors in the picture? Is the picture overexposed? Experimenting with light and color in an image can be a time-consuming task. Consider saving multiple copies of an image as you're working on it so that you can experiment with different combinations of colors and lighting.

Computers and Color

Making a computer display what you see with your eyes is not an easy task. Several kinds of color spaces have been created as the result of different color scientists getting together to solve this task: How do you turn colors into numbers?

A color space defines the way colors can be reproduced, so that a numerical set of values will always generate the same color. Different kinds of computer devices use different color spaces to define color. For example, a computer uses a red, green, and blue color space to determine how to display colors on a monitor. A printer, on the other hand, relies on cyan, magenta, and yellow and values corresponding to the amount of ink and the type of paper to create colors.

note
The definition of the term tristimuli, or tristimuli color system, is located in the section "Calibrating Your Computer," later in this chapter.

You're probably most familiar with the color space of your computer monitor. Some monitors enable you to use hardware buttons to adjust color settings. However, most monitors rely on operating system software, such as a control panel, to allow you to set the way color appears onscreen. For example, the Display Calibrator Assistant, shown in Figure 10.4, enables you to set the white point, gamma, and tristimuli values of the computer monitor.

Introducing Color Space and Color Management

It's important to understand a slight clarification in color terminology. Correcting color can be associated with color-management systems, such as ColorSync. A color-management system is a specific software package designed to work with different input and output devices to produce consistent color. Color-management systems are designed to correct color, and rely on a particular color space, such as CIE, as a reference point for their color-matching engines to work with color profiles. Photoshop Elements can work with ICC color profiles. However, you must save a file with a color profile (see Figure 10.1), and select the color-management option in the Preference dialog box to take advantage of color-management in the work area.

Figure 10.1
Check the ICC Profile check box if you want to save the RGB color profile along with an image.

The terms *color space* and *color management* go hand in hand. A *color space* defines a color based on its relationship to light, or a particular form of color measurement. Photoshop Elements supports the HSB (hue, saturation, brightness), RGB, and hexadecimal color spaces in addition to bitmap, grayscale, and indexed color modes. You've already read about the RGB color space, which is the image mode you'll probably be using most (see Figure 10.2). Most scanners, digital cameras, and computers work well with red, green, and blue color space images. Hexadecimal color values, which commonly represent the 216 colors in a Web-safe color palette, are also important to be aware of if you'll be creating images in Photoshop Elements and using them on the Web.

note
CIE is an acronym for the International Consortium of Illumination. This organization was formed in 1931 to scientifically study the science and art of lighting. CIE is also an acronym used to define one of the settings that can be used to calculate the white point for your computer monitor. Because your computer display enables you to view images that are input and output from your computer, the color space settings for the monitor play a big role in the way color accuracy and color management are defined and converted to other color peripherals. Be sure to calibrate your display before editing any digital images that contain color.

note

ICC is an acronym for the International Color Consortium (www.color.org). This organization was founded in 1993 by eight companies: Adobe, Agfa-Gevaert, Apple, Eastman Kodak, Microsoft, Silicon Graphics, and Sun Microsystems. Its goal is to create standards for color management across computer platforms and imaging input and output devices.

Figure 10.2
The Hue/Saturation window enables you to adjust the hue, saturation, and lightness of an image.

Each color space relies on both hardware and software to work properly. This is referred to as *device-dependent color*. Each computer monitor and printer has its own way of interpreting how to work with color. Some devices, such as a computer monitor, rely on an additive color process to create a full spectrum of colors, while other devices, such as printers, rely on a subtractive color process. A device-independent color space is a color space that can accurately reproduce color no matter which device is being used.

Photoshop Elements doesn't know whether it's displaying an accurate color. It's up to you to choose what you perceive to be the correct color for an image. Monitors create colors based on an additive color process (see Figure 10.3). Red, green, and blue are combined to create magenta, cyan, and yellow as secondary colors. First, you need to have a monitor that supports 24-bit or 32-bit color (thousands or millions of colors for you Mac folks). Plus, you'll need to configure your operating system to display 24- or 32-bit color. If you missed this setup information, go to Chapter 1, "Installing Photoshop Elements," to find out how to set up or check the color setting on your monitor.

Color management describes the software technology that translates a color space from one hardware output device to another, such as monitors, printers, and scanners. ColorSync software on Macintosh computers performs this color manager role. You can choose a color profile for the output device you want to use with the computer. When you print or view a color onscreen, ColorSync tries to make sure the colors match.

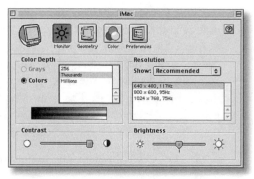

Figure 10.3
Additive colors for the RGB color model are magenta, cyan, and yellow. Computer monitors use an additive color process to create colors on your computer screen. Most computer monitors display 24-bit color. However, you also need to set your operating system to enable your monitor to display 16- or 24-bit color.

Windows also supports color-management color profiles. Right-click on the desktop, and choose Properties to open the Display control panel window. Click the Settings tab, and then click the Advanced button. The Multiple Monitors window opens. Click the Color Management tab, and then click the Add button to choose a color profile for your computer monitor. The color profile files end with an .icm extension. These files are installed in the Windows operating system folder on your hard drive. You can choose the sRGB Color Space Profile or the AdobeRGB1998 color profile for your monitor; both profiles are common to Windows, Mac, and Photoshop Elements.

Every printer, monitor, scanner, or other equipment capable of producing color uses its own method for displaying a range of colors, also called a *color gamut*. For example, the colors you see on a monitor are created using an additive process, where the phosphors in the monitor tube are excited by red, green, or blue colors. On the other hand, printers use a subtractive method based on cyan, magenta, and yellow to create colors. Color representation also varies between different monitor manufacturers. For instance, the colors on a Sony monitor look slightly brighter or bluer than the same colors on an Apple monitor.

In the worst-case scenario, you might be creating an image with an orange color. At least your computer monitor shows the color orange in the picture. When you send that image to a color printer, the printer might need to mix yellow and cyan ink to create orange. The application displaying the image onscreen tells your computer it needs the color orange. The computer sends this information to the printer. The printer gets the message for orange, and tries to create that color. Here's how the exchange might go:

Application: Hey, I need some orange here!

Computer: Printer, make some orange, okay?

Printer: What's orange? Okay, let me mix some ink.

Printer: Okay, I'm printing orange.

Computer to the Application: Hey, the printer made orange.

Application: Okie dokie!

You: This isn't orange, it's pink ink covered with yellow ink!

Gamma and Web Colors

Recall that gamma affects the brightness of the image on a computer monitor. Although Windows and Macintosh computers share the same Web browser color palette, each computer system processes gamma using different hardware technologies. Even though you might pick orange for your Web page on a Windows computer, you will see a slightly different shade of orange on a Macintosh computer screen.

The difference in gamma between Windows and Mac computers is most obvious when choosing colors for a Web page. A solid orange color created on a Windows computer might appear to have more red on a Mac.

The difference in gamma is because each computer system manages color differently. To compensate for the differences in gamma, try choosing colors that look more similar on both computer platforms.

To help hardware devices transform color more accurately from one device to another, the International Color Consortium (ICC) was formed in 1993. The ICC committee defined a workflow for color data to be translated from one device to another. This information was stored in a file, called a color profile.

An application that follows the ICC standards, such as Photoshop Elements, can store a color profile along with an image file. Before a printer uses its own color-management system to put ink on paper, it will load the color profile data (if you saved it with the image). The color profile contains the definition for the actual color data in the image.

For example, if you want to save an RGB image file (that's an image file in RGB image mode), select the Limited color management option in the Edit, Color Settings window to use the SRGB IEC61966-2.1 color profile for a Web graphic. If Full Color Management is selected, the Adobe RGB Color Profile will generate a color profile, which works best with print. Next, choose File, Save As. Check the [ICC Color Profile] (Embed Color Profile) check box in the Save As window and Photoshop Elements will generate ICC color definitions for your image.

note

To find the definitions of CIE and ICC, go to the beginning of the section titled "Introducing Color Space and Color Management" in this chapter.

Devices and Color Management

Most printers use the CMYK color model to print an image. Some devices enable you to modify CMYK settings from your computer. Other devices have a translation system built into them. For instance, some standalone photo printers allow you to insert a Compact Flash or Smart Media card directly into the printer, adjust the image, and print without using a computer. To print more accurate color, many printers include software that can translate an RGB image into a CMYK image. Printers that have this capability can produce printed images that match the colors of the onscreen image.

Calibrating Your Computer

You need to calibrate your computer monitor in order to take full advantage of color management. Calibrating a monitor involves adjusting several video settings: Brightness and Contrast, Gamma, Phosphors, and White Point. The settings you choose in the calibration software determine how other color spaces appear on your monitor, and more importantly, how colors are translated to output devices. You can use the calibration software installed with your operating system or use Adobe's Gamma control panel to calibrate your monitor. If you want to be sure your monitor is set to the correct white point, you can use a desktop colorimeter or spectrophotometer to measure and set its white point.

Photoshop Elements installs the Adobe Gamma control panel in the Control Panel folder on your hard drive. On a Mac, click on the Apple menu, select Control Panels, and then choose Adobe Gamma. On a Windows computer, click on the Start menu, choose Settings, Control Panel, and then select Adobe Gamma from the Control Panel menu list.

Before Calibrating Your Monitor...

To get the best calibration results, perform some of the following suggestions before changing any of your monitor's settings:

- Leave the monitor on for at least 30 minutes.
- Set the monitor to display at least thousands (16-bit) of colors.
- Set your desktop picture or pattern to a neutral color, such as a solid gray color.

The following list provides a brief explanation of the settings you need to calibrate on your monitor and summarizes the settings available in the Adobe Gamma control panel. The Adobe Gamma control panel has a wizard built into it. If you're not sure which settings to choose, use the wizard to help you choose the correct settings for your system.

- **Brightness/Contrast**—The Brightness and Contrast window for the Adobe Gamma control panel appears as a bar if you are adjusting settings manually, or as a black square surrounded by a white border. You can adjust the brightness and contrast settings of your computer monitor by changing the hardware or software settings. The controls will vary depending on the type of monitor and operating system installed with your computer.

  If you're using a Mac, you can adjust the monitor's brightness and contrast setting from the Monitors control panel. The brightness settings for a PC might be located directly on the computer monitor, or you might be able open a control panel window or press the keyboard controls for brightness or contrast on the keyboard. Place the Mac or Windows control panel window beside the Adobe Gamma control panel window on your desktop. Set the monitor's contrast setting to its highest value, and then change the Brightness setting in the (Monitors) [Display] window so that the black square or bar in the

Adobe Gamma control panel is as dark as it can be while keeping the brightness of the white bar as white as it can be.

- **Phosphors**—Monitors use phosphors to emit light and create the colors you can see onscreen. The red, green, and blue phosphors that create colors on your computer screen vary from one manufacturer to another. Select the phosphors for your monitor from the Phosphors drop-down menu. Select EBU/ITU, HDTV (CCIR 709), NTSC (1953), P22-EBU, SMPTE-C (CCIR 501-1), Trinitron, or create a custom phosphor setting. For most computer displays, Trinitron is the best setting. If you're using the Adobe Gamma (Assistant) [Wizard], it will choose a phosphor setting based on the color profile selected in the first step.

- **Gamma**—Gamma settings define the brightness of the midtones on your monitor. Pick the Windows Default gamma setting (2.2) if you're using a PC, or the Macintosh Default (1.8) if you're using a Macintosh computer. Move the slider control below the square in the Gamma section of the Adobe Gamma window to select a custom gamma setting. Calibrate your monitor with a single gamma setting or view or create custom gamma settings for red, green, and blue by deselecting the View Single Gamma Only check box.

- **White Point**—There are two settings for calibrating the white point on your monitor. This will affect how color is translated for other output devices. First, choose a warm or cool white setting for the monitor's white point. 5000K is the equivalent of a white page. 6500K is the default white point for Windows. 9300K is the default white point for Macintosh computers. Next, choose an adjusted white point value that you might want to work with.

note
Gamma defines the mathematical formula that represents the relationship between input and output. Windows and Mac computers each use different gamma processes to display color. In Photoshop Elements, the midtone region in the histogram is synonymous with the term gamma.

Lower values generate warmer, or yellowish, lighting. Colors might appear a little richer, or fuller, in low, or warmer, settings. As the value increases, the white point is cooler, or whiter. Cooler settings can reduce the range of visible colors in an image. The unit for measuring white point is in degrees Kelvin. Kelvin is a scale used to measure the color temperature, or the

note
A color system made of three colors—such as RGB, or CMY—is called a tristimulus. The white point is an achromatic value, meaning it is colorless, and results when all three tristimuli are equal. Setting the white point defines the way other colors will be presented on the computer monitor. It also affects how accurately colors are translated from input devices like a scanner or camera, or to output devices like a printer.

amount of color in a light source. Choose from 5000K (warm white), 5500K, 6500K, 7500K, 9300K, or a custom white point setting.

Some operating systems have calibration software settings enabling you to set the white point for the monitor. Figure 10.4 shows the Calibration settings in Mac OS X for the iMac monitor. Click on a radio button to select the white point of the monitor. Different white point settings will change the way white is displayed onscreen. This can have a significant impact on image editing, especially when you're relying on your computer monitor to determine the color accuracy of a photo.

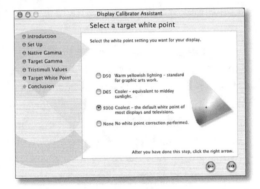

Figure 10.4
Mac OS X enables you to choose from one of three possible white point settings for your monitor.

Choosing a Color Mode

Photoshop Elements uses two color spaces to enable you to view, select, and modify colors. The Hue, Saturation, and Brightness (HSB) color space is based on how people perceive color. The Red, Green, and Blue (RGB) color mode represents the color space for computer monitors. Each color space enables you to view and edit colors. However, the color mode of an image file determines how many colors can be displayed in an image.

note
Almost all the examples in this book require an image to be in RGB color mode.

The following list summarizes each of the color modes in Photoshop Elements:

- **RGB**—New image files opened in the work area are created in RGB mode, and chances are you'll be doing most of your work in this color mode. Most of the tools and commands in Photoshop Elements require an image to be in RGB mode before you can use them.

  RGB mode relies on the RGB color model to assign color values to each pixel. Values range from 0 (black) to 255 (white) for each red, green, and blue channel of the RGB image. To create black, each red, green, and blue value is set to zero (0). White is created when red, green, and blue are each set to 255. Any subsequent combination of equal RGB values results in gray. Each channel contains 8 bits of color. When you work with an image in RGB mode, you can work with up to 24 bits of color.

- **Indexed Color**—This mode supports up to 256 colors. Use this color mode if you want to preserve the quality of the image, while reducing the number of colors and the file size of the image. Photoshop Elements creates a custom color table for the image when you choose this color mode. Any colors that do not map to one of the 256 colors in the color lookup table (also known as a CLUT) are mapped to the closest-matching color.

- **Grayscale**—256 shades of gray are available in this color mode. Zero represents black, and 255 represents white. Grayscale mode is optimal for viewing and editing black and white photographs.

- **Bitmap**—Only two colors, black and white, are available in this image mode. Images in bitmap mode are essentially 1-bit images, with a color depth of one color. Bitmap mode can be used to view, edit, or save line art.

Color and Photoshop Elements

It's now time to get your feet wet. Photoshop Elements contains several tools that enable you to view and customize color settings of an image. The primary tools you will use to select and change colors are the Color Picker window and the Swatches palette. In addition to

note
Photoshop Elements uses the HSB color space in its Color Picker window and its Hue/Saturation Tool. However, no HSB color space is available for creating and editing images.

note
Adobe uses the term *color mode* to describe the RGB, Grayscale, Bitmap, or Indexed Color modes in Photoshop Elements. I frequently use the term image mode in this book. Image mode is synonymous with color mode.

these color-selection tools, you can also correct color using the commands located in the Enhance menu.

The following sections show you how to use the Color Picker, as well as the Brightness/Contrast, Hue/Saturation, and Levels commands to analyze color in an image. You will also learn how to create composite images.

Using the Color Picker

You can use Adobe's Color Picker window to select a foreground or background color for a tool, command or effect. If you prefer to use a color space that's not available in the Adobe Color Picker, such as HSL, choose the Windows or Apple Color Picker. Choose Edit, Preferences, General and then choose (Apple) [Windows] from the Color Picker drop-down menu in the General Preferences window. Figure 10.5 shows the Windows Color Picker window. Click within the boundaries of the large rainbow of colors on the right or click on a color square to choose a new color. You can also type in values for Hue, Sat(uration), Lum(inosity), Red, Green, or Blue to select a color in the Color Picker window.

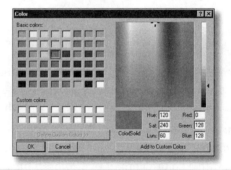

Figure 10.5
The Windows Color Picker supports HSL and RGB color spaces and has a slightly different layout for selecting a color than Adobe's Color Picker. Click on the Define Custom Colors button if you cannot see the custom color selector on the right side of the Color Picker.

When you click on either color box, located at the bottom of the toolbox, the default Color Picker dialog box will open. You can select the color space (such as RGB) that you want to use in the Color Picker dialog box. Figure 10.6 shows the Adobe Color Picker dialog box in Photoshop Elements.

Color wheel bar

Current color

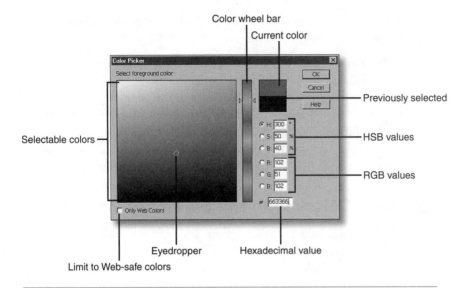

Selectable colors

Previously selected

HSB values

RGB values

Limit to Web-safe colors

Eyedropper

Hexadecimal value

Figure 10.6
Adobe's Color Picker supports HSB, RGB, and hexadecimal color spaces.

Select a color from the Color Picker dialog box to change the color of an object in the image window, or to select a color for a drawing tool, filter, effect, or image-editing tool. Click in the vertical row of colors to pick a basic color. Then click in the large windows on the left to select a more precise shade of color. You can also type in a Hue, Saturation, Brightness, Red, Green, Blue, or Hexadecimal value in the corresponding text box. Click on the two-headed arrow icon located just above the color squares in the toolbox to swap the foreground and background colors.

The foreground color is the square on the upper-left at the bottom of the toolbox. It appears when a drawing or painting tool is applied to the image window. The background color is located in the lower-right square. It appears when the Eraser Tool or (Delete) [Backspace] key is applied to the image window.

The Apple Color Picker enables you to choose from CMYK, HSV, HTML (hexadecimal), HLS, and RGB color spaces. Apple's Color Picker window is divided into two main sections. On the left, you choose a color space. The color wheel settings for the color space appear on the right. The current color appears in the Original color

tip
Choose the Eyedropper Tool (I) from the toolbox. Hold down the Alt or Option key and then click on a color to change the selected background color. The new background color will appear in the toolbox window. You can click on the background color square in the toolbox to choose a new color from the Color Picker window.

swatch. Click and drag the slider controls, or type in a value, to select a new color.

If you don't want to think about color spaces, you can use the Crayon Picker to choose from 60 colors. The Crayon Picker is one of the color spaces located on the left portion of the Apple Color Picker window. Sorry, Windows folks—there's no equivalent to the Crayon Picker available in Windows. Regardless of whether you're using a Mac or Windows PC, Photoshop Elements enables you to work with HSB, RGB, or HTML color values in the work area.

Changing Colors with the Swatches Palette

The Swatches palette enables you to select a color, or load and save a swatch library of colors. You can add or remove a color square from the Swatches palette. If you have the Info palette open, you can also use the Swatches palette to "look up" a color value in your image (see Figure 10.7).

Figure 10.7
Add custom colors to the Swatches palette, and view any color in the image window from the Info palette.

By default, 116 colors appear in the Swatches palette. You can load new swatch libraries by clicking on the arrow drop-down menu and choosing from the Mac OS, VisiBone, VisiBone2, Web Hues, Web Safe Colors, Web Spectrum, and Windows color palettes. Although your monitor might be set to display thousands or millions (16-bit or 24-bit color) of colors, the Swatches palette will usually not contain more than 256 colors.

You can use the Swatches palette to store particular colors from an image file, in addition to any Web-safe, or OS-specific colors. Or you can create a custom palette for a series of color images. This can be helpful when you are creating an image using a specific set of colors such as for a logo or Web site.

To add a color to the Swatches palette, do the following:

1. Click on the Eyedropper Tool in the toolbox.

2. Click on the color you want to add in one of the image windows.

3. Next, click below the last row of color squares in the Swatches palette. When you place the cursor below the bottom row of color squares in the Swatches palette, its icon will change from an eyedropper to a Paint Bucket icon. The Color Swatch Name window appears.

4. Type in a name for the color square, and then press OK. The new color square will appear at the bottom of the Swatches palette.

To remove a color, click and drag the color to the Trash icon located in the lower-right corner of the Swatches palette.

Photoshop Elements Color-Correction Tools

The manual process of color correction in a digital photo is what most of this book is about. The complexity of a project depends on the quality and clarity of the original image. Photoshop Elements has a couple of tools that offer a quick-fix solution for certain kinds of pictures. However, the automatic level and contrast tools can work great with some images, but might not be helpful with other images. Try out the Auto Levels or Auto Contrast commands to see if they improve the image. If you like the change, save the image. Otherwise, you can choose Undo from the Edit menu to undo the automatic changes and make the improvements yourself.

note

A Web-safe color palette consists of 216 colors. These colors are the common colors Windows, Mac, and Linux computers share out of a total system color palette of 256 colors. If you choose a color on a Mac that isn't apart of the 216 Web-safe colors, another computer platform might not have that color. If this is the case, the browser or operating system will convert the missing color to what it thinks is the closest matching color available.

Consider the following issues before taking a first step to correct color. First, determine whether this is the best image you can work with. Is there another image or photo that the image will need to match? Is there a set of colors or light conditions that might need to match each other if you plan to create a composite image?

Next, determine what types of media to which the image will be output. Will the image be printed or posted to a Web page? Finally, be sure you have plenty of disk space, memory, and backup media for any projects you can't afford to lose. The following sections show you how some of the Enhance menu tools affect an image.

Hue and Saturation

A computer creates colors using primary colors. Of course, primary colors are the exception to this rule. Each color space defines it own unique primary colors. For example, red, green, and blue are the primary colors for the RGB color space, which is what your computer monitor uses. Cyan, magenta, and yellow are the primary colors for the CMYK color model, used in print output. When you change a color's hue, the computer adds or subtracts values from a color. When you move the hue slider control, it is similar to choosing a different color by moving around the color wheel.

Saturated colors are either primary or secondary colors. These colors are based on one or two primary colors with the third primary color set to zero. Choose Hue/Saturation from the Enhance, Color menu to open the Hue/Saturation window shown in Figure 10.8.

When you adjust the saturation level from the Hue/Saturation dialog box, one of the primary colors is removed from the selected color, or from all colors in the image (see Figure 10.8). When you move the Saturation control, you can increase or decrease the amount of gray mixed with the colors in the image. The Lightness slider control enables you to add a primary color back into the hue/saturation settings.

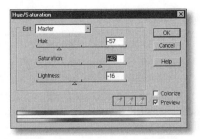

Figure 10.8
Adjust the mixture of colors using the Hue, Saturation, and Lightness slider controls in the Hue/Saturation window.

Color correction is usually a tedious task. Don't be surprised to find yourself experimenting with the Hue/Saturation command to correct colors, or change a color just to compare the results to another color-correction tool in Photoshop Elements. The following list describes situations in which you might want to use the Hue/Saturation command:

- **Color**—If you want to adjust a color in part of an image, you can use a selection tool to highlight the pixels you want to modify. Then open the Hue/Saturation command from the Enhance, Color menu (Cmd-U) [Ctrl+U] and slowly move the Hue control slider. If the Preview check box has been selected, you can watch the color of the selected pixels change as you move the slider.

- **Color Purity**—The Saturation control in the Hue/Saturation dialog box enables you to set the amount of gray level or *chroma* in a color. You might want to adjust this setting if a portion of an image needs a little less gray, and a little more color, than the rest of the image. You can adjust the saturation level of a specific color channel in an image, or of all the channels.

- **Color Brightness**—The Lightness slider control enables you to remove or add light to all or part of an image. This setting can help lighten or darken colors in an image, or help create more even lighting in part of an image.

note
The Hue slider control enables you to change a range of color values in the active image window. This method of changing colors creates a smoother color transition across all colors in the image, or in the selected area of the image. If you use the Swatches palette, you can easily change the color of a specific pixel. However, it's not quite as easy to tweak the colors of the surrounding pixels without spending a lot of time mixing and matching colors.

Brightness and Contrast

The Brightness control enables you to increase or decrease the amount of light in an image, whereas the Contrast control enables you to increase or decrease the amount of dark and light pixels in an image. Choose Brightness/Contrast from the Enhance menu. This dialog box enables you to increase or decrease the overall tonal range of an image. Each slider control has a zero value at the midpoint of the slider, going from –100 to 100, or a range of 200 settings.

Check the Preview check box to preview your changes in the image window. This tool provides a more general way to adjust the tonal range of an image. The Levels command enables you to more precisely modify the tonal range of pixels in an image. The Brightness/Contrast dialog box, for example, has one slider control to enable you to adjust the brightness of all the selected pixels (see Figure 10.9). A higher brightness value increases the highlights in the image. A lower brightness value decreases the highlights, and increases the shadows in the image.

You can increase the shadows and highlights in an image by increasing the value of the contrast slider control. Decreasing the contrast setting lowers the values of the shadows and highlights in the image.

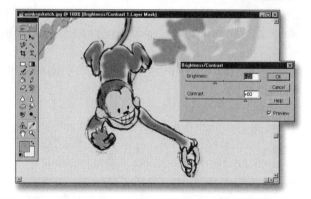

Figure 10.9
The Brightness/Contrast dialog box enables you to adjust the ratio of dark and light pixels, as well as the amount of light exposed to the colors in an image.

The Levels dialog box contains three slider controls: one each for highlights (lighter grays), midtones (grays), and shadows (darker grays). You can adjust the tonal range for all three channels in an image, or customize each channel separately. The Levels command enables you to apply broad or precise changes that can affect some or all of the pixels in an image.

Brightness and Contrast Versus Tonal Range

If you're not sure whether to use the Levels command instead of the Brightness/Contrast command to adjust the tonal range in an image, create an adjustment layer for each command. Click on the eye icon for either setting to compare one set of tonal range settings to another. It's not uncommon to use both commands to apply tonal corrections to an image.

Adjusting Tonal Range Using the Levels Command

The Levels command enables you to adjust black (shadows), white (highlights), and middle tones (midtones). You can adjust pixels dynamically with the Levels command. For example, if you want to make the tonal range of highlights lighter, the midtone and shadow pixels will not be changed. You can use the Levels command to adjust the distribution of pixels in an image by either resetting the shadow/black, neutral gray/mid-point, or highlight/white point of an image (see Figure 10.10). When you adjust the settings in the histogram, you are changing the input levels of all the pixels in the image. You can also change the black and white output levels of the image by moving the arrow controls located at the bottom of the Levels dialog box.

Finding Black and White Points

If you cannot visually identify a black or white color in an image, you can use the Threshold command to find them for you. Defining the black and white points in an image will help you adjust the image's tonal range settings.

First, open an image in the work area. Adjust the size of the image so that the full image is viewable in the work area. Then choose Threshold from the Layer, New Adjustment Layer menu. Type a name for the Threshold layer, and then click on the OK button. The Threshold dialog box will open.

note
A histogram is a visual representation of the number of pixels distributed in an image. Darker shades of pixels are located on the left side of the histogram, and lighter pixels on the right. Black vertical bars in the histogram indicate how many pixels share a common gray value in the image. View a histogram of an indexed color, RGB, or grayscale image. Choose Histogram from the Image menu to open the Histogram window. To find out more about how to read the data in the Histogram window, see Chapter 11, "Tonal Range and Color Correction."

continued

View the histogram of the tonal distribution of pixels. Move the slider to the far left until you can barely see any black in the image. Note the number in the Threshold Level text box. This number represents the black point of the image. Observe the location of the black point in the image.

Move the slider control to the right end of the histogram. Look for the first appearance of the color white to appear as you move the slider from the right end of the histogram to the left. The first white pixels to appear constitute the white point for the image. Note the number in the Threshold Level window. You can use the black point and white point values to set the image's shadow and highlight values, respectively, in the Levels window.

tip
If you want to apply the Levels command without altering any pixels in the original image, add a Levels adjustment layer. You can apply all the same great tools in the Levels dialog box in an adjustment layer except that the changes are stored in a separate layer until you're ready to merge them into the final image.

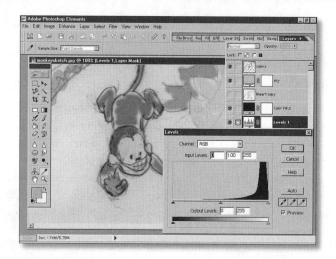

Figure 10.10
A scanned image before adjusting its tonal range—note the absence of data in the darker tonal range.

Choose Enhance, Brightness/Contrast, Levels to open the Levels dialog box. The histogram displays the tonal range of an RGB image. You can use the Levels command to modify all the pixels in an image by choosing the RGB option in the Channel menu. You can also view and edit the Red, Green, or Blue tonal ranges of the image. This enables you to customize a specific set of pixels in an image, reducing potential image data loss that can result from making broader tonal corrections with all three channels. If you've opened a grayscale image, a single window containing the distribution of grays will appear in the Levels dialog box (see Figure 10.11).

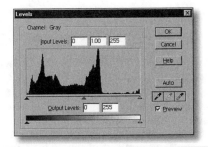

Figure 10.11
Moving the black and mid-range levels makes the darker shades of the image stand out.

You can use the Levels dialog box to do more intensive tonal range correction, too. The three eyedroppers located in the lower-right corner of the Levels dialog box enable you to set custom black, gray, or white points for the image. The Eyedropper Tools will reset the input settings in the Levels dialog box. The Eyedropper Tools are not designed to make tonal corrections. You can use them to make small adjustments to correct the targeting of black, white, and grays in the image.

You can use the Levels Eyedropper Tools in two ways. You can choose an arbitrary color from the Color Picker window. Double-click on the Eyedropper Tool for which you want to set a target color, and then choose a color from the Color Picker window. Or, you can select one of the Eyedropper Tools from the Levels dialog box and then click in the image window to select the new black, gray, or white point for the image.

note
To find out more about tonal correction, go to Chapter 11.

Color and Composite Images

You can apply any of the color or tonal correction commands to a single image, or to a combination of images. When you copy and paste one image into another you create a composite image. The connecting edges of the composite image might not blend in with the composite colors in the background image. Color mismatches and rough edges in composite images can result in a final image that lacks realism.

caution

Each time you apply any of the image-editing tools, you can change and delete a large number of pixels from the original image. As you apply multiple tools to an image, more and more data is lost. In contrast, if you create adjustment layers, and merge them together at the same time, you'll lose less image data than when applying each tool one by one.

note

To find out more about adjustment layers, see Chapter 13, "Working with Layers and Layer Styles."

Feathering Selections

Blur the edges of a selected image before copying it. First, choose a selection tool and highlight an area of pixels in the image window. Then, choose the Feather command from the Select menu to feather the edges of the copied image to allow for better blending between the images.

The Feather command enables you to blend the color of the pixels located at the edge of the selected area. When you choose the Feather command, the Feather Selection dialog box opens. Type a number into the text box to adjust the number of pixels you want to blend with the edge pixels. The higher the number, the more pixels will be blurred at the edges of the selected image. Three to five pixels is a good value to apply with the Feature command. You can increase or decrease the number of pixels that will be feathered until you create the effect that works best with the image you're working with. Click OK to apply the command to the selected area. You should be able to see a slight blur at the edge of the selected image.

Choose the Copy command, and then paste the image into another image window. The pasted, feathered image should blend into the background image.

Figure 10.12 shows two images that have been added to a third image window. To create this image, I used the Magnetic Lasso Tool to select each image. Then I used the Copy and Paste commands to move the selected image to the middle window. Notice how the edges of the cat image are slightly blurred around the edges. The Feather command was not applied to the rabbit.

When you paste an image into an active document window, Photoshop Elements converts the color mode of the pasted image into the image mode of the active image window. To preserve all the color information of a composite image, open an image in RGB color mode, or create a new document window and choose RGB Color from the Image, Mode menu. RGB color mode supports up to 16.7 million colors. It's okay to paste an image in Indexed Color, Grayscale, or Bitmap color modes into an image window in RGB mode. The composite image will retain its resolution and color data.

224

Figure 10.12
Copy and paste images to create a composite image. The Feather command was applied to the cat but not to the rabbit image.

note

A *mask* is a term used to describe a selected area of pixels in an image. A mask protects the unselected areas of an image from being edited, while enabling you to modify the selected area with commands and tools. You can create a simple mask by applying a selection tool to an image in the image window. When you apply the selection tool, the selected area is bordered with a flashing dashed line, or marquee. You can modify the pixels within the marquee. However, the pixels located outside the marquee cannot be edited.

Correcting the color between the two images might be an issue if you're combining images taken under different lighting conditions. For example, an image captured in daylight might not seem realistic if combined with another captured in low light. You can try to correct the highlights, midtones, or shadows of both images by adding an adjustment layer and applying it across layers in the image window. You also can apply the Fill Flash, Adjust Backlighting, Brightness/Contrast, or Hue/Saturation tools to an image before or after combining it with a second image. For best results, try to choose images that share similar lighting and image clarity. The greater the differences between the images, the more time you'll probably be spending trying to correct colors.

Another way to combine images together is to select part of the background image and paste another image into it. Instead of choosing the standard Paste menu command, you can use a selection tool to highlight part of the image in the image window, and then choose the Paste Into command from the Edit menu to create a masked composite image. Many of the same color matching, and lighting issues apply to masked images. Be prepared to spend time correcting and blending colors to try to make the composite image appear more realistic.

note

To find out more about the Paste Into command, go to Chapter 16, "Experimenting with Composite Images."

tip

To find out more about how to create and combine composite images, see Chapter 17, "Creating Complex Images."

A mask can also be used to isolate a particular area of an image where you might want to delete, replace or correct the color. If you've pasted an image into the image window, you can (Command+) [Ctrl-] click the composite image layer in the Layers palette. The image in the selected layer will automatically become selected. You can apply color correction tools to the selected image without affecting other images in the active image window.

A new layer is created for each new image pasted into the active image window. You can use the Move Tool to place the composite image in the image window, or apply the Erase Tool to delete any areas of the composite image that might not fit with the background image. You can use the Eraser, Magic Eraser, or Background Eraser tool to clean up a composite image or remove color from an area of the image.

Select the Eraser Tool (E) from the toolbox. Click and drag it over an image to remove pixels from the image, and create transparent areas in the composite image, or across all layers in the image. A transparent color is actually an absence of color. Transparency is represented by a gray and white checkerboard pattern in the image window. If you see this pattern, no color will appear in the final printed, or Web-published image. To find out more about the Erase Tool, go to Chapter 14, "Adding Text and Shapes to Images."

Tonal Range and Color Correction

Photoshop Elements provides several color correction tools that enable you to replace, adjust, brighten, darken, or remove color from an RGB image. Some tools, such as the Levels and Brightness/Contrast tools, enable you to remap the dark and light pixels in an image. Grayscale and color images are created using a range of black, gray, and white pixels. Some of the tools in Photoshop Elements use the terms shadows, midtones, and highlights to define the range of dark to light colors.

The following sections in this chapter show you how to use selection tools to choose pixels by shape, size, or color. You will find out how to use the histogram, which shows you how pixels are distributed in an image. The selection tools and histogram enable you to perform precise tonal range and color correction changes. You also will learn how to modify the tonal distribution of pixels using the Fill Flash, Adjust Backlighting, Levels, Brightness/Contrast and other tools located in the Image and Enhance menus. These tools enable you to make darker areas of an image more visible, or to add contrast to lighter areas of an image.

Several color-correction tools are also available in the Enhance menu. The Hue/Saturation, Color Cast, Replace Color, and Remove Color tools enable you to customize the entire contents of the image window or focus on a specific selection of pixels. You can use a combination of tonal range and color-correction tools to make a blue sky bluer, remove red eye, or to correct brownish or greenish hues in scanned images of old photos.

Introducing Selection Tools

Although it's appropriate to apply any of the tonal range tools to an entire image, you also can apply them to only selected areas. The selection tools reside in the toolbox and in the Select menu. Each can be used with filters, effects, color correction, and transform tools in addition to the tonal range tools.

You can choose from two kinds of selection tools: ones that allow you to select an arbitrary set of pixels, and ones that help you select a group of pixels based on color or tonal differences. The Rectangular Marquee, Lasso, and Crop Tools fall into the former category, whereas the Magic Wand and Magnetic Lasso Tools fall into the latter category.

Selection tools primarily are used to select the pixels you want to modify, duplicate, or remove from an image. However, you also can use selection tools as a mask. A *mask* enables you to modify a specific area of an image, while all other areas are protected from change. You can apply a filter, effect, drawing, eraser, or any number of other tools to the selected area without affecting the unselected pixels.

The following list describes the selection tools located in the toolbox and Select menu. Each of these selection tools can work with the Clipboard combined with the Cut, Copy, Paste, or Paste Into commands to bring other images into an image window.

You can use each selection tool one at a time or combine them. Hold down the Shift key to add another selected set of pixels to the currently selected set of pixels. Hold down the (Option) [Alt] key and click and drag the cursor over part of a selected area to remove those pixels from the selection area. You can use this tool, combined with the Info palette, to view the size of the selected area. You'll find the following selection tools in the toolbox:

- ▫◯ **Rectangular or Elliptical Marquee**—Create a rectangle or circular selection area in the image window. The marquee selection tools enable you to easily select an area of pixels in a particular shape. Click and drag the cursor in the image window to define the boundaries of the selected area of the canvas.

- ⌗ **Crop**—Apply this tool by clicking and dragging it in the image window. The Crop Tool grays the area surrounding the cropped image, enabling you to preview the cropped area. When you're ready to crop the selected area, press Enter. The image window is resized to the newly cropped image. You can use this tool to remove superfluous outer edges of an image you might want to use for a postcard or photo album.

- ◤ **Magic Wand**—Select, add, or subtract a range of colors with this magical selection tool. Click on a color in the image window to select all immediate occurrences of that color. If you hold down the Shift key, you can add any nearby pixels of another color to the selected area. Hold down the (Option) [Alt] key and click on a color to remove it from the selection. This tool is great for selecting or deselecting a range of colors you want to correct or replace. Colors in a different location in the image window easily can be added or removed from the selection area.

- ▱▱▱**Lasso, Polygonal Lasso,** or **Magnetic Lasso**—The Lasso and Polygonal Lasso Tools enable you customize the shape of the selection area. Use this type of selection tool to choose odd-shaped areas, or to select pixels that you aren't able to select with the Marquee or Magic Wand. Click and drag the Lasso Tool to define the selection area. The Polygonal Lasso Tool enables you to click to define each side of the selection area. Click on the first point again to close the selection area.

The Magnetic Lasso Tool probably is the smartest selection tool of them all. Click in the image area to define the starting point of the pixels you want to select. Drag the cursor around the image you want to select, and the Magnetic Lasso will create selection points. Unlike the other lasso tools, you don't need to click to create each point of the selection area. As you move the cursor around the edge of the image you want to select, this tool will try to create new selection points along the edge of the image based on the current selection points. Press the Backspace key to remove a selection point, or click in the image window to create a new selection point. Click on the first selection point to close the selection area.

Selection commands in the Select menu include

- **All**—Select all pixels in the image window by choosing this command. You can use this command to select or deselect all pixels in a layer.

- **Deselect or Reselect**—After you've applied one of the selection tools, you might notice the selection marquee remains active after you click outside the selected area. If you want to remove the selection marquee from the image window, choose the Deselect command from the Select menu. You can press (Command-D) [Ctrl+D] or (Ctrl-) [Right-] click in the image window and choose this command as well. If you've deselected a selected area, press (Command-Shift-D) [Ctrl+Shift+D] to reselect it, or (Ctrl-) [Right-] click in the image window to choose the Reselect command from the shortcut menu.

- **Inverse**—Use this command to invert the selected area of pixels in the image window. This command will deselect the initial pixels and select all the other pixels in the image window.

- **Feather**—Blurs the pixels along the border of the image with the pixels in the previous layer of an image. Feathering helps reduce hard edges on images that are copied and pasted from one image window to another. The Feather command can improve the way composite images blend together in an image. You can modify the Marquee and Lasso Tools to automatically feather the edges of the selected area by typing in a value in the Feather Text box, which is located in the selection tool's option bar. To find out more about how to apply the Feather command, go to Chapter 16, "Experimenting with Composite Images."

- **Modify**—Four menu commands are stored in the Modify menu: Border, Smooth, Expand, and Contract. Each one adjusts the size and appearance of the selected area of pixels. Use one of these commands if you already have created a selection area but need to expand or contract the selection area to include more or less image information.

- **Grow or Shrink**—Enables you to select pixels that share a similar color to those in the initial selection marquee. These commands work similarly to the Magic Wand Tool, selecting pixels by color value and not only by physical proximity.

Applying the Rectangular Marquee Tool

The Rectangular and Ellipse Marquee Tools are shape selection tools. Applying these selection tools to the image window is nearly identical to applying any of the shape tools—except, of course, you're using these tools to select pixels, not add them to the canvas. The marquee selection tools select an area of pixels in any rectangular or ellipse shape you want.

To use the Rectangular Marquee Tool, click its icon in the toolbox and the tool's settings appear in the options bar.

Click and drag the cursor in the image window. A *marquee* (a broken white line, also called "marching ants," that appears in the image window) marks the boundary of the selected pixels. The marquee that appears when you select pixels in the image window looks similar to the tool's icon in the toolbox. It also represents the selected pixels in the active layer in the Layers palette. The pixels will remain selected until you either choose and apply the selection tool again, or press (Command-D) [Ctrl+D] to deselect the selection.

After you've selected a group of pixels, you can delete the selection, copy it to another image window, apply an effect to the selection, or make other changes that apply only to the selected pixels. If you have a problem copying text from the image window, be sure you have the correct layer selected in the Layers palette.

tip
Hold down the (Command) [Ctrl] key and click on a layer containing an image object. This key combination automatically selects the image object in a layer. This is a great shortcut to use if you want to select an odd-shaped image that resides in its own layer in the Layers palette.

Applying the Magic Wand Tool

You can use the Magic Wand Tool to select a particular range of colors in an image. The Magic Wand icon shows a wand topped with a pixel. You can click on a color in the image window to select all pixels within its immediate proximity that share the selected color. The Magic Wand Tool works great if you're working with images isolated in separate layers in an image. You can use it to pick colors that need to be corrected, deleted, or merged with another image.

Applying the Magnetic Lasso Tool

My favorite selection tool is the Magnetic Lasso Tool. The Rectangular Marquee Tool comes in as a close second. The Magnetic Lasso Tool is a lasso selection tool with smarts. It tries to determine which set of pixels you're trying to select based on the pixels that are not being selected in the image window.

To select pixels with this tool, first you must click in the image window. The first click creates an anchor point in the image. A single-pixel line appears as you drag the cursor away from the anchor point. If you hold the cursor over the edge of the pixels you want to select, the Magnetic Lasso Tool creates additional anchor points automatically. You don't need to click to define the selection area. To close the selection area, click on the first anchor point or double-click in the image window.

The selected area in Figure 11.1 was created with the Magnetic Lasso Tool. Making this type of selection "by hand" using the regular Lasso Tool would be a very painstaking process and probably wouldn't be nearly as accurate as the Magnetic Lasso Tool.

tip

Use the selection tools and the Paste Into command to merge an image stored in the Clipboard into a selected image in the image window. Open two images in the work area. Apply a selection tool to the first image. This selected area is where the second image will be pasted. Apply a selection tool to the second image. Choose the Copy command from the Edit menu. The selected image will be moved to the Clipboard. In the first image, click on the layer with the active selection (where you want to add the image).

Choose the Paste Into command located in the Edit menu. The second image is added to the layer in the first image.

Figure 11.1
Click along the edge of an object in a picture. If you drag the Magnetic Lasso Tool along the edges of the image you want to outline, it will create anchor points for the selection. If the dashed line of the marquee matches the color of the pixels in the image, the marquee might not appear to completely surround the selection area.

Correcting Tonal Range

The term *tonal range* defines how pixels are distributed across the black, gray, and white areas of an image. Many of the tonal range tools use a histogram to illustrate how pixels are distributed across an image. A *histogram* is a bar graph representing the pixel distribution of an image. The more pixels in the white or highlight areas of the histogram, the more light in the overall picture. The histogram shows a taller spike where more color pixels are located in an area of an image, and a shorter spike, or no spike, if few or no pixels are present in that color area of an image.

Some tools, such as the Levels and Threshold commands, use the histogram to display the tonal range of the image. Other tools, such as the Fill Flash and Adjust Backlighting commands, do not use a histogram to illustrate the tonal range of the image. Instead, these tools use slider controls, enabling you to adjust the settings for each of these tools. Although the histogram is a very informative tool, and probably the most effective tool for viewing tonal distribution, most commands in Photoshop Elements rely on slider controls to enable you to view or change tonal or color settings.

note
Histograms are covered in more detail in the next section of this chapter.

Highlights, Midtones, and Shadows

Although an image should not contain a huge spike of pixels in any one area of the histogram, it's also somewhat rare to view an image that has equal distribution of pixels across the full spectrum of black through white pixels.

You can take a look at how the histogram changes by creating a new window and viewing the histogram as you change the colors in the window. Choose New from the File menu. Type a width and height for the new window. Select RGB for the image mode and then select the White radio button to a new window with a white background. Next, choose Image, Histogram to open the Histogram dialog box. Be sure the dialog box shows RGB in parentheses at the top. If it says Gray, go to Image, Mode and change the image mode to RGB. Choose any channel from the Channel drop-down list at the top of the Histogram dialog box and notice there are no pixels in the histogram, although in a 200×200 pixel window, 40,000 white pixels are present.

Now, close the Histogram dialog box and choose black as the foreground color by clicking on the foreground color swatch at the bottom of the toolbox. The Adobe Color Picker window opens. Click in the lower-left or lower-right corner of the Select foreground color section of the Color Picker window. Click OK to exit the Color Picker window. The foreground color in the toolbox (left color square) should be black. Next, select the Paint Bucket Tool, and click in the image window. The white background should turn to black. Next, choose Histogram from the Image menu to open the Histogram dialog box. You should see pixels on the left side of the histogram (Level 0) extending from the bottom to the top of the histogram.

For our next trick, choose the Gradient Tool from the toolbox. Click on the linear gradient icon on the options bar, and then click and drag the cursor in the image window. The black background in the window changes into a white to black gradient. Next, open the Histogram dialog box and notice the pixel distribution is spread somewhat evenly across the histogram (see Figure 11.2).

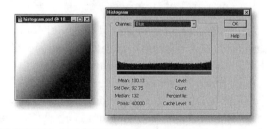

Figure 11.2
This black-and-white gradient generates a relatively flat histogram.

Balancing Foreground Light with Fill Flash

The Fill Flash, Adjust Backlighting, and Red Eye Brush Tools are designed to be quick fixes for some fairly easy, and commonly made, photographic errors. The Fill Flash Tool corrects photos in which the light source is behind the subject. This usually creates a dark foreground. The Fill Flash Tool lightens shadows in an image.

To apply the Fill Flash Tool, do the following:

1. Open an image file.

2. Choose Fill Flash from the Enhance menu. The Fill Flash dialog box will open.

3. Click and drag the arrow slider to lighten the shadows in the image. The Fill Flash value can be adjusted to a value between 0 and 100.

4. Check the Preview check box if you want to view your changes in the image window.

5. Click on OK to save your changes. View the modified image in the active image window.

The next time you open the Fill Flash Tool, the Lighter value will be set to zero.

Figure 11.3 shows an original picture in which the foreground images on the left and right are covered in shadows. Figure 11.4 shows the same image after the Fill Flash Tool has been applied to it. Notice that the foreground images, such as the chairs on the left, are more recognizable. The brighter images in the center and background area of the picture are also lighter.

tip
Brightness is a separate attribute that can affect how we perceive color. The intensity of light on a color affects how brilliant or dull a color appears. Before modifying an image, note the differences in the way your monitor displays light and compare it to the original photograph, or to a reference image. Also, keep in mind that some monitors display colors equally well, whereas other monitors aren't as efficient displaying all three colors equally well.

CHAPTER 11 Tonal Range and Color Correction

Figure 11.3
The foreground images are much darker than the background images in this picture. The camera focused on the background light as the white point for this picture.

Figure 11.4
Lightening the foreground image with the Fill Flash Tool also lightens parts of the background image.

Bringing Out the Background with Backlighting

Another common flaw a camera can make when taking photographs is making the background area of the image too bright. You can darken the tonal range of an image by applying the Adjust Backlighting Tool. Like other tonal range tools, you can apply the Adjust Backlighting Tool to the entire image, or to just a selected part.

Monitor Settings, Colors, and Tonal Range

Although most monitors can only display 24 bits of color, most scanners can capture more data, in some cases up to or more than 48 bits of color. Even though you cannot see these additional colors on your computer screen, when you modify the tonal range, or adjust color hues or brightness or contrast settings, the additional color information can bring out additional colors or details in the image. Keep in mind that you'll get the best results working with an image originally created with the highest resolution and sharpest, fullest color. Tonal range and color corrections are less effective with low-resolution images.

Choose Adjust Backlighting from the Enhance menu to open the Adjust Backlighting dialog box. Figure 11.5 shows the image before the Adjust Backlighting Tool has been applied to it. In this image the background sky is a little too bright. Figure 11.6 previews the same image with the Adjust Backlighting setting applied to it. Adjust the slider control and choose a value between 0 to 100. Then click OK to save your changes. View the modified image in the active image window.

Figure 11.5
Bright background images can cause the foreground image to become underexposed.

237

Figure 11.6
Decreasing the amount of backlight dims the background image, neutralizing the overall image.

Using the Histogram with Tonal Range Tools

Each scanned or photographed image contains thousands of pixels, each capable of representing a million possible colors. You can modify an image by choosing a pixel's physical (x and y axis) location in an image, or by selecting and modifying colors. However, you can also modify an image's tonal range. The tonal range of an image represents how many pixels are distributed across each red, green, and blue channel in an image. Photoshop Elements provides the histogram to enable you to view how pixels share a particular tonal value in an image. You can use the Levels command to modify the tonal range settings in an image.

Tonal Range and the Histogram

A histogram shows you how many pixels exist in its y axis, with each possible shade between 0 and 255 represented along its x axis. Although it's possible for an image to look fine if true blacks or whites are missing from the histogram, images that appear over- or underexposed to the naked eye are usually missing pixels in the shadow or highlight regions of the histogram. You can find the black and white point in an image by locating the darkest and whitest areas of the image. The color that most closely matches black will be the black point for the image, and the closest white color will be the white point.

Photoshop Elements enables you to view the red, green, blue, and luminosity information for an RGB image using a histogram. The histogram is also used as a part of the Levels and Threshold color-correction commands. You can use these tools to view and remap the tonal distribution of pixels in an image. Each red, green, and blue channel stores different kinds of image information. For example, you are likely to find warmer colors, such as red and orange, in the red channel of an RGB image (see Figure 11.7).

note
Most of the images you'll be working with in Photoshop Elements use the RGB color mode and color space. If an image is in RGB mode, you will see the letters RGB in parentheses following the name of the image in the title bar of the image window. Photoshop Elements opens an image file in RGB color mode by default.

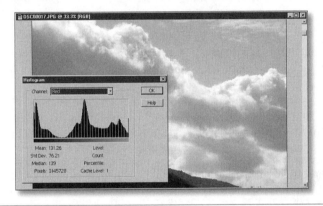

Figure 11.7
Although there are a couple of spikes, pixels are somewhat evenly distributed across the red area of the histogram. The single row of gray banding indicates pixels have been removed from the image. The absence of pixels in the left and top right of the image indicate there are more pixels in the midtone and high-light range of the image.

Open a color image in RGB color mode, and then choose Histogram from the Image menu to open the Histogram dialog box. Select a channel from the Channel drop-down menu if you want to view the histogram for a particular red, green, blue, or luminosity channel in the image. The following list describes the various information you can get by looking at the image's histogram:

* The values representing the Mean (average intensity value), Standard Deviation (difference in variance of intensity values), Median (the middle value for the range of intensity values), and

239

the total number of pixels in the image appear in the left column of the Histogram window.

- The Cache Level appears at the bottom of the right column of the dialog box. This setting can be changed by selecting the "Use cache for histograms" check box, located in the [Memory & Image Cache] (Image Cache) Preferences dialog box. If this check box is checked, the histogram information will sample the data using a faster algorithm. Instead of displaying actual pixel information, the cached histogram will display pixel values based on a representative sampling of pixels in the image.

- Move the cursor over the black areas of the histogram to view the level (intensity level), percentile (compares the number of pixels in the selected level with the rest of the pixels in the image), and pixel count (for the selected level) of the selected channel. The levels, percentile, and pixels values change as you move the cursor over the histogram. The black areas of the histogram represent pixels in that tonal range.

note

If you're working with a grayscale image, the histogram window will display the tonal range for the gray channel: 254 shades of gray, plus white and black. The gray channel is the only channel in a grayscale image.

Bands in the Histogram

If you see regular intervals of missing pixels in the histogram window, this usually indicates the image has been modified. Each time a tool, such as the Brightness/Contrast Tool, modifies an image, pixels are removed linearly from the image. For example, apply the Auto Levels or Auto Contrast commands to an image. Then open the histogram window. The banding that appears in the red, green, and blue histograms confirms pixels have been removed from the image.

Pixels that characterize the sharpness of an image, as well as pixels that contain contrast, tend to be stored in the green channel (see Figure 11.8). When viewing a histogram, more pixels in a particular tonal range appear as a higher bar in the histogram window. Areas with more pixels are the darker areas of the image. Areas of the histogram containing no pixels signify that no data exists for that tonal range in the image. Click and drag the cursor in the histogram if you want to view Count and Percentile data for a group of levels in a channel.

Figure 11.8
View the tonal distribution of grays that represent the green channel in an RGB image by choosing the Green menu item in the Histogram window.

The blue channel tends to store blurrier, garbage aspects of an image (see Figure 11.9). Because the blurrier, distorted artifacts in an image tend to reside in the blue channel of an image, you might be able to more easily identify an area of an image that needs more work by viewing the contents of the blue channel in the image window. You may want to identify where most of the pixels are distributed in the image when you view the pixel distribution of the blue channel in the histogram. Cleaning up or removing blurry elements in an image may improve the overall picture.

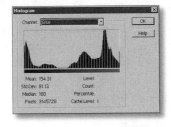

Figure 11.9
You can view the pixel distribution for the blue channel of an RGB image in the blue histogram window.

Although the RGB channels combine to make a 24-bit image, a digital image actually consists of 32 bits of data. The remaining 8 bits of information define luminosity, or the tonal distribution of light in an image (see Figure 11.10). You can view the luminosity levels of an image in the Histogram dialog box. Zero represents black, and 255 represents white. The luminosity histogram represents the tonal

note
Luminosity is visible only in a color image.

range distribution of the pixels in an image as if it were in grayscale mode. When you modify colors or tonal ranges in an RGB image, the luminosity of the image also changes. You can use the luminosity histogram to see how many pixels are distributed in the shadows and highlights of an image and determine whether any true black or white image data exists.

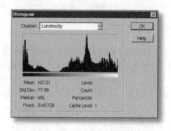

Figure 11.10
View the pixel distribution for light-related elements in the Luminosity histogram.

Adjusting Tonal Range with the Levels Tool

note
The Auto Levels command is a quickie version of the Levels command. It redistributes the midtone-range pixels for each channel in an RGB image.

You can make permanent changes to a layer by choosing Levels from the Enhance, Brightness/Contrast menu. However, in most cases, it's more efficient to create a Levels adjustment layer so that you can adjust the tonal range of all or each channel in an RGB image without altering any of the original pixels in the image. Choose Levels from the Layer, New Adjustment Layer menu. The New Layer dialog box opens. Type a name for the new layer, click on OK, and the Levels dialog box will open.

Finding Black and White Points

If you cannot visually identify a black or white color in an image, you can use the Levels dialog box to find them. Defining the black and white points in an image will help you adjust the tonal range settings for an image.

First, open an image in the work area. Adjust the size of the image so that the full image is viewable in the work area. Then choose Levels from the Layer, New Adjustment Layer menu. The New Layer window opens. Type a name for the Levels layer into the Name text box, and then click OK. The Levels dialog box will open. This new layer will affect only the layers below it. If you want the changes in the adjustment layer to affect all layers in the image, move it to the top of the Layers palette.

View the histogram of the tonal distribution of pixels for the image. Hold down the (Option) [Alt] key and then click and drag the left (black color) arrow-shaped slider control to the right until you see the first shades of black appear in the image. Note the number in the left Input Levels text box. This number represents the black point of the image. Observe the location of the black point in the image.

To find the white point of the image, hold down the (Option) [Alt] key and click on the arrow-shaped sliding control on the right, below the histogram. Move the slider control toward the left end of the histogram. Look for the first appearance of the color white to appear as you move the slider from the right end of the histogram to the left. The first white pixels to appear represent the white point of the image. Note the number in the right Input Levels text box. The input levels will automatically change as you move the triangle slider controls located below the histogram.

You can use the black point and white point values to set, remap, and preview the shadow and highlight values for the image in the Levels dialog box. You can use the level controls to correct areas of an image that may be too light or too dark.

Upon first glance, the Levels dialog box looks like a treasure trove of slider controls, text boxes, eyedropper tools, and buttons. What it's really showing you is the input and output information of the selected pixels in the image window. You can perform tonal corrections to all channels by choosing RGB from the drop-down menu. Perform more precise contrast adjustment by modifying each red, green, or blue channel, one at a time. Choose the channel you want to view from the Channel drop-down menu.

The input and output level controls enable you to remap the way pixels are distributed in an image by increasing or decreasing the amount of contrast in the image. These controls can help you to correct over-exposed or under-exposed images. The input levels of the shadows, midtones, and highlights are shown in the Input Levels text boxes. The histogram displays how pixels are distributed across the tonal levels in the image. Notice the three triangle-shaped sliding controls located at the bottom of the histogram. As you move each control toward the middle of the histogram, the amount of contrast in the image increases.

- The black triangle on the left, below the histogram, represents the shadow input slider. You can move the black triangle icon to change the zero value of the input level of the image.

- The white triangle on the right represents the highlight. You can move it to change the white, or 255, value of the input level of the image.

- The gray triangle in the middle of the histogram represents the midtone, or gamma, pixels in the image. You can adjust the lightness or darkness of the midtones without affecting the darkest or lightest tones in an image.

You can change the value of the shadows, midtones, and highlights independently. This means that if you change the pixels in the shadow tonal range of an image, the pixels in the midtones and highlights will not be modified or removed from the image. Moving the black and white slider controls toward the middle of the histogram will increase the contrast of the active image.

Figure 11.11 shows the selected image after adjusting the shadow and highlight input settings in the Levels dialog box. The selected image shows more contrast after the black and white points for the selected pixels are remapped to match the selection's pixel distribution. By decreasing the highlight input level from 255 to 169, the Levels command redistributes the pixels in the image so that all the pixels between 169 and 255 are changed to white, or 255, and the pixels between the midtone, or gamma, setting are redistributed using 169 as the new highlight value of 255.

Figure 11.11
Adjust the highlight and midpoints to lighten the selected item in the picture.

Output level information is located at the bottom of the Levels dialog box. A grayscale gradient represents the 0 to 255 range of output settings for the image. You can move the black or white slider toward the middle of the grayscale bar to change the output level settings.

Moving the left output slider toward the middle of the histogram will lighten, or neutralize, the darker pixels in the image. Conversely, moving the right output slider to the left will darken the highlight pixels in the image. The output level settings can be used to remap any adjustments to the input level settings made in the Levels dialog box.

You can set the target color for the highlights, midtones, and shadows using the eyedropper tools in the Levels dialog box. Use the eyedropper tools to manually set these values, or click on the Auto button to let Photoshop Elements reset these values. The following steps show you how to manually pick the black, white, and gray points in an image using the Levels dialog box controls:

1. Choose the Eyedropper Tool from the Toolbox. Then, choose a Sample Size from the options bar. Adjust the Eyedropper Tool in the toolbox so that it can sample a portion of the image that's at least three by three pixels. Then set the image window to view the image at 100%.

2. Open the Info palette in the work area. Then open the Levels dialog box. Move the Eyedropper Tool around the image and try to identify x and y coordinates in the image that are good examples of highlights, midtones, and shadows in the image window. Note the RGB color values for the image areas you want to use to sample highlight, midtones, and shadow values for the image.

3. Double-click on the Set White Point eyedropper button in the Levels dialog box. The Color Picker window will open. Input the color values you want to use for the highlight color. For an RGB image, a good highlight color might consist of the RGB values of 244, 244, and 244.

note
The Auto Levels and Auto Contrast commands redistribute tonal range values in between the shadow and highlight settings. They attempt to correct any extreme dark or light areas in an image.

4. Double-click on the Set Gray Point eyedropper button in the Levels dialog box. The Color Picker window will open. Type in the value for the midpoint color you want to use. Enter equal values for red, green, and blue to set the midtone values for an RGB image.

5. Follow the steps for setting the white and gray points using the Black Point Eyedropper Tool. Some sample RGB values for shadows might be 10, 10, and 10.

Changing Colors with Color Effect Tools

If you explore the Image menu, you'll find several commands in the Image, Adjustments menu. The Equalize, Gradient Map, Invert, Posterize, and Threshold commands each have a unique way of changing the brightness and color values in an image. These commands are most commonly used to create image effects, but occasionally can help correct color in an image. Each of the examples in this section uses the image shown in Figure 11.12.

Figure 11.12
This purple orchid may have too much detail for some print media. Experiment with some of the tonal range tools to simplify the image.

Equalizing an Image

Adjust the brightness of an image using the Equalize command. This command uses the lightest and darkest levels in an image to define the white and black points of the image. All the in-between values are evenly distributed so that the brightness values of the overall image are, well, equalized. Figure 11.13 shows the results of applying the Equalize command to the image window.

Figure 11.13
Redistribute the brightness levels in an image by applying the Equalize Tool.

Changing an Image with Gradient Maps

You can apply the Gradient Map command to apply a map of colors to an image. Choose from a range of color or grayscale gradient maps from the Gradient Map window, or create your own in the Gradient Editor window. The Gradient Map command has similar controls to the Gradient command. You can select a gradient by clicking on the right edge of the gradient in the Gradient Map window. Double-click on the gradient to open the Gradient Editor window.

A Gradient consists of at least two colors. The Gradient Map connects highlights to one of the endpoints of the gradient, and the shadows to the opposing endpoint. Midtones are distributed across the in-between colors in the gradient. Figure 11.14 shows the Gradient Map dialog box, and the resulting grayscale image.

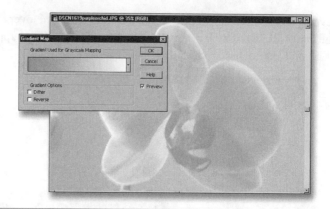

Figure 11.14
Map a grayscale gradient to an image by applying the Gradient Map Tool to an image.

Inverting the Colors in an Image

If you're working with a color image, the Invert command will replace the current color with its complementary color from the color wheel. Figure CS.6 in the color section, for example, shows that if you invert a purple orchid, it becomes green. Grayscale images invert black with white, and darker shades of gray with lighter shades of gray.

Posterizing an Image

The Posterize command enables you to reduce the number of colors in an image. The command remaps the image data in each channel of an RGB image to the number of levels of brightness input into the Posterize window. For example, if you define four levels for the image, 12 total colors—four each for red, green, and blue—will be used to create the posterized image. The resulting image probably will lack the clarity of the original. However, the hue and saturation settings are preserved.

Choose the Posterize command from the Image, Adjustments menu to open the Posterize dialog box. You can set the number of brightness levels, which are also called the tonal levels, of the resulting image. The Posterize dialog box is shown in Figure 11.15. The number you type into the Levels text box is applied to each channel in the image to determine the total number of colors used in the final image.

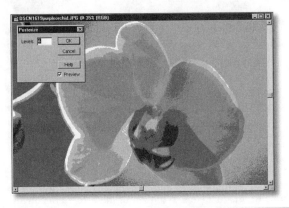

Figure 11.15
Set the number of brightness levels with the Posterize Tool. This command remaps colors to the closest matching level, or reduces the number of gray levels in a grayscale image.

The Posterize command can help simplify an image for low-resolution printing. For example, if you have to print an image with a limited number of colors, you can experiment with different values in the Posterize dialog box until you find the right combination of colors that best matches the resolution of the printer.

Adjusting an Image's Threshold

The Threshold command remaps colors to black and white in an image. Colors that are lighter than the threshold setting change to white, and those that are darker change to black. That's probably why this command is great for finding the black-and-white points in an image. The histogram in the Threshold dialog box displays the pixel distribution of 255 grayscale shades in the overall image. The arrow control located at the bottom of the Threshold dialog box, shown in Figure 11.16, determines which pixels are changed to black or white. The numeric value for the Threshold appears in the text box at the top of the window.

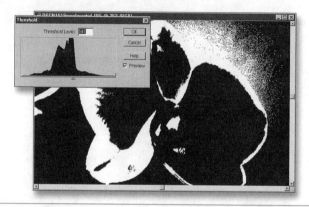

Figure 11.16
The Threshold command enables you to adjust the black-and-white contrast in a grayscale or color image. Pixels to the left of the arrow are converted to black, and pixels on the right to white.

Replacing Colors

Most of the color-correction tools mentioned previously involve tools and commands based on the concept of a color wheel. These tools rely on the color wheel, or Color Picker, to change all the colors in an image. You can type in a color value or move a slider control to select a new color. The Replace Color command works similarly, but enables you to target specific pixels. You can add or subtract pixels to add or remove colors that you might want to replace in the image window. The following sections show you how.

Preparing the Image

Before choosing the Replace Color command, open an image and adjust the Levels and Brightness and Contrast settings. Figure 11.17 shows the Levels command applied to the image that demonstrates how the Replace Color command works. As an alternative, you also can choose the Auto Levels and Auto Contrast commands to see whether any highlights or shadows become neutralized.

Figure 11.17
Before correcting the color, look at the highlights and shadows in the image to
see whether it needs tonal range corrections.

Because the amount of visible color is dependent on light, you might
want to adjust the highlights, shadows, or midtones in the Levels
dialog box and see whether changing these settings reduces any
extreme light or dark areas in the image.

Next, take a closer look at the image and look for any brightly lit
areas that, for example, might be created due to reflected light from
a flash or direct sunlight. Choose Brightness/Contrast from the
Enhance menu to open the Brightness/Contrast dialog box. Move
the Brightness slider control to the left to darken the image, or to
the right to add more light. The contrast slider control will reduce
highlight and shadows in an image as you move it to the left, and
increase these levels if moved to the right.

Replacing Colors

You can replace colors in an image. First, choose a selection tool and
highlight part of the image in which you want to replace colors.
Next, choose Replace Colors from the Enhance, Colors menu. The
Replace Colors dialog box opens. Figure 11.18 shows a set of pixels
that will interact with the Replace Colors settings. Click on the color
square (where it says Sample), and then choose a color from the
Color Picker dialog box to define the replacement color. Check
the Preview check box to view the replacement color in the image
window.

Figure 11.18
Use the Add to Sample and Subtract from Sample Eyedropper Tools to select or deselect the colors you want to replace.

To replace a color in the image, click on the Eyedropper Tool in the Replace Color window. Then, click on a color in the preview image located in the Replace Color window. Move the Hue, Saturation, and Lightness controls to choose the replacement color. The replacement color can replace more than one color in the image window. Check the Preview check box to preview your changes in the image window.

Choose the Add to Sample (with the plus [+] sign) Eyedropper Tool in the Replace Color window if you want to include an additional color to replace. Then, adjust the hue, saturation, or lightness settings to change the selected colors to the color of your choice.

tip
Double-click the Hand Tool in the toolbox to view the full image within the image window.

If you select a color you don't want to include, choose the Subtract from Sample Eyedropper (the eyedropper tool with the [-] sign), and then click on the color you want to remove from the image window. Figure 11.18 shows how the colors in the image window are replaced after using the eyedropper tools to define which colors should be replaced. After you have replaced the colors in the image, choose Deselect from the Select menu, and then save the image to your hard drive.

Correcting Color Cast

The Color Cast command is another color correction command located in the Enhance, Color menu. If you've scanned a photo that has an all-over color tint, you can use the Color Cast command to correct it. The Color Cast command uses an eyedropper tool to enable you to choose the gray, white, and black colors in an image. The Color Cast Correction dialog box appears in Figure 11.19. The tough part is trying to determine which colors to use to define white, gray, and black.

Figure 11.19
Click on a gray, white, and black area of an image to adjust the color cast.

Click once on a black color. Then click on a white, and then gray color in the image window. You should see the tint of the image change after the third click of the eyedropper in the image window. Don't be surprised if the color cast doesn't give you the results you expect. Click on the Reset button to revert the image to its original, incorrectly tinted state. Then, click on the white, gray, and black colors of the image to see whether the color cast changes provide more accurate results.

Removing Color from an Image

You can remove all the color from an image, or use a selection tool to remove color from a selected part of an image, as shown in Figure 11.20. This command highlights a color element in a photo, or de-emphasizes an object by making it a grayscale image.

note
After previewing the replacement color, you can click and drag the slider controls to change the hue, saturation, and lightness to choose the replacement color. Click and drag the Fuzziness slider to experiment with how the replacement color integrates with the other colors in the image window. The Fuzziness slider affects the range of colors that will be included in the color mask in the image. The higher the fuzziness value, the smoother the edges of the mask will become when the color change is applied to the image.

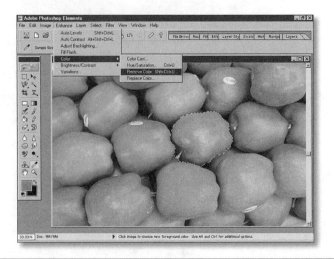

Figure 11.20
Remove the color in a selected area of an image with the Remove Color command.

Choose Remove Color from the Enhance, Color menu. If you're working with a large image, or a relatively slow computer, you might see a progress bar appear at the bottom of the image window. Photoshop Elements will remove all color from the image. When the color is gone and the image is saved to your hard drive, there is no way to restore it.

Grayscale Image Mode

An alternative way to remove color from an RGB or Indexed Color image is to choose Grayscale from the Image, Mode menu. A dialog box will appear asking you whether you want to discard color information. Click OK to remove the color, or choose Cancel if you do not want to remove it.

Changing the color mode from color to grayscale will remove all color information from the image. Don't worry; as long as you don't close the image window, you can press (Command-Z) [Ctrl+Z] to undo the color removal. If you close the image window and save the image file, you cannot restore any color information.

Introducing Color-Correction Tools

After you've checked and, if needed, adjusted the tonal range of the image you're working on, you can start to explore using the color-correction tools. Like the selection tools, you'll find some of the color-correction tools stored in the toolbox, and others in the form of menu commands.

The Red Eye Brush Tool is probably the most obvious color-correction tool in the toolbox. Of course, the Eyedropper, Paint Bucket, and Eraser Tools can also technically be grouped with color-correction tools. However, these tools are explained in more detail in the previous chapter, "Digital Images and Color." The majority of the color-correction tools are found in the Enhance, Color menu. The Color Cast, Hue/Saturation, Replace Color, and Remove Color commands enable you to correct your colors. The Variations command is perhaps the most versatile color-correction tool. You can use it to correct highlights, midtones, and shadows, as well as the saturation. The following list summarizes what each of these color-correction tools can do.

- **Red Eye Brush**—You can use this tool to remove red-eye from your photo subjects. Select a target and replacement color for this tool from the options bar. The target color will be the red eye in the image, and the replacement color will be the natural eye color for the photo subject. Choose a brush size and apply it to the red-eye pixels in the image window to apply the correct color to the image.

- **Dodge**—The icon for this tool looks like a lollipop. Use the settings in the options bar to work with highlight, midtone, or shadow tones of an image. Applying this tool to pixels will lighten their tone.

- **Burn**—Located with the Dodge Tool in the toolbox, this tool will darken the highlight, midtone, or shadow tones of the pixels in an image. The hand icon for this tool appears to be pinching something.

- **Hue/Saturation**—Adjust the color, gray level mixture with color, and lightness values by moving the slider controls in the Hue/Saturation dialog box.

- **Variations**—Open the Variations dialog box to preview color correction options for the active image window. Click on a thumbnail image to change the highlights, midtones, shadows, and saturation of color in an image. Compare the original with the current, modified image and decide whether you want to keep the changes made to the image.

- **Replace Color**—Select one or more colors to replace in an image window by choosing this command. Use the Eyedropper Tool to define the initial color to be replaced, and then modify your settings with the plus and minus eyedropper tools. Change the Hue, Saturation, and Lightness settings for the image to define the replacement color for the active image area.

- **Remove Color**—Performs the same feat as choosing Grayscale from the Image, Mode menu. All color information is removed from all or part of an image.

- **Color Cast**—Change the black, white, and gray points of an image by clicking in gray, white, and black areas in an image. This tool enables you to remap the way colors are mapped to an image based on the colors you want to use to define black, white, or gray.

Adjusting Hue and Saturation Settings

The Hue, Saturation, and Brightness (HSB) or Hue, Lightness, and Saturation (HLS) color model uses three settings to define color. Hue represents one of 360 possible colors on a color wheel. The lightness, or brightness, level can be a value between 0%, or black, and 100%, which is white, or full illumination. The saturation level also ranges from 0 to 100%. 0% represents the full gray, or mid-tones, of a color, and 100% represents the full nongray-containing color value.

You can customize the hue, saturation, and lightness of an image to intensify the color of an image (see Figure 11.21 and CS.7 in the color section). Choose the Hue/Saturation command from the Enhance, Colors menu. The Hue/Saturation dialog box, shown in Figure 11.22 (CS.8 in the color section), contains a slider control for hue, saturation, and lightness settings for all channels combined in an RGB image, or each individual channel in an image.

Figure 11.21
This image contains reds, greens, and blues with both strong highlights and strong shadows. You can use the Hue/Saturation window to make the colors show more blue and red by increasing the saturation level of the image.

The Hue settings, shown in Figure 11.22 (CS.8), can change a green color into blue or turn orange to red. The hue slider control represents the full spectrum of colors on the color wheel. You can change the color values in the image window by moving the slider control to the left or right. Click and drag the slider control and preview the colors in the image window. Wait until the colors in the image change to match another photo, or until the colors look accurate to your eyes.

Figure 11.22
Use the master settings in the Hue/Saturation window to adjust the colors in the image window.

The Saturation and Lightness controls work similarly to the Hue control. Drag the slider control to change the setting. As you move the saturation control to the left, the image should become grayer. As you move it to the right, the colors in the image should stand out, as any shades of gray dissipate. If you want to correct an image by bringing out the blue color in a sky, or a red color in a dress, select the item with which you want to work in the image window. Then move the Saturation setting to the right of the slider to see whether the corrected color meets your needs.

The Lightness control adjusts the shadows and highlights in the image. Zero is the center point value for this setting. Moving the slider control to the left darkens the image, whereas moving it to the right brightens it.

Customizing Channel Hue and Saturation

You can also adjust the color ranges for red, green, blue, cyan, yellow, and magenta. Notice the three color bars located at the bottom of the Hue/Saturation window. Choose one of the colors from the Edit drop-down menu to view the color range. Figure 11.23 shows a modified red color range.

The range of the adjustment slider represents two settings for the selected color, shown in Figure 11.18. The middle area of the slider represents the range of the color. The areas to the left and right of the middle represent the falloff range for that color. Although it's not likely you'll use this method to correct a color, you might want to experiment with these settings to see how color changes when the hue or saturations color ranges are changed.

tip

An alternative to choosing Hue/Saturation from the Enhance/Color menu is to create an adjustment layer. Choose Hue/Saturation from the Layer, New Adjustment Layer menu to add a modifiable Hue/Saturation layer to the image. You can hide or show the Hue/Saturation settings by clicking on the eye icon for this adjustment layer in the Layers palette.

Figure 11.23
Customize the range and falloff settings for a color in the Hue/Saturation
window.

Color Bar Shortcut

Hold down the (Command) [Ctrl] key, and then click and drag the cursor to the left or right in the color bar area of the color bars in the
Hue/Saturation window. The cursor will change from an arrow to a
hand icon when you click on either one of the color bars in the Hue/
Saturation window. The colors will scroll off the right and reappear on
the left end of the color bar. You can use this shortcut to change the
color that appears in the middle of the color bar.

Correcting Colors with the Red Eye Brush Tool

Most digital cameras automatically activate a flash if the light levels
are too low. If you're taking a picture of a person or pet, the brightness of the flash may bounce off the back of the person's eye before
their eyes can adjust to the bright light. This causes the familiar "red
eye" you often see in photos.

Some digital cameras have red eye reduction flashes. These flashes
actually flash twice. The first time, the flash is a brief one, allowing
the iris to contract before the second, brighter flash occurs when the
camera captures the picture.

You can apply the Red Eye Brush Tool to scanned photos or digital
pictures to take care of any red-eye problems. The Red Eye Brush
Tool enables you to select the colors you want to replace, and then
apply the brush to the red areas of the eye. Figure 11.24 shows how
red eye can add a spooky look to the photo's subject.

259

Figure 11.24
Red eye occurs when the flash bounces off the retina before the eyes can adjust to the brightness of the flash. This is a common result with photos taken with a flash.

The following steps show you how to apply the Red Brush Tool to correct red eye in the active image window:

1. Open an image in the work area, and then select the Red Eye Brush Tool from the toolbox.

2. Click in the options bar, shown in Figure 11.25, to select a brush size. I recommend using a soft-edge brush, not a hard-edge one.

Figure 11.25
Choose a replacement color and apply the Red Eye Brush Tool to correct the red eye.

3. Next, choose the color you want to remove by clicking in the red eye in the image window. The target color appears on the right end of the options bar.

4. Then choose a replacement color by clicking in the eye. You also can choose a different brush size from the options bar. Click on the Brush drop-down menu to view a list of brush options. You can load a new set of brushes by clicking on the right-arrow button located on the right side of the Brush option drop-down window. The number below each brush size indicates the number of pixels in that brush tip.

   In the default set of brushes, the first row of brush sizes are hard-edge brushes. These brushes will create a solid-color pixel edge when applied to the image window. The brush sizes in the second row are soft-edge brushes. The pixels on the edges of the soft-edge brushes will blend in with the colors of the surrounding pixels. Soft-edge brushes produce great results with the Red Eye Brush and Clone Stamp Tools.

   The tolerance setting, located in the options bar, enables you to define the range of the target color that's applied to the replacement color. A higher value replaces a wider range of colors.

   The Sampling drop-down menu, located in the options bar, consists of two options: First Click, and Current Color. The default setting is First Click. Simply click on the red-eye color in the image window to pick the target color. Choose Current Color if you want to select a custom target color. Click on the Current color square in the options bar to select a new target color.

5. Drag the tool over the red-eye area in the image window to replace any colors that match the red, or target, color with the replacement color.

If you don't like the results, choose the Undo command from the Edit menu, or click on a previous action in the History palette to revert the document to a previous state before the Red Eye Tool was applied to the image.

Color-Correction Variations

The Variations command is probably the easiest color correction tool you can use in Photoshop Elements. A different set of options is available for grayscale versus color images. However, both enable you to preview changes in a thumbnail window without sacrificing the original image.

The following sections show you how to correct the color of an image taken in low light using the tools in the Variations dialog box.

Grayscale Variations Options

note
You can adjust the intensity of the color or grayscale variations in the Variations window by moving the Finer/Coarser slider control. Variations will be more subtle as you move the slider control toward the Finer settings, and colors or grays will change more dramatically as you move the slider to the right, toward the Coarser settings.

Although you'll probably want to work with a color image with the Variations command, you can work with a smaller set of variations settings with a grayscale image. You can change a color image into a grayscale image by choosing the Remove Color command from the Enhance, Color menu. If the image is in RGB or Indexed Color mode, you can choose Grayscale from the Image, Mode menu to remove the color from the image. After you have the active image window set to grayscale, choose Variations from the Enhance menu to view the grayscale options in the Variations window.

If you've opened an image that does not have any color information, you'll have fewer options to work with in the Variations dialog box, shown in Figure 11.26. Click on a thumbnail above the original image to lighten the image, or click on one of the images at the bottom of the window to darken the image. Compare your change to the original image located in the upper-left corner of the Variations window. Click and drag the slider control to choose how fine or coarse you want the changes to be.

Color Variations Options

If you've opened a color image in RGB mode, you can correct color for highlight, midtones, shadows, or saturation levels in the image using the Variations command. Choose Variations from the Enhance menu to open the Variations dialog box, shown in Figure 11.27. Then click on a radio button to choose highlight, midtones, shadow, or saturation. The Midtones radio button is selected by default.

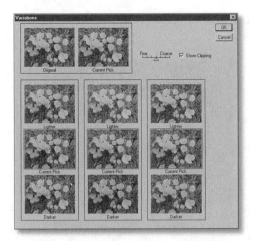

Figure 11.26
You have only a few variations when tweaking grayscale images.

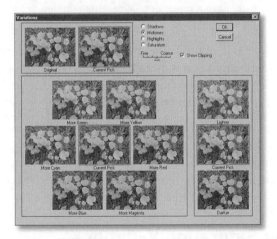

Figure 11.27
You can adjust tonal range and color settings by clicking in a thumbnail setting in the Variations dialog box.

Warming Up an Image with Midtones

Highlights, midtones, and shadows thumbnails enable you to preview the image if red, green, blue, or cyan, yellow, or magenta hues were applied to it, as shown in Figure 11.28. Click on a thumbnail image to change the color of the original image. Compare the

263

change in the Current Pick thumbnail image located at the top of the window.

Figure 11.28
Low-light shots can be taken indoors or outdoors during dusk or evening hours. These images usually have a green or blue cast in them due to the light from a tungsten or fluorescent bulb.

On the right side of the Variations window, you can click on the lighter thumbnail if you want to increase the brightness of the image. Alternatively, you can click on the darker thumbnail image if you want to decrease the brightness of the image.

In Figure 11.29, I clicked on the More Red and then on the More Magenta thumbnail images to add warmer colors to the image. Because this image was taken in low light, and the pumpkin is already orange, the color correction seems to only affect the skin tones and reflected light in the image.

Modifying Saturation Variations

You can click on the Saturation radio button to adjust the gray levels with the Variations window. Click on the Less Saturation thumbnail image to increase the amount of gray mixed with the colors in the image. Clicking on the More Saturation thumbnail adds more color to the image.

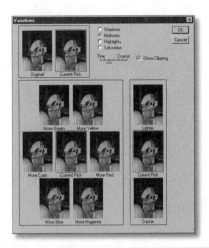

Figure 11.29
Adjust the colors in the midtones of the image. In this example, I chose the
More Red and More Magenta options to add warmer colors to the picture.

The settings in the Variations dialog box don't work exactly the same
as when you're applying color-correction tools directly to the image
window. For example, the Undo command won't work in the
Variations dialog box. However, you can undo all the changes created by the Variations dialog box when you're in the work area. If
you're experimenting with color correction, you might want to make
small changes to allow yourself to become familiar with how the colors in the image interact with different color-correction settings in
the Variations dialog box. Then, save a copy of the different color
variations to your hard drive if you want to compare them side by
side on your desktop.

Applying Filters and Effects

Applying a filter or effect to an RGB or Gray-scale image is as easy as dragging and dropping a filter or effect into an image window. Filters and effects enable you to correct, destruct, or apply an artistic pattern to an image. You can view or choose filters from the Filter menu. Better yet, you can preview each filter and effect from the Filters or Effects palettes.

Previewing Filters and Effects

The Filters and Effects palettes enable you to view available filters or effects in List or Thumbnail view (see Figure 12.1). You can get a pretty good idea of how each filter and effect will change an image by taking a look at the thumbnail image for each one. Each thumbnail image represents how the image might look if you apply that filter or effect to it. In List view, you can preview a filter if you click the name of the filter in the list. The thumbnail image can be viewed for the original and selected filter or effect in List view.

Thumbnail view enables you to see each filter as it will be applied to a sample image. The name of each filter or effect appears below each thumbnail image, and an original thumbnail appears in the top corner of the palette. Filters can be organized in the palette windows as they appear in the Filter menu, or you can view all of them at once in the palette window. You can view or choose a group of filters or effects from the drop-down menu list, located at the top of the palette window. Choose All to view all groups in the palette window.

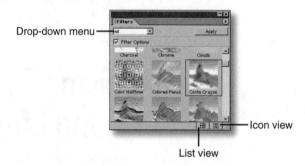

Figure 12.1
Click one of the view icons in the Filters or Effects palettes to view filters or effects in list or icon view.

Filters Versus Effects

Filters and effects enable you to modify images with special effects. So why use two terms to describe special effects?

Filters represent individual effects. When you choose a filter from the Filters palette or Filter menu, you apply one filter to the image. Some filters enable you to customize one or more settings to create customizable effects. Effects, on the other hand, run a preconfigured set of filters. You can take the resulting effect as-is or reject it.

Effects are accessible only from the Effects palette, and most involve applying multiple filters to an image. Some effects require a text or selected object in the image window before you can apply it.

Introducing Filters

Filters enable you to apply special effects to images. In order for a filter to work, there must be a visible image in the image window, or the equivalent of an active layer in the Layers palette. The image must also be in RGB or Grayscale mode before you can apply a filter. You can preview or apply a filter from the Filter menu or Filters palette (see Figure 12.2). Some filters analyze the pixel color or tonal range of an image to manipulate the appearance of the images, while other filters apply an arbitrary change based on the proximity of each pixel in the image.

Figure 12.2
Preview each feature in the Filters palette. Drag and drop a filter into the image window to apply it to an image.

A dialog box might open when you choose a filter command from the Filter menu or Filters palette, enabling you to customize settings for that filter. The Filter dialog box contains a thumbnail-size preview window, enabling you to view the filter's effect on the image before you actually apply the selected settings. You must view or adjust these settings and choose OK before the filter can be applied to the image. After a filter has been applied to an image, that filter command becomes selectable from the top of the Filter menu, or by pressing (Command+F) [Ctrl-F].

Adobe groups filters in categories, which you can view in the Filter menu or the Filters palette. Click on the drop-down menu located at the top of the Filters palette to view or choose the way the filters are grouped in the Filters palette. The Filter menu displays all installed filter plug-in files on your hard drive, grouped by category. The following list contains a brief description of each category of filters. In general, filters can correct, destruct, texturize, or add an artistic stroke to an image.

note
To find out more about color modes, go to Chapter 10, "Digital Images and Color."

note
Adobe installs all filters into the Filters folder and all effects into the Effects folder of the Plug-Ins folder in the Photoshop Elements folder on your hard drive.

- **Liquify**—The Liquify Tool actually consists of seven effect tools. Each effect can be applied with a brush stroke. To find out more about this filter tool, go to Chapter 17, "Creating Complex Images."

- **Artistic**—Each of these filters opens a window of customizable settings. Choose from Colored Pencil, Cutout, Dry Brush, Film Grain, Fresco, Neon Glow, Paint Daubs, Palette Knife, Plastic Wrap, Poster Edges, Rough Pastels, Smudge Stick, Sponge, Underpainting, and Watercolor.

- **Blur**—Smooth hard edges with up to six blur filters. Select one or combine the Blur, Blur More, Gaussian Blur, Motion Blur, Radial Blur, and Smart Blur filters.

- **Brush Strokes**—Change a photo into a drawing by applying one of these stroke filters to an image. Experiment with Accented Edges, Angled Strokes, Crosshatch, Dark Strokes, Ink Outlines, Spatter, Spray Strokes, or Sunrise. If you like these filters, you might also want to experiment with the Sketch filters.

- **Distort**—The filters in this group fall into the destructive category. Pixels from the original image are removed in order to create exaggerated effects such as Diffuse Glow, Glass, Ocean Ripple, Pinch, Polar Coordinates, Ripple, Shear, Spherize, Twirl, Wave, and ZigZag. If you choose the Distort group from the Filters palette, you can choose the Liquify filter. The Displace filter can be selected only from the Filter, Distort menu.

- **Noise**—Another group of destructive filters, these filters try to re-create many of the artifacts you'll try to remove from old, damaged photos in Chapter 15, "Repairing Images." Use Add Noise, Dust & Scratches, Despeckle, or the Median filters.

- **Pixelate**—This group of filters also removes pixels from the original image to create a Color Halftone, Crystallize, Facet, Fragment, Mezzotint, Mosaic, or Pointillize effect.

- **Render**—Most of the filters in this group replace the image in the image window. The 3D Transform effect has its own set of tools. It enables you to create a 3D object from some of the pixels in the image. The Clouds, Difference Clouds, and Lens Flare filters enable you to add custom elements to an image. If you click the Filter, Render menu, you can choose the Texture Fill filter. You can select a texture file on your hard drive that can be used to create a filter effect with the selected image in the active image window. The Lighting Effects filter enables you to change the lighting in an image. For more information about the Lighting Effects filter, go to Chapter 17.

- **Sharpen**—Sharpen filters try to create a clearer, crisper image by enhancing contrasting colors in an image. For most images, you might not notice a change in the image after applying the Sharpen, Sharpen Edges, or Sharpen More filters to an image. The Unsharp Mask filter is sort of an antisharpen filter. Although it is designed to add a slight blur to an image, it uses an algorithm designed to blend contrasting pixel colors closer together. This filter is commonly used to polish a multilayered, or composite digital image.

- **Sketch**—Yet another group of stroke-like filters, these can turn a photo into a drawing. Choose from Bas Relief, Chalk & Charcoal, Charcoal, Chrome, Conté Crayon, Graphic Pen, Halftone Pattern, Note Paper, Photocopy, Plaster, Reticulation, Stamp, Torn Edges, or Water Paper.

- **Stylize**—Diffuse, Emboss, Extrude, Find Edges, Solarize, or add Glowing Edges, Tiles, Wind, or Trace the Contours of an image with the filters in this group.

- **Texture**—Create special effects with a photo. Select from the Craquelure, Grain, Mosaic Tiles, Patchwork, Stained Glass, and Texturizer filters to turn a photo into a unique piece of art.

- **Video**—The De-Interlace and NTSC Colors filters can convert the colors in an image for use with a television. Television broadcasts each successive image using odd and even horizontal lines of the television screen. The De-Interlace filter can replace missing lines of an image captured from video. The NTSC filter adjusts the colors in an image to match a set of colors that are acceptable for television broadcast. This set of colors is designed to prevent oversaturated colors from bleeding into television scan lines.

- **Other**—Although the Dither Box, High Pass, Maximum, Minimum, and Offset filters are located in this menu, any third-party filters will also share this menu space.

- **Digimarc**—Choose the Read Watermark filter to check an image for the presence of a watermark. Watermarks are sometimes used to copyright an image. This filter is available only in the Filter menu.

You can adjust the size of the Filters palette by clicking and dragging the lower-right corner of the palette window. If the palette is in thumbnail view, the number of thumbnail images will increase or decrease to match the size of the palette window. The scroll controls along the right side of the window enable you to view or select any filter in the palette.

tip

You can install third-party Photoshop plug-ins and use them with Photoshop Elements. Installing filter plug-ins is similar to installing TWAIN plug-ins for Photoshop Elements. To find out more about how to install plug-in files, go to Chapter 5, "Scanning Images into Photoshop Elements."

Applying Multiple Filters

You can apply a filter more than once to an image. However, each filter alters the original pixels in an image. It is difficult to predict the resulting image after several filters have been applied to an image. The Preview window can help you visualize how the current filter will change the image.

When you place the cursor over the Preview area of the filter window, the cursor icon will change from an arrow to a hand. You can click and drag the cursor to move the viewable area of the image that appears in the preview window. Click on the minus (–) button to zoom out from the image. Or click on the plus (+) button to zoom into the image in the preview window.

If you're experimenting, you can use the Undo command to view the image before and after applying a filter.

Introducing Effects

Effects are similar to filters and often are the equivalent of applying a combination of filters in a particular sequence in order to produce a complex special effect. Like filters, you can preview each effect from the Effects palette (see Figure 12.3). However, you cannot customize each effect. You can only choose to keep it, or not. You'll also see a dialog box appear after applying an effect to an image. You'll be asked, "Do you want to keep this effect?". Click Yes if you want to keep the effect. Click No if you want to return to the original image. If you check the Don't Show Again check box, the effect will be applied and the dialog box will stop appearing after any effects are applied.

Figure 12.3
Preview the result of each effect by viewing each thumbnail image in the Effects palette.

Although you can find filters in the Filter menu, effects are only accessible from the Effects palette. The following list describes the categories of effects available from the Effects palette:

- **Frames**—Each of these effects adds a custom picture frame to the image in the image window. Some frames, such as the Cut Out, Recessed Frame, Text Panel, and Vignette effects, require you to use a selection tool to select the part of the image window to which you want to apply the effect. Choose from Brushed Aluminum Frame, Drop Shadow Frame, Foreground Color Frame, Photo Corners, Ripple Frame, Spatter Frame, Strokes Frame, Waves Frame, Wild Frame, or Wood Frame.

- **Textures**—Add a texture to an image. Select from Asphalt, Bricks, Cold Lava, Gold Sprinkles, Green Slime, Ink Blots (layer), Marbled Glass (layer), Molten Lead, Psychedelic Strings, Rusted Metal, Sandpaper, Sunset (gradient layer), Wood-Pine (layer), or Wood-Rosewood. Textures followed by (layer) indicate that a separate layer is created for that effect. You can adjust the transparency level of the layer to tweak the effect.

- **Text Effects**—Apply a special effect to a text object. Choose from Bold Outline, Brushed Metal, Cast Shadow, Clear Emboss, Confetti, Medium Outline, Running Water, Sprayed Stencil, Thin Outline, Water Reflection, or Wood Paneling.

- **Image Effects**—Each effect applies a set of filters to an image. Choose from Blizzard, Colorful Center, Fluorescent Chalk, Horizontal Color Fade, Lizard Skin, Neon Nights, Oil Pastel, Quadrant Colors, Soft Flat Color, Soft Focus, or Vertical Color Fade.

Undoing Effects

Because almost all effects involve resizing an image, pressing the Undo command will not undo an entire effect, only the last steps in the sequence of events for that effect. Consider increasing the number of Undo steps in the General Preferences window if you want to use the Undo command with effects. Type a higher number into the History States text box in the General Preferences window. You also can save a copy of the image with a unique filename before experimenting with any number of effects.

Each history state is stored in the History palette. As long as you don't save the image, you can click on a previous state in the History palette to undo a change in the active image window.

Click the Step Backward command in the toolbar to step through each filter or effect applied to the active image window. To redo each filter, click the Step Forward button in the toolbar. These buttons perform the same tasks as the Undo and Redo commands in the Edit menu.

Different Ways to Apply Filters and Effects

Filters and effects can be applied to the entire image, or to a selected area of pixels. You can apply a filter to an image in three primary ways. The easiest method is to drag and drop the thumbnail image of the filter or effect onto the image window. If there are multiple layers in the image window, a filter can be applied to an individual image layer. Figure 12.4 shows an image before a filter has been applied to it. Figure 12.5 shows the same image after the Gaussian Blur filter has been applied to selected areas of the image.

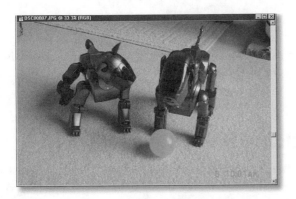

Figure 12.4
The first- and second-generation Aibo dogs before a filter is applied.

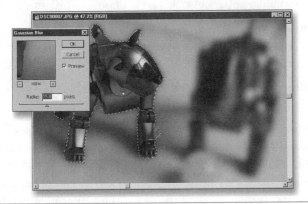

Figure 12.5
The Magnetic Lasso Tool selects one of the Aibo dogs. Choose the Invert Selection command to select everything except the dog. Then apply a filter to the selected area of the image. The Gaussian Blur filter was applied to the image in this figure.

You can double-click a filter or effect in the palette window, or click on a filter or effect, and then click the Apply button to apply an effect. The active image window will be the target of the filter or effect. If the filter has a dialog box, view the settings, and then click OK to dismiss the dialog box. Wait for the filter or effect to process the image. Then view the resulting special effect. Figure 12.4 shows the result of applying the Gaussian Blur filter.

Yet one more way to apply a filter is to choose a filter command from the Filter menu. The Filter menu enables you to view each filter in its category. This can help you quickly navigate different groups of filters although you won't have any idea how any of these filters will change the image.

Introducing Blur Filters

The Blur filters are helpful tools if you're trying to smooth rough areas of an image, reduce detail in an area of a picture, or if you want to hide information that you don't want to share with your picture-viewing audience. The following list contains a brief description of each of the blur filters installed with Photoshop Elements.

- **Blur**—Smooths transitions between colors by averaging the color of the pixels beside hard edges of color, defined lines, or shaded areas.

- **Blur More**—Increases the degree of the blur by three or four times.

- **Gaussian**—In simple terms, this filter blurs an image by enabling you to customize the range of pixels affected by the blur. When the Blur filter is applied to an image, Photoshop Elements gives each pixel a weight value and applies a blur based on the average value of the pixels. This filter increases low-frequency detail combined with the adjustable settings you select in the filter settings window to create a hazy blur on the image.

- **Motion**—Blur an image from –360 to +360°. You can also adjust the intensity of the blur from 1 to 999. Try applying this filter to a moving object in a photo. This filter gives the illusion of motion.

- **Smart**—Enables you to create a specific kind of blur by setting the radius of the blur, quality, threshold, and difference between pixels.

- **Radial**—Creates a circular directional blur. Adjust the radius and number of pixels to be blurred with the Radial Blur settings. Create spin, zoom, or specify a degree of radial blur with the radial blur filter.

Introducing Filter Effects with Toolbox Tools

In addition to the Filter menu and the Filters and Effects palettes, you can also apply a few filters as toolbox tools. Being able to apply a filter as a tool enables you to focus on an area that might be difficult to select and experiment with smudging, saturating, blurring, or sharpening it. Like menu or palette-based filters and effects, these toolbox tools can be applied only if an image is in RGB or Grayscale color mode. The following list contains a brief description of the filter tools available in the toolbox:

- **Smudge**—The Smudge Tool enables you to smear selected pixels in the direction of your brush stroke. You can customize the brush size, blending mode, pressure, and brush dynamics from the options bar. This tool can be applied across all layers of an image or to a single layer. Check the Finger Painting check box if you want to paint with the foreground color.

- **Sponge**—Choose desaturate or saturate blending mode, or a custom brush size, pressure, or brush dynamics for the tool from its options bar. Apply the Sponge Tool to adjust the saturation level of the pixels in an image.

- **Impressionist Brush**—Select a brush size and adjust its settings in the options panel. Applying this brush to an image will enlarge, blur, and mix the pixels as you move the brush around.

- **Blur**—Apply the Blur filter to an image using a preset brush size chosen in the options bar. This is a great alternative if you don't want to use a selection tool combined with a filter command to change a small area of an image. You can adjust the brush size, blending mode, pressure, and brush dynamics from the options bar. Check the Use All Layers check box if you want to apply the Blur Tool across all layers of the active image window. Uncheck this check box if you want to apply it to the selected layer in the Layers palette.

- **Sharpen**—Choose this tool to intensify the colors wherever you apply this filter using a particular brush size chosen from the options bar. This is a handy tool if you're curious to see whether the Sharpen filter will have any impact on sharpening a slightly blurry area of an image. Like the Blur Tool, you can adjust the brush size, blending mode, pressure, affected layers, or brush dynamics from the options bar.

Variations with Blur Filters

tip
You can apply a selection tool by clicking and dragging the cursor in the image window. The selected area will appear with a flashing dashed line surrounding its border.

If you miss part of the image with the selection tool, hold down the Shift key and select the overlapping area using the same or different selection tool. The original selection area will grow to include the overlapping selection area.

Filters can subdue or bring out areas of an image. For example, if you're creating screen shots of your computer settings for a manual, you might want to blur some of your personal information from the captured images. If you're preparing a photo for publication, you might want to blur elements of the photo that might distract from the main subject. The previous example shown in Figures 12.3 and 12.4 illustrated how the Gaussian Blur filter can highlight one element in a photo. The next example shows you how to selectively blur part of an image.

Using the Blur Filter to Emphasize Part of an Image

Choose one of the many selection tools available to select the area of the image you want to blur. In this example, I chose the Magnetic Lasso Tool to select shoes on the right side of Figure 12.6.

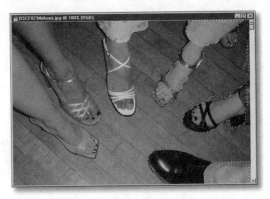

Figure 12.6
The before shot of the shoes.

Choose the Blur More filter from the Filters palette, or from the Filter menu. The selected area of the image should appear slightly blurry. The Blur More filter will appear at the top of the Filter menu, as shown in Figure 12.7. Choose the filter once more if you want to make the selected area more blurry.

Figure 12.7
When a filter is applied to the image window, it appears at the top of the Filter menu.

You can apply more than one kind of Blur filter to the selected area to create blur special effects. The Gaussian, Motion (see Figure 12.8), and Radial filters enable you to create directional blurs, which can make the original image pattern unrecognizable. Blurring part of an image can hide sensitive information, such as a license number or password, without taking away too much from the bigger picture you want to share with your Web viewers or readers.

Sharpen Filters

If you're impressed with the Blur filters, you might think the Sharpen filters can correct a blurry photo. Unfortunately it's easier to blur an image than to sharpen it. The Sharpen filters interpret the pixels in an image and try to increase the amount of color based on the local neighborhood of pixels. Depending on how blurry the original image is, the Sharpen filters might not be able to improve the clarity of an image. They're actually more likely to make an image look flatter, or make the edge of something in the image look harder, rather than softer.

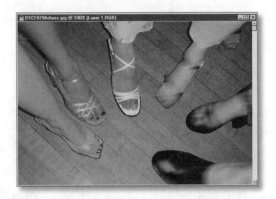

Figure 12.8
A motion blur applied to the selected area of the image makes the rest of the shoes in the picture stand out—no pun intended.

Polishing the Final Image with the Unsharp Mask

The Unsharp Mask filter is an unlikely but great tool for polishing an image before you save or print it. The Unsharp Mask filter looks for edge details in an image and makes the darker side of an edge darker, and the lighter side of an edge lighter. This filter can help sharpen an image as shown in the before and after shots seen in Figure 12.9.

Before

After

Figure 12.9
The Unsharp Mask filter being applied to an image. The original image is on the left, and the Motion-blurred, Unsharp-masked image is on the right.

A Helping Hand

You can click and drag the preview image in any of the filter settings windows. If you place the cursor over the image in the preview window, the cursor will change to a hand. Click and drag the cursor in the preview window to move the image. Click on the minus (–) button to zoom out from the image, and click on the plus (+) button to zoom into it.

If you have selected part of the image in the image window, move to the selected area to zoom into a particular area of pixels to which the filter might apply (see Figure 12.10). Adjust the settings for the filter and use the image in the preview window to optimize the filter effect. Then click OK to apply the filter to the image.

Figure 12.10
You can move the image in the filter window to preview specific areas of the image before you apply a filter to it.

Applying Artistic Filters

Although you'll find fifteen groups of filters in the Filter menu, there are two general groups of filters: those that enhance (or degrade) an image, and the kind that apply some sort of effect, such as a brush stroke or stained-glass window effect. The Blur and Sharpen filters are image-enhancing filters. This section explores some of the more artsy filters.

Applying an Artistic Filter to a Selection

The artistic filters in Photoshop Elements enable you to apply fine-art, or paint-related enhancements to all or part of an image. For example, you can apply the Dry Brush filter to change a photo into an image painted with a dry brush. Similarly, the watercolor artistic filter can help you visualize how an image might look if you painted it with watercolor paint. The Sketch and Brush Strokes filters can create similar paint-like filter effects as those in the Artistic group of filters.

You can apply an Artistic filter to an entire image, or to a selected area of an image. If you choose a selected area, you can make part of image stand out. For example, if a picture of flowers had one flower with the Colored Pencil filter applied to it, the colored pencil flower would stand out from the others.

Conversely, you can apply a filter to everything except the selected item to make it stand out. First, you use one of the selection tools to highlight an area of the image, such as the flower shown in Figure 12.11. You also can apply the Select, Inverse command to deselect the flower and select all the other pixels in the image. This command comes in handy when you want to apply the filter to everything in a picture except for a particular area of the image, or as you'll discover in this chapter, when you want to apply more than one filter to different areas of an image. Figure 12.12 shows the same image after the Colored Pencil filter has been applied.

Figure 12.11
The Inverse command enables you to exclude a particular part of an image so that you can apply the Artistic filter to only the selected portion or to everything but the selected portion.

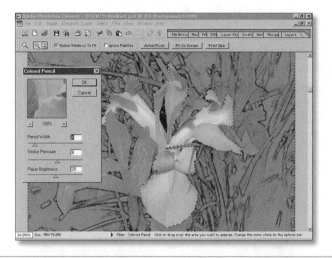

Figure 12.12
The Colored Pencil filter is applied to all selected areas of the image window.

Accented Edges

The Accented Edges filter is located in the Brush Stroke submenu of the Filter menu. This filter intensifies the edge colors in an image. You can increase the slider control, shown in Figure 12.13, to brighten the edge colors in the image to resemble white chalk. Lower Edge Brightness values darken the edge colors to resemble black ink.

Figure 12.13
The Accented Edges filter softens the background images. You can adjust the settings before applying it to the selected areas of the image.

The Edge Width slider control enables you to determine how many pixels to use to define the edges in the image. This value is used with the Edge Brightness value to create the accented effect. Increasing the Smoothness value improves the smoothness of the color transitions between the original image and accented edges. Click the OK button to apply the filter settings to the image. The resulting image is shown in Figure 12.14.

Figure 12.14
The realistic-looking flower stands out because the Accented Edges filter was applied to the rest of the flowers in this picture.

Artistic Filter Variations

You can see how filters interact with different kinds of images by applying different filters to the same image. Figure 12.15, for example, shows the previous picture of the Irises with a Water Paper filter. The Water Paper filter belongs to the Sketch family of filters. It adds a pattern to the image so that the image appears to be printed on a wet, thick-fiber type of paper.

Applying the Conte Crayon Filter

The Conte Crayon filter creates a paper effect shown in Figure 12.16. Like the Water Paper filter, it is a Sketch filter. Conte Crayons consist of colors ranging from dark gray to bright white (black, sepia, and sanguine). The Conte Crayon filter takes the foreground image and uses it to create the darker areas of the image. The background colors create the light areas of the effect.

Figure 12.15
The Water Paper filter blends chunks of pixels together to create the illusion that the image is printed on wet, fibrous paper.

Figure 12.16
The Conte Crayon filter uses the foreground and background colors in the image to create extreme dark and light crayon strokes.

Combining Filters in an Image

In a previous section of this chapter, you saw how the Inverse command could select everything except the pixels you want to preserve. This enables you to apply a filter to the area of the image that isn't the focal point. Figure 12.17 shows the ZigZag filter, one of the Distort filters, applied to the Irises photo. Choose the Inverse command from the Select menu again to reselect the iris in the photo if you want to apply a different filter to it, such as the Plastic Wrap filter also shown in Figure 12.17.

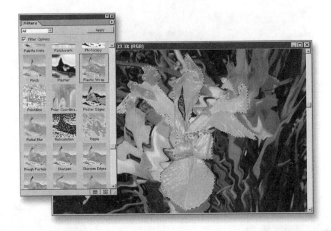

Figure 12.17
Two in one. The Plastic Wrap filter has been applied to the flower and the
ZigZag filter to the rest of the image.

Applying Halftone Filters

There are two halftone filters from which you can choose in
Photoshop Elements: Color Halftone (choose Filter, Pixelate, Color
Halftone) and Halftone Pattern (choose Filter, Sketch, Halftone
Pattern). Both reduce the number of pixels in the image by breaking
an image into rectangles and replacing each with a line, circle, or dot
to simulate a halftone screen used in printing. The tonal range is
preserved in the image, as shown in Figure 12.18, keeping the picture recognizable. However, a distinctive pattern is added to the
image.

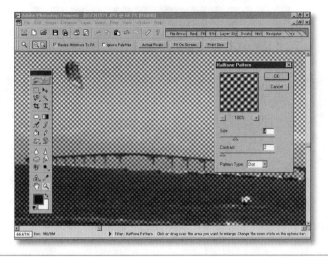

Figure 12.18
The Halftone Pattern filter reduces the resolution of an image without affecting the range of tones.

Exploring Effects

Effects can consist of adding a particular kind of gradient layer, or a combination of filters, to an image. Effect categories are Frames, Textures, Text Effects, and Image Effects. To apply these effects, the image must be in RGB or Grayscale mode and unlocked in the Layers palette. For some effects, a specific object must be in the image window, such as text for use with the Text Effects.

Applying Effects

There are three ways you can apply effects to an image: double-click an effect, drag and drop one from the Effects palette into an image window, or click a thumbnail and then click the Apply button. Watch the progress bar at the bottom of the image window as the effect is applied to an image. Figure 12.19 shows the result of applying the Lizard Skin effect to an image.

Figure 12.19
Drag and drop the Lizard Skin thumbnail onto an image to apply this effect.

Applying Image Effects

Most of the Image Effects apply Artistic filters to an image. There might be one or two destructive effects, such as Blizzard and Fluorescent Chalk. However, most produce visually interesting effects, like the Soft Flat Color effect shown in Figure 12.20. Unlike most filters, you cannot adjust settings for effects. If you like the preview image in the thumbnail, drag and drop the effect onto an image to see whether you like the resulting image.

Figure 12.20
Another image effect, Soft Flat Color, makes this image look as if it were painted.

caution
Some effects involve applying multiple filters to the image window. If you have the level of Undo set below the number of filters that will be applied by the effect, you won't be able to reverse an effect after it has been applied to the image.

If you initially choose Yes after applying an effect to an image, and then want to undo the effect, open the History palette and choose a previous state of the document where the effect has not been applied. You also can click the Step Backward button in the toolbar to see whether you can revert the image to its original state. You might want to save a copy of the image before applying an effect, just to be safe.

Applying Texture Effects

Most Texture Effects add a new layer to an image. When the effect is first applied, the new layer will cover the entire image window, blocking the background image. To combine the texture with a background image, you must decrease the opacity value for the texture effect layer. Select the texture effect from the Layers palette, and then type in a value less than 100, such as 60, in the Opacity text box. Figure 12.21 shows how the Sunset effect adds a gradient layer to the image. Notice that the texture effect is selected, and it has an Opacity setting of 45 percent in the Layers palette.

note
To find out how to use the Horizontal or Vertical Type Tool, go to Chapter 14, "Adding Text and Shapes to Images."

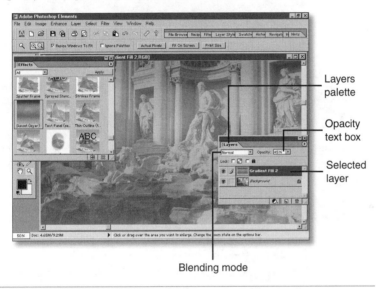

Layers palette

Opacity text box

Selected layer

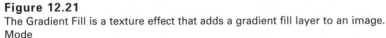

Blending mode

Figure 12.21
The Gradient Fill is a texture effect that adds a gradient fill layer to an image. Mode

Applying Text Effects

Several effects can be applied only to text objects. The Water Reflection text effect appears on the text object in Figure 12.22. Before you can apply a text effect, you must first use the Horizontal or Vertical Type tool to add text to the image window. You can use the Move tool to select the text object from the image window or the Layers palette. Then, apply a text effect to the text object. Choose Text Effects from the Effects palette if you only want to view the text effects in the palette. A text effect changes only the text layer in the image window.

289

CHAPTER 12 Applying Filters and Effects

Figure 12.22
Apply a text effect to a text object. The Water Reflection text effect was applied to the Statue text in this image.

The Quadrant Color effect adds four big squares of colors to an image. Figure 12.22 shows the text and image effects applied to the text and image layers, respectively. You can view this image in full color in the color pages of this book (see Figure CS.9).

Combining Effects

Several effects can be applied to individual image and text objects, or to the full image (see Figure 12.23). You can apply a selection tool to part of an image to apply a Cut Out or Recessed Frame effect. Then, add a text object to the image. Select the text object, and choose an effect to customize the text in the image window. Texture effects enable you to blend a text layer with the rest of the image. A texture effect can help pull together different images and image effects by adding a common look to the picture. You can hide and show layers to create custom effects for images that have been copied or pasted into the image window. Then, flatten the layers together and apply one or more effects to the final image.

Figure 12.23
The original image before any effects are applied to it.

The original figure, shown in Figure 12.23, can be changed into a picnic invitation, shown in Figure 12.24. Some effects, like the Recessed Frame effect, can be applied only to a selected area of an image. Next, a text object must be created and selected to apply a text effect. Other effects, such as the Rusted Metal effect, add a new layer to the image. You must adjust the opacity level to blend the texture effect with the other image layers.

Figure 12.24
The same image after applying the Recessed Frame, Sprayed Stencil, and
Rusted Metal effects.

Working with Layers and Layer Styles

Layers are a part of every document created by Photoshop Elements. For example, when you open an image file, the image is placed in the background layer of a document. A new layer is created whenever an image is pasted into the image window. You can also add Fill and Adjustment layers to correct colors to some or all layers in the document. Select, add, or remove layers from the Layers palette. The full capabilities of layers run deep and wide.

Layer styles enable you to customize the contents of a layer. You can add one or several layer styles, such as a drop shadow, bevel, or glow to an image, text, or graphic object in a layer. You'll find eight groups of layer styles at your disposal in the Layer Styles palette.

Introducing the Layers Palette

The kinds of layers that you'll find in the Layers palette are the background layer and any layers above it. A layer can consist of a text, vector, or bitmap object. You can also create or delete a layer in the Layers palette, or add fill or adjustment layers and apply them to all or part of the image window. Using layers makes it quick and easy to make changes or improvements to an image or text without affecting the original object. Adding layers to your image essentially is like creating a stack of transparent pages with different colors, objects, or effects on each one. If at any point you don't like the effect that a layer has on the image, you can remove, change, or hide it without affecting any other layer in the image. Layers also enable you to do things such as image repair and correction without actually working on the original image so that you can make different corrections on various layers and hide and show them one at a time to see which has the desired result. As you work on an image, or are ready to finalize it, you can merge the layers, thereby converting any text or vector graphics into bitmap graphics.

Each layer has a unique group of settings. By default, each layer has a blending mode, opacity, lock, and lock transparency setting. Select the Layers palette from the palette well in the work area to view any layers corresponding to the image in the image window. Click in the left column next to the layer to show or hide the contents of that layer in the image. You can click on a layer in the Layers palette to choose the contents of that layer in the image window.

Three shortcut icons appear at the bottom of the Layers palette. These small icon buttons enable you to view or apply a layer style, create or duplicate a new layer, or delete a layer. Drag and drop a layer over the Trash icon to delete it.

If all this information about layers seems a bit overwhelming, it might be easier to understand all the possible kinds of layers by taking a peek at a document that's already chock-full of them. Figure 13.1 deconstructs each item in the Layers palette.

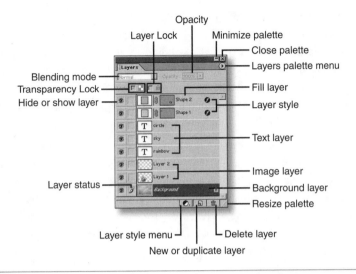

Figure 13.1
You can select any layer from the Layers palette. Here you can create, delete, or modify a layer with a layer style.

Each layer acts as a separate sheet of transparent paper, enabling you to combine images into the image window, while keeping them separate. The order of layers in the Layers palette will match the order each layer is applied to the image window, unless you change their order in the Layers palette. You can choose one of the commands in the Layer, Arrange menu, or click and drag a layer to move it to a new location in the Layers palette. The background layer is always at the bottom of the heap, with each new layer added on top of it (see Figure 13.2).

note
You must have at least two editable layers in the Layers palette before you can access the Layer, Arrange menu commands.

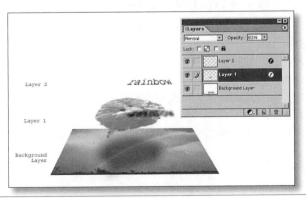

Figure 13.2
The background layer is the bottom-most layer in the document. Each new object is added to a new layer in the document.

There are several different ways you can add layers to the active image window. You can choose the New command from the Layer, New menu, or select one of the Layer, New Fill Layer, or Layer, New Adjustment Layer menu commands. Choose a selection tool from the toolbox and select part of the background image. Then, choose the Copy and Paste commands to add the selected image to a new layer in the Layers palette.

You also can create a new layer to add text or graphics to the image window by clicking on the Create a New Layer button located at the bottom of the Layers palette to create a new, empty layer. You then can use a shape or painting tool to create an object in the new layer. You can drag and drop a layer over the Create a New Layer button to duplicate the contents of a layer into a new layer.

You can click and drag a layer to change its order in the Layers palette, which in turn changes the way the layer is displayed in the image window. Click on a layer to select it. Then drag the layer above or below another layer in the palette to move it up or down in the layer order. You also can move the position of the layers using the Layers, Arrange menu command. The Arrange menu command consists of the following: Bring to Front, Bring Forward, Send Backward, and Send to Back. The Bring Forward and Send Backward commands move a layer up or down in the list of layers in the Layers palette. Bring to Front moves the selection to the top of the Layers palette, and Send to Back moves it to the bottom, right above the background layer.

Layer Palette Menu Options

Several menu commands can be accessed from the Layers palette menu. You can select this menu if the Layers palette is located in the palette well by clicking the right-arrow icon located immediately to the right of the palette tab. If the palette is open in the work area, click the right-arrow button located in the top-right corner of the Layers palette. The following list describes each menu item in the Layers palette menu:

- **Help**—Choose the Help menu item to open a new browser window that shows the Photoshop Elements Help Contents. Navigate the help content, find information in the index, or search for a help topic. To find out more about how to use the help system, go to Chapter 4, "Using the Quick Start Window and the Help System."

- **New Layer**—Select this command to create a new layer in the Layers palette.

- **Duplicate Layer**—Duplicate a layer that contains a bitmap or vector graphic object such as images, text, or shapes.

- **Delete Layer**—Remove a layer from the Layers palette.

- **Rename Layer**—Select an editable layer to choose this menu item from the menu list. The Layer Properties window opens. Type a new name for the layer into the text box, and then click OK to save the new name to the Layers palette.

- **Simplify Layer**—Choose a shape tool from the toolbox and add a shape to the image window. Select the shape layer from the Layers palette, and then choose Simplify Layer from the menu list to combine the shape object with its linked color. The two thumbnails will merge into a single thumbnail image, and the vector shape will become a bitmap. You can apply the Paint Bucket Tool to the simplified shape if you want to change its color.

- **Merge Down**—Click on one of the middle layers in the Layers palette, and then choose the Merge Down command from the menu list to combine all layers below it into a single layer. Any layers above the selected layer will remain in the Layers palette.

- **Merge Visible**—Click on the left box for each layer to show or hide the layers you want to merge. Choose the Merge Visible command to merge all visible layers in the Layers palette. Hidden layers will not be merged and will remain in the Layers palette after the visible layers have been merged.

- **Flatten Image**—Select the Flatten Image command to merge all visible layers into a single layer in the Layers palette. Hidden layers will be permanently removed from the document.

- **Palette Options**—Choose Palette Options from the menu list to open the Layers Palette Options window. You can select from three different thumbnail image sizes, or click on the None radio button if you don't want to see a thumbnail image in each layer. Click OK to save your changes.

- **Close Palette to Shortcuts Well**—Almost all the commands accessible from the Layers palette are also available in the Layer menu.

Introducing Blending Modes

note
You can lock all settings in a layer by checking the Lock check box for the selected layer in the Layers palette. Check the Transparency Lock check box if you do not want any pixels added to the transparent areas of an image. A lock icon will appear to the right of the layer name if either lock is applied to a layer. Uncheck the Lock check box to unlock a layer. Double-click the background layer to convert it to an editable layer.

A blending mode enables you to mix the color of the selected layer with the colors of the images in the layer directly below it. You might want to apply a blending mode to a layer if you want its colors to blend in with the colors or content in the layer below it. Choose one of 17 blending modes for any layer. Normal is the default blending mode for any newly created layer. The following list briefly defines each blending mode used in RGB images. The selected layer refers to the base, or original colors, whereas the term *blending color* refers to the colors in the layer directly below the selected layer. Blending and base colors are required in order to create a result color produced by choosing a particular blending mode.

- **Normal**—No blending is applied to pixels in this default mode. Colors are represented as-is. Referred to as Threshold mode if you're working with a bitmap or Indexed Color image.

- **Dissolve**—Pixel colors are randomly replaced with the base or blend color, using the opacity of any pixel in the image to set the color of the dissolved pixels. Try this blending mode with layers containing large Airbrush or Brush stroke graphics.

- **Multiply**—Multiplies the base color of each channel with the blend color. The result is similar to applying overlapping strokes of a felt tip pen, which darkens the original color.

- **Screen**—Multiplies the opposite of the blend and base colors to create the resulting color, which is usually lighter than either of the original colors.

- **Overlay**—Preserves the lightness or darkness of the base color and multiplies or screens it before mixing it with the blend color.

- **Soft Light**—Darkens or lightens the base color depending on whether the blend color is lighter or darker than 50% gray. The result is lightened, which is similar to applying the Dodge Tool, if the blend color is lighter than 50%, or darkened, which is similar to the Burn Tool, if it's 50% darker than the blend pixels.

- **Hard Light**—Screens or multiplies the base color depending on whether the blend color is lighter or darker than 50% gray. If the blend color is lighter than 50%, the result is a lighter color. Otherwise, the result is darker if the blend color is also darker than 50%. The resulting effect, if darkened, adds shadows to an image.

- **Color Dodge**—Brightens the base color after checking each channel in the RGB image and reflects the blend color. Blending with black produces no change.

- **Color Burn**—Darkens the base color after checking each channel of the RGB image and reflects the blend color. Blending with white produces no change.

- **Darken**—Picks the darker of the base or blend color after checking each channel and replaces pixels lighter than the blend color.

- **Lighten**—Chooses the lighter of the base or blend color after checking each channel color and replaces pixels that are darker than the blend color.

- **Difference**—Subtracts the blend from the base color if the base color is darker than the blend color. The brighter of the two colors is subtracted from the other. Blending with black produces no change, while blending with white inverts the base color values.

- **Exclusion**—A lower-contrast color (compared to the Difference blending mode above) is created. This blending mode adds the blend or base color depending on the brightness values of the colors in each RGB channel.

- **Hue**—Combines the saturation and luminance of the base color and the hue of the blend color to produce the resulting color.

- **Saturation**—Combines the hue and luminance of the base color with the saturation of the blend color to produce the resulting color. The blend color must contain gray to produce a different color.

- **Color**—Mixes the luminance of the base color with the hue and saturation of the blend color to produce the resulting color. Can be used to colorize grayscale images or add tinted color to images.

- **Luminosity**—Creates a resulting color by mixing the hue and saturation of the base color with the luminance of the blend color, creating the opposite effect of the Color blending mode.

You can also simplify and combine layers as you complete all or part of an image. The Simplify Layer command enables you to combine linked components of a layer. You might apply this command to a fill or adjustment layer as you finalize each layer setting for an image.

When you create a fill or adjustment layer, a multi-part layer is created in the Layers palette. The linked color and shape elements enable you to easily change the color of the fill layer, or unlink the shape from the fill component. Choose the Simplify Layer command from the Layer menu if you want to merge the parts into a single bitmap layer. You will no longer be able to modify the fill or adjustment layer after it has been simplified.

Convert the Background Layer into Layer 0

If you want to modify or move the background layer up in the Layers palette, you can change it to a nonlocked, regular layer. Double-click on the Background Layer to open the Layer Properties window. If you want to, you can type a new name for the layer. Photoshop Elements changes its name from the Background Layer to Layer 0.

The Background Layer is a locked layer, but Layer 0 is not locked and is fully editable just like any other layer in the Layers palette.

Modifying a Layer with Layer Styles

Pump up the content in a layer by applying one or more layer styles to it. Layer styles enable you to quickly add one or several effects to a text or graphic object in a layer. Choose from eight installed groups of Layer styles. Figure 13.3 shows the Drop Shadows group of layer styles.

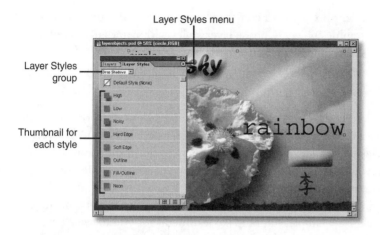

Layer Styles menu

Layer Styles group

Thumbnail for each style

Figure 13.3
Preview a set of layer styles in the Layer Styles palette.

You can view and choose layer styles from the Layer Styles palette. Like the Filters and Effects palettes, you can preview thumbnail images of each layer style in the Layer Styles palette. Click on the icons located at the bottom of the Layer Styles palette to change the way a group of layer styles is shown in the Layer Styles palette. For example, you can add a drop shadow or a bevel layer style to a shape or image object in the active image window. The following list briefly describes each set available in the Layer Styles palette.

- **Bevels**—Adds a three-dimensional edge to the borders of text or a graphics object. Great for creating Web graphics buttons.

- **Drop Shadows**—Creates a drop shadow below the text or graphics object.

- **Inner Glows**—Adds a custom pattern to the inside of the selected graphics object.

- **Inner Shadows**—Applies a shadow effect to inside the borders of the selected object.

- **Outer Glows**—Creates a colored border effect around the selected object.

- **Visibility**—Shows, hides, or creates a ghosting effect with a graphics object.

tip
You also can adjust some of the layer styles from the Style Settings window. If you're not sure which layer styles you've applied to an object, you can double-click the f icon located on the right side of a layer in the Layers palette. The f icon will appear if a layer style has been applied to a layer.

The Style Settings window opens. If you applied a drop shadow, bevel, or glow layer style to an object, the corresponding slider control will be selectable in the Style Settings window.

- **Complex**—Adds a combined texture and color pattern to a graphics object. Choose layer styles with names like Rainbow, Rivet, Star Glow, and Woodgrain.
- **Glass Buttons**—Changes the selected object in a layer into a colored glass button shape.

Be sure you have more than one layer of images to work with in the image window. If this is your first time experimenting with layer styles, you might want to use the Shape tools in the toolbox to create a few graphic objects in an empty, new document window so you can more easily see each layer style as you apply it to an object. You also might want to select a light foreground color for the graphic object. Black, for example, might make it difficult for you to see a bevel style that's been added to an object. To apply the layer style to your image, do the following:

1. Choose the Move tool from the toolbox. Click on the object to which you want the style applied. You also can hold down the Shift key and click on several objects if you want to select a group of objects.

2. Choose a set of layer styles from the Layer Styles palette pop-up menu.

3. Click on the desired layer style to apply it to the selection in the document window. You also can drag and drop the layer style onto the document window. You will see an f icon appear in the selected layer if a layer style has been applied to it.

4. Apply additional layer styles as needed to get the desired result. New objects you create will use the last set of layer styles applied to an image in the work area.

Removing Layer Styles

Each group of layer styles has a default style (none) located in the upper-left corner of the Layer Styles palette. The icon is a white square with a black border with a red, diagonal line running through it. Select the object in the image window, and then click on this Default Style (none) option to remove all Layer Styles from the selected object.

In addition to applying layer styles to your selections, most of the styles sets have certain settings that you can fine-tune to get exactly the effect that you want. Double-click on the f icon in a layer that contains a layer style to open the Style Settings window shown in Figure 13.4. You also can choose Style Settings from the Layer, Layer Styles menu. Each of the slider control settings becomes active if a layer style from the corresponding layer style group is applied to a layer.

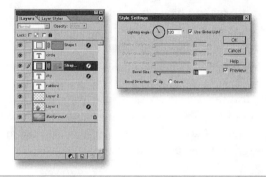

Figure 13.4
Customize layer styles by changing settings in the Style Settings window.

Renaming a Layer

As you add objects and create new layers, it's helpful to rename each one so you can quickly hide, show, or select a layer as you need to work on it. In the Layers palette shown in Figure 13.5, you can see how easy it is to identify layers with custom names versus layers with generic names. Double-click on the name of a layer in the Layers palette to open the Layer Properties dialog box. Type a name for the layer into the Name text box. Then click on the OK button to view the newly named layer in the Layers palette.

Figure 13.5
Type a name for a layer in the Layer Properties window.

Introducing Fill Layers

Adjustment and fill layers are yet two more kinds of layers you can add to a document. You can use solid, gradient, or pattern fill layers to correct colors, or enhance a graphic design. You can add fill layers to an image to apply a color tint or color correction to any layers located directly below it in the Layers palette. This section shows you how to add a solid color fill layer to a selected area of an image.

If you want to make a blue sky bluer, you can apply the Magic Wand Tool to select a color in the image window. Then add a blue, solid color fill layer to it. Adjust the opacity level of the fill layer to adjust the blue color of the sky. Figure 13.6 shows the blue sky in a picture surrounded by a selection marquee, which was created by the Magic Wand Tool. If the sky consists of more than one shade of blue, you can hold down the Shift key to add other colors to the selected area. The solid color fill layer can be applied to a selected area or to the entire contents of the image window.

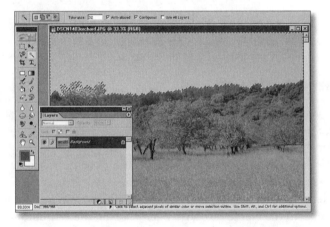

Figure 13.6
The Magic Wand Tool can help select a particular color in the image window with a single click.

Adding a Solid Color Fill Layer

One way to enhance the color of the sky is to add a solid color fill layer to the picture. The following steps show you how:

1. Choose Solid Color from the Layer, New Fill Layer menu. The New Layer dialog box will open.

2. Type in a name for the fill layer and choose any custom settings you want to use (see Figure 13.7). Then click on OK.

Figure 13.7
Type a name for the new fill layer, and then choose the blending mode and opacity settings for the new fill layer.

3. Next, the Color Picker window will open. Pick a color for the fill layer. Then click on OK.

A new fill layer will appear in the Layers palette. The contents of the image window will also change to show the color of the fill layer you just selected (see Figure 13.8). Reduce the opacity setting for the solid color fill layer to blend the fill layer color with the layers located directly below it in the Layers palette.

Adjusted color (image window)

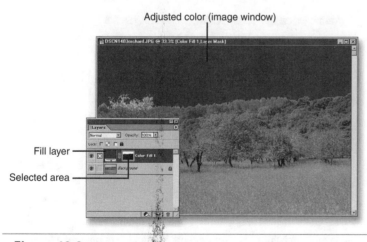

Fill layer

Selected area

Figure 13.8
Adjust the opacity value for the solid color fill layer to blend the blue color of the fill layer with the other layers in the image. The solid color fill layer added a nighttime look to this daytime shot.

Click on the fill layer in the Layers palette. Then click on the Opacity slider control and decrease the value in the text box. As the fill layer becomes transparent, you'll be able to see the graphics in the layers below the selected fill layer.

Gradient Fill Layers

A gradient fill layer can be added to an image to create a controlled, but general, directional lighting effect, or a general background pattern. A gradient consists of at least two colors, and is a gradation of tones changing from one color to the next. A gradient can add depth to an image. If applied correctly, it can imply a light source for other objects, or enhance a graphic composition.

Choose Gradient from the Layer, New Fill Layer menu to add a gradient fill layer to the Layers palette. Type a name for the gradient fill layer, and then click OK. The Gradient Fill dialog box opens. Click on the Gradient drop-down menu to choose the colors for the gradient. Select one of five kinds of gradients in the Style drop-down menu in the Gradient Fill dialog box, shown in Figure 13.9. Then, click OK to add the new gradient fill layer to the Layers palette.

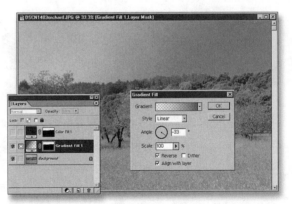

Figure 13.9
A gradient fill layer consists of two components in the Layers palette: a layer effect and the layer graphic. Double-click a gradient fill layer to open the Gradient Fill dialog box. You can customize the gradient colors, style, angle, or scale from the Gradient Fill dialog box.

Double-click the gradient fill layer to open the Gradient Fill dialog box. You can modify the gradient fill without affecting any of the pixels in the other layers in the image. Click and drag the radius in the circle graphic in the Angle area of the Gradient Fill dialog box if you want to change the angle of the gradient. You also can type an angle value into the Angle text box.

You can reverse the direction of the gradient by checking the Reverse check box. Select the Dither check box if you want to reduce color banding in the gradient. Check the Align with Layer check box if you want the Gradient Fill layer to align the gradient component with the graphic object in the Gradient Fill layer.

The following list briefly describes the five gradient styles you can choose from:

- **Linear**—Creates a horizontal gradient from left to right in the image window.
- **Radial**—Draws the gradient outward from the center of the selected area.
- **Angle**—Applies a gradient at an angle in the selected area of the image.
- **Reflected**—Adds a horizontal bar in the image window, and draws the gradient upward and downward in the image window.
- **Diamond**—Creates a diamond out of one gradient color, and fades outward in all directions to the next color.

Modifying a Gradient

Click on the gradient box in the Gradient Fill window to open the Gradient Editor window. Each square located in the Present area of the window represents a gradient you can choose. Click on a gradient square to select the colors for the gradient fill layer. Select a different group of gradients by clicking on the arrow pop-up menu. Each of the items at the bottom of the menu list represents a group of gradients. Choose a custom group of gradients, such as Color Harmonies 1, Color Harmonies 2, Metals, Noise Samples, Pastels, Simple, Special Effects, and Spectrum. Choose Reset Gradients to show the original gradients' presets.

Type a name for the gradient into the Name text box. Click on the New button to add the gradient settings to the Preset area of the

Gradient Editor window. Choose between a Solid or Noise from the Gradient Type drop-down menu. Choose a percentage value from the Smoothness drop-down menu; a lower value produces a coarser blend of gradient colors.

The selected gradient's colors appear at the bottom of the Gradient Editor window (see Figure 13.10). Click below the gradient bar to add a new color to the gradient. Click on the color slider control to view the gradient color in the color box. Click in the Color box to choose a different color for the gradient. Click on one of the square controls located above the gradient bar. Customize the Opacity setting for that location of the gradient. Move the square along the gradient bar to change the location of that part of the gradient, or type in a different percentage value into the Location text box. Click OK to save your changes and return to the Gradient Fill window.

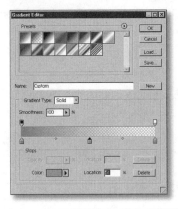

Figure 13.10
Pick a different gradient or customize your gradient colors in the Gradient Editor window.

Combining Fill Layers

You can add more than one solid color, gradient, or pattern layer if you want to hide or show different effects and preview different combinations of colors without modifying the original image (see Figure 13.11). You can move each fill layer above or below other layers to change the color of specific layers, or preserve the colors of other layers. Try choosing a blending mode for a fill layer to experiment with different color effects between two layers.

Figure 13.11
Add more than one gradient fill layer to experiment with color changes in the
image window. Modify a fill layer by removing the link between the fill and
graphic components in a layer.

Pattern Fill Layers

You can create an adjustment fill layer that contains a pattern, too.
Choose Patterns from the Layer, New Fill Layer menu. Type a name
for the pattern fill layer, and then click OK. The Pattern Fill dialog
box appears. Here you can choose a pattern from the pattern drop-
down menu. You can adjust the scale of the pattern file by choosing a
percentage from the Scale drop-down list. You can choose from two
groups of patterns.

Check the Link with Layer check box if you want the pattern to
move along with the fill layer. Press the Snap to Origin button if you
want to set the position of the pattern to match the grid or ruler settings for the document window. Finally, you can save your pattern
settings by clicking on the New Document icon (white rectangle
icon). Click on the OK button to add the pattern fill layer to the
active image window.

Introducing Adjustment Layers

Adjustment layers are similar to fill layers in that both create modifiable layers in the Layers palette. Adjustment layers enable you to
customize Levels, Brightness/Contrast, Hue/Saturation, Gradient
Map, Invert, Threshold, or Posterize effects with an image in RGB

mode without sacrificing any of the original pixels in the image window.

If you plan to combine two images with disparate lighting, you can use adjustment layers to correct the color difference between the two images instead of using the same tonal range tools available in the Enhance menu. The tonal range tools permanently remove or remap the pixels of the original image. Using an adjustment layer enables you to experiment with tonal and color corrections without having to worry about degrading the quality of the image. Figure 13.12 shows a sample base image to which to apply adjustment layers. Figure 13.13 shows the secondary image, selected with the Magnetic Lasso Tool before it is placed into Figure 13.12.

Figure 13.12
Open an image file that needs tonal range corrections.

Figure 13.13
Select and copy the second image you want to combine with the first image. The Magnetic Lasso tool marquee surrounds the selected image. However, the bounding box appears if you select the marquee object with the Move tool.

The selected image in Figure 13.13 was copied to the Clipboard and then pasted into the background image shown in Figure 13.12. The pasted image appears in its own new layer in the Layers palette. You can click and drag the corner handles of the pasted image to scale it to fit with the background image. Choose the Move Tool from the toolbox and place the pasted image in the image window.

Making Changes with a Levels Adjustment Layer

For this example, the image needs help with a level adjustment to correct the tonal ranges and to bring out the detail in the image. Choose the Levels menu item from the Layer, New Adjustment Layer menu. The Levels dialog box will open. Click and drag the slider controls to adjust the highlight, midtones, and shadow settings for the RGB image. Then preview the changes in the image window, as shown in Figure 13.14. Like any other layer, an adjustment layer will only affect all layers below it in the Layers palette. If you want an adjustment layer to affect all layers in the image, move the adjustment layer to the top of the Layers palette. Similarly, you can exclude layers from the adjustment layer by moving them up, positioned above the adjustment layer.

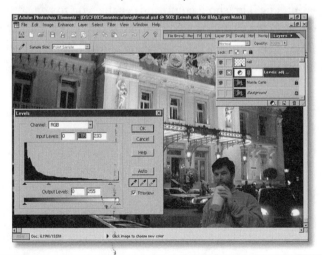

Figure 13.14
Adjust the tonal range in the Levels adjustment layer window.

note

Many of the adjustment layer tools are also selectable as permanent color correction tools, located in the Image and Enhance menus. To find out more about these commands, go to Chapter 11, "Tonal Range and Color Correction."

Each of the adjustment layer tools functions exactly the same way as the matching menu commands located in the Enhance menu. Creating an adjustment layer brings the flexibility of being able to modify any of these settings before changing the original image. You can also click in the left column in the Layers palette to show or hide each of the adjustment layers. Compare different tonal range tools and pick the best combination of settings to create the best-looking image. The following list briefly describes each of the adjustment layer tools.

- **Levels**—Enables you to adjust the tonal range of the image.
- **Brightness/Contrast**—Increase or decrease the amount of highlight and shadow in an image by adjusting the brightness or contrast settings.
- **Hue/Saturation**—Add or decrease the amount of color, gray level in a color, or the amount of lightness in the image.
- **Gradient Map**—Apply a grayscale gradient to the image window.
- **Invert**—Apply the opposite color from the color wheel.
- **Threshold**—Choose the black and white midpoint for an image, if you want to compare the results with the Levels adjustment layer. The Threshold commands enable you to adjust the threshold level for changing a color or grayscale image into a bitmap.
- **Posterize**—Reduce the number of colors by choosing the number of posterize levels in an image.

Blending Composite Images

When you copy an image and paste it into any other image window in the work area, one of the first things you might notice are the differences between the colors of the two images. You can use the Move Tool to adjust the scale and location of the composite image. However, because each image can have unique color and light characteristics, it would be difficult to apply a levels or color correction command to change both images at the same time. Fortunately, you can add a fill or adjustment layer to correct any subtle color differences between the two images.

When an image is pasted into an image window, Photoshop Elements creates a transparent layer containing the pasted or composite image. You can ignore the transparent areas in the image layer by holding down the (Ctrl)[Command] key while selecting the layer. The image will be surrounded by a selection marquee. Alternatively, you can select the layer and click on the Transparency Lock icon to prevent any of the transparent areas from being modified in that image layer.

Now, if you add a new fill or adjustment layer, it will be applied only to the selected area in the image window. Figure 13.15 shows the before and after image of adding a gradient fill layer to the secondary image. The gradient fill layer contains a few of the colors in the background image. In this particular example, the pasted image was taken under fluorescent light.

Adding the gradient fill layer, and reducing the opacity level of the gradient, enables the image to share some of the same colors of the background image, creating a very subtle color blending effect in the composite image. Figure 13.16 shows final blending mode and opacity settings for the gradient fill layer.

tip
Most of the adjustment layers can quickly be modified if you double-click on the adjustment layer from the Layers palette. You can also click on a layer, and then choose the Layer Content Options command from the Layer menu to modify an adjustment layer.

CHAPTER 13 Working with Layers and Layer Styles

Figure 13.15
Select the object in a graphic layer by holding down the (Ctrl) [Command] key
and clicking on the layer. Then choose the fill or adjustment layer you want to
apply to the selected layer.

Figure 13.16
Adjust the opacity value for a gradient layer to match the colors between two
images.

Correcting Images with Layers

You can use layers to temporarily store pixels as you correct an image. Figure 13.17 shows the before image that has several small dust and spec marks that need to be removed. If you look closely at the left and bottom areas of the image, you should see many small black specs. In this example, an empty layer is created to store corrections to the background layer. The Clone Stamp Tool is used to sample the image across layers.

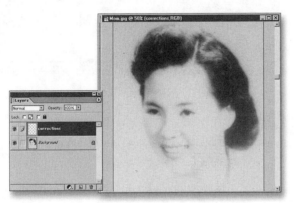

Figure 13.17
Click on the Create a New Layer icon to add a transparent layer to the image. Then check the Use All Layers check box to grab pixels from the background layer with the Clone Stamp Tool and add new pixels to the correction layer.

To apply the Clone Stamp Tool to an image, do the following:

1. Hold down the (Alt) [Option] key and drag the Clone Stamp Tool in the image window to capture the location where you want to sample pixels. Release the (Alt) [Option] key.

2. Click and drag the Clone Stamp Tool in the area where you want to apply the sampled pixels to the image.

3. A circle will appear in the image window indicating the location of the pixels being replaced. A circle icon will appear over the area of pixels being sampled, as shown in Figure 13.18. The size of the circle will match the brush size selected for the Clone Stamp Tool in the options bar.

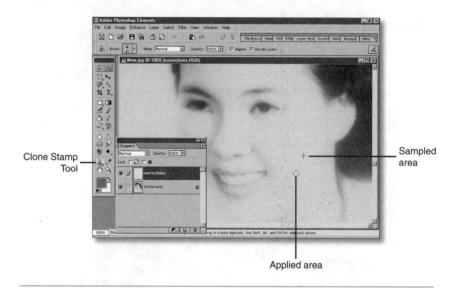

Clone Stamp
Tool

Sampled
area

Applied area

Figure 13.18
Zoom into the image and apply the Clone Stamp Tool to remove dirt or dust
from the photo.

4. Click on the correction layer in the Layers palette. Sample and
apply the Clone Stamp Tool in small areas of the image window
until the dust and specs are cleared away from the image window
as shown in Figure 13.19.

Figure 13.19
Use the History palette to undo a change or use the Erase Tool to remove pixels
from the correction layer.

Although the Layers palette offers great image editing flexibility with fill and adjustment layers, try to work with the highest resolution possible to get the best results. If the image was scanned, you might want to consider rescanning the image at a higher resolution to capture more detail, or to work with a different image that has better tonal range, color, and detail.

Merging Layers

As you finalize image and settings between the content of layers, you will want to simplify an image by merging layers. Simplifying an image will not only reduce the size of the file, but will also permanently merge two or more layers of images into one. Click on the eye icon to hide a layer you don't want to merge, or click to show a layer. Then choose the Merge Visible command, shown in Figure 13.20, to turn any visible layers into a single layer.

note
Fill and Adjustment layers affect any layers that appear below them in the Layers palette. You can change the way the resulting image looks by changing the order of the layers in the Layers palette. Click and drag any layer and drop it above or below any other layer in the palette window to perform a re-org.

Figure 13.20
Use the Merge Visible command to flatten layers that you want to finalize.

Flattening Layers

The Flatten Layers command will combine all layers in an image into a single layer. The before and after images are shown in Figure 13.21. If you've created an image file with multiple layers, you can preserve layers by saving the file as a PSD, the native Photoshop Elements file format. However, if you want to save the file in any other file format, such as JPEG, GIF, or PNG, you must first flatten all layers before you can save the image as a file.

Removing Hidden Layers

Click on the left column beside one of the layers in the Layers palette. The eye icon appears, indicating the layer is visible. Its blending mode, lock check boxes, and opacity fields become selectable. You should be able to see the contents of the image layer in the image window.

Click in the box once more. The eye icon disappears, and the blending mode, opacity field, and lock layer settings are deselected.

Choose Merge Layers. All visible layers will be merged into a single layer. If any layers are hidden in the Layers palette, they will be permanently discarded from the image file when the Flatten Layers command is executed.

If you accidentally select this command before closing the image window, you can choose Undo from the Edit menu to restore any layers. Alternatively, you can open the History palette and click on a previous state to revert the document back in time and show any layers you want to preserve.

tip
Hide a layer in the Layers palette, and then choose the Merge Visible command from the Layer menu. Only images appearing in the image window will be combined into a single layer. You can use the Hide Layer command to preserve changes you're not quite ready to save along with the rest of the image.

Figure 13.21
The Flatten Layers command merges all layers into a single background layer.

Adding Text and Shapes to Images

To most people, the terms images and graphics might be synonymous. However, some people use the term *graphics* to refer to text or hand-drawn vector or bitmap graphics. Photos created with a camera or scanner are considered images, not graphics. Whatever term you might prefer, Photoshop Elements enables you to create, edit, and delete graphics and images.

This chapter shows you how to add fabulous horizontal and vertical text to an image using the Horizontal or Vertical Type Tools. Find out how to format text and create special effects with the Warp Text Tool. Learn how to add and modify graphics with the Pencil, Paintbrush, Airbrush, and the shape tools.

Introducing the Type Tool

Adobe uses the term *type* to describe what you and I call text. Type refers to a set of alpha, numeric, and symbolic characters that can be defined as a typeface, or font. The most commonly used formats for typefaces are PostScript and TrueType.

Photoshop Elements enables you to enter text horizontally or vertically in an image window. The Horizontal and Vertical Type Tools share one location in the toolbox. You can press the letter T to select this tool, or use the mouse to click on its icon in the toolbox. More importantly, the type tools enable you to format the font, font style, and font size, as well as choose from a small set of layout options and one or two special effects. I refer to these tools using the general term *Type Tool*. You can use either one to add text to your image file.

To add text to an image, do the following:

1. Select the Horizontal or Vertical Type Tool from the toolbox.

2. Click on the image window. Depending on which tool you chose, either a vertical or horizontal line appears where you clicked, indicating where the text will appear.

3. Type a few keys on the keyboard to add text to the image window, as shown in Figure 14.1.

Text Option

Figure 14.1
The text shown here was created with the Horizontal Type Tool. The Horizontal and Vertical Type Tools (Type Tool) enable you to add text to an image. Choose from several text settings in the Type Tool options bar.

4. The text color is the foreground color selected in the toolbox. You can use the Type Tool to select text, and then modify the text using any of the Type Tool settings in the options bar.

Formatting Text

When you add text to the image window, a text layer is created in the Layers palette. You can click on this layer to select the text as an object. Click and drag a handle with the Move Tool to resize the text object in the image window. If you want to modify the font size or style, click on the Horizontal or Vertical Type Tool, and then triple-click on the text in the image window to select it (see Figure 14.2). The options bar will show the Type Tool settings.

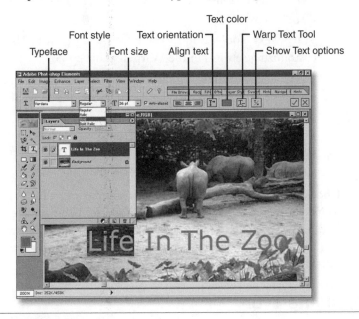

Figure 14.2
Choose a font style from the drop-down menu in the Type Tool's options bar.

The following list contains a brief description of each of the Type Tool settings located in the options bar:

- **Typeface**—Choose a font from the drop-down menu. Any font installed with Windows or Mac OS will appear in the menu list.

- **Font Size**—Font sizes appear in points. Smaller numbers represent a smaller size font; larger numbers represent larger fonts. You can also use the Transform and Move Tools to enlarge text beyond the numbers in the menu list.

- **Font Style**—Add a bold, italicized, or bold italicized font style to a font, or remove styles by choosing Regular. The font style menu is shown in Figure 14.2.

- **Anti-aliased**—Smooth the edges of a font by checking this check box.

- **Align Text**—Align the text object to the left, center, or right of its location in the image window.

- **Text Orientation**—Draw the text horizontally or vertically in the image window.

- **Warp Text Tool**—Add special effects to the text by choosing or customizing settings in the Warp Text dialog box.

- **Show Text Options**—Additional formatting options appear when you click on the right-most button in the Type Tool's options bar. The contents of the drop-down menu vary depending on which typeface you're using. Apply faux bold, faux italic, underline text, or strikethrough text by checking the corresponding check box in this window.

Choose different combinations of font settings to find the right text to match the message and the image. You can modify any text object as often as you like. Create a copy of a text object on a separate layer and hide and show different combinations of text settings to compare different text settings with each other.

Modifying Type

You must select the Type Tool before you can modify a text object. The Move Tool only enables you to select and scale the text object in the image window. You can select all or part of a text object in the image, and format a single word, or all words in the text layer. Figure 14.3 shows the first and last word in the text layer formatted with a larger font size, with a custom style setting.

caution

If you want to add type to an image, the image must be in RGB or grayscale mode. Bitmap and Indexed modes do not support layers, and you cannot add text or use the Type Tool when an image is in either of these image modes.

Figure 14.3
The Type Tool enables you to add, modify, and select text. You can modify one or several characters with the formatting settings in the options bar. The word "Life" is in boldface, and the selected word "Zoo" is in bold, italic.

Virtually all the text formatting settings in the options bar can be applied to individual characters. The Warp Text Tool, however, can only modify all text in the selected text layer. If you want to customize a few characters in a text object, first choose the Type Tool. Next, highlight a specific character, word, or words in the image window. Then, choose a font, font style, or font size from the options bar. The highlighted text will change to match the settings you choose in the options bar.

Text objects are created as vector graphics. One way you can tell if you're working with a vector graphic is to scale it up in size. If you don't see any jagged edges, you're working with a vector graphic. Vector graphics are great for generating crisp, concise graphics. However, they usually create a slightly larger file, and can only be customized in the application in which they're created.

note
If you're working with several layers of images, you can create different effects with text depending on where the text layer is located in the Layers palette. Drag and drop the text layer to move it above or below other layers in the document. Remember the top layer in the Layers palette represents the top layer in the image window. If you can't see a text object, you probably need to bump it up to a higher layer in the Layers palette.

To use text in other ways, such as filling it with an image, you first must convert the text into a bitmap. When a text object is converted into a bitmap, the mathematically calculated pixels are changed into a fixed set of pixels. You can apply filters, effects, and other tools and color-correction commands on the bitmap text as long as the image window is in the proper color mode for the tool you want to use. However, you cannot modify bitmap text with the Horizontal or Vertical Text Tools. The following steps show you how to convert vector text into bitmap text:

1. Press the (Command) [Ctrl] key and click on the text layer in the Layers palette. The outline of the text should be highlighted with a dashed line.

2. Choose the Copy command from the Edit menu, or press (Command-C) [Ctrl+C] to copy the selected text to the Clipboard.

3. Then select the Paste command from the Edit menu, or press (Command-V) [Ctrl+V]. The vector text object will be pasted as a bitmap into the active image window and a new layer will be created in the Layers palette.

The following list describes the benefits of working with vector text:

- **Scalable**—Text will look crisp and clear whether you increase or decrease its size.

- **Editable**—You can select the Type Tool and modify the Text object layer at any time.

- **Filters and Effects**—You can drag and drop a filter or effect onto the text object to blur, sharpen, texturize, or give it an artistic look. Once a filter or effect is applied to a text object, that text is permanently converted into a bitmap.

- **Layer Styles**—You can drag and drop a layer style onto a text object to give it a three-dimensional look, or to add other spiffy effects. Layer styles can turn two-dimensional text into professional-looking, Web-ready graphics. If you drag and drop a layer style onto a text object, the text is converted into a bitmap graphic.

Bitmap Text and the Paste Into Command

Convert a vector text object, which is the default state of a text object, into a bitmap by copying and pasting the vector text into the image window. First (Command) [Ctrl] click on the text layer to select each character in the text layer. The highlight should surround each letter in the text layer. Then choose Copy from the Edit menu, or press (Command-C)[Ctrl+C] to copy the image to the Clipboard. Then choose the Paste command from the Edit menu to create a new layer containing the bitmap text.

The letter T will appear as the thumbnail image for a vector text layer, regardless of the text in the layer. A tiny image of the bitmap text object will appear as the thumbnail image for a bitmap text layer. After you create the bitmap text layer, you might want to hide the vector text layer, so that only the bitmap text appears in the image window. Click in the left box beside the vector layer. The eye icon should disappear from the box, indicating the layer is hidden from the image window.

After you've converted the text object to a bitmap, you can copy an image into the Clipboard. Open a new image file, and then use a selection tool to select all or part of the image in the image window. Then choose the Copy command from the Edit menu, or press (Command-C) [Ctrl+C] to copy the selected image to the Clipboard.

Next, select the bitmap text by (Command) [Ctrl] clicking on the bitmap text layer in the Layers palette. Then choose the Paste Into command from the Edit menu to paste the image from the Clipboard into the bitmap text object. The image will appear in each character of the selected text object.

note

Drag and drop a Bevel layer style onto a text object to give it a three-dimensional look. When a layer style is added to a layer, an f icon appears on the right side of the layer. Double-click on the f icon in the text layer to customize the bevel settings in the Style Settings dialog box.

Warping Type

When a piece of text is highlighted with the Type Tool, the Warp Text button appears to the right of the text color well in the options bar. The icon for the Warp tool resembles the letter T with an arched line below it. Click on the Warp Text button to open the Warp Text dialog box shown in Figure 14.4.

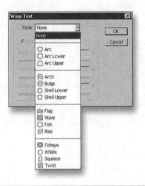

Figure 14.4

Apply special effects to text by choosing one of many styles from the Warp Text dialog box.

Click on the Style drop-down menu to view a menu list of fifteen warp styles you can apply to the selected text object. The following list briefly describes each of the four groups of Warp Text effects. Choose None if you do not want to apply a Warp Text effect to the selected text object.

- **Arc**—Raise the top or bottom area of the text object by choosing Arc Lower or Arc Upper. Make the entire text object arc by choosing Arc.

- **Arch**—Arch or bulge the midsection of the text object. Choose Shell Lower or Shell Upper to push out the upper or lower mid-section of the selected text object.

- **Flag**—Makes the text object take the shape of a waving flag. Choose the Flag, Wave, Fish, or Rise style.

- **Miscellaneous**—The styles located at the bottom of the menu list are a collection of miscellaneous effects. The Fisheye effect bloats the middle area of the image, Inflate bloats the entire text object, Squeeze puckers the entire image, and Twist twirls the text object.

The settings in the Warp Text dialog box will remain un-selectable until you choose one of the warp text styles from the Style drop-down menu, shown in Figure 14.4. You can only apply one style to each text object. Each style changes the entire text object. You cannot apply a warp text effect to individual characters or words in a text object.

After you choose a style, you can customize the Horizontal or Vertical direction, Bend, Horizontal Distortion, and Vertical Distortion of the warp text style. Figure 14.5 shows the settings for the Fish style in the Warp Text dialog box. Drag the sliders to control the warp effect. You can preview your changes in the image window. Click on OK to apply the Warp Text settings to the text object.

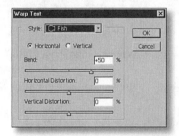

Figure 14.5
Customize warp text effects by moving the slider controls in the Warp Text window.

The letter T appears in the text object thumbnail box in the Layers palette. The T icon indicates the text object is editable with either the Horizontal or Vertical Type Tool. If you apply the Warp Text Tool to a text object, the letter T in the Layers palette will change into the Warp Text icon (the letter T with an arc line below it), as shown in Figure 14.6.

The Warp Tool will affect every character in the text layer. However, you can continue to modify the formatting and style settings of any character in the text object that has been warped. Select the Horizontal or Vertical Type Tool and click on the warped text in the image window to highlight the characters or words you want to modify.

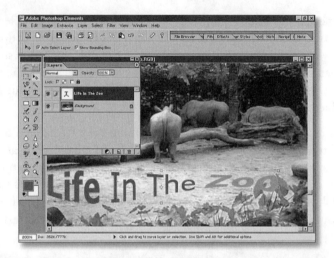

Figure 14.6
The Type icon in the Layers palette changes if the Warp Text Tool is applied to a text layer.

Adding Graphics to an Image

In addition to all the fabulous bitmap-editing tools it has, Photoshop Elements enables you to create customized effects with painting and drawing tools. Painting tools such as the Paintbrush and Airbrush Tools enable you to apply a color with a brush tip of your choice. The shape and line tools are drawing tools, enabling you to add geometrically shaped objects to the image window.

Introducing Painting Tools

The Paintbrush, Airbrush, and Pencil Tools are the three painting tools available in the Photoshop Elements toolbox (see Figure 14.7). Click on a tool to view its option settings on the options bar. The Paintbrush and Pencil have custom brush settings, blending modes, and opacity settings. The Airbrush Tool has brush, blending mode, and pressure settings, but no opacity setting, in its options bar. Click and drag the cursor in the image window to apply the foreground color to the selected layer in the Layers palette.

Airbrush   Paintbrush   Pencil

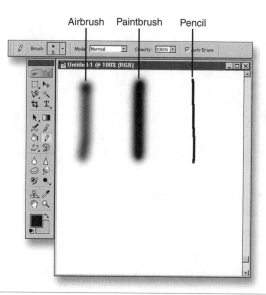

Figure 14.7
Each paint tool applies color in a slightly different pattern.

The Paintbrush and Airbrush Tools have a wider selection of brushes available to them. Experiment with different brush sizes in addition to different types of brushes, such as hard-edge and soft-edge brushes. The following list summarizes how each of the paint tools, plus the Eraser Tool, work.

- **Airbrush**—A spray effect is created with this paint tool. The longer you leave this tool over the image window, the darker the foreground color will become in the image window.

- **Paintbrush**—Creates an even-pressured stroke of color to the selected layer.

- **Pencil**—Creates a hard-edge pixel stroke.

- **Eraser**—Applies the background color to the image window. The Magic Eraser deletes the first color you click on in the image window. You also can use the Magic Erase Tool to change pixels to the background color, erase to transparency, or erase contiguous or all similar pixels in a layer. The Background Eraser removes all color from the layer or layers.

note
Although you can't draw or paint with the Eraser Tool like you can with the Paintbrush, Pencil, or Airbrush Tools, you can use the Eraser Tool to remove any strokes created by the paint and drawing tools. In fact, you can customize the mode of the Eraser Tool to match the settings in the Paintbrush, Airbrush, or Pencil tools by choosing one of these painting tools from the Eraser Tool's Mode drop-down menu, located in the options bar.

Each paint tool has several settings that you can customize in the options bar. Select one of the paint tools from the toolbox. Then view each of the settings in the options bar. The following list briefly describes each paint tool setting:

- **Brush**—Choose a brush size and style from the drop-down menu. The number below each brush indicates the number of pixels that are in that brush tip. You can customize the hardness, angle, spacing, and roundness of each brush. Click on the arrow button to choose a different set of brushes.

- **Mode**—Select a Blending mode for the foreground color applied by the paint tool.

- **Opacity**—Set the transparency level of the color. This setting is not available for the Airbrush Tool.

- **Pressure**—Choose a percentage value to set the pressure of the Airbrush Tool. The longer you hold down the mouse, the more pressure will be applied to the tool, increasing the amount of color that appears in the image window.

- **Wet Edges or Auto Erase**—Adds an effect to the applied color for the Paintbrush, making the color appear darker toward the edge of the stroke. If the Pencil Tool is selected, the Auto Erase check box enables you to erase the foreground colored pixels with the background color.

- **Brush Options**—Customize the Size, Color, and Opacity settings of the selected brush.

The Eraser Tool can remove any strokes created by the Paintbrush, Airbrush, and Pencil Tools. It can also erase strokes created by other bitmap-editing tools, such as the Clone Stamp Tool. You can use three eraser tools from the toolbox: Eraser, Background Eraser, and Magic Eraser. Figure 14.8 shows how each type of eraser affects a set of paint strokes created in the same layer.

note

The Smudge, Blur, Sponge, and Sharpen Tools in the toolbox also enable you to customize the Pressure setting in each tool's options bar.

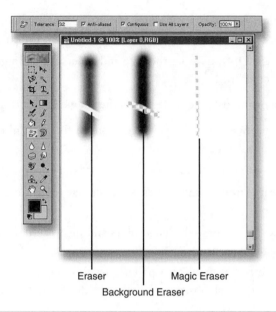

Eraser

Background Eraser

Magic Eraser

Figure 14.8
The Eraser Tool replaces the foreground color with the background color. The
Background Eraser removes the foreground and background colors, and the
Magic Eraser can be configured to remove a selected color, all similar colors,
erase with the background color, or to transparency.

Each eraser tool has a unique group of settings. The Eraser Tool can
share many of the same settings as the Paintbrush, Airbrush, or
Pencil Tools. For example, if you select Paintbrush from the Mode
window of the Eraser Tool's options bar, you will see the following
options appear along with the Paintbrush setting: Brush, Mode,
Opacity, Wet Edges, and Brush options for the Eraser Tool from the
options bar. The Airbrush Tool will enable you to adjust the pressure
of the Eraser Tool in Airbrush mode. The Pencil mode enables you
to adjust the opacity of the Eraser in Pencil mode. You can choose
Block mode if you want to use the Eraser Tool without any special
Painting Tool options.

The following list briefly describes each of the settings of the
Background Eraser Tool:

* **Brush**—Select a brush size from the drop-down menu.
* **Limits**—Choose either Discontiguous to erase the sampled
  color only, or Contiguous if you want to erase connected areas
  of sampled color.

333

- **Tolerance**—Drag the slider control or type a value into the text box to adjust how much color is erased from the path of the tool.

- **Brush Options**—Set the Size and Tolerance settings for the selected brush.

The following list briefly describes the Magic Eraser Tool's settings:

- **Tolerance**—Enables you to customize the amount of color removed from the selected layer.

- **Anti-aliased**—Smoothes the edges of the erased colors.

- **Contiguous**—Only erases pixels similar to the color you initially sample.

- **Use All Layers**—Deletes colors and pixels across layers in the image window.

- **Opacity**—Sets the transparency level of the erased color by moving the slider control, or by typing in a value into the Opacity text box.

Bitmap Versus Vector Graphics

Paint tools create bitmap patterns of color in a layer. These images will not scale well if increased in size. If you plan to use a paint tool, try to draw the image to scale, or larger than the actual size you need.

Drawing tools, on the other hand, are created as vector graphics. Vector graphics use a mathematical algorithm to retain their original shape if increased or decreased in size. If you want to create dynamic graphics, use the drawing tools, such as the shape tools, to create your graphics.

Introducing Drawing Tools

You'll find seven shape tools sharing one location in the toolbox. This strategic toolbox design is for a very good reason. You can select any shape tool from the options bar, regardless of which icon is selected in the toolbox.

You can create rectangles, circles, lines, and custom shapes with the drawing tools, as shown in Figure 14.9. The drawing tool creates two components in each shape layer: the color component and the shape. The link icon between the two layer components enables you to select and move the object in the image window. Click on the link icon if you want to modify the shape or color. Click on the color thumbnail to choose a new color from the Color Picker window.

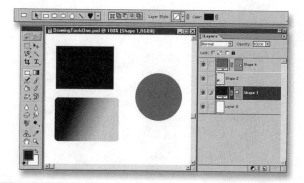

Figure 14.9
Master the drawing tools by adding shapes to the image window.

The following list briefly describes each shape drawing tool:

- **Rectangle**—Draw a square or rectangle with this tool.

- **Rounded Rectangle**—Identical to the Rectangle Tool, except each corner is rounded. Great for creating signs and buttons.

- **Ellipse**—Click and drag this tool to create a circle, oval, or ellipse.

- **Polygon**—Draw a multisided graphic.

- **Line**—Draw a straight line. Click on the Shape drop-down menu, located on the right end of the shape selection window in the options bar. Click on the Start or End check boxes if you want to add arrowheads to either end of the line.

- **Custom Shape**—Choose a custom shape from one of over a dozen custom shape libraries. Click on the Shape drop-down menu to choose custom shape options.

- **Shape Selection**—Pick a shape that has been added to the image window. Check the Show Bounding Box check box if you want to view the selected shape's bounding box.

Each shape can have unique settings. For example, you can apply a gradient or effect to a shape to create great looking graphics as shown in Figure 14.10. The following list briefly describes each setting in the shape options bar:

- **Shape**—Click on a shape icon to choose the shape you want to create in the image window.

Figure 14.10
Simplify a shape, and then apply effects to create custom graphics.

- **Radius**—This option enables you to set how many pixels each corner is rounded if the Rounded Rectangle shape is the selected shape.

- **Create New Shape Layer**—Creates a new layer in the Layers palette for the shape that will be drawn in the image window. This icon is located in the middle of the options bar when a shape tool is selected. It is grouped with the Add/Subtract, Intersect, and Exclude Shape icons.

- **Add/Subtract from Shape**—Choose the Add setting to add a new shape to an existing shape. Or subtract a shape from an existing shape in the image window.

- **Intersect Shape Areas**—Preserves the overlapped area of two overlapping shapes.

- **Exclude Overlapping Shape Areas**—Preserves the non-overlapping area of two overlapping shapes.

- **Layer Style**—Add a Bevel, Drop Shadow, Glow, or other effect to the shape by choosing a layer style from the drop-down menu.

- **Color**—Select a color for the shape or line.
- **Simplify**—Merge the color and shape components in a layer into one component. This command converts a vector graphic into a bitmap graphic.

Variations—Creating Signs with Drawing and Painting Tools

You can enhance your photos by combining painting and drawing tools to design custom graphics. For example, you can use the paint tools to add graffiti to the wall or sidewalk of the storefront shown in Figure 14.11. In this example, two kinds of signs will be created with shape and text tools.

Figure 14.11
The storefront before graphics and text are added.

You can combine shape tools and Layer styles to create a three-dimensional sign, shown in Figure 14.12. Or you can create a text object and change the Opacity and Blending mode settings to create a window sign.

To create a sign using the drawing and painting tools, do the following:

1. Select the Rounded Rectangle shape to create the sign. A separate layer will be created in the Layers palette for the rounded rectangle. You can change its color or shape by selecting either component in the Shape 1 layer.

Figure 14.12
The same photo after two signs are added to it.

2. Next, choose a custom shape to place in the center of the sign (see Figure 14.13). In this example, I chose a symbol shape from the People library. You can choose a library from the drop-down menu located in the Shape window of the Symbol Shape Tool options bar. Use the Move Tool to place the custom shape on the rounded rectangle.

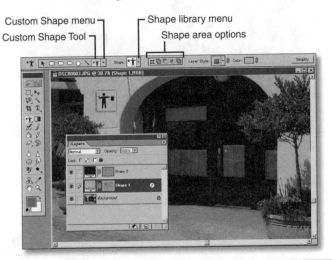

Figure 14.13
Use the Shape and Custom Shape Tools combined with Layer styles to create a sign.

3. Place the cursor between the two shape layers in the Layers palette.

4. Hold down the (Option) [Alt] key. The cursor icon changes from an arrow to a small arrow with two overlapping circles. Click on the line between the two layers. Then release the (Option) [Alt] key. A down-pointing arrow, shown in Figure 14.14, will appear in the top layer, indicating the two layers are grouped together. You can group two layers together to preserve their order in the Layers palette.

Figure 14.14
Group the two shape layers in the Layers palette.

5. Select the Horizontal Type Tool and type some text into the image window. Use the Move Tool to line up the text object with the background image.

6. You can apply the Transform commands to add perspective, or scale the text to fit with the rest of the image. If you want the text object to blend in with the background image, choose a Blending mode and decrease the Opacity value in the Layers palette.

When you select a symbol shape, a Shape selection window appears in the options bar. Click on the shape window to view the drop-down menu. You can choose from five views to navigate through each of the custom shape libraries. The following list briefly describes each view:

• **Text Only**—Lists each shape without any visual aides.

• **Small Thumbnail**—Probably the ideal view for custom shapes. Enables you to view all images in a library without scrolling.

note
A list of all the Symbol Shape Tool libraries is provided at this end of this section.

note
When two or more layers are grouped together, the bottom layer defines the boundary of any layers that are a part of the group. The name of the bottom layer of the group will become underlined in the Layers palette. You can ungroup two layers by holding down the (Option) [Alt] key and clicking on the group icon (two overlapping circles), which is located between the two grouped layers in the Layers palette.

note

Grouping two layers together is different than linking layers together. Linking two or more layers together preserves the location of each object to each other in the image window. Whenever you move the primary object in the link, all other linked objects will adjust to the new location.

You can link together two or more layers in the Layers palette. First, select the layer to which you want to link other layers. Then, click in the right check box beside a second or third layer to link those layers to the selected layer.

- **Large Thumbnail**—Doubles the size of the small thumbnail images.

- **Small List**—Organizes the library items in list view with a small icon in the left side of each item name.

- **Large List**—Same as the small list, except uses larger icons.

You can use 14 custom shape libraries to create professional-looking graphics for Web or print. The following list briefly describes each of the custom shape libraries:

- **Animals**—Includes butterflies, deer, cats, and dogs.

- **Arrows**—Contains fancy arrow shapes.

- **Awards**—Includes trophy and flag silhouettes.

- **Default**—Contains an assortment of shapes, such as a heart, a moon, a barefoot icon, and directional arrows.

- **Frames**—Contains more than a dozen frame shapes.

- **Fruit**—Includes cherries, pineapple, apple, pear, and other fruit icons.

- **Miscellaneous**—Contains an assortment of puzzle shapes, keys, and cutlery icons.

- **Nature**—Includes sun, moon, stars, sky, and water shapes.

- **Office**—Contains shapes of pens, paper, and phones.

- **People**—Contains gender-neutral symbols of people, ideal for creating a sign or for marking a handicapped parking space.

- **Plants**—Contains 10 leaf icons.

- **Signs**—Includes various traffic-related sign shapes.

- **Talk Bubbles**—Contains more than a dozen cartoon-like bubble shapes.

- **Travel**—Includes airplanes, cars, and suitcase icons.

Designing Bitmap and Vector Graphics

Because most of the tools in Photoshop Elements are bitmap tools, you won't be creating vector graphics unless you're working with the Type or Shape Tools. Nevertheless, you can combine bitmap and vector graphics in the same file or image window.

Combining these two different kinds of graphics isn't really the big issue. The big concern is usually whether you should create a graphic as a bitmap or vector graphic. As mentioned previously, vector graphics are great because they keep their sharpness whether you grow or shrink them. However, bitmap graphics are made up of a fixed set of pixels. Growing a bitmap image generally results in creating a bigger bitmap, with chunkier, squarish-looking pixels.

Because vector graphics are so flexible and dynamic, they carry more information along with them, which usually increases the overall file size. In general, the same size bitmap graphic will be smaller than, and possibly not as crisp as, a vector graphic of an equal shape and color.

Drawing a Bitmap Graphic

Open an image file such as the one shown in Figure 14.15. In this example, bitmap and vector graphics will be added to this image. Follow these steps to add a bitmap graphic to an image:

Figure 14.15
The background layer stores the locked image of a newly opened document.

1. Choose Layer from the Layer, New menu, or click on the Create a New Layer button at the bottom of the Layers palette to create a new layer. Select the new layer in the Layers palette. Choose a paint tool from the toolbox.

2. Choose a brush size and style, as shown in Figure 14.16. Specify the blending mode and opacity of the brush.

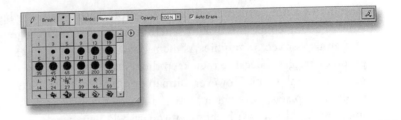

Figure 14.16
Choose a brush from the options panel for the Pencil Tool. The fish on the bottom of this figure was created with a hard-edged brush with the Pencil Tool. The fish above it was created with a soft-edged brush with the Paintbrush Tool.

3. Click and drag the tool in the image window to draw the image.

4. Scale the graphic to fit with the background image. You can experiment with different compositions, such as the one shown in Figure 14.17.

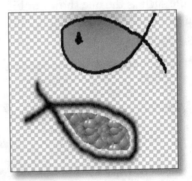

Figure 14.17
You can enlarge the shape of each graphic or move each one around in the image window.

Creating Transparent Text

You can adjust the transparency setting of a text object from the Layers palette. Lowering the text object's opacity settings can help it blend in with any of the image layers directly below it. The Opacity setting in the Layers palette enables you to add transparency to an object by decreasing the value in the Opacity text box. You can create transparent text or graphics that blend in with the background image like the text object shown in Figure 14.18.

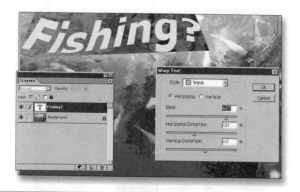

Figure 14.18
You can adjust the opacity setting of text before or after applying an effect to it.
The Warp Text Tool can add instant special effects to a picture.

The following steps show you how to add text to an image, apply the
Warp Tool, and then adjust the text object's opacity settings (shown
in Figure 14.18):

1. First, select the Text Tool and type some text into the image
   window.

2. Click on the tools in the options bar to format the text. Choose
   the Warp Text button to open the Warp Text window.

3. Then choose a warp style and adjust the warp text effect.

4. Click on OK to save your changes.

5. Next, select the text layer in the Layers palette. Click on the
   drop-down arrow to move the slider control for the Opacity
   setting.

6. Set the opacity to roughly 50 to 70%, as shown in Figure 14.19.
   The background should show through the solid regions of the
   text.

You can place the text anywhere in the image window. Use the Move
Tool to select and move the text object. Place it over a part of the
background image that might show a pattern or object through the
letters of text.

Figure 14.19
Adjust the Opacity level of the image to blend the text with the background image.

Modifying Custom Shapes

You can choose a shape tool from the toolbox to add a simple geometric shape to a photo. When you apply the shape tool—or any other vector graphic tool—to the image window, Photoshop Elements creates a new layer to store the new graphics. This new layer is usually created above the selected or active layer in the Layers palette, enabling you to overlap the graphic with the picture.

If drawing tools don't do the trick for you, try adding text or paint to a picture in the image window. You can apply the Type or Paint tools to any image window. Text and graphics can overlap with each other, in addition to overlapping with the background image. You organize the order that text and graphic objects appear in the image window by changing their order in the Layers palette. For instance, you can place a particular text or graphic object in front of or behind other objects by placing it above or below other layers in the Layers palette.

To add a drop shadow or reflection to a text object, select the layer you want to copy and drop it over the Create New Layer icon in the Layers palette. Photoshop Elements will create a new layer containing the contents of the original layer. The following steps show you how to add a new shape to an image window:

1. Select the Shape Tool from the toolbox.
2. Then click on the custom shape in the options bar.
3. Click on the Shape drop-down menu to view the shapes loaded from the currently selected library, as shown in Figure 14.20.
4. Click on the right-arrow button in the drop-down menu to view or select a different shape library. In this example, I chose a fish from the Animals library.

Figure 14.20
Choose a custom shape form the built-in library of images.

To add a color or layer style to the custom shape, perform the following steps:

1. After the shape is added to the image window, the link icons will appear beside the Layer Style and Color boxes in the options bar.
2. Click on the Layer Style menu button, shown in Figure 14.20, to view and select a layer style. You can drag and drop the layer style onto any object in the image window to enhance the target object.
3. Click on the right-arrow menu, also shown in Figure 14.21, to choose a different layer style library.

tip
To find out more about layer styles, see Chapter 13, "Working with Layers and Layer Styles."

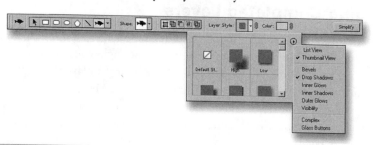

Figure 14.21
Drag and drop a layer style onto the custom shape.

You can change the color of the custom shape by clicking on the Color swatch in the options bar. The Color Picker window will open. Choose a color for the graphic in the Color Picker window, and then click on OK. The new color will appear in the left thumbnail beside the shape thumbnail in the shape layer of the Layers palette. You can change the shape color as often as you like as long as you do not simplify the shape layer.

The Transform commands enable you to grow, shrink, skew, distort, apply perspective, and rotate a shape in the image window. Click on the Image, Transform menu to view the Transform commands. You can also press (Command-T) [Ctrl+T] to choose the Free Transform command to the selected layer.

If you want to experiment with the Transform commands, create a copy of a custom shape. Select the shape layer of the graphic, and then drag and drop it over the Create a New layer icon in the Layers palette. The copied layer will appear in the Layers palette and the copied shape will appear over the selected shape in the image window. Select the Move Tool to move it to a new location in the image window.

Select the Move Tool and drag the copy of the shape to a new location in the image window. Select a custom layer style and color for the shape. In this example, I reduced the size of the copied shape, and then flipped it horizontally, as shown in Figure 14.22. If you want to permanently keep the shape settings and prevent the shape from being edited, select it, and then choose Simplify Layer from the Layer menu. The color and shape thumbnails will merge into a single thumbnail image.

Merging Completed Layers

As you put together different graphics and images, you might want to merge some layers together to make those changes permanent. You can combine two or more layers by hiding all layers except for the ones you want to merge. Then choose the Merge Visible command from the Layer menu. Photoshop Elements will convert the layers that appear in the image window into a single layer in the Layers palette.

Figure 14.22
Combine layer styles and linked elements by simplifying a layer.

If you want to make the shape part of the background image, first show the two layers in the Layers palette. Then choose the Merge Visible command from the Layer menu. You can also press (Shift-Command-E)[Shift+Ctrl+E] to merge any visible images in the image window. The two layers will be merged into a single layer.

Applying Effects with the Impressionist Brush

Photoshop Elements has a full suite of filters and effects you can apply to your background images and shapes. If you want to apply an impressionist effect to a specific graphic, or to an area of a bitmap image, you can choose the Impressionist Brush, shown in Figure 14.23, to paint with stylized strokes. The Impressionist Brush gives a photograph a unique look by blending the colors and images of a particular layer together.

You can adjust the brush settings to experiment with different kinds of impressionist effects and different types of images. Select the Impressionist Brush from the toolbox to view its settings in the options bar. The brush settings are located on the left side of the options bar. If you're working with an image that consists of more than one layer, select the layer to which you want to apply this tool from the Layers palette. Then click and drag the brush over the image window to texturize the pixels in the image window.

Figure 14.23
You can use the Impressionist Brush to blend a custom graphic into your background image. The Impressionist Brush was applied to the bottom half of the fish graphic.

In addition to the Mode and Opacity settings, which are also available with the Paintbrush and Airbrush Tools, there are several other settings you can customize when using the Impressionist Brush. The following list briefly describes each setting:

- **Brush**—Pick a brush tip for the Impressionist Brush.
- **Mode**—Select a blending mode from the drop-down menu.
- **Style**—Control the shape of the painted strokes. Choose a Tight Short, Tight Medium, Tight Long, Loose Medium, Loose Long, Dab, Tight Curl, Tight Curl Long, Loose Curl, or Loose Curl Long style from the menu list.
- **Fidelity**—Decide how much the paint color changes between the new and old colors in the image window. A lower percent adds more color to the resulting stroke.
- **Area**—Type the number of pixels you want the brush to affect.

- **Spacing**—Enter a percentage to restrict the way the paint stroke is applied. A lower value enables you to paint anywhere in the image window. A higher value limits the colors the brush can change.

- **Brush Options**—Adjust the size and opacity settings of the brush stroke.

Previewing the Final Image

You can now place each graphic in the image window and view the final image before saving it for the Web or before you print it. If you are going to use the image on the Web or send it via email, you can optimize the final image by choosing Flatten Image from the Layer menu. Then adjust the color palette in the Save for Web dialog box to a Web safe palette, or just convert the image to Indexed Color mode. With the exception of Photoshop native and TIF formats, most file formats will automatically flatten all layers into one in order to create the final image. Figure 14.24 shows the final text and graphics photo. If you have the hard drive space available, save a copy of the image as a PSD file to preserve its layer information.

Figure 14.24
The final photo. It's a good idea to save a copy of the image as a PSD file to preserve its layer information.

chapter 15

Repairing Images

Restoring damaged photos is definitely a challenging task. It's no picnic trying to re-create missing portions of an image, or trying to determine the original colors of a worn, faded photo. However, the reward can be extraordinarily worthwhile in sentimental value alone. Repairing a worn or torn image helps preserve the look and feel of earlier photography as well as family history and heritage.

Repairing Folds and Tears

It would be nice if we all kept two copies of important photos: one in a photo album, in pristine condition, and another one in our wallet or in a picture frame. Unfortunately, this usually isn't the case. Sometimes photos are accidentally folded or torn as they are shuffled from album to album, or from home to home over the years. Figure 15.1 shows a color photo that has been folded and gathered dust and stains over the years.

Figure 15.1
The before photo with torn, folded paper.

My mother asked me to repair the photo in Figure 15.1. She didn't have the negative, and requested any size print I could muster up, expecting me to repair any wear and tear accrued over the years. Before I started to work on this image, I tried to assess the different kinds of work and tools I might need to use for this project.

The Clone Stamp Tool definitely was my tool of choice. It enables me to sample from the selected layer, or across all layers, and then apply the sampled pixels to the active layer. This is helpful for using undamaged areas of an image to repair missing, torn, or worn areas of an image.

I also wanted to keep my repairs on separate layers, so that I could undo any area I incorrectly tried to fix. Several tools, such as the Clone Stamp, Blur, Smudge, and Eraser Tools, can be applied to either a single layer or across all layers in an image. Working with these tools and keeping my corrections on separate layers enables me to experiment with different repair techniques without altering the original image.

In addition to the torn, folded edges that create x and y axes in the photo, the white areas of the photo had dust, stains, and coloring imperfections. There also were several speck marks in various places in the image, probably created when the original print was made. I decided to experiment with different soft-edge brush sizes with the Clone Stamp Tool to repair these smaller areas of the image. I created a correction layer in the Layers palette to store the dust and speck corrections.

note

To find out more about how to create a new layer and how to work with layers in the Layers palette, go to Chapter 13, "Working with Layers and Layer Styles."

Straightening an Image

Before you start to repair a photo, make sure the image is properly aligned in addition to performing any tonal or color corrections. Sometimes images are scanned with a slight rotation. If you weren't using a tripod when taking a digital photo, you might have under- or over-rotated the camera.

You can correct these crooked images by applying one of the Straighten commands. First, click on a layer in the Layers palette. Then, choose the Straighten Image command from the Image, Rotate menu. Photoshop Elements first will create a new, empty layer, and then apply the Image Skew and Rotate commands to the image in the selected layer. The corrected image is placed in a new layer.

You also can apply a selection tool to straighten and crop a particular part of an image. First, choose a selection tool, such as the Rectangular Marquee Tool from the toolbox. Apply the selection tool to the image window. Then, select the Straighten and Crop Image command from the Image, Rotate menu. Photoshop Elements will adjust the axis of the image, and then crop out the nonselected areas of the image. The cropped image will be created in a new layer in the image window, but also will replace the background image.

Not all images work well with the Straighten command. If you apply this command to an image and don't get the results you expected, choose Undo from the Edit menu, or select a previous state of the document from the History palette. If the Straighten command fails to straighten an image, the Straighten and Crop command might produce similar, unstraightened, results for the same image.

Eliminating Wrinkles and Torn Areas

You can apply tools directly to the background layer of an image to repair damaged areas, and save different copies of the image file to your hard drive until you create a repaired image you want to publish or print. However, it's best to create one or several new layers in the Layers palette, as shown in Figure 15.2, to store any corrections. Click in the left column on the eye icon in the Layers palette to hide a layer, or click on the empty box to make the eye icon appear and show the selected layer in the image window. You can hide or show the corrected areas of the image and quickly compare them to the original. You can apply the Erase Tool to the correction layer to remove any corrected areas you're not happy with.

Figure 15.2
Create a new layer for the corrections.

You might want to keep different kinds of corrections in different layers so you can keep track of what is changing. You can also compare different corrections, or experiment with different methods of repairing the image, without altering the actual pixels of the scanned or photographed image. The following list highlights a few of the common kinds of image damage and suggestions for repairing or correcting each one. You can create a separate layer for each type of correction you want to perform on an image that you want to repair.

- **Heavily damaged areas**—Removing torn or folded paper and replacing it with an image can be a cumbersome task. You can create a new layer and apply the Clone Stamp Tool to sample an undamaged portion of the original image, and apply that to a correction layer. If you like the changes, you can replace the torn image in the lower layer with a reconstructed image in the correction layer.

- **Color-correction areas**—You might want to create a fill or gradient layer to correct aged photos or color casts created by flash or internal lighting.

- **Changes in color**—Consider creating separate layers for skin tones versus clothes, furniture, or other items in the photo.

- **Dust and specks**—Sometimes it's difficult to discern a dust spec from actual image details. Keeping these corrections on a separate layer can help restore detailed elements in an image.

- **Mold and stains**—Tiny areas of color distortion might be difficult to correct. You can adjust the brush size of the Clone Stamp, Smudge, or Blur Tools to try to remove small sets of pixels that need to be repaired.

You can repair an image with the image window set to any view. However, in most cases, it will be easier to repair an image if you use the Zoom Tool to magnify the area on which you want to work. Click on the Zoom Tool, and click on the area you want to magnify. Press the (Option) [Alt] key and click on the image if you want to zoom out from the image. You also can set the image window view to 200% or 300%. Click in the text box located in the lower-left corner of the image, and type 200 or 300, or choose the Zoom In command from the View menu until the text box shows 200 or 300. Adjust the view so that you can see all or part of the image you want to repair in the active image window.

When you're ready to begin repairing the image, select the layer in which you want to store the corrected pixels. Then, magnify the image in the image window. Figure 15.3 shows the torn area of the image before and after applying the Clone Stamp Tool to the image. If you select the Clone Stamp Tool from the toolbox, check the Use All Layers check box. This setting enables you to sample pixels from any layers located below the active layer in the Layers palette. Select the correction layer from the Layers palette. Then, sample and apply the Clone Stamp Tool in the image window, and repair areas close to the damaged area without altering the original image.

Keep these issues in mind when making image repairs with the Clone Stamp Tool:

- Choose a brush with a soft edge so that the edges of the brush strokes blend into the surrounding pixels.

- Pick a brush size that covers part of the torn area of the image. You can compare the torn area with the repaired pixels in the image. If the repair looks like it matches the rest of the image, you might want to repair the remaining torn area, or resample pixels close to each area of the torn image before applying the replacement pixels. Don't try to use a brush that's too large or too small to repair damaged areas in the image.

note
To find out more about how to use the Clone Stamp Tool, go to Chapter 2, "Navigating the Work Area."

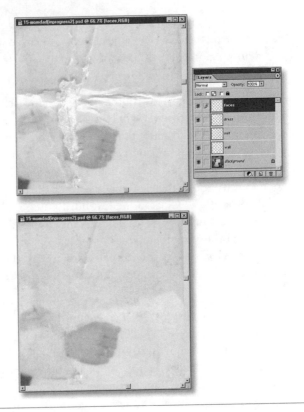

Figure 15.3
Create a new layer for different repair areas of the image. Compare the image before and after applying corrections by hiding and showing the correction layer in the Layers palette.

- Try to avoid sampling discolored or shaded areas of the image. If you sample damaged or worn areas of the image, they will be applied to the correction layer in other areas of the image. If you can't avoid sampling part of the damaged image, try choosing a smaller brush and reconstructing smaller portions of the damaged area.

- Avoid creating long strokes. Make a few small corrections, and then zoom out to a wide view to see whether the corrections match the surrounding image, as shown in Figure 15.4.

Figure 15.4
Zoom out to view the repaired portion of the image and compare it to the rest
of the photo.

Removing Aged Color, Dust, and Stains

Although you can remove dust and stains before or after repairing an
image, you might find it is easier to make small corrections to an
image after fixing the bigger problems. For example, Figure 15.5
shows how it is a little easier to identify the stains and dust after the
folds and tears have been removed.

note
To find out more
about each of the
settings available
for the Clone
Stamp Tool, go to
Chapter 2,
"Navigating the
Work Area."

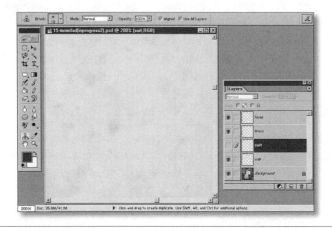

Figure 15.5
Stains and dust cover most of the scanned photo. This is a close-up of the white
jacket shown in Figure 15.4. You might need to look closely to find the faint
hues of the stains.

Again, you can apply the Clone Stamp Tool to remove dust, stains, or discoloration in an image. Use the following steps to correct a damaged image:

1. Click on the Clone Stamp Tool in the toolbox, and then choose a soft-edge brush from the options bar. Be sure to use a brush size that roughly covers part of the size of each stain. Also, check the Use All Layers check box. This setting enables you to sample pixels in any layer below the selected layer. Then, apply the sample pixels to only the selected layer.

2. Look for an area of pixels near the stained pixels.

3. Sample a set of pixels about half the size of the stained area by holding down the (Opt) [Alt] key while moving the cursor over the area to be sampled. The tool will sample the image from the background layer.

4. Select the correction layer in the Layers palette. Apply the Clone Stamp Tool to the correction layer. Remove a small portion of the stain, and hide and show the correction layer to see whether your correction matches the unstained areas of the image.

5. Repeat these steps until the dust or stain is removed. Then, clean up the area in the image window, as shown in Figure 15.6. The Clone Stamp Tool is the most commonly used tool for removing dust and scratches. However, you might want to experiment with the Smudge, Blur, or Magic Eraser Tools to see whether they are easier to use or provide better results for the image you're working with.

You can apply the Undo command to remove any corrections added to the image window. If you like part of a correction, try applying the Eraser Tool to the corrections layer. Remove any undesired pixels from the correction layer to restore the original pixels.

You can choose from three kinds of Eraser Tools in the toolbox. In addition to the standard Eraser Tool, you can remove a range of colors with the Magic Eraser Tool. It works similarly to the Magic Wand Tool, except it removes any color you click on in the image window. The Eraser and Magic Eraser Tools can be used to remove specific-colored pixels, or pixels in a certain location in a correction layer.

tip

Hold down the Shift key and press the letter E to cycle through each Eraser Tool in the toolbox.

Select the Eraser, Magic Eraser, or Background Eraser Tool. Hold down the (Command) [Ctrl] key to change the cursor to the Move Tool.

Figure 15.6
After applying the Clone Stamp Tool, the stains and dust are removed from the photo.

You also can use the Background Eraser Tool to remove the pixels in a correction layer, thus exposing transparency. It can override the Lock Transparency setting if it has been applied to a layer. The Background Eraser Tool can show the previous layer through the layer where this tool has been applied.

Fine-Tuning the Image

To fine-tune an image, you have to move to different parts of the image and gradually repair small areas of the image. Compare the before and after areas as you progress to see whether the corrected image resembles the original. This can take quite a bit of time. Patience plays a big role, especially if you want to preserve as much of the original picture as possible.

After you've corrected most of the problems in the image, you might want to add a fill or adjustment layer to pull together any disparately lit areas of the picture. Figure 15.7 shows a fill and adjustment layer added to the repaired image to warm the colors in the photo. Adjust the settings in the fill or adjustment layers if needed, and then merge any visible layers you want to keep in the final picture.

You can add adjustment layers to correct any areas of the image that are too light or too dark. Apply a fill layer and adjust its opacity level to add color to the image. You can create adjustment or fill layers for

note
To find out more about how to use the Eraser Tool, go to Chapter 14, "Adding Text and Shapes to Images."

a selected area of the image, and then merge the correction layer and the fill or adjustment layer to make those changes permanent.

note

To find out more about how to create fill or adjustment layers, or when to merge layers in an image, go to Chapter 13, "Working with Layers and Layer Styles."

Figure 15.7
Merge layers together as corrections are made. Apply adjustment and gradient fill layers to pull the final image together.

Comparing Images

Before saving the final image, compare it to the original, damaged photo. You might want to keep one or two visual defects in the digitally retouched photo if you want to preserve the look and feel of the original photo. Figure 15.8 shows the final, flattened image.

Figure 15.8
After repairing folds, tears, and stains, the image should resemble the original.

If you want to post the image to a Web site, you can resize it after the layers have been flattened into a JPEG file. You might want to choose the Save for Web command from the File menu to optimize the file size of the Web file. However, if you want to print the image, it's best not to remove any pixel information by shrinking it.

Save the final image to your hard drive. Compare the original, damaged photo with the restored photo by zooming into both images. In Figure 15.9, notice that the original image has a little more detail than the restored image. However, it is difficult to tell where the damaged areas were upon examining the restored image.

Figure 15.9
Zoom into the original and compare it to the final image.

Rebuilding a Damaged Photo

Worn photos might also be missing portions of the original image. You can use the Clone Stamp Tool, and, if needed, additional photos, to reconstruct missing areas of a scanned image. Figure 15.10 shows the before and after pictures of a photo of my great grandmother. Wear and tear removed most of the left side of the photo. The following sections show you how to restore the missing areas of the image, and then re-create the tattered, frayed areas of the photo.

Figure 15.10
A photo of my great grandmother before and after repairing it.

Sorting Out Tasks By Layer

First, create a separate layer for each area of the photo that you want to correct or repair, as shown in Figure 15.11. In addition to the damaged areas on the left side of the picture, there are a few small scratches on the right. Apply the Clone Stamp Tool to sample and correct the scratches in a correction layer.

Figure 15.11
Create a separate layer for each area of the image that needs to be repaired.

Assess the different kinds of damage before applying any tools to the image window after selecting the appropriate correction layer in the Layers palette. You might want to save a copy of the image as you work on it if you want to experiment with different techniques for repairing the image. You also can duplicate and show or hide different correction layers. You can delete a layer if it turns out you don't need it as you repair the image with other correction layers.

Removing Scratches and Dirt

It can't hurt to remove any scratches or dirt from an image before you start to rebuild the missing areas of the image. For example, if you plan to sample from an area of an image that contains scratches, it will be easier to reconstruct the missing areas after you remove any specks, dust, or scratches from the images. Then the reconstructed image will not inherit these defects.

Before you begin to sample or repair the scratches or dirt, first zoom into a damaged portion of the image, as shown in Figure 15.12. Try to identify the original color or tonal range of the image. Also try to differentiate the paper and backdrop in the photo from the subject of the photo.

The following steps show you how to remove scratches or dust from the photo:

1. Click on the Create a New Layer button at the bottom of the Layers palette. A new layer with a transparent background will appear in the Layers palette.

2. Select this new layer in the Layers palette. Click on the Zoom Tool (Z) in the toolbox, and magnify the area of the image you want to rebuild (see Figure 15.12).

3. Choose the Clone Stamp Tool from the toolbox. Check the Use All Layers check box. Select a brush size to match the thickness of the scratch. Then, use the Clone Stamp Tool to sample undamaged pixels and replace the scratches and specks with the sampled pixels. In this example, the Clone Stamp Tool will sample pixels from the background layer and apply them to the new layer to repair the scratches and dust in the image.

Figure 15.12
Zoom into the image and try to identify as much detail about the original image as possible.

Replacing Missing Pieces of the Image

There are a couple of different ways you can replace a missing piece of an image. One way is to sample small portions from the existing image and reconstruct the missing area. The second way is to copy and paste part of an image from a different image file. This second method works well for replacing unique images, or images that are missing larger portions of an image. The first method is effective for reconstructing images missing small sections of an image.

The general process for replacing a missing portion of an area is fairly straightforward. First, select a correction layer in the Layers palette. Then, apply a tool, such as the Clone Stamp Tool, to the image window. Check the Use All Layers check box, and then sample a whole, undamaged area in the image. Apply the Clone Stamp Tool to fill in a missing chunk of the image with the sampled pixels. Zoom out to see whether the repaired area visually matches the rest of the picture.

Repeat these steps until the missing areas of the image are reconstructed. Try to use other photos of the subject to restore hairstyle or clothing patterns, if you have them. Figure 15.13 shows the repaired image after tediously applying the Clone Stamp Tool.

Figure 15.13
Use the Clone Stamp Tool to reconstruct missing areas of the image.

Creating the Final Image

If the backdrop area of the photo is seriously damaged, it might be easier to reconstruct as much of the subject as possible. Move the subject to a new image window. Then create a new backdrop by adding fill layers.

The following steps show you how to move the subject in the damaged photo to a new image window:

1. Use a selection tool, such as the Magic Wand Tool, to select the subject in the damaged photo. You also can press the (Command) [Ctrl] key while clicking on the layer containing the image you want to select to highlight the image. Then, choose the Copy command from the Edit menu.

2. Choose New from the File menu and create a new document. Photoshop Elements will automatically input the width and height of the image into the New dialog box. Select a transparent background for the new window.

3. Choose Paste from the Edit menu to add the selected image into the new image window (see Figure 15.14).

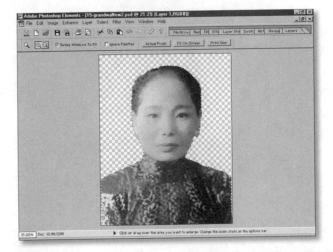

Figure 15.14
Copy the selected image and paste it into a new image window. The gray and white grid indicates the background is transparent.

4. Choose Gradient from the New, New Fill Layer menu. Type a name for the gradient layer, and then click OK. Click on the gradient in the Gradient Fill window. The Gradient Editor window opens.

5. Click in each square slider control located below the gradient bar in the Gradient Editor window. Click in the Color box to choose a new color for the gradient. Then, click OK in the Gradient Editor. You might want to adjust the angle of the gradient to match the angle of the light source in the image window. Click OK in the Gradient Fill window to add the Gradient Fill Layer to the image window.

6. Select the Solid Color command from the Layer, New Fill Layer menu to add a fill or adjustment layer to the image (see Figure 15.15). You can adjust the colors and opacity levels of these layers and place them in the background and foreground of the image to help blend the colors of the pasted image with the gradient and fill layers in the image window.

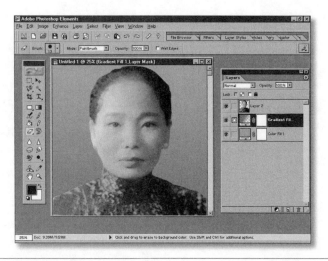

Figure 15.15
Re-create the background of the original image by adding gradient and solid color fill layers to the image.

The final image can consist of three layers. In Figure 15.16, the subject is first copied into its own layer. Then a fill layer is created to create the backdrop. The Merge Visible command combined the subject with the new backdrop. Then, I pasted the selected subject into the image window one more time. Finally, I added a gradient layer to the foreground of the image to blend the highlights, shadows, and colors of the image together.

Figure 15.16
The final image after moving it to a new image window.

Experimenting with Composite Images

A *composite image* is created when one or more images are placed in an image window and blended together to create a unique composition. Photoshop Elements enables you to combine multiple images into a single document. Each image you paste into the image window is placed into its own new layer, above the background layer in the document. You can use Photoshop Elements to blend pixels between any two layers, or apply tools to blend the edge pixels of one image with another image to make the final picture appear realistic. This chapter introduces you to a few basic techniques you can use to create composite images.

Creating Composite Images

Creating a composite image involves three steps: selecting an image, copying it, and then pasting it into the image window. Although the selection tools enable you to define the secondary image in a composite, the copy and paste commands enable you to duplicate and add images to an image window. A fourth step, moving and transforming the image, is optional but very likely to be part of your workflow when creating any realistic composite image.

Two scenarios exist for creating a composite image. The first one involves layering and possibly resizing selected images within the same image window. The second scenario involves adding one or more images to the active image window. The four-step process defines the workflow for both scenarios. The following steps walk you through this four-step process and explain some of the issues that might arise when creating a composite image.

1. **Selecting the image**—To define the image you want to copy, you must use a selection tool. The Magnetic Lasso Tool is probably the most helpful tool you can use to define the edges of a selection. However, you also can use the Marquee or Lasso selection tools to crop or copy a set of pixels you want to use with a composite image.

2. **Copying the image**—The Copy and Paste commands are located in the Edit menu. The Copy command enables you to duplicate pixels selected in the active image window and copy them to the Clipboard. The Clipboard is a Windows and Mac OS operating system resource designed to work hand in hand with the Copy and Paste commands. To place the contents of the Clipboard into the work area of the active image, you simply apply the Paste command.

3. **Pasting the image**—If you've already pasted an image into an image window, you've created a composite image. Each time you paste a new image into an image window, you will see a new layer appear in the Layers palette. The pasted image is also converted to the color mode of the new image window.

4. **Moving and transforming the image**—Although you can create a montage of images of any size or shape with composite images, you can also try to make the elements of the composite image blend together. The goal in this case is to make both images match the perspective of the background image, or create a logical spatial relationship resulting in a more believable

tip

If you want to experiment with a composite image before pasting it into another image window, you can copy and paste it into its own image window and adjust its size and color settings there before combining it with other images. You also can modify each pasted image in its own layer. Select an image layer by clicking on a layer in the Layers palette. To find out more about layers, go to Chapter 13, "Working with Layers and Layer Styles."

picture. You probably will need to rotate or resize each composite image to make them fit with the rest of the picture.

If you're not sure which images you want to combine, you can save the images separately, each in its own layer. Choose the File, Save As command to open the Save As dialog box. To preserve each image in the composite in its own layer, save the image file as a Photoshop (PSD) file. Select Photoshop from the Format drop-down menu, and then click on Save to save the PSD file to your hard drive. When you are ready to save the final image, you can flatten all the layers into one. You also can optimize the color palette, change color modes, or apply any final adjustment layers or color corrections to the image before saving the final image to your hard drive.

tip
To find out more about Photoshop Elements' native file format (PSD), see Chapter 8, "Saving and Sharing Files."

Choosing Images

It's important to pick an appropriate starter image as the backdrop for the second, third, or fourth images as you define the composite image. Figure 16.1 shows a picture of daisies; it will be used as the backdrop for this first example, which will show you how to create a composite image.

Along with the content of an image, you need to consider the dimensions of the background image. Decide whether the width and height of the background image match the composite images you want to place there. Also, check the resolution of the background image. Make sure you're working with the original, unedited source image, preferably in RGB color mode. If you plan to correct colors, apply a filter or effect, or modify the background image, you will get the best results if the image contains as many colors as possible.

Select an image you want to combine with the background image. You will want to choose an image that is slightly larger or one that matches the dimensions of the background image. For example, if the background image is 2000 pixels wide and 1500 pixels tall, choose a composite image that was also created at that size. Smaller images can also be added to the background image. However, if the smaller image needs to be resized into a larger, rather than smaller scale, its resolution will degrade, resulting in a pixelated image that won't match the higher-resolution background image.

caution
One of the limitations of the Copy and Paste commands is that the Clipboard can store only one image at a time. When you choose the Copy command, the previous image stored in the Clipboard is deleted, and a new one is added in its place. If you want to create a composite image containing several pasted images, save each one as an original, unedited file on your hard drive.

Before

Figure 16.1
The backdrop image has the proper dimensions and resolution for the images that will be placed here.

Although each image you add to the background image defines the composition, the backdrop image can make or break a composite image. Figure 16.2 shows a pair of daffodils added to the foreground of the first image. Notice the edges of the daffodils are soft so that they blend into the background image.

After

Figure 16.2
Adding daffodils into the backdrop photo results in a composite image.

Applying Selection Tools

Open an image file that contains the backdrop image you want to use to create the composite. Then, choose a selection tool from the tool-box. Use it to highlight the image you want to paste into the background image (see Figure 16.3). You can soften the edges of the selected image with features like the Feather command and the Blur Tool before moving it to another image window. You also can apply a filter or effect to the selected image, or rotate or transform the image before copying it to the Clipboard.

tip

To find out more about using the selection tools, see Chapter 11, "Tonal Range and Color Correction."

Figure 16.3
The daffodils selected in this photo can be pasted into the image of the daisies.

note

You can copy an image from one layer into the selection area of a different layer to create a mask. First click on a layer in the Layers palette. Use a selection tool to outline the border of the image you want to copy. Choose the Copy command from the Edit menu, and then select the Paste Into command. The highlighted image in the selected layer acts as a mask to the pasted image.

The selected area in the image window behaves like a mask. The pixels located inside the marquee are editable. Pixels outside the selected area are not affected by any tools, filters, effects, or commands. Once the selected area is defined, you can add adjustment or fill layers to a document. You might want to copy and paste the image into a new document window, as shown in Figure 16.4, if you want to store the selected image as a file on your hard drive.

Figure 16.4
Use a selection tool to select part of an image. Then copy and paste the selected image into a new document window.

Different Ways to Select an Image

You can select the edges of an image in the image window in two ways. The first method involves using the selection tools in the toolbox. Apply the Rectangular Marquee, Lasso, or Magic Wand Tools to an image to select a particular set of pixels in an image. The selected area then is surrounded by a dashed line, called a *marquee*.

The second method requires an image to already be pasted into the image window. Hold down the (Command) [Ctrl]key while clicking on the image layer in the Layers palette. The image in the selected layer will become highlighted in the image window.

Feathering the Selected Image

While the image is selected, you can apply the Feather command to soften its edges before copying it. Choose one of the selection tools to define the image you want to copy or move to another image window. Figure 16.5 shows the dashed line of the Magnetic Lasso Tool surrounding the selected image.

Figure 16.5
The Magnetic Lasso Tool was used to select the daffodils.

Next, choose the Feather command from the Select menu or press (Option-Command-D) [Alt+Ctrl+D]. The Feather Selection dialog box will open (see Figure 16.6). Type a value between 1 and 9999 into the Feather Radius text box. If you want to create a subtle pixel feather effect, type 3 or 5 into the text box. Type a larger number, such as 12 or 15, if you want to create a more dramatic feathering effect. Click on OK to apply the effect to the selected area.

Figure 16.6
The Feather Selection dialog box enables you to determine how many pixels are
blended along the edges of the area of selected pixels.

Color Modes and Composite Images

Photoshop Elements supports four color modes: Bitmap, Grayscale,
Indexed Color, and RGB. When you paste an image created in one
color mode into another window that uses a different color mode,
Photoshop Elements will convert the first image into the color mode of
the target window.

RGB color mode was used to create all the images for this book. This
default color mode supports the largest number of colors. If you're
working with Grayscale or Indexed Color, based on a 256-color palette,
you might want to convert the color mode of the composite image
before pasting it into the target window. When you convert an image
made up of hundreds of colors into two colors—for example, if you
convert an RGB or Indexed Color image into a bitmap—you might not
recognize the image as a bitmap. A bitmap only consists of black and
white colors. A color image may turn into splotches of unrecognizable
black and white patterns after you convert it to a bitmap.

On the other hand, when you convert a bitmap image into a higher-
resolution color mode, the original image will be preserved. Because
black and white are part of all the other color modes, Photoshop
Elements does not need to convert them when the bitmap's color
mode changes. To find out more about color modes, see Chapter 7,
"Creating, Opening, and Converting Images."

Copying and Pasting the Image

Check the color mode of the image window containing the selected
image before copying it. If you are planning to create composite
images in Grayscale, Bitmap, or Indexed Color mode, you might
want to change the color mode of an RGB image window to match
the smaller-sized color palette of the target image. On the other
hand, if you have converted an RGB image to Grayscale or Indexed
Color mode, you might want to reopen and reselect the image in
RGB mode so that you can copy as much color information as
possible to the Clipboard.

When you paste an image into an image window, Photoshop Elements converts it to the color mode of the target image window. If the target window has a higher color depth than the image pasted into it, the color depth of the composite image will be preserved. However, if the target window has a lower color resolution than the pasted image, Photoshop Elements will remove color information from the composite image before adding it to the target window.

The following list describes the different kinds of images and the color modes you can use with them to compose a composite image:

- **Line art**—You can work with vector graphics and Encapsulated PostScript files (EPS) in Photoshop Elements. This type of graphic image includes line art, shapes, and other black-and-white graphics, including text, with the color mode set to Bitmap. You can create composite images solely from bitmap images, or you can start from a bitmap image and then change the color mode of the document to RGB or Indexed Color if you want to add color composite images to it. For example, if the background image was created in Bitmap mode, you can change the color mode of the image window to RGB. Then you can paste Grayscale, Indexed Color, or RGB images into new layers without affecting the black and white background image.

- **Black-and-white photos**—You can work with black-and-white photographs in Grayscale color mode. You can combine two or more black and white photos, and view the composite image with a fixed palette of 256 shades of gray. This can help you pinpoint black and white levels in each image layer, and help maintain continuity across images in the final, flattened picture.

- **Color images**—If any of the images you want to use in the composite contain color, change the color mode of the image window to RGB color mode. Choose RGB color from the Image, Mode menu. RGB color mode supports millions of colors, and can help preserve the sharpness and quality of each image as you scale, rotate, or flip it in the image window.

- **Color graphics**—*Color graphics* is a term that can refer to different kinds of graphics. The first kind of color graphic is a color image captured by a camera. The other is a color drawing or painting. In some cases, you might not be able to work with the original, full-color image that contains the RGB color information. If you plan to combine color graphics that contain 256 or fewer colors, you can work with these composite images in Indexed Color mode. However, Indexed Color mode restricts the maximum number of colors you can work with to 256. For best results, work in RGB mode until you finalize the location of each composite image and the order of each composite image layer. Then flatten the image into a single layer before converting it to Indexed Color mode.

tip
To find out more about color modes, see Chapter 10, "Digital Images and Color."

Can't Paste?

If you cannot paste an image into an image window, check your computer to see if it is running low on memory. Click on the Applications menu if you're running Mac OS, or take a peek at the taskbar in Windows. If you have several applications open, save any files you have open, and then (Quit) [Exit] as many as you can to make more memory available for Windows or Mac OS.

The Clipboard can store a fairly large-sized image. However, the amount of memory available depends on how many other applications are running on the computer, and how much memory is available to the operating system. If Photoshop Elements cannot save an image to the Clipboard on Windows or Mac OS, you might need to (Quit) [Exit] one or more applications, or restart the computer.

You can view the contents of the Clipboard on a Mac by choosing Show Clipboard from the Edit menu in the Finder. If the copied image does not appear in the Clipboard window, or if no image can be pasted into the image window, the Copy command was not able to copy the selection into the Clipboard. You can clear the Clipboard by choosing Purge, Clipboard from the Edit menu.

You must use several commands to copy an image into the same window or move an image from one image window to another. Before copying or pasting an image click on the source and target image's status bar to check the color mode of the image. The following list reviews the copy and paste commands available in Photoshop Elements:

*   **Copy**—Creates a copy of the selected image and puts it in the Clipboard.

*   **Cut**—Moves the selected image to the Clipboard, and deletes the original from the active image window.

- **Copy Merged**—Copies the contents of all layers of the selected area in the image window.

- **Paste**—Moves the image from the Clipboard to the active image window, creating a new layer for the image in the Layers palette.

- **Paste Into**—Enables you to paste an image in the Clipboard into the selected layer of the active image window instead of pasting it into a new layer. For example, you can use this command to paste an image into another selected image, such as a bitmap text or graphic object.

- **Duplicate Image**—Creates a new image window containing the contents of the previously active window. This command can help you view the same image at different magnification levels, or show and hide different layers in different windows.

Before you can paste an image, you must first select the image you want to copy. Then choose the Copy command from the Edit menu, or press (Command-C) [Ctrl+C] to copy the selected area to the Clipboard. Next, click on the image window where you want to add the selected image. This can be the same window you already have open, or another image window. Then choose the Paste command from the Edit menu or press (Command-P) [Ctrl+P]. The selected image will appear in the active image window. It is added to the document in a new, transparent layer. Select the Move Tool and click on the new layer in the Layers palette. Click and drag the image in the selected layer to move it to a new location in the image window.

Variations—Pasting Images

Because Photoshop Elements creates a new layer for each image you paste into the image window, anything you paste into an image window becomes a composite image. You might have noticed that there are two Paste commands in the Edit menu. The Paste command enables you to add a new image to a new layer in the active image window. The Paste Into command enables you to add an image into an existing, unlocked layer. If you choose the Paste Into command, the selected image in the target layer becomes a mask for the pasted image. The pasted image will only appear within the boundary of the selected image, despite the fact that it might be taller or wider than the selected image.

note

The Composites recipe is located in the Add Elements group of recipes. Select the Add Elements group from the drop-down menu in the Recipes palette. Then, choose the Composites recipe to find out more about how to use selection tools, menu commands, and transform commands to work with composite images.

You can also follow recipes to find out how to remove or replace a background layer by choosing one of these topics in the Recipes palette.

You can apply the copy and paste commands to duplicate all or part of an image within the same image window. For example, you can enlarge or shrink a particular object in the image window, and then paste a second image behind it. The following sections show you how you can make the subject of a photo stand out from the background.

Follow the same four steps introduced in the beginning of this chapter. Except this time, you copy and paste part of the background image to place the composite image within the target image. First, use a selection tool to highlight the subject of the photo, as shown in Figure 16.7. Then, copy and paste the selected image into the same image window.

Figure 16.7
Place an image behind the flower by selecting, copying, and pasting the flower into its own layer.

After you paste an image into an image window, a new layer containing the selected area will appear in the Layers palette, as shown in Figure 16.8. If you're pasting the selected area into the image window from which it originates, the image window will look the same before and after the image is pasted. However, you can view the copied image in its new layer from the Layers palette.

Figure 16.8
The image remains the same. However, you can see that the flower now is on its own layer in the Layers palette. Now, you can insert another image into the scene behind the flower layer, without changing the background.

Next, open the image you want to paste behind the duplicate composite image in the target image window. Figure 16.9 shows two yellow poppies that have been highlighted with a selection tool. Select the portion of the image you want to paste into the target image window. Then, choose the Copy command from the Edit menu, or press (Command-C) [Ctrl+C] to copy the selected image to the Clipboard.

Figure 16.9
Select the image you want to add to the first. Then add it using the Paste command.

Click on the target image window. In this example, it's the image window that already contains the composite image of the closed poppy. Then choose the Paste command from the Edit menu. The selected image will appear in the image window (see Figure 16.9). You can use the Move Tool to change the location of the selected image in the image window. If you want the second composite image to appear behind the first one, you might have to adjust the order of the image layers in the Layers palette. In this example, the layer containing the two poppies is sandwiched between the composite image of the closed poppy and the background image (see Figure 16.10).

Figure 16.10
You can modify the background layer by converting it to a regular layer in the Layers palette.

Working with the Background Layer

When you open an image file, the image is created in a locked, background layer. You cannot change the opacity or Blending mode settings for the background layer. However, you can apply selection tools, and copy and paste all or part of the background layer image into a new layer in the same image window. Depending on the image, you might want to duplicate the background by dragging and dropping it over the New layer icon in the Layers palette. You can work with the copy of the background image, while keeping the background layer locked and hidden. This is a great way to keep a backup image close by if you do not want to work with multiple image windows in the work area.

Because composite images are stored in their own layer, you might want to change the state of the background layer into a regular layer. You can convert a background layer by double-clicking on it in the

continued

Layers palette. The Layer Properties window will open. The name of the background layer will change to Layer 0 (see Figure 16.10). Click on the OK button in the Layer Properties window to complete the conversion. Now you can apply filters, effects, or any toolbox tools to layer 0.

Putting Two Subjects Together

Composing a picture with objects is a little easier than trying to place two more people in the same picture. You don't have to worry about eye contact between people or with the camera when composing a picture of flowers or other objects. Creating composite images with people or pets involves a little more work to make the images appear as if they were truly in the same place at the same time. This section shows you how to work with the Levels Adjustment layer to help two images blend together.

The background image can consist of any particular setting or location. However, the image resolution and dimensions of each of the subjects must be similar if you want the image to appear as realistic as possible. Each of the subjects can be rotated, flipped, or transformed to match each other's height or make eye contact. When choosing the subjects for your composite picture, try to work with images that share the same color mode, and try to choose subjects that share the same general shape and size. Figure 16.11, for example, shows a cat that will be added to the picture of a dog.

Figure 16.11
Apply a selection tool to highlight the cat, which will become the composite image.

The easiest way to create a composite image with two or more subjects it to select a starting photo that contains at least one subject you want to include in the final picture. Next, choose a photo of another subject you want to add to the first picture. Apply a selection tool to the image to select only the portion you want to include in the final picture. Choose the Copy command from the Edit menu to move the selected image to the Clipboard. Then, click on the first image window and use the Paste command to add the second subject to the first picture, as shown in Figure 16.12.

Figure 16.12
Use the Paste command to add one image to another. You can use Photoshop Elements to create portraits that are difficult or impossible to set up in the real world.

As you combine live subjects into the same picture, you might need to correct color, or make tonal corrections to the background or composite images. For example, you might need to correct or adjust the tonal range, such as the highlights and shadows, so that two images from different photos fit in with the lighting in the new picture. In almost all cases, you can work on images with color correction, as well as other image-editing tools the same way that you work with a noncomposite image.

Before you adjust the tonal range in either image, you might want to sample the black and white points of an image to determine the best tonal range. The black and white points in an image represent the darkest and lightest pixels. You also can use the Threshold command to view the black and white points in an image. The following steps show you how to find the black and white points in an image using the Threshold command.

tip
To find out more about correcting colors, or correcting the tonal range in an image, go to Chapter 11.

1. Open an image in RGB mode.

2. Select a layer in the Layers palette.

3. Choose Threshold from the Layer, New Adjustment Layer menu. Click on OK.

4. Click on the slider control located on the left end of the Threshold window (see Figure 16.13). Gradually move it to the right until you can see the first hints of black in the image window. Note the threshold value in the text box in the Threshold window. That's the black point. Remember the location of the black point in the image window. You can use this pixel location to click on with the Eyedropper Tool if you need to sample the black point of the image.

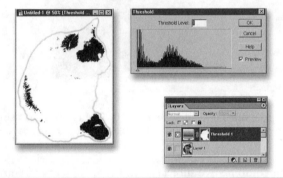

Figure 16.13
The black pixels in the image represent the black point of the image.

5. Next, click on the slider control on the far right in the Threshold window (see Figure 16.14). Gradually move it to the left until you can see the first hints of white in the image window. Note the threshold value in the text box in the Threshold window. This value is the white point for the image. Remember the location of the white point in the image window. You can click on this pixel location if you need to sample the white point of the image.

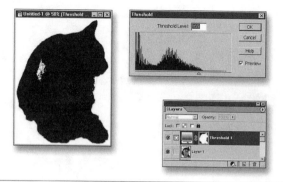

Figure 16.14
The first white pixels you can see in the image window represent the white point in the image.

You also can use the Levels dialog box to view the black and white points of an image. The Levels command is located in the Enhance, Brightness/Contrast menu, or the Layer, New Adjustment Layer menu. The Levels dialog box (see Figure 16.15) enables you to remap the tonal distribution of pixels in an image to reduce any extreme dark or light areas of an image. Press the (Option) [Alt] key to put the Levels window into Auto Range Mode. Then click on the black triangle control below the histogram and slide it to the right until the first black pixels appear in the image window. These pixels represent the black point in the image. If you continue to move the slider control to the right, you can see which pixels are being clipped to black. Perform these same steps with the white triangle control to identify the white points in the image, or to see which pixels are clipped to white.

Saving the Final Image

When you're ready to save the image for the Web or for printing, flatten the layers in the image. Select the Save for Web command from the File menu if you want to optimize the image for the Web. The Save for Web window enables you to customize color, file type, and other settings and preview the changes in a single window. Figure 16.16 shows how a frame is added to the border of the image by checking the Matte option in the Save for Web window. You can also choose the Save or Save As command from the File menu to save the file to your hard drive.

note
When the (Option) [Alt] key is held down in the Levels window, the Auto button will change to Options. You can adjust the Auto Range settings for the black and white clip values in the Levels window. You can enter a value between 0.00 and 0.99 percent in each text box of the Auto Range window. Click on the Reset button (which replaces the Cancel button when the (Option) [Alt] key is held down) to reset the values in the Levels window to the original values when the window was first opened.

note

To find out more about how to find the black or white point in an image, go to Chapter 11, "Tonal Range and Color Correction."

Figure 16.15
The Levels dialog box enables you adjust the way pixels are distributed across the tonal range of the image. You also can use it to find the black and white points in an image.

Figure 16.16
Add a matte around the border of the image from the Save for Web window.

Creating Special Effects with Composite Images

If you're a special effects fan, you'll be happy to know you can create special effects with composite images. Like the other examples in this chapter, the Select and Move Tools and the Copy and Paste commands play a big role when bringing two or more images together.

The transform commands also help scale and size an image to fit in with the background image.

The special effects in an image can be defined purely by combining composite images that have filters or effects applied to them. You can also grow or shrink the composite image, turning a person into a giant or a midget. You can remove the color from a composite image to make that image stand out against a color background image, or add color composite images to a grayscale background image.

Choosing the First Image

One of the first things you'll need to decide is what kind of effect you want to create. This will help you pick the images you will use to create the composite image. If you're not sure where to start, pick the background image first. Figure 16.17 shows a close-up picture of a flower. Looking at this photo, you might not expect a special effect to be the first vision to pop into your head.

Figure 16.17
The original image, before any changes are made.

Because the flower takes up most of this photo, I added a relatively tiny person to create a giant flower effect. Take a look at the dimensions of each image you want to use before combining them. The flower is a 3-megapixel image, and the image of the person is a 640×480 pixel image. Both images are in millions of colors, and the target image window is set to RGB color mode. The dimensions and resolutions of both images enable them to come together nicely to create a composite image.

tip

If you want a composite image to appear semi-transparent, like a ghost, you can lower the opacity value of the composite image in the Layers palette. Select the layer that contains the composite image in the Layers palette. Then type a lower value, such as 60 or 70, into the Opacity text box. The lower the value you type, the more transparent the image will appear.

tip
To find out more about how to use the transform commands, move ahead to Chapter 17, "Creating Complex Images." The rotate commands are explained in more detail in the following sections.

Figure 16.18 shows the completed image. The Move Tool and the transform commands are used to modify the composite image so that it fits in with the rest of the picture.

Figure 16.18
The same image after adding a composite. The size of this flower makes the man at the top seem very tiny.

Transforming the Composite Image

There are many ways to transform an image in Photoshop Elements. You can resize, rotate, skew, and change its perspective, or flip it horizontally or vertically. In order to apply a transform command, you must first select the image.

Pick a selection tool from the toolbox and use it to highlight the composite image you want to paste into the target image window. The Magnetic Lasso Tool was used to select the image shown in Figure 16.19. When the image is selected, you can choose the Feather command to soften the edges of the selected image, or apply a filter, effect, or layer style to it. You also can apply the Rotate or Transform commands (from the Image menu) to the selected image. However, it's easier to modify the selected image if you have the background image in the target window behind it.

Figure 16.19
Select the composite image and copy it to the Clipboard.

Scaling Objects with the Transform Commands

Transform commands enable you to skew, distort, and apply perspective to an image. You can also grow or shrink the size of an image object.

You can press (Command-T) [Ctrl+T] to activate the Free Transform command. Most objects go into Free Transform mode when you select them with the Move Tool.

Transform commands are particularly helpful for scaling images that are pasted from one image window into another. You can shrink a large image so that it fits with the scale of the objects in the background layer of an image.

When you're ready to move the selected image to the other image window, choose the Copy command from the Edit menu or press (Command-C) [Ctrl+C]. The selected image will be copied to the Clipboard. Next, click on the target image window, which is the image window with the background image. Then choose the Paste command from the Edit menu, or press (Command-P) [Ctrl+P]. The selected image will appear in the active image window, as shown in Figure 16.20.

note
In Figure 16.20, the image on the left was captured as a 640×480 pixel image. It appears slightly blurry, or pixelated, because it has been magnified to 300 percent of its original size. The image of the flower on the right was captured at 2000×1500 pixels and contains more color and image data than the image on the left.

Figure 16.20
Paste the selected image on the left into the target image window. Use the transform commands to size the image. Then use the Move Tool to compose the new picture.

Working with Multiple Composite Images

Creating an image consisting of two or more composite images is pretty similar to putting together a single composite image. The only real difference is that there are more images to coordinate in the final composition. Figure 16.21 shows the background image that's used to create the multi-image composite image in this section.

Figure 16.21
A field of lilies is the background photo for this composite image.

Figure 16.22 shows the field of lilies after the mammalian images were added. I've added three cats and a squirrel to the field of lilies. Each composite image originated from a different photo, all taken at different times. Larger images were scaled down to fit in the image, whereas smaller ones were placed in perspective to the background.

Figure 16.22
The field of lilies after three cats and a squirrel are added.

> **note**
> You don't have to have a background to create a composite image. You can paste images into a new document window with a white, transparent, or colored background. Then use the Move Tool to arrange the images into a photo-composition.

Stacking Up Composite Images

If you're working with 2- and 3-megapixel images, you will want to preserve the dimensions of each image in addition to all the color and image data for the selected image by working with each image in RGB color mode. If you plan to paste several images into one file, keep an eye on the status bar. The file size of the target image will increase as you add or copy images in the Layers palette or image window.

One way to minimize the file size of a composite image is to work on some of the images prior to pasting them into the target image. Figure 16.23 shows a picture of a cat created by a 3-megapixel digital camera. The cat was selected, feathered, and copied to a new document window. Saving each image in a separate image file enables you to correct colors, or simply preserve the original image by itself instead of saving or modifying it with a group of composite images.

Figure 16.23
You can select, copy, and paste a composite image into its own image window.
If you plan to layer several composite images together, you can place each one
in a separate image window and perform any color corrections or image tweaks
before combining them in the final image.

Rotating Images

When an image is pasted into an image window, it will appear in the
same orientation and size as it was saved to the Clipboard. Although
you can move an image using the Move Tool, you might also need
to flip it horizontally or vertically, or rotate it clockwise or counter-
clockwise in order to make the image fit in with the rest of the
picture. Rotating and flipping an image are the most common corrections performed on composites. You must use several commands
to rotate or flip an image. The following list briefly describes the
rotate commands located in the Image, Rotate menu.

- **Free Rotate**—Rotates the selected image in any direction you
  choose. Click outside the border of the selected image. Then
  drag the mouse up or down, as desired.

- **90 Degrees Left or Right**—This moniker is somewhat of an
  oversimplification. But a 90-degree angle is about the same size
  as a quarter slice of pie. Rotate the selected image 90 degrees
  clockwise or counter-clockwise by choosing either of these
  commands.

- **180 Degrees**—Flips the selected image across the X axis. If the
  selected image is right side up, this command will rotate it so
  that it becomes upside down.

- **Flip Horizontal or Vertical**—Flip the image along an X or Y axis. If you copy and paste the selected image, each of these commands can be used to create a mirror image of the original.

- **Rotate Canvas Commands**—The same commands can also be applied to the entire canvas area.

Rotating and Resizing Selected Image Objects

You can freely rotate a pasted image using the Move Tool. First use a selection tool to select a portion of the background image in the window. Then copy and paste the selected area in the same image window. Select the new layer in the Layers palette. If you place the cursor beside the selected image, the cursor will change from an arrow to the rotate cursor (a double-headed arrow icon turned 90 degrees). Click beside the highlighted boundary (marked by a dashed line) and drag the mouse to rotate the selected image. You can grow or shrink the image by clicking and dragging any of the square handle boxes located on the boundary of the selected image.

Composing a New Picture

Each image added to a picture can either do nothing for the original, or completely change the tone. Having the freedom to put together any combination of digital images can be extremely easy, if the source images are similar and are taken with similar cameras. Combining images that have more differences than similarities, such as combining a black-and-white image with a color one, can be a tedious task. Photoshop Elements enables you to work with any kind of image. However, the amount of time you'll spend fine-tuning the final composition will vary depending on what you're trying to accomplish, and the quality of the photo resources you have available to work with.

The composite image shown in Figure 16.24 shows how images taken with different cameras can be prepared and placed in an image window to create a complete, unique picture. When you combine images from a diverse set of source images, you likely will spend more time adjusting each image's perspective and scale using the transform commands. The Move Tool is another indispensable tool to change or tweak the location of each image. Try experimenting with the order of each of the image layers in the Layers palette. For example, you can make one image appear in front of another by dragging its layer above the other layer in the Layers palette.

tip

To find out more about how to flatten an image, go to Chapter 13. To find out more about how to optimize an image, go to Chapter 8.

Figure 16.24
Paste each cat into the active image window. Use the Move Tool to move each image and compose a new picture.

Layers and Blending Modes

Another way you can blend composite images is by choosing a different blending mode for the image that resides in the top-most layer in the Layers palette. You can change the order of layers by clicking and dragging them in the Layers palette. Blending modes affect the way pixels interact with the image layer directly below it. The colors in the top layer are combined with the color in the layer directly below it to create a new, result color. To find out more about how to apply a blending mode to a layer, go to Chapter 13, "Working with Layers and Layer Styles."

tip

To find out more about saving files and file formats, go to Chapter 8, "Saving and Sharing Files."

Finally, preserve the composite image and all the layer information and settings in your image file by first saving it as a native Photoshop file (*.PSD). The Photoshop, or PSD file format, preserves each layer in the image file. This enables you to continue editing each composite image at any time.

Flatten the layers to create the final image. Remember that after you flatten an image, it will be difficult to edit it as freely as you did when each composite image was in its own layer. Before you save the final image-flattened file on your hard drive, you can experiment with different optimization settings if you want to reduce the overall file size of the image. Once the final file is saved, you might want to add copyright, source filenames, or photographer information into the image's File Info window.

part

V

DESIGNING COMPLEX IMAGES

chapter

17

Creating Complex Images

Effects, reflections, light, and shadow are some of the key elements that might not necessarily jump out at you in every photo, but are definitely elements that can make or break a picture. Some effects can improve the original composition, while others enable you to create entirely new ones. This chapter introduces the Liquify and Paste Into commands and teaches you how to create some cool effects. You also learn how to add a reflection or light source to an image, as well as remove shadows from an image.

Melting Images with the Liquify Filter

The Liquify filter consists of eight tools. Pucker, bloat, warp, reflect, or shift the pixels in an image with this powerful, yet simple, tool. There's also a Reconstruct Tool, which will undo any of the twisty effects created by the other tools in case you want to recall what part of the original image looked like.

Open any image in RGB mode to apply the wondrous effects to an image in the Liquify dialog box. If you are working with an image that contains more than one layer, you can select a layer from the Layers palette and apply the Liquify tools to part of an image. If you want to apply this tool to all layers, you'll need to choose the Flatten Image command from the File menu to merge all layers into one first. Then, open the Liquify filter window and apply any of the tools to the image.

Applying Liquify Tools

To open the Liquify dialog box, choose Liquify from the Filter menu or press (Shift-Command-X) [Shift+Ctrl+X]. Click on either the Twirl Counter Clockwise, Twirl Clockwise, Pucker, Bloat, Shift, or Reflection Tool located in the upper-left corner of the Liquify dialog box, as shown in Figure 17.1. Then, click and hold down the mouse on the image to apply a tool. To apply the Warp Tool, you'll need to drag the cursor over the image. The Reconstruct Tool enables you to reverse the effects created by the other Liquify tools.

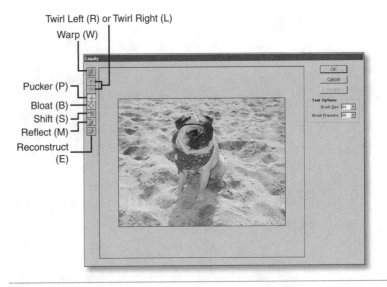

Figure 17.1
Choose from eight Liquify Tools in the Liquify dialog box.

The following list briefly describes each tool in the Liquify dialog box:

- **Warp**—Melts pixels in the direction that the cursor moves.
- **Twirl Left**—Moves pixels downward and around in a clockwise direction.
- **Twirl Right**—Pushes pixels downward and counter-clockwise in a circular direction.
- **Pucker**—Bends the pixels towards the center of the brush.
- **Bloat**—Pushes pixels from the center of the brush outward.
- **Shift**—Moves pixels perpendicular to the direction the cursor moves.
- **Reflection**—Copies pixels below the brush location in the image to the brush area. You can apply this tool by clicking and dragging the cursor on the image. The set of pixels below the brush will be reflected. If you (Option-Drag) [Alt+Drag] the pixels located above, the brush will be reflected in the opposite direction of the cursor movement. You can overlap strokes to create a reflection effect.
- **Reconstruct**—Restores pixels to the original location when the Liquify dialog box is open. You also can press the (Option) [Alt] button to change the Cancel button into the Reset button. Click on the Reset button to remove any of the tools that have been applied to the image in the Liquify dialog box. The Revert button performs a similar task. If you apply one of the Liquify tools to the image, the Revert button becomes active. Click on the Revert button to restore the image to its original state when the Liquify dialog box opened the image for the current session.

You can customize the brush size and pressure in the Liquify dialog box. Type a value into the Brush Size text box, or click on the arrow and use the slider to set the brush size on the Liquify Tools. The larger the number, the larger the brush. Similarly, the number you type in the Brush Pressure text box will determine how quickly the selected Liquify Tool applies the effect to the image. Figure 17.2 shows how the Warp Tool enables you to push pixels around with a 64 pixel-size brush.

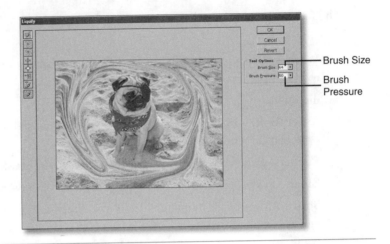

Figure 17.2
Melt pixels as you move the cursor around in an image with the Warp Tool.

You can apply one tool to create an effect, or combine more than one tool to create elaborate effects. Figure 17.3 shows the image after the Bloat, Pucker, and Twirl effects have been applied to the image. As you can see, the Liquify Tools can easily make the original picture unrecognizable, yet can also result in an interesting-looking picture.

Figure 17.3
Expand pixels with the Bloat Tool, contract with the Pucker Tool, or twirl the pixels.

Reverse Effects with the Reconstruct Tool

The Reconstruct Tool enables you to undo any Liquify Tool applied to an image. You can also press the Revert button to return the image to its first open state. Figure 17.4 shows how the Reconstruct Tool restored the face of the subject. The Reconstruct Tool can undo any Liquify Tool applied to the image. However, when you close the Liquify dialog box, the tool changes are saved to the active image. As you work on an image in the Liquify dialog box, you can also use (Command-Z) [Ctrl+Z] with each tool to undo each step of the previous task in the image area of the Liquify dialog box.

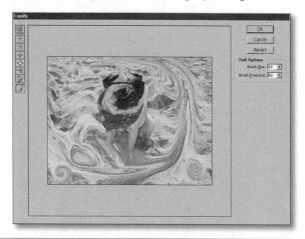

Figure 17.4
Undo any of the other tools by applying the Reconstruct Tool.

tip
Hold down the (Option) [Alt] key, and the Cancel button in the Liquify dialog box will change to Reset. Click on the Reset button to remove any of the tools applied to the image. The Revert and Reset buttons perform the same task, restoring the image to its original state when first opened. However, the Revert button also returns each tool to its original settings in addition to returning the image to its original state.

When you click on OK, any changes you made to the image in the Liquify dialog box will be applied to the active image window. You can choose a previous state of the image from the History palette, or choose Undo from the Edit menu if you decide not to keep any of the Liquify filter changes.

Pasting an Image Into Text

The Liquify filter provides a set of tools that enable you to create great-looking, sophisticated, special effects. Another way of creating a special effect is to paste an image into text. You can do this by choosing the Paste Into command after applying the selection tools

note
You can choose the Paste command if you want to paste an image from the Clipboard into a new layer of the active image window. This is the most common way the Paste command is used with graphics and text.

Photoshop Elements also provides the Paste Into command, which enables you to paste an image from the Clipboard into a selected area of the active image window. You can click on a layer in the Layers palette to pick the image layer you want to combine with the Clipboard image and the Paste Into command.

and the Copy command to an image. Unlike the Liquify filter, the Paste Into command involves following a set of steps to create the resulting special effect.

The Paste Into command pastes a bitmap from the Clipboard into a selected object in the image window. The bitmap image can be added to a selected set of pixels in an existing layer in the Layers palette. The following example shows you how to fill an image into text using the Paste Into command.

Creating Text to Fill with an Image

The Horizontal and Vertical Type Tools enable you to add text to a layer in the active image window. Click on the Horizontal or Vertical Type Tool in the toolbox, and then click in the image window. Adjust the Horizontal or Vertical Type Tool settings in the options bar. Then type some text. The text will appear in the image window (see Figure 17.5).

Figure 17.5
Add text with one of the type tools. Then, scale it to a larger size with the Move Tool.

Text objects are vector graphics that use a mathematical algorithm to preserve their size and shape, especially when enlarged. The Horizontal and Vertical Type Tools create vector text objects when you apply them to an image. If you want to apply the Paste Into command to text, the text object must be converted into a bitmap. Bitmap graphics can be reduced in size. If a Bitmap graphic is enlarged, its edges will pixelate, causing the edges of each letter to appear jagged. You can convert a text object into a bitmap by

(Command) [Ctrl] clicking the text layer, as shown in Figure 17.6. Then copy and paste the text object into the image window. A bitmap image of the text will be created in a new layer.

Figure 17.6
Select the text object and copy and paste it to convert it to a bitmap image. Copying the image to the Clipboard converts the vector text object into a bitmap graphic.

Bitmap Versus Vector Graphics

If you're not sure whether to use a bitmap or vector graphic, first decide what you want to do with the text object. If you want to choose or change a font, font size, font style, or format of the text object, you'll want to preserve the original text layer created by the Type Tools.

You can take advantage of hiding and showing layers and convert any text object into a bitmap if you want to experiment with a filter or effect, or apply the Paste Into command to a bitmap text object. To find out more about graphics, see Chapter 14, "Adding Text and Shapes to Images."

note
You might need to increase the size of the text object if you want to see more of the image that is pasted into the text. Click on the layer containing the text object from the Layers palette. Then, select the Move Tool from the toolbox. The grow handles will appear on the borders of the text object. Click and drag the corner handles away from the center of the text object to grow the size of the text object.

Selecting the Image for the Text

Open another image that you want to place inside the text object. In most cases, the shape of each letter of text will prevent the image from being recognizable. Choose an image based on the way color and tonal range are distributed. Then, use a selection tool to choose the area of the image you want to paste into the text, as shown in Figure 17.7. Then select the Copy command from the Edit menu or press (Command-C) [Ctrl+C].

Figure 17.7
Select the image to be pasted into the bitmap text object.

note
To find out more
about how to use
the Horizontal and
Vertical Type
Tools, go to
Chapter 14,
"Adding Text and
Shapes to
Images."

In the image window that contains the text object, (Command) [Ctrl] click on the layer that contains the bitmap text object to select it. If you don't select the text object, Photoshop Elements won't know what to paste the second image into. Choose the Paste Into command from the Edit menu or press (Shift-Command-V) [Shift+Ctrl+V]. The image of the mushrooms will be pasted into the text object, as shown in Figure 17.8. Because both images are bitmaps, you can't modify the text or the pasted image after choosing the Paste Into command.

Figure 17.8
Choose the Paste Into command to add the image to the text object.

You can apply filters, effects, or layer styles to the bitmap text object. For example, in Figure 17.9, the Simple Emboss layer style was applied to the text object. The Bevel layer style gives the text object a three-dimensional look. You can apply more than one layer style, as well as any filter or effect. Use the History palette to revert the image window to a previous state, or create a copy of the text object layer and hide it to create a backup of your work.

Figure 17.9
Add a layer style to the text object to enhance the effect.

Double-click on the f icon—located on the right side of a layer that has had a layer style applied to it—to open the Style Settings dialog box. You can customize any of the layer styles applied to an object from the Style Settings dialog box shown in Figure 17.10. Set the lighting angle, use of global light, shadow distance, outer glow size, inner glow size, or bevel size and direction and preview any changes in the active image window.

Each layer style setting has a slider control combined with a text box. You can type in a value in the text box, or move the slider control to choose a new value for a style setting. If you want to save your changes, click on OK. Select Cancel if you do not want to save any changes you've made.

note
To find out more about how to choose and apply layer styles, go to Chapter 13, "Working with Layers and Layer Styles."

Figure 17.10
Customize the layer style settings in the Style Settings dialog box.

You also can adjust the tonal range and color settings of the bitmap text object. Select the text object by (Command) [Ctrl] clicking in its layer to create adjustment or fill layers specifically for this text object. Experiment with different settings until you find the right combination. The final image appears in Figure 17.11.

Figure 17.11
The image in the text object is barely recognizable in the final picture.

Adding a Reflection to an Image

Reflections, lighting, and shadows are some of the elements that make photos seem real. For example, if you see a reflection of an image on the surface of a wall, you might think the wall is made of glass or is a mirror. You can use the Copy and Paste Tools, combined with the Rotate and Transform commands, as well as the layer blending and opacity settings, to create custom reflections in an image.

For this example, a composite image is added to a background image. Then a reflection of the composite image is added to give the overall image a sense of realism. Figure 17.12 shows how the Magnetic Lasso Tool selects an Aibo dog, which is copied and pasted into a picture of a sunset.

Figure 17.12
Select the composite image for the picture you want to create.

caution
Bitmap graphics don't retain their image quality if you try to make them larger. Photoshop Elements will interpolate the pixels to create the larger image. It does this by creating more pixels for each existing color, creating a squarish-looking, blocky image, also referred to as pixelation.

You might need to scale the pasted image so that it matches the dimensions of the background image. The new image is pasted into its own new layer. If you see the small square handles shown in Figure 17.13, you can click on one of these handles to grow or shrink an image. Click on one of the handles on the border of the pasted image and drag it to resize the image. The border of the transform box won't always cover the borders of the composite image. Click on the Move Tool, and move the image to a new location in the image window.

Although an image can be transformed when you first paste it into the image window, you can apply the Transform commands in several other ways. The following list shows you the many ways to activate the scale, skew, distort, and perspective Transform commands.

note

To find out more about how to use the rotate commands, see Chapter 16, "Experimenting with Composite Images."

Figure 17.13
Scale the composite image to fit with the background image.

- **Move Tool**—Select the Move Tool from the toolbox. Then, click on an image in the image window to select it and activate the Transform commands. You can click and drag the side or corner handles on the selected object to grow or shrink it.

- **Layers palette**—Click on a layer to select the objects in the image window. If layers are linked, the transformations affect all linked layers.

- **Shape Selection**—Choose the Shape Tool from the toolbox, and add a shape object to the image window. Then, choose the Shape Selection Tool (black arrow icon) from the Shape flyout menu in the toolbox. Click on the shape object with the Shape Selection Tool, and then choose the Move Tool to resize the shape object.

- **Transform menu**—Although some of these options are also accessible from the options bar when certain tools are active, you can skew, distort, or change the perspective of the selected object by choosing the corresponding command from the Transform menu, shown in Figure 17.14.

You must select a shape or image object before you can use one of the Transform commands. First, choose a selection tool and select part of an image in the image window. Then, copy and paste the image into the same window. You also can create a shape using one of the shape tools in the toolbox, or choose Select All from the Edit menu to select the image in the active layer. Next, choose one of the Transform commands from the Transform menu.

Figure 17.14
Apply the Transform commands to add perspective to the composite image.

note
When you apply a Transform command to an image object, you can preserve the original width and height relationship of the image by holding down the (Option) [Alt] key. Preserving the original proportions of the image enables you to limit the amount of distortion to the original image as you grow or shrink it.

When you select Free Transform, Skew, Distort, or Scale from the Transform menu, several settings appear in the options bar. Choose from the buttons in the middle of the bar to rotate, scale, or skew the selected object. You can use any combination of Transform commands before saving the final transformed object.

On the far left side of the options bar is a rectangle shape with a square on each corner and midpoint of each line, plus a square at its center. Click on a square in the options bar to set the center point of the selected object. Experiment with different center points combined with different Rotate commands.

A Width, Height, and Rotate text box are also present in the options bar. You can type a new size or angle for the selected object into each text box, or click and drag the handles of the bounding box in the image window to change the size of an object. Click on the link icon if you want to preserve proportional relationships between the width and height of the object whenever a new value is typed into the width or height text box.

The following list briefly describes how each of the Transform commands works:

- **Transform**—Rotates the image clockwise or counter-clockwise, or grows or shrinks the selected object.

- **Skew**—Extends or contracts one side or corner while preserving the proportions of the object. Creates a slanting effect.

- **Distort**—Collapses or expands a side or corner of the selected object. Stretches or squishes part of an image.

- **Perspective**—Grows or shrinks any side of an object to apply perspective to the bounding box.

After you've transformed and shaped it, you can move the image to a new location in the image window to create your composition. Identify a light source in the background image, and try to decide where the reflection of the composite image should be located. You might also want to make any tonal or color corrections to the composite or background image.

Creating the Reflected Image

The key to creating the reflection of the composite image is the Opacity setting in the Layers palette. Many of the skills you mastered while using the Transform and Rotate commands can also be used to create the reflected image. To create the reflection of the composite image, follow these steps:

1. (Command) [Ctrl] click the composite layer, and then copy and paste the image into the image window. A new layer will be created with the copied image.

2. Use the Move Tool to select the copied image. Then choose Flip Vertical (or Flip Horizontal) from the Image, Rotate menu.

3. Select the layer containing the reflection, and decrease the Opacity setting from the Layers palette, as shown in Figure 17.15.

Composing the Final Image

If the background image does not contain an obvious light source, move the composite image and its reflection to different locations in the image to see which positions fit best with the light and shadows in the background image (see Figure 17.16). You might also want to experiment with different opacity settings for the reflection.

note
In the Layers palette, click on the eye icon beside the layer that contains the reflected image. The reflected image will not appear in the image window. Click on the left column box once more to show the reflection. The eye icon will appear beside any layer that appears in the image window.

Figure 17.15
Create a copy of the composite image and then paste and flip it vertically. Decrease the Opacity value to create the reflected image.

Figure 17.16
Move the reflection around in the image to see how it matches up with the primary composite image.

After you've finalized the placement of the composite image and its reflection, as shown in Figure 17.17, you can create one more copy of the composite image for use as the composite image's shadow. Like the reflection, you can use the Transform and Rotate commands to create the shadow. Except with the shadow, you can add a Gradient Fill layer to darken the resulting image, and fade it into the background image.

411

Figure 17.17
Click on a tool in the toolbox to save the changes to the transformed image. This figure shows the reflected image after the Transform commands have been applied to it.

You also can add a solid or gradient fill layer to the overall image to bring the composite and background image together. For example, if the background image contains a sunrise or sunset, you might want to consider adding a orange fill or gradient so that the composite image shares similar hues as the background image, as was done in Figure 17.18.

Figure 17.18
Determine the light source in the picture, and then move and rotate the reflection to match it. The background image is dimmed in this figure to emphasize the location of the drop shadow for the composite.

Lighten and Remove Shadows

Another conundrum of working with digital pictures is how to add more detail to dark, shadowy images. Starting with a 2- or 3-mega-pixel image can make a big difference. The more image data in the image file, the higher the possibility you might be able to lighten the image, although the tonal and color information won't match the rest of the lighter areas of the picture.

You can use many techniques to lighten dark areas of an image. The best approach is to work with smaller areas of the image instead of trying to fix the entire image in one fell swoop. Figure 17.19 shows an area selected with the Magic Wand Tool. You can apply the Dodge Tool to lighten the shadows in the selected area.

Figure 17.19
Select a shadow in the image with the Magic Wand Tool. Then, apply the Levels or Brightness/Contrast commands to lighten the selected area.

Color-Correction Recipes

The Recipes palette contains a short list of instructions you can follow to learn how to use different tools in Photoshop Elements. For instance, you can learn how to correct colors using the Brightness and Contrast, Hue and Saturation, Tonal Range, and Replace Color commands.

Some steps have a green arrow button beside them. Click on the button to choose a menu command or toolbox tool, or to open a tool window.

Cleaning Up Shadows with Layers

note
To find out more about how to work with the Levels command, go to Chapter 11, "Tonal Range and Color Correction."

Add a new, blank layer to the image if you want to experiment with making shadows lighter. In Figure 17.20, I've created a copy of the background layer as a backup layer for the background layer. Then, I clicked on the eye icon to hide the copied layer in the Layers palette. Next, I added a new layer that I renamed Shadow Removal. You can select dark areas of the original image and copy and paste them into this new layer to see whether the tonal range tools can lighten and blend these areas before merging any changes with the original image.

Figure 17.20
Create a new layer so you can apply any tools or effects to the image without affecting the original.

You can add a Levels adjustment layer to the image to remap the shadow, or dark pixels in the image. To select the shadowy areas of an image, do the following:

1. Open an image file. Choose the Magic Wand Tool from the toolbox.

2. Click on the darkest areas of the shadows in the active image window with the Magic Wand Tool. Any similarly shaded pixels will be selected in the image window.

3. Choose Levels from the Layer, New Adjustment Layer menu. The Levels window will open as shown in Figure 17.21.

Colorize Shadows

You can add color to the shadows in an image by creating a layer, applying painting tools to it, and then adjusting the transparency of the colors in the layer. First, open an image file, and then click on the Create a New Layer button in the Layers palette to create a new layer. The new layer will be created above the background layer that contains the image. Next, select the new layer in the Layers palette, and then choose Color for its blending mode.

Now you can apply a painting tool to the image window. Choose the Paintbrush Tool from the toolbox. Customize the brush size and any settings from the options bar, and then select a foreground color by clicking on the left square in the toolbox. The Color Picker window will open. Select a color, and then click OK.

Next, add color to the new layer by holding down the mouse and dragging the Paintbrush Tool over the shaded areas of the image. The color should appear in the image window. With the new layer selected, decrease the Opacity setting in the Layers palette to blend color into the shadows.

Figure 17.21
Select darker pixels with the Magic Wand Tool, and then adjust their visibility with the Levels Tool.

4. Move the left slider to adjust the shadows level for the selected area in the image window. Then move the right slider to change the input level of the highlights. Changing the highlight setting should bring out more details in the shadowy areas.

5. Click on OK to save your changes to the adjustment layer.

You can hide or show this layer if you want to compare the adjustment layer to the original image.

The lightened area of the selection might appear slightly off-color from the rest of the image. Choose Hue/Saturation from the Layer, New Adjustment Layer menu. The Hue/Saturation dialog box will open, as shown in Figure 17.22. Move the Hue slider control to adjust the color of the selected image area. The Saturation control will add or remove gray levels from the selected image area. Increase or decrease the amount of light in the selection by moving the Lightness slider control. If you're able to match the colors in the selected area with the rest of the image, click on OK and save your changes to the adjustment layer. Otherwise, click on Cancel.

Figure 17.22
Try to match the color of the lightened pixel with the Hue/Saturation command.

note

To find out more about how to correct colors, or remap dark and light pixels in an image, go to Chapter 11, "Tonal Range and Color Correction."

Neutralizing Pixels with the Dodge and Burn Tools

If you still have an active selection, deselect it by pressing (Command-D) [Ctrl+D]. Then take a look at the whole image. Compare the lightened areas of the image to the unchanged areas. You might find that parts of the image are a little too light compared to the rest of the picture.

You can use the Burn Tool from the toolbox to darken pixels in the image window, as shown in Figure 17.23. The mushroom caps in this figure have been darkened to better match the overall tone of the image. When using the Burn or Dodge Tools to darken or lighten pixels in an image, you'll want to use the Brush Size, Range, and Exposure settings from the options bar. Select a brush size that generally matches the area of the image you want to correct. In Figure 17.23, I chose a soft edge brush size of 65 pixels.

You can choose to darken the highlights, midtones, or shadows in the image window using the Range menu. Choose Highlights if you want to darken the brighter areas of the image. The Exposure slider control enables you to set a percentage (a value between 1 and 100) of how much the Burn or Dodge Tool affects the pixels in the image window. A lower value creates a more transparent effect. A higher value enables the Burn or Dodge Tool to function more like a brush with paint, having a stronger effect on any pixels touched by the tool.

note
Press the Tab key to hide the tool-bars and palette windows from the work area. Only the image window will remain visible. Press Tab once more to show the toolbars and palette windows.

Press the Shift+ Tab keys to only hide the palette windows. Press Shift+Tab a second time to show the palette windows.

Figure 17.23
Darken pixels that stand out using the Burn Tool.

The Dodge Tool lightens highlights, midtones, and shadows in an image. The Dodge Tool creates the opposite effect of the Burn Tool. You can lighten any dark areas in the image by clicking and dragging the Dodge Tool in the image window, as shown in Figure 17.24.

As you work on the image, compare the edited image to the original by opening a backup of the original image, or by hiding the layer containing the work in progress, and showing the original back-ground image. Figure 17.25 shows the original photo. The edited image reveals details that were previously hidden by shadows.

Dodge Tool

Lightened pixels

Figure 17.24
Lighten pixels by applying the Dodge Tool to the image window.

Figure 17.25
Compare the lightened image with the original.

Adding a Light Source

A photo can have one or several light sources. Even if you can't iden-tify a light source in a photo, you know that photos are not possible in the absence of light. Light plays a big role in any photo, and can also be the subject of a photo.

The Lighting Effects filter, located in the Filter, Render menu, enables you to choose from seventeen lighting effects. Figure 17.26 shows a photo taken on a cloudy day. Although the colors are clear and the image is crisp, the lighting appears to be weak in this photo.

Figure 17.26
Start with a photo that lacks an identifiable light source.

Choosing the Right Light

Open the Lighting Effects dialog box by choosing Lighting Effects from the Filter, Render menu. Several settings appear on the right side of the Lighting Effects dialog box, and a preview pane is located on the left side. Choose a light source from the Style drop-down menu, located at the top of the Lighting Effects dialog box.

The light style shown in Figure 17.27 is the 2 o'clock spotlight. The type of light for the style appears in the Light Type drop-down menu. Choose from a Directional, Omni, or Spotlight. You can turn the light on or off by checking or unchecking the On check box. Click and drag the slider controls to adjust the Intensity and Focus of the type of light.

note
The amount of light exposed to an object affects the amount of visible color. If you're adding light to a photo, check the resulting colors in the photo to see whether they are accurately rendered based on the position of the light source. Also check to see whether shadows or reflections need to be added to supplement the existing light.

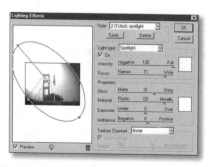

Figure 17.27
Preview the light effect in the preview window.

Customize the properties of the light by adjusting the settings for the Gloss, Material, Exposure, and Ambience slider controls.

Choose different lighting styles to find the right light for your photo. Figure 17.28 shows some of the lighting styles available. I've selected the Parallel Directional light for this photo.

Figure 17.28
Pick a lighting effect from the Style drop-down menu.

Duplicate a Light

Hold down the (Option) [Alt] key in the preview area of the Lighting Effects window. Then click on the center, white circle in the light source and drag it to a new location in the preview window. Release the mouse to add the new light source to the image.

A white circle will appear in the preview pane, indicating where the first light source is positioned. Add as many light sources as you like to the image.

Click on the Save button if you want to save the customized settings for the light. Type a name for the light settings, and then click on OK. The new light should appear in the Styles list in the Lighting Effects window.

Applying Another Light Source

The parallel directional light brightens up the large portion of the photo dedicated to the gray, cloudy sky. The parallel directional light breaks up the upper-right half of the image by adding a gradient light pattern. However, the bridge and the flag are the subjects of the photo. Add another light source to the photo to highlight these subjects. I've chosen the Crossing light, shown in Figure 17.29, to point toward the subjects in the photo.

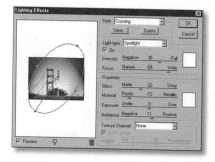

Figure 17.29
Adjust the properties of the light in the Lighting Effects window.

Viewing the Final Image

As you add each light source to the image, view the full image and decide whether the light source is worth keeping, or whether you should undo it and try adjusting some of the settings to create a more realistic lighting effect. Figure 17.30 shows the photo after the Parallel Directional and Crossing lights have been added to it. Although the image in the photo is essentially identical to the original, the additional light sources make it more colorful and visually interesting.

Figure 17.30
The photo after adding the Parallel Directional and Crossing lighting effects.

note
Although you cannot apply the Lighting Effects filter to a grayscale image, you can apply the Remove Color command to an image to make it seem black and white. Choose the Blue Omni or RGB Lights to add color to the lit areas of the image.

Applying Texture Channels

The Lighting Effects filter and its dialog box enable you to add texture to an image (see Figure 17.31). First, select the image layer you want to modify with the Lighting Effects filter. Then, choose Lighting Effects from the Filter, Render menu. The Texture channel settings are located at the bottom of the Lighting Effects window.

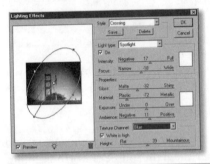

Figure 17.31
Adjust texture channels settings in the Lighting Effects dialog box.

You can create a texture based on a red, green, or blue channel in the image by choosing one of the options in the Texture Channel drop-down menu. Adjust the height of the texture by moving the Height slider control to a value between 0 and 100. Check the White Is High check box if you want the lighter colors to rise from the surface to create the texture.

Click and drag a slider control to adjust any of the lighting effects settings before applying the texture channel settings to the image. Check the Preview check box, located in the lower-left corner of the Lighting Effects dialog box, if you want to view your changes in the active image window. Click on OK to apply your changes, or click Cancel to return to the active image window (see Figure 17.32).

Figure 17.32
The final image after modifying the texture channel.

chapter 18

Animating Images

The human eye has a way of interpreting a series of changing images as motion. Animation can consist of two or more images that are played one after the other, or repeated over and over again. Cartoon characters such as Bugs Bunny and Mickey Mouse are probably the first things you think of when you see the word animation. However, over the years, digital imaging (also known as CGI, computer generated images) and digital special effects have put animation center stage in live-action television and film as well as for computer generated and hand-drawn cartoons. The animation examples in this chapter show you how to create animation with photographed or scanned images.

Creating the First Frame

Some images naturally hint at motion by the way the characters are positioned. Try to find a photo containing several discrete objects. It's easier to animate a small, recognizable object, rather than to try to animate something abstract, like colors or shadows.

note
To find out more about how to reduce the size of a file, go to Chapter 8, "Saving and Sharing Files."

Next, decide how many frames of animation you want to create. If you want to create real-time motion, the frame rate can range from 18 to 32 frames per second (fps), although you really need 24 or more frames per second if you want to create quality animation. Depending on the size of each frame of animation, this can create a gigantic animation file.

For example, if one frame of animation contains a 1-megapixel image (approximately 500×700 pixels in a 1MB file), three frames will grow to be approximately 2MB to 3MB. You can reduce the overall size of the animation by reducing a 2000×1500 pixel image to a 640×480 pixel image. The best way to keep the file size small is to design an efficient animation. Keep an eye on the file size as you work on your animation.

Composing with Composite Images

If you're creating an animation that will share the same background image across frames, you'll probably be copying and pasting other images into each frame to create the animation. When you paste one or mores image into the image window, each is added to the document as a new layer. Because the pasted image is placed on a layer above the background image, the resulting image is referred to as a composite. You can paste as many images as you like into the image window. Figure 18.1 shows two Aibo dogs copied from separate image windows into the background photo for the animation.

Figure 18.1
Combine a photo with composite images to create an interesting animation.

Use the Move Tool to place each image in the image window and compose the first frame of animation. As you put together the animation, try to decide how you want to light and frame the subjects in the animation. Try to think of a message, or give the animation some sort of theme. The following list describes important elements to consider when putting together an animation:

note
Multiply the size of the initial image in the first frame of animation by the number of frames you want to create to determine how large the file will be when you're finished. The more frames, or layers in this case, the larger the resulting file will be. Be sure you have plenty of hard drive space and memory available.

- **Lighting**—The central subject of a photo should be well-lit, crisp, and free of shadows.

- **Scale**—Larger images usually are perceived as closer to the viewer. Images that are smaller give the illusion of being farther away.

- **Perspective**—Exaggerating the background image or any props in a photo can distract the person from viewing the actual subject of a photo. Keeping the subject somewhere in the foreground of the photo in perspective with the background images can make animation easier to follow.

- **Shadows**—First, it's easiest to animate frames of animation if most of each frame is completely black or white. Regardless, keep an eye on how the shadows fall in each frame. Shadows and light give animation a three-dimensional look but are harder to animate.

- **Number of frames**—Adding more frames to an animation enables you to create smoother, more believable, motion. Another way to simulate smoother motion is to add blur to one or more frames of the animation.

Finalizing the First Frame

Copy and paste as many images as you need to create the first frame of animation. Hide any layers in the Layers palette of images you might not want in the first frame. You can also apply filters, effects, and layer styles to add any final touches to one or all the images in the animation.

After you've decided which layers you want to use in the first frame of the animation, create a copy of the background layer so that you can create any additional frames using the same background image, as shown in Figure 18.2. Hide the copy of the background layer in

note
Save your finished animation, or one in progress, as a PSD file to preserve the layer information. Each layer represents a frame of animation in a Photoshop (PSD) file. Saving in other file formats will flatten the image into a single layer.

the Layers palette. Then use the Merge Visible command in the Layer menu to merge all visible layers in the image window. Voila! You've created your first frame of animation!

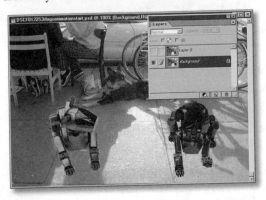

Figure 18.2
Merge visible layers to create the first frame, or layer, of animation.

Animating Composite Images

Add or select the second layer in the Layers palette to create the next frame of animation. You can approach putting together an animation in several ways. The traditional way is to create the first and last frames of animation. Then, create key frames of motion between the first and last frames, adding in-between frames to smooth out any motion between any of the key frames. However, you can also create each frame of animation sequentially.

It's All in the Layers

The trick to creating live motion in photos is to capture sequential images with a digital camera or video camera. If you want to experiment with motion, you can use a poseable figure and shoot it in different positions to create key frames of animation. Figure 18.3 shows two Aibo dogs placed in slightly different positions in the first and second layers of the animation.

Figure 18.3
Hide and Show previous layers to place the composite images into the next frames of animation.

These images were copied and pasted into the second layer of the document. Then the Merge Visible command was applied to the images needed for the second frame of animation. You can hide and show the first and second layers to play back the animation.

Copy and paste another set of composite images to create any additional frames of animation. In this example, two frames, or layers, are used to create a simple animation. Hide and show layers to make sure each object lines up with the previous object in the first and second layers of the animation. Then make each layer of the third frame visible. Choose Merge Visible to create the third layer in the Layers palette. Now you're ready to turn the animation into a full-fledged animated GIF file.

Creating an Animated GIF

An animated GIF is the file format used to store several frames of animation. It's popular because Internet Explorer and Netscape Navigator support this file format by default. You don't need to install a plug-in file to play an animated GIF in a browser window.

Photoshop Elements enables you to save layers as frames of animation. Choose Save for Web from the File menu to open the Save for Web window. Then choose GIF from the Settings drop-down menu. The GIF setting, located in the top-left drop-down menu, activates the Animate and Transparency check boxes shown in Figure 18.4.

note
You can break an animation down into two groups of images. The first group, *key frames*, is the first and last frames of an animated sequence. For example, if you want to animate a stick figure walking from the left of the screen to the right, the first key frame would show the stick figure on the left side of the screen, and the last key frame would show the stick figure on the right side of the screen.

The second group is called *in-betweens* (or "tweening," which is the creation of these in-between frames). In-between images contain the frames of animation between the first and last key frames.

note

You can decrease the opacity setting on a visible layer if you want to see how one layer of images overlaps with the previous layer. This is similar to a technique used in animation called *onion skinning,* in which transparent sheets of paper hold each frame of the animation. These sheets enable the artist to see through each "frame" and make the slight adjustments from one page to the next that result in the animation you see when the frames are played in succession.

Check the Animate check box if you want Photoshop Elements to treat each layer as a frame of animation. You also can choose a palette, dither options, and the number of colors in the color palette from the Settings drop-down menus.

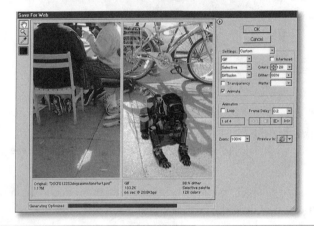

Figure 18.4
Check the Animate check box to turn the image file into an animated GIF.

Click on the arrow buttons in the Save for Web window to view each frame in the animation. Adjust the view of the image in the preview windows. The image on the left side of the Save for Web window is the current image in the active image window. The image on the right side of the window is the image as it would appear if the settings located on the right side of the Save for Web window are applied to the original image. I refer to the image on the right as the optimized image.

The Hand, Zoom, Eyedropper, and Color Picker Tools are located in the upper-left corner of the Save for Web window. You can use the Hand Tool to position the preview images in their respective windows. The Zoom Tool enables you to adjust the view of the original and optimized image in the Save for Web window. Select the magnifying glass icon and click in either window to zoom into the image. Hold down the (Option) [Alt] key and click to zoom away. Select the Eyedropper Tool if you want to sample a color from the image windows in the Save for Web window. Click the Eyedropper Tool icon to select it. Then, click on a color in the original or optimized image. The color square located below the Eyedropper Tool will change to the selected color.

Adjusting Playback Settings

Each of the settings in the Animation section of the Save For Web window work independently of each other. For instance, the Frame Delay setting does not affect the number of frames, and can be changed whether the Loop box is checked or unchecked.

You can adjust the amount of time between each frame of animation by typing in a value in the Frame Delay text box, shown in Figure 18.5. Click on the drop-down menu arrow to choose 0, .1, .2, .5, 1.0, 2.0, 5.0, or 10 minutes. The best way to decide whether you like the frame delay settings is to preview the animation in a browser window, as described next.

note
To find out more about how to save image files, go to Chapter 8, "Saving and Sharing Files."

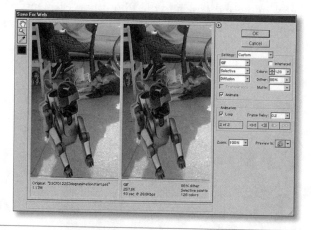

Figure 18.5
Customize playback by selecting frame delay and loop settings in the Save for Web window.

If you want the animation to play forward repeatedly, like some of the annoying Web ads you might find on some Web site, check the Loop check box, shown in Figure 18.5. The Loop feature can help you analyze the smoothness of animation playback, as well as enable you to view frame delay timing over and over without having to keep reloading the file in the browser window.

Previewing the Animation

Choose the settings you want for your animation. Then click on the Preview In drop-down menu to select a browser. The icon for the browser will appear in the Preview In menu. Click on the browser icon to preview the animation in a browser window. Photoshop Elements will generate the animated GIF file, along with some HTML code and open a browser window with the animation, as shown in Figure 18.6.

Watch each animated character in the browser window and make sure each character appears according to the settings you made in the image window. Click on the Back button or Close box to exit the browser window and return to the Photoshop Elements work area. If you want to publish the animation as a file, click on OK and then type a name for the file to save it to your hard drive. Otherwise, click on Cancel to return to the work area. Don't forget to save the animation as a PSD file to preserve the layers of animation.

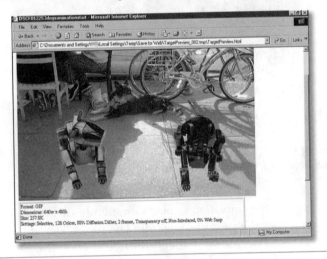

Figure 18.6
Click on the browser button in the Save for Web window to preview the animation in a browser.

Variations—Animating People

Perhaps one of the more difficult subjects to animate is the human body. In addition to the myriad lighting and shadow effects to which you must pay attention, there are also just as many issues related to motion of both the body and clothes. The detail needed to animate human-like subjects leads to the problem of size—image file size, animation playback speed, and memory.

Creating the First Frame

Although you can create a computer-generated background using the animated person as a composite image, this example shows you how to animate a person in an existing photo, shown in Figure 18.7. In fact, no composite images are used in this example.

Figure 18.7
Add layers to a picture to turn a still picture into an animation.

Double-click on the background layer in the Layers palette and rename it so that you can identify it as the first frame of animation. Click and drag the first frame over the Create a New Layer icon at the bottom of the Layers palette to duplicate the first layer twice. Two new layers will appear in the Layers palette. Rename this layer to reflect the second and third frames of the animation, as shown in Figure 18.8.

Figure 18.8
Select the subject of the animation and paste it into the same image window twice to create two new layers.

note
To find out more about the Clone Stamp Tool, go to Chapter 2, "Navigating the Work Area." To find out how to apply the Clone Stamp Tool across layers, go to Chapter 15, "Repairing Images."

Select the first frame of the animation. Apply the Magnetic Lasso Tool to select the subject of the photo. Then click on the Move Tool and enlarge the image by about 10 to 20 percent. In this example, the animation makes the small child appear to be sliding down the beach. The first frame contains a larger image of the child. The second frame will show a slightly smaller image, and the third frame will contain the original photo.

With the image in the first frame still selected, choose the Feather command from the Select menu. This command will blend the pixels at the edge of the selected image with the pixels surrounding it. The Feather command helps images blend in with the background image, as shown in Figure 18.9. Set the number of pixels in the Feather command to a range of 3 to 5 pixels. Choose a smaller number of pixels if you're working with a relatively small image, or choose a larger number if you're working with an image with a relatively large width and height. Finally, fill in any transparent areas of the image by applying the Clone Stamp Tool.

Figure 18.9
Show the layers in the Layers palette to work on the contents of the first frame.
Apply the Transform Tool to enlarge the image. Fill in any transparent areas of
the image with the Clone Stamp Tool.

Creating the In-Between Frames

Next, create the in-between frame of the animation. Follow these
steps to do so:

1. Click on the second frame of the animation. This frame will
   actually be a layer located in the Layers palette, but this layer
   represents a layer that will be used to create a frame of animation. Use a selection tool to highlight the image in the second
   layer, or copy and paste the image from the first frame into the
   second one.

2. Select the Move Tool to scale the image so that it is smaller than
   the image in the first frame, but larger than the one in the third
   frame. You can experiment with the size of the subject in the
   second frame by pasting it into a new layer and adjusting its size,
   as shown in Figure 18.10.

3. Finalize the second frame by pasting the final image of the subject into the appropriate layer. Then delete any layers you do not
   want to use to create the final animation.

note

If you want to be a little less ambitious, you can use the animation feature in Photoshop Elements to create a simple slide show. Simply copy and paste each image into the image window so that each image is added into its own layer in the Layers palette. You can hide the layers if you want to be sure a specific image has indeed been added to a document. To turn a set of layers into a slide show, set a longer frame delay in the Save for Web window, which is explained in more detail at the end of this chapter.

Figure 18.10
You can customize animation by pasting the image and transforming it to create additional frames.

Exaggerating Images

View each frame of the animation by hiding and showing each layer in the Layers palette. What's been created so far is a shrinking baby, which in and of itself is cute, but not very dramatic.

The very nature of animation encourages exaggeration to emphasize certain shapes or expressions to make the animation more entertaining. Figure 18.11 shows frame 2 of the animation in the Liquify dialog box. I've selected a fairly large 64-pixel brush and applied it with the Pucker Tool to create a different facial expression.

Save the changes to the Liquify dialog box. Then select the before and after frames in the animation, as shown in Figure 18.12, to see whether the Liquify effect is distinguishable compared to the other frames. In this example, the Liquify filter was also applied to frame 1. The 64-pixel brush was used to apply the Shift Tool to the lower portion of the subject's face.

note
To find out more about the how to apply the tools in the Liquify dialog box, go to Chapter 17, "Creating Complex Images."

Figure 18.11
The Liquify Tool can warp, twirl, pucker, bloat, reflect, or shift pixels.

Figure 18.12
Hide and show layers to compare the exaggerated layer with the previous or following layer.

Filters and Effects

You can also apply a filter or effect to exaggerate an image. To find out more about filters and effects, go to Chapter 12, "Applying Filters and Effects."

Finalizing Tweaks and Previewing the Animation

Open the Save for Web dialog box to make any final optimizations or changes to the animation file. Many of the settings chosen in the animation created earlier in this chapter have also been selected in this example, as shown in Figure 18.13. Choose GIF and select the Animated check box to access the animation settings for the active image window.

Figure 18.13
Adjust the loop and frame delay settings in the Save for Web window.

There are several default settings for the animated GIF image file. Photoshop Elements will select the optimal color palette and dither settings for the animation. If there are any transparent areas of the image, check the Transparency check box if you want them to remain transparent in the final image. The animation will loop indefinitely, and each frame has a delay of 20 seconds.

Before saving the file to your hard drive, preview it in a browser window. The animation should play back the same way in Internet Explorer 5 and Netscape Navigator 4.7. Click on the browser icon in the Preview In menu to preview the animation in a browser window, as shown in Figure 18.14.

Figure 18.14
Preview the final animation in a browser window before saving the final ani-mated GIF file.

If you like the animation as it appears in the browser window, close the browser window and then click on OK in the Save for Web window. Otherwise, go back to the file and change the Frame Delay set-ting, or experiment with a different GIF palette setting before saving the final file. Once the file has been saved, you can upload it to a Web server and share the URL for the animated GIF file with your friends and family.

Stitching Together a Panorama

Ever want to capture all the colors of a beautiful sunset along with the color reflecting across the local hillsides and plains? This can be an expensive task to perform with even a traditional 35mm camera. First you would have to shoot each picture of the panorama, and then you'd have to print them and lay them out to identify the overlapping areas.

This more expensive process can involve splicing together the negatives, or exposing separate negatives to a large-sized sheet of photography paper. The inexpensive way to create a panorama is to mount the images to a piece of cardboard, or align them in a picture frame.

Photoshop Elements enables you to create multi-picture panoramas by laying out each picture and then merging them into a new document window, as shown in Figure 19.1.

Figure 19.1
Combine similar photos with the Photomerge command.

Shooting and Choosing Images

The first step to creating a panorama is to take several pictures of a skyline or horizontal or vertical view of some sort of scenery. Try to apply many of the basic photography practices in order to take an appealing, well-composed picture. Each picture can overlap 30% to 50% with other pictures in the panorama. Also, you might want to set up a tripod to take pictures. Try not to change any of the camera settings as you take each picture.

Photo Composition for Panoramas

A panorama is comprised of several photos that move along a horizontal or vertical axis. It can be difficult to decide where your panorama should start and end. Depending on how much of the view you want to include, it can be difficult to decide how much sky, or other objects, you should include in the panorama composition.

As you look through the viewfinder of the camera, try to frame the view into thirds: one-third sky, one-third hills or water, and one-third foreground or flat ground area. Composing a panorama is also much easier when you are taking pictures in daylight. Because digital cameras can capture dark photos, resulting in unsightly tints, shadows, or hues, consider taking your first panorama photos in daylight. Figure 19.2 shows the first picture in a multishot panorama.

Figure 19.2
Include the skyline or other common elements in each picture you want to use in the panorama.

A tripod can help you maintain consistency in each picture you take for the panorama, although all the panoramas created in this chapter were shot by hand, without the aid of a tripod. However, you'll notice the overall horizontal area of the panorama is slightly smaller because of fluctuation in overlapping areas across pictures. When I took the picture shown in Figure 19.3, I tried my best not to change the position of my arms and of the camera, overlapping part of the picture in Figure 19.2 so that I could match similar elements in both pictures.

Figure 19.3
Include some overlapping areas across photos.

note
The number of files, combined with the width and height of each image file, can help you estimate the final dimensions of the panorama. If you want to reduce the resulting image, you can do so by choosing a menu item from the Image Size Reduction drop-down menu. Don't forget the pictures will overlap about 30% to 50%, too.

Each file you add to the panorama will increase the file size of the final image. However, be sure to capture each photo at the highest possible resolution so that you have as much image information to work with if you need it. Adobe recommends using image files that are 2 megapixels in size. The images used to create the examples in this chapter were all 3-megapixel images. If you want to reduce the size of the images for the panorama, you can choose from 12.5%, 25%, 50%, or 75% from the Image size reduction drop-down menu located in the Photomerge dialog box.

For example, Figure 19.4 contains a person moving along the horizon. Because I took this picture with a 3-megapixel camera, I can use the Clone Stamp Tool to remove whatever I don't want to appear in the final panorama. If I make the image smaller, thus removing image data, the edits to the image might not be as easy to make.

Figure 19.4
Don't worry if movement is absent from neighboring shots. You can edit them out if you don't want to include them in the panorama.

Before taking any of the pictures, determine where the light source is. Try to stand in front of the light source. If the light source is in front of you, the foreground objects in the picture will be underexposed, or too dark compared to the light source. If at all possible, try not to include the light source in the panorama. The brightness of the sun, or other light source, can overexpose the immediate area surrounding the light.

As you take each picture for the panorama, try to look for any landmarks, such as a tree or sign (see Figure 19.5). Distinct objects that appear in two or more images can help you reassemble each picture of the panorama in Photoshop Elements. In this example, the figures standing along the shoreline, plus the tree, and props along the right side of the image in Figure 19.5 helped me match the overlapping areas of the images in the Photomerge dialog box.

Tree

Boats

Figure 19.5
Look for a landmark or other object to end the panorama.

After you've taken the first set of panorama pictures, you might want to change the zoom settings, or, if your camera has manual options, adjust the shutter speed or aperture settings. You might want to wait for the lighting to change. Then take another set of panorama pictures. You can use a second or third set of pictures to create and choose the best-looking panorama. Copy the pictures you want to use from your digital camera to your computer's hard drive.

Before creating the panorama, you can use Photoshop Elements to correct any color differences between the pictures, or to clean up any objects you don't want to appear in the final image. However, you can also edit the image after the panorama has been created.

Introducing Photomerge

Adobe includes a panorama feature in Photoshop Elements. It's the Photomerge command, located in the File menu. Photomerge enables you to select two or more pictures that you want to combine to create a panorama.

Choose the Photomerge command from the File menu to open the Photomerge dialog box. There are two main Photomerge dialog boxes. The first window, shown in Figure 19.6, enables you to select files and choose from three options that you can apply to each image as it is opened.

note

The optimal number of photos in a panorama depends on how much of the view you want to show, and how many pictures you've taken. If you're trying to determine how many photos to take, experiment with creating panoramas with anywhere from two to eight photos.

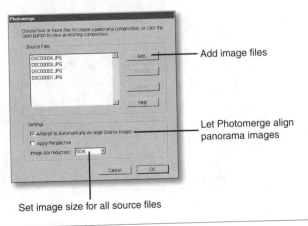

Add image files

Let Photomerge align panorama images

Set image size for all source files

Figure 19.6
Select the Image files you want to use for the panorama in the Photomerge dialog box.

To easily locate each image you want to include in the panorama, store all the files in the same folder on your hard drive. You can hold down the Shift key and click on more than one file in the Open window to add multiple files to the Photomerge dialog box list, as shown in Figure 19.7. If you're not sure which photos you want to use, choose more, rather than fewer, files. You can always remove a photo from the final panorama in the second Photomerge dialog box.

Figure 19.7
Shift-select multiple images in the Open window.

You can choose from several options at the bottom of the Photomerge dialog box. The following list describes how each check box and field in the Photomerge dialog box affects the panorama:

- **Attempt to Automatically Arrange Source Images**—Check this check box if you want Photomerge to arrange the pictures into a panorama for you.

- **Apply Perspective**—Enables you to set the center point of the panorama. Photoshop Elements grows the size of each end of the panorama. Apply Perspective is not selectable (grayed out) if Attempt to Automatically Arrange is not checked.

- **Image Size Reduction**—Choose the percentage you want to use to resize all the selected photos. Select 12.5, 25, 50, 75, or None from this drop-down menu.

- **Add, Remove, Open, Help**—Each of these buttons performs important roles for the Photomerge command. Choose Add to add a file to the Photomerge dialog box. Click Open to pick the photos with which you want to work. Select Remove to delete an item from the window list.

note
Pay close attention to the setting in the Image Size Reduction text box. This setting determines the width and height of the final panoramic image. You can modify the settings generated if the perspective or auto-arrange check boxes are selected in the first Photomerge dialog box.

Arranging Images in the Panorama

Add the files to the Photomerge dialog box that you want to use. Click on OK and wait for Photoshop Elements to resize each image according to the selected setting in the Image Size Reduction box. You can watch Photoshop Elements open, resize, and then close each image in the work area. It will finally create a new document to fit all the selected images.

When the batch script has completed all its tasks, a new, larger Photomerge dialog box will open in the work area, as shown in Figure 19.8. If you checked the Attempt to Automatically Arrange Source Images check box, Photoshop Elements will present what it thinks the panorama should look like in the larger area of the Photomerge dialog box.

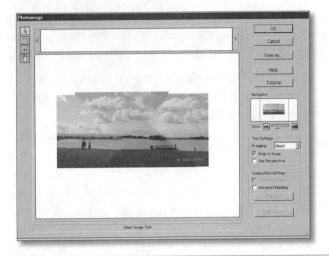

Figure 19.8
View the panorama in the Photomerge dialog box.

note
The Photomerge
dialog box enables
you to choose any
combinations of
photos you want
to use to create a
panorama. If you
check the Attempt
to Automatically
Arrange Source
Images check box,
Photoshop
Elements will try
to arrange the
selected images
into a panorama. If
it fails, the follow-
ing message will
appear:
"Photomerge
could not auto
place any of the
images." Click on
OK, and manually
place each image
in the Photomerge
dialog box to
create the
panorama.

The Photomerge dialog box is divided into three general sections.
The middle of the window contains two window areas. The top window stores any images selected in the first Photomerge dialog box
that do not appear in the second, larger window. To the left of the
windows are four tools. To the right are several functional buttons,
such as OK, Cancel, and Save As. Below the buttons is a mini-
Navigator window. It works almost exactly like the Navigator palette.
Tool settings and Composition Settings are located in the bottom-
right corner of the Photomerge dialog box.

Moving Panorama Images with the Arrow Tool

If you chose to have Photoshop Elements automatically place the
images, they should appear to fill the large, lower section of the window. Click and drag the slider control in the Navigator palette to
reduce the size of the images. Note the four tool buttons located in
the upper-left corner of the Photomerge dialog box. Click on the
Hand Tool to move the viewable canvas area along with the image in
the Photomerge dialog box so you can see how the entire series lines
up from one end to the other.

If you did not select the Attempt to Automatically Arrange Source Images option, the chosen images should all appear in the smaller window at the top of the Photomerge dialog box. Click on the arrow icon to activate the Select Image Tool to select and move images into the Photomerge dialog box. Figure 19.9 shows all four images in the top window section. Use the Select Image Tool to move an image from the top portion of the window and place it in the larger window to compose the panorama. You can move an image within the larger window, or drag and drop it into the top window area to exclude it from the final panorama.

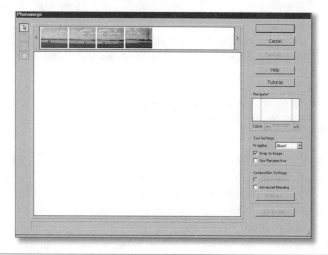

Figure 19.9
Use the Select Image Tool to drag any of the images in the top window to the bottom window if you want to put the panorama together from scratch.

Identify the image with which you want to start building the panorama. Then click and drag each surrounding image and see how close of a match the two images are, as shown in Figure 19.10. The two images might not line up exactly with each other. This results in a panorama that is not completely horizontal. The corner areas of two or more pictures might not overlap with each other, creating a staggered, slightly vertical panoramic image. Focus on the central content of the images to piece together the panorama.

note

Check the Snap to Image check box if you want the Photomerge command to help you align the photos in the panorama. Choose either Ghost or Blend Dragging to define how the selected image should be drawn when it is being dragged in the Photomerge dialog box. Choose Ghost Dragging if you want to view a partially transparent image as you drag it around in the Photomerge dialog box to help you find appropriate placement. Select Blend Dragging if you do not want the image to appear as you drag it around.

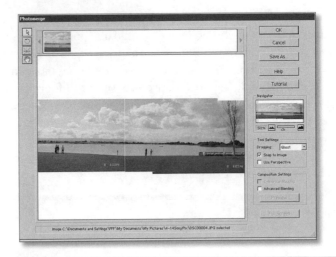

Figure 19.10
Select and place each image in the panorama in the Photomerge dialog box. Scale the panorama by moving the Navigator slider control located on the right side of the window so you can view the entire panorama at once.

After you select an image in the lower, larger area of the window, you can click on the Rotate Image Tool (second from the top) if you want to rotate the image. When you place the cursor over the larger window, it will change from an arrow icon to the rotate icon. When this happens, click beside the image and drag the mouse. The selected image should rotate along its X axis as you move the mouse up or down in the window.

Adding Perspective

The Use Perspective check box works in conjunction with the Set Vanishing Point Tool. Check the Use Perspective check box if you want the panorama to be drawn so that the outer images grow large as they get farther away from the vanishing point. To set the vanishing point, click on the Set Vanishing Point Tool, and then click in the center of the panorama images. The panorama will be redrawn, as shown in Figure 19.11.

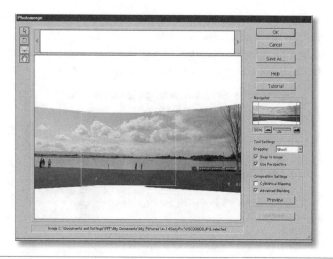

Figure 19.11
The Set Vanishing Point Tool works with the Use Perspective check box,
enabling you to distort each end of the panorama.

Publishing the Panorama

When you're ready to turn the panorama in the Photomerge dialog
box into a new image window, click on OK. Photoshop Elements
will resize each image, create a new document window, and arrange
the images to mimic the panorama defined with the Photomerge
command. The final panorama will be opened in the work area, as
shown in Figure 19.12.

Figure 19.12
A perspective panorama with the center image used as the vanishing point.

note
Check the
Advanced
Blending check
box before choos-
ing the vanishing
point in the
panorama. Wait
for the perspective
to be applied to
the panorama.
Check the
Cylindrical
Mapping check
box. Then press
the Preview button
to view the
panorama.
Cylindrical map-
ping makes the
vanishing point
photo larger than
the left or right
photos, whose
ends taper off into
slightly smaller
images. Click on
the Exit Preview
button to return to
the Photomerge
dialog box.

note
Select the Advanced Blending check box if you want Photoshop Elements to blend the colors and tonal range across the images in the panorama. You can preview this feature by pressing the Preview button. The blended image will appear in the Photomerge dialog box. If you like what this setting does to the panorama, leave the Advanced Blending box checked. If you don't like the preview, click on the Exit Preview button and then uncheck the Advanced Blending check box.

After you create the final panorama image, you cannot return to the Photomerge dialog box. Be sure you like the settings before you click on the OK button. Figure 19.13 shows the same panorama used in Figure 19.12, but without the perspective settings.

Figure 19.13
The same panorama minus any composition or perspective settings.

Cleaning Up the Final Image

Take a close look at Figure 19.13. Notice that most of the image is surrounded by white space, and some of the images have dates or timestamps. If you like the way each of the images fits together in the image window, the first thing you should do is save the file to your hard drive. Because all the images used to create this panorama were originally JPEG files, I chose to save the panorama as a JPEG file, too.

You can choose from several options to perform the final cleanup of the panorama. You can apply the Clone Stamp Tool to fill in the white areas in the image window, and apply the Crop Tool to trim away the incongruous edges of the panorama, as shown in Figure 19.14.

Figure 19.14
Apply the Crop Tool to trim the edges of the incongruous areas of the panorama. Then use the Clone Stamp Tool to clean up any unwanted items in the final image.

Cleaning up the image also involves removing any visual glitches or unwanted graphics. For example, the digital timestamp from the camera was removed with a 21-pixel, soft edge Clone Stamp Tool. You can also remove any people, or other small objects, from the image depending on what you want the panorama to focus. Sometimes having a person in an image reveals the true scale of the panorama.

Variations—Working with Different Photo Elements

You can create a wide range of landscapes—from scenic hillsides or lakes, to urban cityscapes or skylines. Panoramas can contain vertically overlapping images, too. Figure 19.15 shows a pastoral hillside near Page Mill Road in Palo Alto, California. I tried to capture the dramatic cloud cover in addition to the green hillsides when I took these photos.

note

If you want to check out Adobe's Help files of the Photomerge dialog box, click on the Help button. Photoshop Elements will open a browser window showing the help pages from the manual.

You can also click on the Tutorial button if you want to navigate Adobe's built-in tutorial. It shows you how to compose and stitch together a panorama.

Figure 19.15
Although a group of images might be a great fit logistically, tonal range differences can be difficult to correct after the panorama has been created.

Color and tonal corrections are particularly difficult to perform on panorama images because it is difficult to know which areas of an image will overlap. For example, the top-middle portion of the panorama in Figure 19.15 is the result of two slightly lighter and darker images overlapping, resulting in a visual glitch in the image. Try correcting this tonal difference with the Dodge or Burn Tools to lighten or darken areas as needed. You can also apply the Blur Tool, located in the toolbox, to blur the edges of the overlapping areas to help bring them together.

note
Select an image with the Select Image Tool in the Photomerge dialog box. Then, choose the Rotate Image Tool to freely rotate any image. Once the image is rotated, it will remain in that orientation. A subtle rotation might enable you to exaggerate part of an image, such as the slope of a hill or skyline.

Resizing the Canvas

Choose Canvas Size from the Image, Resize menu to open the Canvas Size dialog box. This dialog box enables you to increase or decrease the width and height of the active image window. The current size of the file appears at the top of the dialog box, followed by the width and height. The new settings appear at the bottom of the dialog box. You can increase the size of the canvas without changing the dimensions of the image.

Click on the Width or Height drop-down menu to choose the unit of measurement: percent, pixels, inches, centimeters, points, picas, or columns. The canvas size will be displayed in the measurement you choose.

You can customize how the new canvas size affects the current canvas size in the active image window by clicking an anchor button in the Canvas Size dialog box. The Anchor portion of the dialog box consists of nine squares. Click on a square to pick the anchor point. The canvas size is adjusted based on the anchor point selected. Type the new width and height of the window into the corresponding text boxes. Then, click OK to change the canvas size of the active image window.

You can also experiment with foreground and background composition in panoramas. Figure 19.16 contains a bench in the left foreground with the panorama of the east bay skyline in the background. Because the skyline is a fairly small area of the panorama, it can be difficult to line up each of the images. You can try to use the clouds in each of the pictures to determine whether you've overlapped two images correctly.

Although you can place each image in the Photomerge dialog box, you cannot modify individual images in the panorama once the new document window has been created in the work area. Look closely at the left-middle skyline area of the panorama in Figure 19.17. Even though the pictures appear to be a match in the Photomerge dialog box, the final image is slightly off-kilter. You can apply the Clone Stamp Tool to correct this visual glitch. You might also have noticed the overlapping corners of the middle images are slightly darker than the rest of the blue sky in each photo. You can apply the Blur or Clone Stamp Tools to lighten the border resulting from the overlapping images.

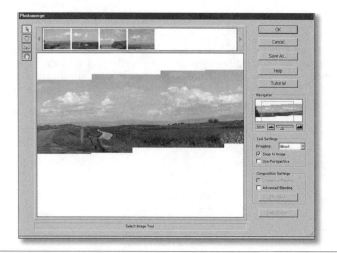

Figure 19.16
If you're not sure how many photos to use, choose more than you need and piece together a panorama with the images of your choice.

Figure 19.17
You will want to fill in the rest of the panorama with other images, or crop the continuous area of the image.

Printing Panoramas

Depending on the paper size supported by your printer, you might not be able to print your panorama on a single sheet of paper. You can use the Print Preview command in the File menu to scale the panorama so that you can print it on an 8×10 or 11×14 sheet of paper.

The Print Preview button enables you to position and scale the active image window. You can adjust the scale of the image by typing in a percentage value in the Scale text box. You also can type in a value in the Height and Width boxes. You can view the height and width of the scaled image in inches, centimeters, points, or picas. Check the Scale to Fit Media check box to let Photoshop Elements set the print size of the image based on the height and width of the paper size. Then click on OK to print the image.

continued

Check the Show More Options check box to choose output and color management settings for the image. You can customize the border, background, and encoding settings for the Output settings. The encoding settings enable you to choose the type of encoding that's sent to the printer. This will depend on the type of printer you are using; refer to the printer's manuals for information.

Creating a Web Photo Gallery

Photo albums contain a treasure chest of photographed memories. You can create traditional photo albums by printing photos to glossy paper using a color printer, a computer, and Photoshop Elements. To share their photo album with friends and family, more and more people are creating photo albums on the Web. Photoshop Elements enables you to create four kinds of customizable Web photo galleries.

Choosing a Gallery Style

Adobe has four gallery styles you can choose for your Web Photo gallery (see Figure 20.1). You can choose from two categories of styles: frame and nonframe based galleries. A frame is a part of the HyperText Markup Language (HTML) and enables a single Web page to be divided into two or more parts. A frame-based gallery enables Photoshop Elements to place thumbnail images of your photos on one frame, while showing the full-sized image in the other frame. You can

note
Many Web sites, including www.yahoo.com and www.msn.com (communities.msn.com/PictureIt), enable you to create and upload digital photos if you create an account on the Web site. Other Web sites, such as www.kodak.com and www.shutterfly.com, also provide Web photo album services, plus additional services such as converting printed photos into digital files, or printing your digital pictures onto glossy photo paper.

choose between vertical or horizontal frame designs for your Web gallery.

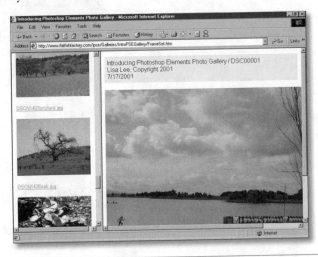

Figure 20.1
A Web photo gallery enables you to surf your digital photos on your hard drive or on the Internet.

The other two gallery styles are titled Simple and Tables. The simple gallery uses HTML tags to format the thumbnail images on a Web page. Click on a thumbnail to view the full-sized photo on a different Web page. Tables are another construct of HTML. Tables enable a Web page to group text or images into columns or rows, similar to the way a spreadsheet groups its data. The Tables gallery places each thumbnail image in a cell of the table in a Web page. Click on a thumbnail image to open a new Web page containing the full-sized image.

Creating a Frame-Based Gallery

Choose the Web Photo Gallery command from the File, Automate menu. Photoshop Elements uses a set of scripts to automate resizing each image file, and then generates the HTML and JavaScript code to create the Web photo gallery. The Web Photo Gallery dialog box, shown in Figure 20.2, will open. The Web Photo Gallery dialog box is divided into three sections: Styles, Options, and Files. The Banner setting will appear as the default item in the Options text box. You can type the site name, photographer, and date of the photo gallery into each text field (see Figure 20.2).

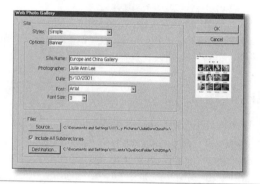

Figure 20.2
Choose a gallery from the Styles menu. You can type the name of your photo gallery into the Banner Options text fields.

The Styles drop-down menu contains the four styles available for the Web Photo Gallery. The selected style determines how the final gallery is formatted. Preview the layout in the right column of the Web Photo Gallery dialog box. The following list describes each gallery style you can create with the Web Photo Gallery command:

- **Horizontal Frame**—Places the full-sized image at the top of the Web page, and a thumbnail along the bottom of the page.

- **Vertical Frame**—Splits the Web page vertically. The thumbnail images are located on the left side of the page, and the full-sized image is on the right.

- **Simple**—Creates a Web page consisting of a specified number of columns and rows of thumbnail images. Click on a thumbnail image to go to another Web page to view the full-sized image.

- **Table**—Each thumbnail image is placed in a table, which can be customized with an HTML editor program. Click on a thumbnail image to go to another Web page to view the full-sized image.

Select the Source and Destination buttons located at the bottom of the Web Photo Gallery dialog box to choose the source and destination directories for the gallery. The source directory contains the files you want to include in the photo gallery. The destination directory will contain the Web photo gallery files created by Photoshop Elements. If you have several directories of files—for example, folders containing other folders of image files—check the Include All Subdirectories check box if you want Photoshop Elements to add all folders in the selected directory to the Web gallery.

Setting Site Options

Each of the Site Options can be applied to any gallery style. You can review each set of options by choosing each menu item from the Options drop-down menu. Customize settings for the banner, gallery images, gallery thumbnails, and custom colors. Each Options menu item changes the text boxes and settings that appear in the Options region of the Web Photo Gallery window.

If you're not sure whether you should customize the numbers of rows or columns in a gallery, leave the default settings untouched, and create a gallery. The horizontal frames gallery is shown in Figure 20.3. Each of the images in this gallery was scanned into a computer. The original image was resized down to 350 pixels, which is more than half as small as the scanned image size. Photoshop Elements converts the resolution of each image to 72 dpi.

note
You can customize the size of each full-sized and thumbnail image for each Web gallery you create with Photoshop Elements. If you're not worried about the amount of time it will take for your Web site visitors to download images from your Web site, feel free to select the full width of the image in the Web Gallery window (see Figure 20.2). If you are concerned about the amount of time it might take for your Web site visitors to download the images in your Web photo gallery, choose a smaller image size, such as 300 pixels wide for the full-size image, and 100 pixels wide for the thumbnail images.

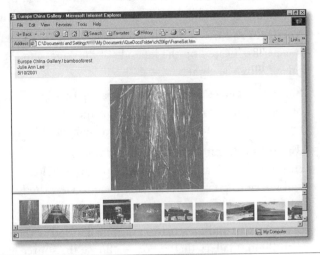

Figure 20.3
Photoshop Elements can create a fully functional Web photo album with a folder of images.

Notice that each thumbnail image is not exactly the same size. Photos taken in portrait mode are not turned on their side. Similarly, vertical photos that remain in landscape mode are not automatically turned right side up.

The following list summarizes each of the menu settings available in the Options menu list:

note
To find out more about how to resize a document and set the resolution of an image, go to Chapter 7, "Creating, Opening, and Converting Images."

- **Banner**—Type in the site name, photographer, date, and font settings for the gallery. This information is added to every page of the gallery.
- **Gallery Images**—Choose the border size, image size, and JPEG image quality for the full-sized image that will appear in the photo gallery.
- **Gallery Thumbnails**—Select a caption, font, font size, image size, and number of rows and columns for the thumbnail images (if you're creating a simple or tables gallery). You can also change the border size of each thumbnail.
- **Custom Colors**—Modify the HTML color settings of the background, banners, text, links, active links, and visited links for each Web page in the gallery.

You can navigate the Web gallery in two ways. To view a larger version of a thumbnail image, click on the thumbnail image. The full-sized image will appear in the browser window. Some Web galleries include navigational arrows enabling you to move from one page of thumbnail images to another. Frame-based galleries, like the horizontal gallery shown in Figure 20.4, enable you to click on a thumbnail to change the full-sized image in the larger frame in the browser window. The Simple Gallery, shown in Figure 20.6, enables you to click on an arrow button to navigate through each page of thumbnail images.

note
If you want to discourage unauthorized publication of your Web photos, add copyright information to the banner settings in the Web Photo Gallery window. Some digital photographers also add a watermark to their images, or add their name and copyright information to each photo just to make sure their work can be easily identifiable.

Figure 20.4
Click on a thumbnail image at the bottom of the browser window to make a larger-size image appear in the top frame.

Creating a Simple Gallery

The Simple gallery style enables you to navigate pages of thumbnail images by clicking on arrow buttons. Click on a thumbnail image to view the full-sized image. The simple gallery Web page layout, shown on the right side of Figure 20.5, does not use any fancy HTML elements like frames or tables to create the gallery layout, just straight, simple-as-can-be HTML tags. This gallery format works with any browser program.

If you want to see how each gallery layout looks and feels with your photos, choose a different Destination folder, and select a different style each time you open the Web Photo Gallery window. You can view each gallery from your hard drive by opening the index.html file with a browser application. Open the folder containing the Web gallery images. Then drag and drop the index.html file into a browser window. Figure 20.6 shows the images previously shown in the horizontal frame gallery laid out as a simple gallery.

note
To find out more about how to view watermarks in an image, go to Chapter 12, "Applying Filters and Effects."

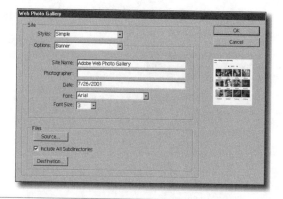

Figure 20.5
The Preview window on the right side of the Web Photo Gallery dialog box enables you to preview the chosen gallery—in this case, the simple photo gallery.

Figure 20.6
Compare different gallery styles and decide whether you want to use custom settings for thumbnails or gallery images.

Making a Table-Based Gallery

You can customize your gallery's colors to create a unique color scheme. Click on the Options drop-down menu and choose Custom Colors to view the custom color settings, shown in Figure 20.7.

Choose a custom color for the background or banner areas. Or select a custom color for static or link text.

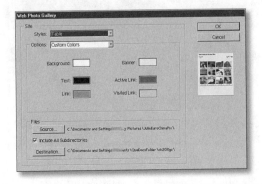

Figure 20.7
Customize colors for the Web-generated elements in the gallery by choosing the Custom Colors option.

Customizing Thumbnail Settings

Gallery thumbnail images exist in each gallery style. Unlike the frame-based galleries, which show a gallery image beside the thumbnails, the simple and table gallery styles use only thumbnail images in the Web gallery index pages. You must click on a thumbnail image to view the larger, full-size gallery image.

You can choose Gallery Thumbnails from the Options drop-down menu to view the page layout settings of the thumbnail images in the gallery. Check the Use Filename check box if you want the name of each filename to appear below each thumbnail image, as shown in Figure 20.8. The filename will appear below the thumbnail if you choose any gallery style except for the horizontal frames gallery, where the name appears in the upper-left corner of the browser window. You also can determine the size of each thumbnail image, as well as how many rows and columns of thumbnail images you want to appear on each Web page.

Try to keep the thumbnail images in smaller columns and rows. More images will mean that each page takes more time to download. And more than likely, your Web visitors will need to scroll through three or more rows of images if they don't have the luxury of a huge desktop.

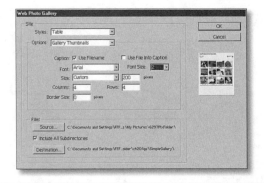

Figure 20.8
Try making the columns and rows larger so that the thumbnail images are easier to see in the table gallery.

Creating Custom Web Galleries

The gallery template files are stored in the Preset folder, located in the Photoshop Elements folder on your hard drive. Open the WebContactSheet folder to access the template files for the Horizontal Frame, Simple, Table, and Vertical Frame HTML files that Photoshop Elements uses to lay out the Web galleries.

Make a copy of any template you want to modify. Then customize the HTML files using an HTML editor application such as BBEdit, Adobe GoLive, or Macromedia Dreamweaver. Choose Web Photo Gallery in the File, Automate menu to view your new gallery template, or select it to make a new gallery.

Navigating the Gallery

After you've added your custom information to the banner, gallery thumbnail, gallery image, and color settings for the photo gallery, click on OK. Photoshop Elements will generate the resulting HTML and image files for your gallery, as shown in Figure 20.9. The table gallery creates an HTML table, similar to a spreadsheet. Photoshop Elements also adds a texturized background image to each Web page of the table gallery.

As part of your gallery options, you can customize the size of each thumbnail image. Figure 20.10 shows what the gallery looks like in its final form with larger thumbnail images previewed in a browser window. The person viewing the images will have to use the horizontal and vertical scrollbars in the browser window to gain access to all the thumbnails.

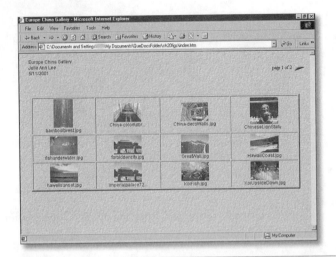

Figure 20.9
Navigate a table gallery using the arrow buttons located at the top of each page.

Figure 20.10
Customize the size of the thumbnail images to fill the layout with larger-sized photos.

Relative and Absolute Paths

Each Web page is a text file that can be stored in any directory on your hard drive, or on a Web server. Photoshop Elements uses relative paths to locate the image and Web files created for each gallery.

This means you can move the gallery folder to a Web server or any directory on your hard drive, and each link will work. Each picture will appear in the browser window when you load any of the HTML files in a browser window. A relative path might look like this: \images\GreatWall.jpg.

One thing to avoid using is an absolute path. An absolute path includes an exact directory path to each Web page, link, or image. An absolute path might look like this: C:\ProgramFiles\MyWebGallery\Images\GreatWall.jpg. If you move the gallery out of the ProgramFiles folder, this link no longer will be able to locate GreatWall.jpg. The lesson here is to use relative paths whenever possible.

Working with the Photo Gallery HTML Files

Photoshop Elements creates each Web gallery by processing each image in the source directory and creating full-size and thumbnail images. Then, it generates HTML code for each Web page in the photo gallery. As mentioned earlier in this chapter, HTML is an acronym for HyperText Markup Language, the language that enables a browser to view a Web page. When you create a Web photo gallery, Photoshop Elements creates several folders on your hard drive. The images folder contains the full-size images for the gallery. The thumbnails folder stores all the thumbnail images, and all the HTML files for the gallery are located in the pages folder.

You can view the HTML code for one of the Web pages in the gallery in one of two ways. One way is to drag and drop the HTML file into a browser window to view an HTML file as it will appear in a browser window of any Windows or Mac desktop. This enables you to view the file located on your hard drive. The other method is to post the file on a Web server and visit the Web site. In both cases, you can choose the Source command from the View menu to take a closer look at each Web page in your photo gallery. Although you don't need to have an understanding of HTML to create a Web photo gallery, the following sections provide a brief overview of the HTML code that is used to create the Web photo galleries in Photoshop Elements.

note
Another way to share a Web photo gallery with others is to copy the Web photo gallery directory to a CD-ROM drive. Most CD software, such as Adaptec's Easy CD Creator or Toast software, enables you to create CD-ROMs that work on Windows and Macintosh computers. If you want your CD-ROM to work on both Macintosh and Windows computers, format the CD with the ISO format. To reduce navigating problems with the Web photo gallery on the CD-ROM, try to keep the names of each image file as short as possible (around eight characters).

Viewing the Photo Gallery's HTML Source Code

While viewing the Web photo gallery in the browser, you can take a look at the HTML source code for the Web page. The HTML source code enables you to view the tags and URLs for each image and file in the gallery, and can be helpful if you want to troubleshoot any problems navigating the gallery images. If you're using Internet Explorer, choose the Source command from the View menu, or press (Command-E) [Ctrl+E]. If you're using Netscape Navigator, choose Source from the View menu. A window will open containing the HTML code, as shown in Figure 20.11.

This code is interpreted by the browser program, which enables you to view a Web page in a browser window. If you look closely you'll notice some of the text matches what you see in the initial browser window. Viewing the source code can be helpful if you notice a typo or misspelled word in your photo gallery and want to find out where that word appears in the HTML code for that Web page. You also can use a text editor program to view and modify the HTML code for the Web photo gallery pages.

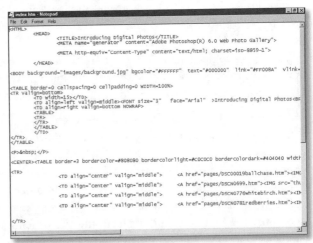

Figure 20.11
Choose the View Source command in Internet Explorer to view the HTML code.

Modifying the Gallery with a Web Editor

You can customize any of the HTML code in any pages of the Web photo galleries using an HTML editor application such as Notepad in Windows, or SimpleText on a Mac. Several commercial HTML editor applications are also available, enabling you to view the HTML source code, find errors in your HTML code, and other helpful features. Some of the more popular HTML editor applications are Microsoft FrontPage, Macromedia Dreamweaver, Adobe GoLive, and for Mac users, BBEdit.

The home page of the Web gallery will have the filename of either FrameSet.htm or index.htm. In addition to having a separate thumbnail image, each image in the photo gallery will have its own HTML page. Each Web page is named with the filename of each image file in the photo gallery. If you want to customize text on each Web page, you must open each one and modify the text in the gallery.

The first index.htm file contains the main layout of the gallery. The following examples use Microsoft FrontPage to open the gallery HTML files. Choose Open from the File menu. The Open File window, shown in Figure 20.12, will open in the work area. Double-click on the index.htm file.

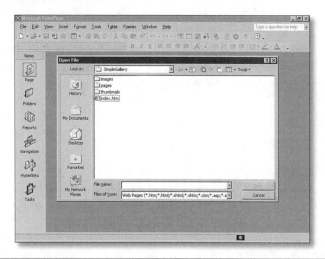

Figure 20.12
Open the index.htm file to modify the main page of the table gallery.

Although you can customize some of the text that appears in each page from the Banner Options settings in the Web Photo Gallery dialog box, you can add other kinds of information using a text editor. The following list outlines some of the elements you might want to add to each gallery Web page:

- **Titles**—The site name of the Banner options page appears as the title on each Web page of the photo gallery.

- **Copyright**—You can type copyright information into the Photographer or Date fields in the Banner options settings in the Web Photo Gallery dialog box. You also can customize each image with the Horizontal or Vertical Type Tool, and add copyright information to each image before you create the photo gallery.

- **Captions**—Photoshop Elements can add the filename for each thumbnail image as the caption. Check the Use Filename check box in the Gallery Thumbnails options page in the Web Photo Gallery dialog box if you want to add this information to each file in the photo gallery. You can modify the name of an image by changing its name in the index.htm and changing the filename for the HTML file for that image in the Pages folder of the photo gallery.

- **Links**—Photoshop Elements creates a link for each image in the photo gallery and places it in the index.htm or FrameSet.htm file. If you change the name of an html file in the photo gallery, be sure to also change the filename in the link in the index HTML page, too.

HTML Tags

The index.htm file opens in the FrontPage work area. HTML uses language elements referred to as *tags* to define how the text appears in the browser. Each tag, such as <HTML>, begins and ends with a bracket (see Figure 20.13). The text following this tag follows the language syntax associated with the <HTML> tag. Each tag also has a closing tag, noted by the forward slash (/). If you scroll to the bottom of the index.htm file, you'll find a </HTML> end tag.

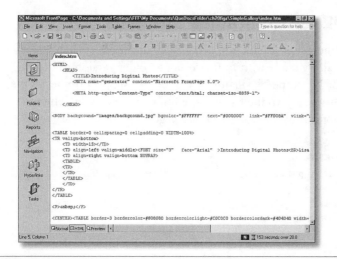

Figure 20.13
The `index.htm` page open in FrontPage.

note
To find out more about HTML and Web-related languages, visit www.w3.org, www. htmlcompendium.org, www.webmonkey.com, or www.webreview. com.

The HTML language has changed over the years. The World Wide Web Consortium (W3C) was created in 1994 and is responsible for defining new additions to HTML, such as XML. It currently has more than 500 member organizations, 50 team members, and an advisory board. However, each browser can implement HTML, as well as any other Web language, such as JavaScript, as they like. Keep this in mind if you notice your Web photo gallery appears with a slightly different layout in browser program, but not another.

There are many tags you can use to put together an HTML Web page. Photoshop Elements uses only a subset of HTML tags to create the Web photo galleries. The following list reviews some of the HTML tags used to create the Web photo galleries:

- **Page-related tags**—Such as `<HEAD>`, `<BODY>`, `<TITLE>`

- **Formatting tags**—Such as `<CENTER>`, `<P>`, `<bgcolor="#FFFFFF">`

- **Table-related tags**—Such as `<TABLE border=0 cellspacing=0 cellpadding=0 WIDTH=100%>`, `<TR>`, `<TD>`

- **Frame-related tags**—Such as `<FRAMESET frameborder=1 rows="80%,20%">`

- **Link-related tags**—Such as `<A href="index_2.htm">`

- **Tags for images**—Such as `<IMG src="images/next.gif" height="30" width="30" border="0" alt=Next>`

471

HTML for Nonframes Browsers

Photoshop Elements shows an error message when you try to view a gallery made with frames using an older version of Internet Explorer or Netscape Navigator (which do not support frames). Open the FrameSet.htm file to view the frame-related code. The following code appears at the bottom of the page:

```
<NOFRAMES>
<BODY>
Viewing this page requires a browser capable of displaying
frames.
</BODY>
</NOFRAMES>
```

If someone visits your Web site using a browser that cannot display frames, the message located between the <BODY> tags tells the viewer that this page requires a browser that can display frames.

GLOSSARY

A

adaptive color table   A variation of the color lookup table, used with images. An adaptive color table specifically contains colors required to display an image.

adjustment layer   A special kind of layer you can add to an image that enables you to adjust the levels, brightness/contrast, hue/saturation, gradient, invert, threshold, or poster-ize commands without altering the image layers located below the adjustment layer in the Layers palette.

analog-to-digital converter (ADC) A device containing one or more chips that converts analog data into digital data. For example, a charge couple device (CCD) converts light information into digital image infor-mation. CCDs are used in scanners and digital cameras.

animation   Two or more images that play back and forth to create the illusion of motion. Photoshop Elements enables you to use layers to create an animated GIF, a commonly used file format for animation files viewable on Web pages.

anti-alias   A software option that enables the program to smooth out the edge pixels in an image, blending them with the background color.

aperture   In a digital camera, the aperture setting determines the amount of light exposed to the CCD. Increasing the aperture can affect the depth of focus on the camera.

automate commands   The tech-nique of making an iterative or redundant task automatic. Choose an Automate command from the File menu and create a picture package, contact sheet, or Web gallery.

B

background color   The color of the background of the image window in the Photoshop Elements workspace. It also can be the background color of a Web page.

background layer   The bottom layer of an image file, or the bottom layer in the Layers palette. *See Also layer.*

bitmap graphics   A matrix of pixels that form an image. Digital pictures are created as bitmap graphics. Most of the tools in Photoshop Elements enable you to work with bitmap graphics. See also *vector graphics*.

BMP   A standard bitmap file format supported by Photoshop Elements, and more commonly created and used with PC computers.

brightness   The luminance of a color across pixels in an image.

browser   An application that can read Hypertext Markup Language (HTML) documents.

Burn Tool   A tool that resides with the Dodge Tool in the toolbox. It can darken pixels in the image window.

button   A graphic element used in applications to enable users to perform specific actions, such as to accept changes or to bring up a new dialog box. If clicked, a button indicates a transition to a unique set of information in the same or different window, toolbar, or dialog box.

C

calibration   The process of configuring one device, such as a monitor, to match certain settings. These can be color settings, a predefined set of values, or the values of a second device, such as a printer or scanner. You can use the Adobe Gamma control panel to calibrate your computer monitor.

canvas   Actual work area of an image file. Non-canvas areas of an image window are marked with a gray color.

cast   A light shade of a color, usually created by a reflection of a brighter color in an image.

CCD   An acronym for Charge Coupled Device. CCDs are used with most popular digital cameras and scanners. A CCD is a device the size of a microchip. It contains a group of light-sensitive components that translate light into digital data, which is in turn processed and stored as a file on a camera's storage card or sent from the scanner to a computer.

channel   In an RGB image, a channel consists of 8 bits of red, green, or blue image information. Each channel contains a set of pixels that can range in value from 0 to 256. You can view the pixel distribution for each channel from the Histogram or Levels window.

check box   A graphic element used in an application which, when checked, indicates that a particular feature is active. If unchecked, the feature is not active.

chroma   Synonymous with saturation color levels.

CIS   An acronym for Contact Image Sensor. A low-cost image sensor used in some scanners.

Clipboard An area of memory managed by the operating system that stores cut or copied data from an application. Images stored in the Clipboard can be pasted into an image window.

Clone Stamp Tool A tool located in the toolbox that enables you to copy part of a bitmap image and apply it elsewhere in the image window.

CMOS An acronym for Complimentary Metal Oxide Semiconductor: a method for building low-power chips. CMOS chips are used by some digital cameras and scanners to capture light information.

CMYK An acronym used to express Cyan, Magenta, Yellow, and Black color values. Each color component has a value between 0 and 255. Some applications and printers do not use the black channel of a CMYK image file. Photoshop Elements does not support opening or converting images to CMYK. It supports RGB, grayscale, indexed color, and bitmap image modes.

Color Picker A window containing a palette of colors. Select a color from the Color Picker window. Click on a foreground or background color in the toolbox to open the Color Picker window. You also can choose between the Adobe or Windows or Mac OS color picker window from the General Preferences window.

ColorSync Apple's name for its color management software installed with Mac OS 9 and Mac OS X. Choose ColorSync from the Apple, Control Panels menu to assign a color profile for your computer monitor.

composite image An image created by combining multiple images. For example, if you paste an image into another image file, the new image is placed in a new layer located above the image in the layer below it. The resulting single image is called a *composite*.

contrast The difference between light and dark pixel values in an image or object.

convert Usually refers to changing the file format of an image from one format to another.

crop A tool that enables you to retain the subject of a photo, but remove unselected image areas.

D

digital camera A consumer electronic device, similar to a traditional analog camera, that can capture digital images and store them to a removable card.

display Synonymous with show; opposite of hide. To make a layer or image object visible in the image window. Also, a synonym for computer monitor.

Dodge Tool   A tool that resides with the Burn Tool in the toolbox. It can lighten pixels in the image window.

download   To copy a file from another computer on a network or from the Internet to your computer's hard drive. For example, if you want to edit your Web pages, you can log in to your Web site and download a file to your computer using a network connection.

DPI   An acronym for dots per inch, a measurement used to define screen and printer resolution.

E

edit   To change, adjust, or reorganize text or image objects.

editor   An application or feature in an application that edits text or graphics.

effect   One or more ways to enhance the way an image appears in the image window. Most effects consist of a combination of filters that are applied to all or part of the active image window. Some effects can be added as a separate layer, while others are applied directly to the selected image layer.

eraser   This tool erases pixels from an image. Photoshop Elements has three kinds of erasers: Eraser, Background Eraser, and the Magic Eraser Tools.

export   A command used to convert the active image window into a special file format. Export file formats are defined by a plug-in file. Photoshop Elements plug-in files are installed in the Import/Export folder located in the Plug-ins folder in the Photoshop Elements application folder.

eyedropper   A tool that can capture a color from an image and be used as the foreground or background color in the toolbox.

F

f-stop   Also referred to as shutter speed. A setting on a digital camera that can affect the simulated shutter speed. This impacts how long the CCD will be exposed to light.

file format   A generic term for describing the way a file is saved. GIF, PSD JPEG, and PNG are examples of graphic file formats.

filter   Photoshop Elements includes image-editing filters that adjust contrast, brightness, and other types of filters to improve your images. You can view filters in the Filters palette or the Filter menu.

font   A character set of a specific typeface, type style, and type size. Some fonts are installed with the operating system on your computer.

foreground   The front-most layer of objects or images in an image window. Also, the top layer in the Layers palette.

foreground color   The upper-left color in the color well in the toolbox. If the Pen, Pencil, Paintbrush, or other drawing tool is selected, the foreground color is used with the selected tool.

frames   A feature of HTML that can be used to divide a Web page, enabling you to view and navigate more than one page in a browser window. Photoshop Elements enables you to create a Web photo album containing frames.

FTP   File Transfer Protocol. You can use a browser application to download files from an FTP site. An FTP application enables you to upload or download files to the Web or network server that has an FTP server.

G

gamma   Also known as the gamma correction setting. Not synonymous with Grandma. You can adjust the gamma setting for your monitor from the Adobe Gamma control panel. In the Levels window, gamma is synonymous with midtones.

GIF   Pronounced "gif," (with a hard "g") the Graphics Interchange Format is one of the two most common graphic file formats used on the Web. The GIF format is most effective at compressing solid-color images and images with areas of repetitive color. In addition to supporting background transparency (which is great for animation), up to 256 colors can represent a GIF image. Best used with illustrations, text, and line art.

gradient   A progression of colors that gradually blend or fade into each other. Create a gradient within an object or across frames and layers.

grayscale   Represents a percentage of black where 0 is white and 100 is black and intermediate colors are shades of gray.

H

halo   An off-colored ring of pixels that appears around borders of a graphic. Most noticeable around the edges of a mask.

hard disk   A hardware component commonly used in computers to store files and folders of data.

hexadecimal   A term to express red, green, and blue color values. Each component value is represented by a hexadecimal value, such as FF-FF-FF for white.

highlight color   The color used as a visual interface to identify selected text or graphics.

hints   Synonymous with Tooltips. Hints are located in the Hints palette. Click on a tool in the toolbox to view its tool information in the Hints palette.

History palette   Stores a list of states as you work on image files in Photoshop Elements. Each state is a command that has been performed or a tool that has been applied to a Photoshop Elements document. The History palette does not store zoom, or view changes, or the scroll location of the image window.

HTML   An acronym for Hypertext Markup Language, which is the language used to create Web pages. Photoshop Elements generates HTML code to create Web photo gallery files.

hue/saturation   Hue is an adjustable range of colors from 0 to 360, or plus or minus 180. Saturation values encapsulate color intensity within a range of 0 to plus or minus 100.

I

image   A bitmapped matrix of pixels that represent a picture.

Import   The command used to acquire an image from a scanner or digital camera. It can also be used to convert a nonsupported document into Photoshop Elements.

Indexed Color   One of the color modes supported by Photoshop Elements. This color mode uses an indexing algorithm to reduce the number of colors in the image and also reduce its file size. Indexed Color mode enables you to work with up to 256 colors in an image.

Info Palette   Displays the location, size, and colors of a particular object in the image window.

interpolation   The process for calculating color when pixels are added to or removed from an image during transformations. Bicubic interpolation creates the best results, but is usually the slowest method of interpolation. Photoshop Elements also enables you to apply nearest neighbor and bilinear interpolation processes. Choose the Image Size command from the Image, Resize menu to select an interpolation method for an image.

J

JPEG   Created by the Joint Photographic Experts Group, JPEG is a popular graphic file format used on the Web. The JPEG file format preserves broad color ranges and subtleties in brightness and image tones and supports up to millions (24 bits) of colors. JPEG uses a lossy compression format that can remove some of the image data when a file is compressed. Best used with images and photographs. See also *PNG* and *GIF*.

L

Lasso   A selection tool that enables you to select a freeform set of pixels. Photoshop Elements has three kinds of Lasso Tools: Lasso, Polygonal Lasso, and Magnetic Lasso.

layer   A particular plane in a document window that enables you to store simple or complex graphics. You can rearrange, add, remove, show, hide, and lock a layer in Photoshop Elements.

layer styles   A collection of effects that can be applied to a selected object in the image window. Layer styles are located in the Layer Styles palette.

lossy compression   An image file compression format used to compress a JPEG image. Lossless JPEG compression preserves the original image, without losing any image data. Lossy compression can lose image data when compressing a file. Photoshop Elements lets you choose between 12 levels of JPEG compression. The lower the level you choose to save the JPEG image, the more image data is lost due to compression. The image will not lose any additional data each successive time you save a JPEG image at the same compression level.

M

marquee   Rectangular or elliptical tool that enables you to select an area of pixels in an image.

mask   The selected area of pixels that can be modified with a toolbox tool or menu command. The pixels outside the selected area cannot be modified with tools or commands.

megabyte   Abbreviated MB. Equivalent to a million bytes, or more exactly, 1,048,576 bytes.

megapixel   A million pixels. A measurement used by digital camera manufacturers to measure the total number of pixels captured by a camera. Most of today's cameras can capture 2- or 3-megapixel images.

memory   Also known as RAM. Refers to the amount of physical memory (in chips) installed on your computer. Virtual memory is the amount of memory or hard disk space allocated for use by the operating system and applications on a computer. As you use the software on your computer, data is swapped from the hard drive into memory, and data stored in the physical memory chips is swapped to the hard drive.

Photoshop Elements creates a scratch disk with its own form of virtual memory to store image information on the hard drive as you modify an image in the work area. Memory, in regards to an application such as Photoshop Elements, represents the amount of space required for an application to run its routines and functions.

menu   A user-interface element originating from the operating system and containing commands for an application.

O

opacity The degree of transparency applied by a blending mode onto an object.

optimize To reduce the size or image quality of a document in order to decrease the loading time of a Web page.

options bar Contains additional settings and tools in the toolbox. It is located at the top of the Photoshop Elements work area.

P

Paint Bucket Tool A fill tool selectable from the toolbox. Works with the foreground color in the color well to fill a selected object with a particular color.

Paintbrush Tool A drawing tool selectable from the toolbox. You can apply this painting tool to the image window to add graphics to an image.

palette Similar to the term floating palette; synonymous with panel. A window containing a set of tools and icons. Some palettes also contain a custom menu.

palette well Located in the toolbar, this is the storage place for all palette windows.

PDF An acronym for Portable Document Format. A file format capable of preserving text and image information that can be viewed with a PDF viewer application such as Adobe Acrobat.

Pencil Tool A drawing tool located in the toolbox. Used to draw with a single pixel of color in the image window.

pica A format of measurement of approximately 1/6 of an inch. Originated with the typewriter, where 10 characters were roughly equivalent to a horizontal inch, or six lines of type for a vertical inch. You can create a new document with the width and height in picas.

pixel An atomic element of color that can be grouped together to form a picture or image.

Pixels Per Inch (ppi) A measurement of a monitor's screen resolution. This is usually set to 72ppi. For this reason, images created for the Web use the resolution of 72ppi.

plug-in A special type of file that can be placed in a folder on your hard drive. Each plug-in file extends the features available in Photoshop Elements. If the plug-in preferences are configured correctly, all plug-ins will appear in the Filter menu.

PNG The Portable Network Graphic is a newer graphic file format growing in popularity on the Web. Effectively compresses solid-color images and preserves details. The PNG format might require a plug-in to be added to a browser, but can support up to 32 bits of color, in addition to transparency and alpha channels. It uses a lossless form of compression. It is best used for creating high-color graphics with complex live transparency, and general low-color graphics. See also *PSD*, *GIF*, *JPEG*, and *lossy compression*.

preferences   Application and document-specific settings that you can customize to increase your productivity within Photoshop Elements.

process   A set of steps that, when followed, complete a task.

processor   The central processing unit of a computer. A faster processor will display graphics more quickly than a slower processor.

PSD   Photoshop Elements' native file format. Preserve layers, layer sets, channels, and masks by saving them in a Photoshop Elements file. The Windows version of Photoshop Elements shows this file format in the Save As window as Photoshop (*.PSD or *.PDD). The Macintosh version shows this file format as Photoshop.

Q

Quick Start window   The menu window that opens when you first start Photoshop Elements. Open a file, acquire or paste an image, or access the help or tutorial files by clicking on an image in the Quick Start window.

R

radio button   A user-interface element found in applications and Web pages that has an on or off state.

RAM   See *memory*.

Recipe Palette   A window containing a group of instructions for a single task or group of tasks that can be applied to an image, selection object or layer.

resolution   The number of horizontal and vertical pixels that make up a screen of information.

RGB   Red, Green, and Blue values used to express a color. Each value is within a range of 0 to 255.

S

Samples Per Inch (spi)   A measurement used by scanner devices to measure the resolution of captured images. Samples per inch combines the number of sensors (600 to 1200) on the scan bar located below the glass surface with the amount of vertical distance the bar moves for each scanned line.

Save   A command used to convert an image stored in memory into a file on the hard drive.

scale   A term used to indicate the size—larger or smaller—of an original object or image.

scanner   A computer peripheral that usually connects to the USB port. A scanner can be powered by the USB port, or powered by an external power source. Images are captured line by line and converted into digital data, viewable on your computer screen. Today's scanners can capture 24- or 36-bit images ranging from 600 dpi to 2400 dpi, or higher resolutions.

scrollbar   A set of window controls consisting of directional arrows, a scroll button, and a horizontal or vertical bar that you can use to navigate an image window.

shortcuts bar   The toolbar located below the menu bar. Click on a shortcut icon to quickly access a command, such as the Save, Copy, Paste, or Print commands.

show   Synonymous with display, opposite of hide. To make a palette or window visible in the work area, or a layer or image object visible in the image window.

shutter speed   A setting on a digital camera that can affect the simulated shutter speed. This impacts how long the CCD is exposed to light. Synonymous with f-stop.

swatch   Not a watch by any means. A swatch is a single square of color stored in the Swatches palette. The Swatches palette enables you to select, add, or remove a single color, or change to a particular group of colors for the active image.

T

text   Also referred to as type. Alphabetic, nonalphabetic, and numeric characters that make up a font. Use the Horizontal or Vertical Type Tool to add text to an image window.

Transform   A set of commands that enable you to scale, rotate, flip, distort, or skew all or part of an image in the image window.

TWAIN   A special kind of plug-in file that enables Photoshop Elements to communicate with a scanner or digital camera device. Each device installs its own specific TWAIN plug-in file. Any installed TWAIN plug-ins are accessible from the File, Import menu.

tweening   The frames of animation that convey the interim motion between two key frames of animation. You can create an animation file using the layers in the Layers palette, and the Animated GIF file format in the Save for Web window.

U

Undo   A menu command that enables you to reverse a previous command in the image window. Set the number of undo levels in the General preferences window.

update   To make current. Photoshop Elements automatically updates all windows whenever you change a value in one window or palette.

upload   The process of copying a local file or folder to another computer.

URL   An acronym for Uniform Resource Locator. Type a URL (such as http://www.adobe.com) into a browser window to go to a Web site or Web page on the Internet.

V

vector graphics   A type of graphic comprised of paths and points. Vector graphics use an algorithm to retain crisp, high-resolution versions of an image if scaled larger or smaller than the original size.

W

Web   Also referred to as the World Wide Web. A group of computers running Web server software connected to an extended network around the world.

Web client   A computer connected to the Internet and configured with a browser and plug-ins to enable users to surf the Web.

Web server   A computer connected to the Internet and configured with server software to enable it to host one or more Web sites.

X-Y-Z

Zoom Tool   A tool that enables you to magnify the contents of the image window. Use with the Hand Tool (H) to move the page while it is magnified. Press the Z key as a shortcut to select the Zoom Tool from the toolbox. Press the (Command) [Ctrl] plus or minus key combos to zoom into and out of an image in the image window.

INDEX

J-K-L

Other Related Titles

Special Edition Using Adobe Photoshop 6
Richard Lynch
ISBN: 0-7897-2425-1
$39.99 USA/
$59.95 CAN

Special Edition Using Adobe Illustrator 9
Peter Bauer
ISBN: 0-7897-2427-8
$39.99 USA/$59.95 CAN

Flash 5 From Scratch
Cheryl Brumbaugh-Duncan
ISBN: 0-7897-2461-8
$39.99 USA/$59.95 CAN

Photoshop 6 Power Shortcuts
Michael Ninness
ISBN: 0-7897-2426-x
$24.99 USA/$37.95 CAN

The Complete Idiot's Guide to Photoshop 6
Robert Stanley
ISBN: 0-7897-2424-3
$19.99 USA/$28.95 CAN

Photoshop Restoration & Retouching
Katrin Eismann
ISBN: 0-7897-2318-2
$49.99 USA/
$74.95 CAN

The Scanning Workshop
Richard Romano
ISBN: 0-7897-2558-4
$29.99 USA/
$44.95 CAN

www.quepublishing.com

All prices are subject to change.